The Sound and the Fury

a rock's backpages reader

40 years of classic rock journalism

edited by

Barney Hoskyns

BLOOMSBURY

784
SOU

*Dedicated to the memory of Penny Valentine, who
broke into the boys' club and made the Beatles swoon*

Introduction and compilation copyright © 2003 by Barney Hoskyns
and Mark Pringle

Published by Bloomsbury, New York and London
Distributed to the trade by Holtzbrinck Publishers

Library of Congress Cataloging-in-Publication Data has been applied for.

ISBN 1-58234-282-2

First U.S. Edition 2003

1 3 5 7 9 10 8 6 4 2

Typeset by Hewer Text Limited, Edinburgh
Printed in Great Britain by Clays Limited, St Ives plc

CONTENTS

Barney Hoskyns

HAIL, HAIL, ROCK'N'ROLL WRITING!

By Way of Introducing the RBP Reader . . .

I'VE BEEN A rock writer and editor for over twenty years now. Why? Because nothing has ever moved and excited me like great rock'n'roll music – like punk, soul, electro-pop, alt.-country and all the other sub-strata of the Anglo-American *genus* Rock. I've tried over the course of two decades to hail, to champion, the music that's thrilled me and touched me – because I want it to thrill and touch YOU.

The greatest music writers (the ones I grew up reading, many of them in this book) were the ones who got me closest to what rock'n'roll was really about: the irresistible combo of sound and spectacle; of music, performance, image, attitude and ritual.

When, in late 1999, I returned to London from a three-year stint as US Editor of *Mojo*, I had the notion to build an archive of articles by my favourite rock writers – everyone from Al Aronowitz to Jon Savage, Paul Williams to Vivien Goldman, Greil Marcus to Glenn O'Brien. To build it, furthermore, online, creating a virtual library accessible at the fingertips of passionate music fans the world over.

Thus was born Rock's Backpages [www.rocksbackpages.com], home to thousands of classic pieces – reviews and rants, interviews and overviews – by over a hundred writers, male and female, black and white, eclectic and specialist alike. The overwhelmingly positive response to – and use of – the site is testament to the evergreen, universal resonance of music from Elvis to Eminem.

One of the things Rock's Backpages points up is just how free rock writers once were to express themselves: how intense and committed, how irreverent and iconoclastic. Back in the day, few music journalists experienced what writers today do increasingly, which is having their album reviews killed in favour of more positive spins.

The sad truth is that rock journalism has become little more than a service industry, with scant critical autonomy and even less responsibility to its readers. We have all, in our different ways, colluded with the entertainment machine in its canny efforts to dictate what music sells.

Part of the thrill of growing up in the '70s was that rock stars and journalists alike were inventing the rules as they went along. Of course, it couldn't last forever: for the music industry, punk was the last straw, the last time an organic grassroots uprising would properly occur. Ever since, the major conglomerates have done their best to control and commodify rock rebellion.

The music industry's greatest victory has been to make pop music – from boy bands to nu metal – a mere lifestyle choice, a disposable commodity. In a world where Britney Spears is the new Madonna, what does 21st-century pop culture promote other than celebrity as the illusory transcendence of mortality? (When did pop last offer up an icon as ambiguous and unsettling as Prince?)

In this tame new world of fame for fame's sake – and codified Fred Durst rebellion – we are all living out Warhol's nightmare: an endless parade of pneumatic automatons who signify and celebrate nothing other than their own narcissism and greed.

Little wonder, therefore, that teenagers treat pop music like Coke. Trained to consume and dispose by a cynical, junk-food industry, teens ascribe no real value to the acts whose MP3s they swap so freely. The billions of sound files exchanged in the post-Napster pop universe represent not just a voracious consumerism but a loss of faith in pop as *event*, as something that means anything at all. Pop music is no longer a main course, simply a snack between meals. And this has everything to do with the industry's conscious decision not to nurture true talent.

Moreover, it's no coincidence that, just as record sales are plummeting, so the music press is in perilous decline. The *New Musical Express*, despite now having the field to itself as a British rock weekly, is selling fewer copies than ever. (The flipside: *Mojo*, covering the best music from the era when rock still mattered, continues to hold its own.) There is a fundamental loss of faith in the value of pop culture, with so much coverage reduced to bland, consumer-guide homogeneity.

In contrast, just as the internet now offers new means of exchange between artists and fans, so much of the freshest new rock writing can be found on music sites where anything goes and advertising rates are too low to corrupt contributors. Root around a bit and you'll stumble on the new Lester Bangs and Julie Burchills. The decentralisation of new media may be disorienting, but we should all embrace it as a rock'n'roll lifeline.

So what can we in the media *do*? Well, we can resist the relentless banalisation of rock'n'roll. We *must* resist it. We have a sacred duty to inject magic and danger into the bloodstream. We cannot let capitalism erode our souls. Music is about spirit, not matter: it's about our emotional lives, not our material status.

The Sound and the Fury comes at rock's post-Elvis history from several different angles, spanning four decades of Good, Bad and Ugly. It's also a book about how pop has been received, consumed and processed by fans, as well as by the writers themselves.

In the first section, 'Stardust', the phenomenon – as well as the unexpected side-effects – of pop fame is examined, from the laddish solidarity of the Beatles taking America to the problematic celebrity of Kurt Cobain 30 years later. It's also about the construction of stardom and the manipulation of media – and about that moment when hype is either going to break an artist or break his spirit.

In 'Close Encounters' we present some fascinating interfaces with some very different artists. From a pally chinwag 'twixt Madonna and Warhol acolyte Glenn O'Brien to an intermittently sticky exchange between Morrissey and Will Self, these are riveting portraits of artists in all their egocentric splendour.

'Making the Scene' focuses on the sociology of pop trends – the feverish thrills and catty competitiveness of musical micro-communities. The pieces in this section are essentially fly-on-the-wall, packed with vivid detail, whether in the form of gripping investigative drama (John Mendelssohn on NWA) or bemused travelogue (Mick Farren's adventures in mid-'70s Nashville).

In 'Congregations', we zoom back to three great tribal assemblies: to Monterey, the first 'international' pop festival; to Altamont, the Speedway bummer that killed the '60s; and to Perry Farrell's Lollapalooza, a Woodstock for the Kurt Cobain generation. Following swiftly is 'Live and Direct', with reviews and reports (on Otis Redding but also on Grand Funk Railroad!) that capture beautifully the charisma and commotion that live rock'n'roll performance is about.

Finally, in 'After the Fact', six writers look back – in love, in anger – at music and musicians that mattered to them (John Lennon, Abba) or recontextualise rock scenes (psychedelic rock, the Velvets' New York) with the wisdom of hindsight.

The Sound and the Fury anthologises some of my favourite pieces, by some of my favourite writers – heroes both sung (Greil Marcus, Jon Savage) and *un*sung (Bill Millar, Robot A. Hull). Read the words of Michael Lydon and Mary Harron, Mick Farren and John Mendelssohn, Richard Cook and Simon Reynolds. Imbibe Cliff White on Marvin Gaye, Caroline Coon on Johnny Rotten, Will Self on Morrissey. To all future rock'n'roll writers, I say: soak up these timelessly invigorating pieces and consider the opportunity you have to *make a difference*. Let go, tell the truth, express yourselves.

Barney Hoskyns
Editorial Director, Rock's Backpages
London, May 2002

1
STARDUST

Al Aronowitz

THE BEATLES: MUSIC'S GOLD BUGS

The Saturday Evening Post, March 1964

At the old Saturday Evening Post, *the editors were the kind of old-timers who slapped their thighs when they laughed at photographs of long-haired rock'n'rollers. But they claimed to be journalists and if they perceived Beatlemania as some kind of strange monster, it was, after all, a monster which had swallowed England in one gulp and which was about to start chomping on America. When European-based Pete Hamill handed in a piece about the Beatles that the editors considered too superficial, they assigned me to cover the Beatles' arrival in America. That's how come I was at what some people still called Idlewild Airport when the Fab Four emerged from the plane in the February chill to their usual fanfare of teenybopper screeches.*

I was part of a welcoming army of journalists who were equipped with an arsenal of poison pens and whose intentions were more or less to skewer the Beatles if at all possible. We were there to burst the Beatles' bubble if we could, to see if they were for real, to give America a good reason NOT to swallow Beatlemania (because we might choke on it), to debunk the Beatles' stardom, to find an excuse to mock them and to jeer at them and to discredit them, to discover a rationale of why these four Brits-in-need-of-a-barber should be prevented from spreading their craziness to crewcut America. We were hardened veterans. Scepticism and cynicism were our partners.

Immediately, the Beatles had us eating out of their hands. Certainly, the Beatles charmed me. It wasn't with music alone that they conquered the world. On a planet of which the axis is tipped too heavily in favour of heartache, the Beatles were F-U-N!

I had a brilliant editor named Bill Ewald at the Post, *but I'm afraid I wore him out. (I've got a whole WHO'S WHO of people I've worn out.) Bill assigned me to write 3,500 words or so, but longwinded me found myself so dazzled by the Beatles that I handed in a manuscript of some 10,770 words. I told you Bill Ewald was brilliant. Expertly, he whittled the piece down to about 4,000 and, with a photo of the Beatles on the cover, that issue sold more copies than any edition since Ben Franklin founded the magazine.*

AA

BRIAN SOMMERVILLE IS a balding 32-year-old Londoner whose jaw juts out like the southeast corner of England when he thinks he is about to say something important. At Kennedy International Airport in New York on February 7, 1964, Sommerville's jaw was projecting so far he was almost unable to open his mouth to speak. A thousand screaming teenagers were trying to wriggle toward a thin white line of nylon rope that had been stretched across the terminal building lobby. Three thousand more were screaming from behind bulging metal railings atop the roof, where they were the guests of New York disc jockeys, who had invited them to take the day off from school.

Next to Sommerville a New York *Journal-American* photographer was tugging angrily at his arm, shouting, 'We bought an exclusive story, and we can't even get a picture of them looking at us – what did we pay you money for?' At Sommerville's other arm a phalanx of British correspondents was complaining that the police wouldn't let them into the pressroom. There wasn't space left in the pressroom anyway, and one of the cops tried to throw out a Capitol Records executive who had arrived without an identification badge. Disc jockeys equipped with tape recorders were pointing cylindrical microphones at the mob. Flashbulbs exploded. From the back of the lobby came word that two girls had fainted. Hemmed in and harassed, Sommerville's jaw signalled a pronouncement. 'This,' he said in the intonations of a nation that has been accustomed to ruling the world, 'has gotten entirely out of control.' Sommerville is press officer of a rock'n'roll group known as the Beatles. Their plane had just landed.

Amid a fanfare of screeches, there emerged four young Britons in Edwardian four-button suits. One was short and thick-lipped. Another was handsome and peach-fuzzed. A third had a heavy face and the hint of buckteeth. On the fourth, the remnants of adolescent pimples were noticeable. Their names were Ringo Starr, Paul McCartney, John Lennon, and George Harrison, but they were otherwise indistinguishable beneath their manes of moplike hair.

After they were ushered into the floodlit uproar of the pressroom, Brian Sommerville, acting as master of ceremonies, stepped to a microphone, again thrust out his jaw, and addressed the reporters. 'Gentlemen, gentlemen, gentlemen,' he said, 'will you please shut up!' The first question from the American press was, 'Do you believe in lunacy?' 'Yeah,' answered one of the Beatles, 'it's healthy.' Another reporter asked, 'Would you please sing something?' 'No,' replied another Beatle, 'we need money first.' Still another reporter asked, 'Do you hope to take anything home with you?' 'Yeah,' a Beatle replied, 'Rockefeller Center.' At first, few of the reporters could remember which Beatle was which. But by the end of their two-week visit to America, each of them had become a distinct personality. Each of them, in fact, had become a star.

Ringo is the one that some observers have compared to

Harpo Marx. He has bright-blue eyes that remind one of a child looking through a window, although he sometimes deliberately crosses them as he sits dumbly at the drums, playing his corny four-four beat. 'I hate phonies,' he says with the absolutism of somebody who thinks he can spot one a mile away. 'I can't *stand* them.' The most popular of the Beatles in America, he evokes paroxysms of teenage shrieks everywhere by a mere turn of his head, a motion which sends his brown spaniel hair flying. When he flips his wig, the kids flip theirs. 'Riiinngo! Riinngo!' the kids call out. He acquired the nickname because he wears two rings on each hand. He wears different rings at different times, changing them like cuff links. 'I like the gold ones,' he says. 'The fans send a lot of silver ones too, but I send them back.' Then he adds, 'Do you know I have 2,761 rings?' His fame has brought Ringo other treasures, but he seems not to have forgotten what it was like to grow up amid the grimy row-house streets of Liverpool.

He was born Richard Starkey, the only son of a father who was a house painter and a mother who was a barmaid. He never finished school. He was kept out by pleurisy and more than a dozen stomach operations. Also, it seems, he never started growing. Asked how tall he is, he snaps back, 'Two feet, nine inches!' Actually he is five feet seven. 'When I feel my head starting to swell,' says John Lennon, 'I just look at Ringo and I know perfectly well we're not super-men.' Without proper schooling, Ringo worked as an electrician's apprentice and at various odd jobs before turning to drumming.

'When I was sixteen, you know,' he says, 'I used to walk on the road with the rest of the lot and we'd have all our drape coats on and we'd have a few laughs with the rival gangs, and then I got the drums and the bloke next door and I got a job and we started playing together, and another bloke and me made a bass out of an old tea chest and this was about 1958, mind you, and we played together and then we started playing on dances and things, you know, and we took an interest in it and we stopped going out and hanging around corners every night.'

These days still lie close behind him. When an American reporter asked him if he liked fish and chips, he answered, 'Yes, I like fish and chips, but I like steak and chips better.' One of his greatest moments was when the Beatles played before Princess Margaret and the Queen Mother at the Royal Command Performance in London last November. 'It was the first time I ever felt British,' he says. 'You know, you never think about royalty. But the Queen Mother, she was a nice lady.'

He sits with his drums behind the group as the other three perform, and he rarely sings, although that is what he would most like to do. At 25 he is the oldest of the Beatles, but he is at the bottom of what sociologists would call their pecking order. When he joined the group it already had a record contract, and the unspoken feeling in the quartet is that Ringo was hired by the other three. When they disagree on anything, Ringo is the last to get his way. 'You'd be nowhere,' Paul McCartney says to him in the ultimate squelch, 'if it weren't for the rest of us.'

The fans call Paul the handsome one, and he knows it. The others in the group call Paul 'The Star'. He does most of the singing and most of the wiggling, trying to swing his hips after the fashion of Elvis Presley, one of his boyhood idols. In the British equivalent of high school, Paul was mostly in the upper ranks scholastically, unlike the other Beatles. 'He was like, you know, a goody-goody in school,' remembers one of Paul's boyhood friends. He also, as another former classmate remembers him, was a 'tubby little kid' who avoided girlish rejections by avoiding girls.

Paul, who plays bass guitar, wears the same tight pants that are part of the uniform of the Beatles, although he often distinguishes himself by a vest. 'Paul,' says one member of the troupe, 'is the only one of the boys who's had it go to his head.' Sometimes, talking with the other Beatles, he finds himself using accents much more high-toned than the working-class slang of Liverpool, where he grew up. When he does, John Lennon mockingly mimics him.

Paul and John have collaborated in writing more than 100 songs, including such hits as 'I Want to Hold Your Hand' and 'She Loves You'. 'None of us really knows how to read or write music,' says Paul. 'The way we work it is like just whistling. John will whistle at me, and I'll whistle back at him.'

John doesn't smile when he sings. 'That's because,' says Neil Aspinall, the 22-year-old road manager who grew up in Liverpool with the Beatles, 'he's giving you his soul.' He likes to wear sunglasses both indoors and out, as a sort of declaration of privacy. 'John,' says Brian Epstein, the 29-year-old personal manager who discovered the Beatles, 'is the most intellectual of the boys.' Though he has a habit of falling asleep at odd moments, he is also the most intense and has a temper that reddens his face at the slightest rub. At a cocktail party in the British embassy after the Beatles' Washington concert, John found himself besieged by dignitaries, their wives and girlfriends, all of whom were thrusting autograph books at him with such official commands as, 'Look, sign this for my daughter! Can't think why she likes you! Must be out of her mind.' Finally John pushed away the pens. Forcing his way to the bar, he ordered a drink and said, 'These people are worse than the fans. These people have no bloody manners. Now, the Ambassador, I liked him; we talk the same language. But I wouldn't give a thank you for his friends.' At that moment a young embassy official approached John and said, 'Come now and do your stuff.' John glared back. 'I'm not going back through that crowd – I want a drink,' he said. 'Oh yes you are,' the official said imperiously. Livid, John turned to Ringo and said, 'I'm getting out of here!' With a smile, Ringo put an arm on John's shoulder and said calmly, 'Oh, come on, let's get it over with.' The 'stuff' consisted of drawing names out of a box in a charity raffle.

John began with ideas of becoming a painter, spending two years at the Liverpool Art Institute. He also writes short stories and poems, a collection of which, combined with his sketches, is being published in London. He has since written two books, *In His Own Write* and *A Spaniard in the Works*. One editor calls Lennon's literary efforts 'British hip, a sort of conglomeration of funny Lewis Carroll jabberwocky and an almost Joycean wordplay.'

When John first appeared on the *Ed Sullivan Show*, a subtitle identifying him carried the parenthetical message, 'Sorry, girls, he's married'. His wife Cynthia is a quietly beautiful 21-year-old blonde whom he met at the Liverpool Art Institute and whom the newspapers now call, to the Lennons' disgust, 'Mrs Beatle'. When the Beatles travelled from New York to Washington, she wore a black wig so she could get through the crowd. In Washington, she remained alone in her hotel room. In Miami Beach, she sunbathed by herself. 'Ever since the boys became famous,' says Cynthia, 'it's become more and more difficult for me to see John.' They have an infant son, Julian, whom the newspapers call, again to their disgust, 'Baby Beatle'. When the Lennons have business visitors, Cynthia serves tea and recedes into the background.

John is the leader of the Beatles. 'We *have* no leader,' he might argue with some annoyance. 'We're a *team*, y'know, pull together and all that.' As a matter of fact, each Beatle has a veto on what the four of them do together. 'But it's John who usually wins out,' says one of their friends. 'John is the hippest and the sharpest of the lot. They've all learned from him. Even their humour, the way they're always sending people up, they got that from John.'

Just 23, George Harrison is the youngest of the Beatles. 'He doesn't have the maturity of the others, so he tends to play it a little safe,' says a member of the troupe. 'It's as if he is the baby of the family.' Being the baby of the family is a role to which George is accustomed. The son of a bus driver, he is the youngest of four children. 'George was always the one who tried to please,' says his sister, Mrs Louise Caldwell, the pretty platinum-blonde wife of an engineer who lives in the Midwest. 'When the fire needed more coal, he would always say, 'Mummy, I'll do it. Let me get the shovel'. Or when we'd be going to church, George would polish everyone's boots.'

George plays lead guitar for the Beatles, often with a look of unconcern that seems to reflect a desire to be strumming elsewhere. 'Well,' he says, 'the songs that Paul and John write, they're all right, but they're not the greatest.'

His boyhood idols were guitarists Chet Atkins and Duane Eddy, although he recently discovered Andres Segovia. He listens on the radio to other pop artists from the start of his day, which often begins when road manager Aspinall drags the boys out of bed at 10:30 to keep some 10 A.M. date. He keeps a transistor radio in his hand, even during conversations. He adjusts the volume according to his interest in what is being said.

'You have to be very careful of what you say to George,' says disc jockey Murray (the K) Kaufman of New York's WINS, who glad-handed the Beatles when they stepped off the plane in New York and who was George's roommate when the Beatles travelled to Miami Beach. 'You have to be sure that every word means what you want it to mean. He takes what you say very literally.'

'George, as a matter of fact,' says manager Brian Epstein, 'is the only one who asks questions. He's the only one who takes an active interest in the business aspect of the Beatles. He wants to know how I book them, how the discs are distributed, and everything that has to do with the financial working.'

George's ambition, he says, is to retire with 'a whacking great pile of money.' He recalls that in the early days of the group in Liverpool, 'we got what would work out to two dollars a night apiece – and all the soda we could drink. We drank until that stuff came out of our ears, to make sure we got our money's worth.'

Although by no means the quietest of the Beatles, because

none of them really is quiet, George remains the least prominent. At a press conference for fan magazines in New York's Plaza Hotel, a young woman asked, 'Mr Starr is known for his rings, Mr McCartney obviously for his looks, and Mr Lennon for his wife. What about you, Mr Harrison?' George swallowed a bite of chicken sandwich, fluttered his long eyelashes in the same manner that Paul often does, and answered, 'As long as I get an equal share of the money, I'm willing to stay anonymous.'

These are the Beatles – the four young men who brought with them to America a phenomenon known as Beatlemania. So far, Beatlemania has travelled over two continents. In Stockholm, the arrival of the Beatles was greeted with teenage riots. In Paris another congregation held screeching services at the airport and the Beatles' performances at the Olympia Theater were sold out for three weeks. In the Beatles' native Liverpool, sixty youngsters collapsed from exposure after standing all night in a mile-long line of 12,000 waiting to buy tickets to the Beatles' performance. When a foreman shut off the radio in the middle of a Beatles record at a textile mill in Lancashire, 200 girls went out on strike.

While the Beatles toured the United States, three of their singles were in the top six and their albums ranked one and two in the record-popularity charts. Beatle wigs were selling at three dollars apiece, high-school boys were combing their forelocks forward, and hairdressers were advertising Beatle cuts for women. Beatle hats, T-shirts, cookies, eggcups, ice cream, dolls, beach shirts, turtleneck pullovers, nighties, socks and iridescent blue-and-green collarless suits were on the market, and a Beatle motor scooter for children and a Beatlemobile for adults were being readied for production. 'I think everyone has gone daft,' says John. Adds Ringo, 'Anytime you spell "beetle" with an "a" in it, we get the money.' In 1964, Beatle-licensed products grossed $50,000,000 in America alone. As for the Beatles, their total income that year reached $14,000,000.

It all began in Liverpool, a smog-aired, dockfront city that overlooks the Mersey River. When the Beatles first put their brows together eight years ago, there were an estimated 100 rock'n'roll groups in the city. Today Liverpool is the pop-music capital of the British Isles, and what newspapers have come to call 'the Mersey sound' dominates the English hit parade. 'Do you want to know what the Mersey sound is?' says one American critic. 'It's 1956 American rock bouncing back at us.'

In the beginning, the group was called the Quarrymen Skiffle Group, then the Moondogs, and then the Moon-shiners. John, Paul, and George were in the original group; Ringo Starr joined in 1962. Hired in 1959 for a job in Hamburg, Germany, the Beatles worked their way up to a wage of $25 a week, and became one of the main attractions along the Reeperbahn.

'When they got back to Liverpool, that's when they really started to swing,' says Neil Aspinall. It was then that Brian Epstein discovered them. A delicately mannered young man who once wanted to be a dress designer, Epstein at the time was in charge of the television-radio-records department of his father's department-store chain. When several customers began demanding Beatle records, Epstein signed them up, got them a test with Decca Records (they flunked), then brought them to Electric and Musical Industries Ltd.

'They were impressive – it was like striking oil,' recalls an E.M.I. official. 'I remember I gave them back their first tape and told them, "If there's anything you don't like, let me know." And George came right back and said, "Well, I don't like your tie for a start."'

In short order the Beatles had four hits, and teenage mobs began following the Beatles throughout England. But it wasn't until they played London's Palladium and several thousand fans mobbed them that all Beatles became national heroes. They had to be rescued by police. 'Well, there were no assassinations that day,' recalls Brian Sommerville. 'There were no wars, no invasions, no great crises of state, and the Beatles were the only good story the London dailies had, so they gave it a big display.'

In the United States, Capitol Records, which has first rights to any E.M.I. release, originally turned down the Beatles' records. As the craze grew, it not only issued them but poured $50,000 into a promotion campaign. 'Sure there was a lot of hype,' says Capitol vice-president Voyle Gilmore. 'But all the hype in the world isn't going to sell a bad product.'

Nevertheless, that hype helped stir the interest of thousands of fans who greeted the Beatles at Kennedy Airport. Many thousands more waited for them at New York's Plaza Hotel. Outside the hotel, stacked up against barricades, the mob chanted, 'We want the Beatles! We want the Beatles!' According to one maid, the Beatles found three girls hiding in their bathtub. Dozens of others climbed the fire exit to the twelfth-floor wing in which the Beatle entourage had been ensconced. Still others, with the names and pocket-books of prominent families, checked in at the hotel and tried to get the Beatles via the elevators.

On the twelfth floor the Beatles rested in their suite, while the phones rang with requests for interviews and autographs. One call was from a man who wanted to produce Beatle ash trays. Another was from a promoter in Hawaii who wanted to book the Beatles.

Telegrams came in by the handful, and boxes loaded with fan mail. 'We get 12,000 letters a day,' Ringo later said. 'Yeah,' added John. 'We are going to answer every one of them.' The road managers, meanwhile, were busy signing the Beatles' autographs for them, and the room-service waiters kept bringing up tables loaded with all sorts of drinks. Murray the K also came in, bringing with him the Ronettes, an American recording group of three exotic-looking girls. 'We met the Beatles in Europe,' one of them said, as if she were singing it.

As the Beatles' stay at the Plaza extended, so did the

throngs. Each time the Beatles left the hotel, the mobs would break through police lines in a jumble of lost shoes, falling girls, and Beatle sweat shirts. A deputy chief inspector of police accused the Beatles' press agents of bringing in teen-agers by the busload. The Beatles, meanwhile, spent their time watching TV, dining at the 21 Club, sightseeing from their car, twisting at the Peppermint Lounge, and flirting with waitresses.

The remainder of the Beatles' tour of America was more of the same. In Washington, to which the Beatles travelled aboard a private railroad car called the 'King George,' 2,000 teenage fans mobbed the locked metal gates of Union Station. At their concert in the Coliseum that night the Beatles were showered with flash-bulbs, hair rollers, caramels, and jelly beans, in some instances a bagful at a time. 'They *hurt*,' Ringo said afterward. 'They felt just like hailstones.'

When they flew to Miami, they were greeted at the airport by a chimpanzee, four bathing beauties, a four-mile long traffic jam, and 7,000 teenagers, who shattered twenty-three windows and a plate-glass door. The flight engineer of the plane wore a Beatle wig. As they were getting off, the wife of the president of National Airlines came aboard with two teenage girls, but was blocked by Sommerville, who stormed, 'No, no, madam! We cannot spend time giving autographs to employees' families.'

After their American tour, the Beatles flew back to England to make their first movie. When they stopped off at Kennedy Airport to change planes for London, they again found several thousand teenage fans screaming from the observation roof, after waiting there for hours. Four girls collapsed. When it was all over, America relaxed again.

Steve Turner

HOW TO BECOME A CULT FIGURE IN ONLY TWO YEARS: THE MAKING OF DAVID BOWIE

unpublished piece for *Nova*, 1974

One of the most fascinating experiences of my time as features editor of Beat Instrumental *(1971–1973) was witnessing first-hand the rise of David Bowie. I had first met him as a scruffy songwriter dressed in roll-neck and jeans and last saw him as Ziggy Stardust sitting with Iggy Pop in a dressing room at Regent Street Polytechnic in the West End of London.*

Yet, despite having known the 'real' David Bowie, I was surprised to find myself as mesmerised by the new image as any other fan. The more difficult it became to get through to him, the more I wanted to interview him. I knew what he was doing and had a shrewd idea how he was doing it, but the knowledge didn't immediately demystify him.

The story that follows was a breakthrough in style for me. It was not only longer than anything I'd previously written but also more thoroughly researched. The rock journalism I was used to encouraged the celebrity interview rather than background investigation. It was also the first time that I recorded a telephone interview, which I did by Sellotaping the microphone to the earpiece.

It was commissioned in 1974 by Russell Miller, then features editor at Nova, *but wasn't published*

*because the magazine folded (for the first time) later
that year.*

ST

MICKIE BLOOMFIELD IS a 16-year-old shipping clerk living in a
tower block off the Old Kent Road who in order to 'be great
like David Bowie' has had his ear pierced, his hair restyled
and spends up to £17 for a pair of boots with four-inch
platform soles. Roger Swanborough, 23, is a postgraduate
painting student at the Royal College of Art, who feels that by
imitating Bowie he has found expression for a previously
submerged part of his personality. Tony DeFries, 29, is a rock
manager, and wants his product, David Bowie, to become a
'real star' – which, as he points out, is not a Rod Stewart or a
Cat Stevens-type star . . . but a James Dean or a Marlon
Brando-type star.

Over the past two years DeFries hasn't done badly. It must
please him to walk along Kensington High Street on a Saturday morning and see all the heads of cropped Bowie-esque hair
adorning male and female alike, plus the chandelier earrings,
the platform boots and maybe even a handful of guys dabbling
in mascara and rouge. It must please him that his boy's image
has become a cliché, that Mum, Dad, the milkman and the
bank manager all know about him and that little Johnny's
rebelling by cutting off his lovely long blond hair and colouring it red and wearing those ridiculous baggy trousers.

Mr DeFries is a calculating man who tries to blend the
business strengths of his two personal heroes – Colonel Tom
Parker, manager of Elvis Presley, and Allen Klein, sometime
manager of the Beatles. From Parker he learned protective-
ness, the way in which living legends are built not so much
from what's said and seen but from what's unsaid and
unseen. Manufactured mystery. From Klein, who he'd seen
in operation when working as a solicitor in London, he took
the hard bargaining technique, the ability to understand the
intricacies of law and squeeze the best from every deal.

DeFries is admired by those who work with him and frequently despised by those who don't. 'A brilliant man,' says one music journalist. 'He's pulled off a brilliant hype. Bowie wouldn't be anywhere without him.' On the other hand, a former associate of Bowie's, now no longer part of the inner circle, describes him as 'a little Jewish hustler who even Jews don't want to deal with'. Those who admire him do so because of his driving determination to create a superstar. Stuart George, formerly Bowie's personal bodyguard, remembers a meeting in a Kings Road restaurant at which the whole operation was discussed. It was attended only by those involved in the creation of the star. He says: 'DeFries turned to Bowie and said, "Do you want to be a star or do you want to be famous or do you want to be rich, famous and a star?" ' Bowie accepted the third alternative, and the wheels started spinning.

'Once he'd become convinced that things were going to work he was able to project how Bowie would be as a star and make long term plans accordingly,' says American record producer Tony Visconti, a former DeFries client and a close friend of Bowie's. 'What he has is a shrewd sense of perspective,' explains photographer Mick Rock. 'He saw David as a building, waiting I think he said two years, and then making him a landmark.'

Well, two years it was, and the long-haired, stubble-chinned lad from Beckenham – described by his former manager as being 'totally introverted and colourless' – has been transformed from a frustrated songwriter into a cult performer. 'DeFries told me that Bowie was going to be a Dylan for the '70s,' recalls Mick Watts, assistant editor of *Melody Maker*, 'but that he also wanted a James Dean image going at the same time.' Bob Dylan for the head market and James Dean for the body market, eh? There are as many Bowie imitators in the stands at Millwall on a Saturday afternoon as there are in the canteen of the Royal College of Art on a weekday. One group sees him as rebellious and glamorous, while the other sees him as creative and camp.

To be a cult figure you have to recognise the public need and then set out to fill it. Required reading should include all available material on Dylan, Presley, the Beatles, the Rolling Stones, James Dean, Dietrich, Valentino, Garbo and Monroe plus useful guide books like *The Selling of the President* by Joe McGinniss (tips on creating an imaginary human called Richard Nixon and conning the majority of America to vote for him), Vance Packard's *The Hidden Persuaders* (a favourite of Bowie's), *The Image* by Daniel Boorstein and *The Neophiliacs* by Christopher Booker. Then all that's needed is a few original ideas, gleaned from this research, and a sympathetic manager able to bankroll your imagination.

David Bowie had got the theory worked out by 1971. 'I believe in fantasy and star images,' he told the *Cheltenham Chronicle*. 'I am very aware of these kind of people and feel they are very important figures in our society. People like to focus on somebody who they might consider not quite the same as them. Whether it's true or not is immaterial.' Now, the first problem facing potential cult figures is how to become 'not quite the same'. How is it possible to make something extraordinary of an ordinary member of the public? The point is, you don't have to. It's not the person you have to change, it's the public perception of the person. As Ray Price wrote in a memorandum to the Nixon staff during the 1968 election: 'We have to be very clear on this point: that the response is to the image, not to the man, since 99 per cent of the voters have no contact with the man. It's not what's there that counts, it's what's projected.'

But of course! Those who project the image need the manipulation – the journalists, the photographers, the designers and the press agents. If they can be controlled, so can the intensity and power of the image that they will be handling. You don't need Joseph Goebbels to give you tips like that.

Initially, the physical impression of the potential star has to be made into something startling. It should be an image that slightly contravenes current convention but not so outrageous that it won't be accepted by the public. David Bowie, who'd experimented with long dresses and pre-Raphaelite curls earlier in the year, found the necessary balance by chopping off his shoulder-length hair, which had almost become a convention itself, and colouring it a carrot red. It was a good move because male hair styles had reached their length limit, and the Ziggy cut fitted both sexes. Nine months later the *Sun* would give him its centre-spread with the caption 'Now everyone wants the Bowie haircut'.

Bowie also designed suits which, together with the platform boots, suggested science-fiction or DC comics. Superstars are supposed to be other-worldly and Bowie was taking this literally. A show with special lighting, well-rehearsed stage movements and a costume change was developed. Most important of all for a cult figure, Bowie represented a defiance against a particular convention – in his case that of heterosexual relationships being the only acceptable relationships.

Bowie and DeFries understood the psychology of the media. They knew what made headlines. 'DeFries manipulated the media very well,' says Mick Watts. 'He was a good story, he looked good, and he was good for a picture.' The product had to seem rare so that demand would steadily increase. Dai Davis, a former music journalist, was brought in at that end of 1971 to handle press relations. 'The general idea was that Bowie was a phenomenon rather than a pop star,' he recalls. 'After a while it became a question of controlling the press coverage so that we could have prestige magazines and large spaces. You had to ration it out in order to get more. When you have something unique and you make it scarce it adds to its value.' During his first tour of America, DeFries decided that, since Bowie earned over £1,000 an hour for performing, journalists too should expect to pay him at the same rate for an interview with him.

Similar control was exercised over photographers. Right from the very early concerts in England, when Bowie was hardly known as a performer, DeFries issued the instruction: 'There shall be no still, cinema, television, video or other cameras in the auditorium during the performance, except those authorised by MainMan.' The move was calculated to whet media interest while simultaneously ensuring that all published photographs were authorised by Image Control. No photographer was going to catch our David with his frail humanity exposed. 'DeFries likes to be in charge but there's also an element of game to the whole thing,' says Mick Rock, the photographer hired by DeFries to cover the concerts. 'The more you refused people permission to photograph him, the more they wanted to do it. And it was exactly the same regarding interviews.'

Rock regards Bowie as one of the first rock'n'roll people to realise the value of photography in image creation. 'He understood in an intelligent way what pictures could do. It was a refreshing change for me to be involved with someone who saw things in this way. An image is a difficult thing to capture on film. You're basically dealing with a body and yet it's somehow got to be more than that. What you have to do is to try and distil some of the mystery behind it. You can create a feeling of inaccessibility in that you can build an aura by lighting, angle and just the kind of sympathy you can elicit from your subject.'

Brian Ward, the photographer responsible for the covers of Bowie's first two RCA albums, has a similar respect for his understanding of the medium. 'He knows exactly where he's going – he's a very cool person. He always comes to you with a definite idea of what he wants but he also respects what you're doing and leaves you a lot of room to work.' For the *Hunky Dory* album cover, Bowie had arrived at Ward's studio with a book on Marlene Dietrich and pointed out a particular photograph he wanted imitated. For *Ziggy Stardust* he asked him to check out a location for what he described as 'a Brooklyn alley scene' where he'd appear alone like some alien being. 'He was playing on this man-from-

Mars thing,' recalls Ward. 'He wanted to come over like a real stranger, like something out of a science-fiction movie.'

All of Rock's photographs were studied by Bowie and DeFries. Only those that promoted the image were considered for publication and a large proportion of these remained unseen. 'Some of the best pictures have never been released,' says Rock. 'It's nicer that way. They'll mean much more in a few years to come.' Another reason for the concern over photographs was that Bowie's image was still undergoing changes. In the first six months his hair went from a crop to a swept-back style, immediately turning Early Ziggy into a period style. In America he shaved his eyebrows off, adopted different disguises and ended up with a chandelier earring hanging from his left ear. 'The essence of fantasy,' writes Christopher Booker in *The Neophiliacs*, 'is that it feeds on a succession of . . . unresolved images, each of which arouses anticipation, followed by inevitable frustration, leading to the demand for a new image to be put in its place.'

The cult figure needs to cultivate aloofness. It doesn't do to be too open and friendly. In 1971 Bowie explained this to his music publisher and close confidant Bob Grace, who recalls: 'He said that he would have to become elusive. He said it was terribly important.' By the end of that same year Grace couldn't contact him by phone; even his mother's number had been changed. He went to one of his concerts only to find him protected by bodyguards and whisked off by a chauffeur after the show. 'It was that whole image thing,' recalls Grace. 'With all this protection and transport it was obviously costing them a lot more to put concerts on than they were getting at the time, but that was the whole style of it – the Greta Garbo bit.'

'The whole bodyguard thing is another technique of De-Fries',' explains Tony Visconti. 'He knew that the way to become successful is to start acting successful.' William Gavin, writing to the people responsible for promoting Nixon during the '68 elections, put the theory like this: 'He (Nixon) has to come across as a person larger than life, the stuff of legend. People are stirred by the legend, including the living legend, not by the man himself. It's the aura that surrounds the charismatic figure more than it is the figure itself, and that draws the followers. Our job is to build that aura. Attention begets attention.'

Most rock groups tour the States two or three times before they take top billing. Bowie headlined on his first tour. With him were an entourage of 24, including three bodyguards, a hairdresser, a publicity designer, two photographers, a ward-robe mistress and a press officer. Photographs were released of him walking towards the stage flanked by two burly bodyguards – the level of protection one associates with Presley or the President. Anyone who needs looking after that much MUST be important! Attention begets attention.

Key to star creation is the strategic interview. Bowie now looks back to one particular interview he gave to the *Melody Maker* as being the one that 'made him' (his words). It was here that for the first time he openly stated that he was bisexual – an important part of his image. But even this interview was made hard-to-get. 'It seemed that already they were vetting the press,' recalls Mick Watts, who wrote the feature, 'and I thought, Christ, this is heavy, the guy hasn't had a hit in two years.'

When the feature was published it gained him full-page coverage plus the front-page headline and a prediction of his success. 'We took a risk,' admits Watts. 'We put him on the cover when no one had heard of him. We had letters in saying "Who is David Bowie?"' The open statement of his bisexu-ality, an unusual step at the time (months earlier he'd told the *Daily Mirror*, 'I get called queer but my sexual life is normal'), was obviously a good move. With gay lib blossoming and male/female distinctions being challenged Bowie appeared to be on the cutting edge of social change. 'I'm sure he did it for publicity,' says Watts. 'He's a bright boy. I think that he sensed that it was becoming vogue-ish, that the permissive was becoming permissible. Now of course it's trendy to act like a fag. Bowie developed fag chic.'

Later, Watts interviewed both Bowie and DeFries for a *Sunday Times* feature but after it was written a dispute blew up over which photographs were to be used and the project was dropped. DeFries, whose policy is never to be interviewed, wrote to Watts and offered to buy back the feature but this was refused because the paper claimed copyright. In August of the same year Watts wrote another piece for *Melody Maker* in which he almost tarnished the star's image. He quoted Bowie as calling Marc Bolan, then on top of the rock pile, 'prissy and fey – engrossed in his own image.' This quotation did not please image-control one bit. 'I was at a reception,' recalls Watts, 'and DeFries came over to me and said, "You've been a bit of a naughty boy, Michael. You've caused a bit of trouble." From then on I was a bit suspect in the Bowie camp.'

Nick Kent of the *New Musical Express* is also suspect. When the David Bowie Fan Club circulated a list of journalists who had written unfavourable stories, Kent's name was prominent, largely because of three anti-Bowie articles he wrote – one for an American journal and two for his own paper. Since that time he's received hate mail from fans and a threatening phone call.

In order to limit the number of articles that don't promote the image as conceived Bowie's management vet all copy where they have arranged interviews or supplied information. The policy regarding the availability of the product himself is contained in a sheaf of instructions circulated to staff and to promoters. 'The artist will do no press, radio, television or other interviews whatsoever,' it states. 'We need to see the articles so that we can have control over them,' says the General Manager of the company, Barry Bethel. 'Our ideal has always been to see everything that is written about any of our artists so that we can alter or take out anything that would be damaging or which could be misconstrued. After all, we're talking about the image of one of our artists, aren't we? Every move we make is thought out. Every photograph is personally vetted and every article approved of. The benefits are that you end up with the correct sort of stories.' Bowie's more recent reticence to be interviewed is explained by his friend Tony Visconti: 'He's very aware of the mystery he's created and he's keen to keep it that way.'

The flow of information must be controlled. Too much of it and your hero becomes just another person, a celebrated member of the public. Not enough and he sinks back into anonymity. With just enough information, each cult follower can nurture their own dream to fit with their own psychological requirements. 'All fantasy images excite the mind by the fact that they are incomplete and cannot be properly resolved,' writes Christopher Booker. 'They tantalise and egg on the imagination in the same way as an object only seen indistinctly, because it does not provide the brain with sufficient information to clearly make it out, may tease and excite our minds into thinking it larger and more awesome than it in fact is.' William Gavin in his memos to the Nixon staff was also aware of the importance of what was not said. 'What you don't say can be more important than what you do say. What you leave unsaid then becomes what the audience brings to it.'

Every good student of cult figures knows that it's important to either die or disappear from public view before public interest withers away. James Dean and Jimi Hendrix took the first option, the Beatles took the second, while Dylan compromised by almost killing himself and almost disappearing. Bowie chose to do it in grand style with a retirement announcement from the stage at Hammersmith followed by a party at the Cafe Royal.

Mick Watts knew of the retirement plan six months before it took place when DeFries mentioned it to him in New York. No one was really surprised when it happened – at least, no one who was aware of the whole campaign to create super-

stardom for Bowie. It seemed the logical conclusion of everything that had preceded it and many people suggest that it
was even planned back in 1971 along with Ziggy's first
haircut.

After the farewell concert the official fan club mailed the
following plea: 'We firmly believe that with some sincere
persuasion from all of you, possibly in the form of letters to
him via the fan club, we can help change his decision . . . we
need your letters to persuade him to return as a live performer. BRING BACK BOWIE.'

Melody Maker was sceptical about this retirement. In an
article titled 'Is Bowie Really Quitting?', Roy Hollingworth
wrote: 'Would it not be a very super move to "quit" in public
even before he'd reached his peak? To be very famous one has
to pull many tricks these days. And however lovely Bowie is
in your eyes, don't ever think he won't pull tricks. To survive
he has to . . . But don't worry. He'll be back – when everyone's calmed down, and levelled off. It's just tactics. Remember, just tactics.' In a separate interview Bowie's guitarist,
Mick Ronson, was quoted as saying, 'To continue wouldn't
be right. Bowie has to become a legend – it's the only way he
can last.'

How does a cult figure feel at the end of the first two years
as he sees carbon copies of his Ziggy idea walking the streets
and living out the fantasy? How does he feel as he sits out the
retirement period obviously wondering whether the image is
expanding or contracting in the public mind? After all,
Presley, Dylan and the Beatles all lived with their public
for up to five years before they slipped out of reach. 'I don't
feel I'm a person at all sometimes,' Bowie confessed to *Rolling
Stone* during what seems to have been an extremely open
moment. 'I'm just a collection of other people's ideas. The
artist doesn't exist. None of us do. We're in the twilight zone.
We're the original false prophets. We want all the adulation
but we've got nothing to say.'

Although 'the comeback' seems certain to feature prominently in the next part of the strategy it's difficult to visualise what new image he can concoct for the event which won't diminish the aura already created. He has already been advising Lulu and Mott The Hoople that the 'glam' image is passé. 'I don't think that anyone who has manifested as much imagination as Bowie can blow it completely,' admits Charles Shaar Murray, possibly the writer closest to the Bowie camp. 'I do think though that he has come far too near it for comfort. Imagination is not unlimited. In a sense, it's a capital sum reduced by expenditure.'

Jerry Gilbert

IT'S HARD TO BE A SAINT IN THE CITY: BRUCE SPRINGSTEEN ON THE BLOWER

I don't recall the point at which the artist, latterly known as The Boss, handed over his home phone number . . . but trading words over junk food at 4.30 a.m. in a Georgetown diner had provided every facility. The show had been over barely an hour and Springsteen had just ground out over four hours of music spanning two sets at Georgetown University – working himself to the same level of exhaustion that had caused cancellation of the lead-up gigs.

Memory flashbacks of the musician coughing blood, and necking back medicine to mitigate the effect, remain indelible. So, although CBS had invested money in flying me over to cover the show, Bruce's manager Mike Appel was insistent there would be no interview tonight.

Yet The Boss remained resolute, which is how come we ended up talking endlessly in Washington's crepuscular early dawn. It was also the year William Friedkin released The Exorcist, *and so Georgetown had taken on a celebrity of its own.*

However, this is not about that interview.

Four months later the fanzine ZigZag, owned by Tony Stratton-Smith, called up, desperate for an instant cover story. And 13 speculative digits later I was talking to The Man.

I simply phoned Bruce Springsteen at home, on spec, right off the cuff. And found him ready for an emotional heave of epic proportions. Instead of reporter/interviewee the interaction changed to confessor/amanuensis in what became a cathartic experience for both of us. Mr Pitman would have been proud of the accelerated shorthand hybrid.

The conversation itself was conducted in an Embassy-style building in Mayfair – on a Chesterfield surrounded by chandelier, coffee tables, rococo cornice and panelling. I had diurnal access to the office only, as after dark it was used for shooting skinflicks.

And so the fact that the article went fee-free was made all the sweeter by knowing that the cost of the call (which must have been substantial in those days) was being covered by the grubby gains of the tenants.

JG

ALL DRESSED UP AND NO PLACE TO GO

'WHEN HIS TWO-HOUR set ended I could only think, can anyone really be this good: can anyone say this much to me, can rock 'n' roll still speak with this kind of power and glory?'

These questions, which he then went on to answer, were posed by Jon Landau in a May issue of *Rolling Stone*. His 500-word eulogy provided a head-and-shoulders vignette of a New Jersey street poet called Bruce Springsteen. 'I racked my brains but simply can't think of a white artist who does so many thinks so superbly,' went on Landau, stretching out in uncustomary fashion. 'There is no one I would rather watch onstage today . . .' Jeeez.

Landau was announcing the second coming of the man who first appeared from the pens of the scribes as the brother Messiah of Bob Dylan. One way or another, American critics have laid a heavy onus on Springsteen, but I guess it's easier to live up to a placing in just about every US writer's 1974 playlist than to efface the charlatan connotations which accolades pertaining to Dylan invariably conjure up in the eyes of the beholder.

It just so happens that I agree with all Mr Landau's comments and I'm glad that he too can detect the power of Springsteen's band ringing in his tired old bones, just as I'm glad that Mr Springsteen can quote dismissively that 'Dylan influenced me as much as anyone, I guess . . . when I was fourteen, maybe . . . but I don't think about the comparison too much.'

A couple of years after it started, CBS's attitude in building Springsteen into the star the critics say he already is remains bewildering. He's never been to England and currently waits for his new single to be completed with the desperation of a man who's flat broke, pinning his final hopes on the record, wondering whether his band will survive and seeking fit to qualify only that he doesn't feel he's written AM station lyrics. When did he ever?

I've travelled 18,000 miles to see Springsteen twice, courtesy of CBS London, and shared my enthusiasm with other foreign journalists as the Springsteen band have disseminated waves of ecstasy across theatre auditoriums, and yet he maintains that Columbia have been constantly cool in dealing with their wonder talent.

Peter Jay Philbin, a friend of Springsteen's long before joining CBS International press department in New York, claims that it isn't until sales really start to look good that CBS throw the full weight of the heavy artillery into the game, and right now Springsteen may be the critics' fave but he ain't selling albums. All dressed up and no place to go.

'We're at the lowest we've ever been right now,' he told me last month. 'It means that if we don't play every week of the year then we don't have money. Right now we've just come off the road and the guys are getting thrown out of their houses. Hopefully I'll be getting some money from Columbia, and maybe with David Bowie doing some of the songs that'll be good. But that's the only problem right now . . . it's sort of a shame . . . I'd just like to be a little more secure, that's all,' he said in a vain attempt to make light of the problem.

Physically, Bruce Springsteen has all the hallmarks of a guy who's spent his life being dragged through the gutter. He's of frail build, sports a scrubby beard and matted, tousled hair, has an uneven gait (stumbles) uneven speech (mumbles). Shirt tails hang beneath an old leather jacket that's followed him around 1,000 gigs and religiously been thrown from his shoulders at some point during the 120 minutes' worth of music that his band are guaranteed to pound out whether the contract says so or not.

Such was the case at Georgetown University, Washington in March 1974 – a Jesuit college whose only claim to fame is being the centrepiece of Blatty's *Exorcist*. My second visit to the Springsteen show.

The first show opens, and to my delight it belongs to John Hall's band Orleans. Springsteen does his coupla hours. They take a break. Orleans open the second show and the audience bitch for an encore. Springsteen wanders onstage . . . the city orphan who had just cancelled two gigs because he'd been throwing up blood. Homes in on his regular showstoppers, and with all that out of the way, starts pulling up these old R&B classics like 'Walking The Dog' and 'Let The Four Winds Blow' with total disdain of the fact that we're living in the '70s. The show takes on a strange atmosphere that only nocturnal energy can generate and when this spirit in the night staggers off stage, beads of sweat dripping from the huge black frame of number one sideman Clarence Clemons, it's way past three. In the dressing room a grand piano awaits his call and he starts to re-work a theme that he's been trying to mould into a song.

'MANY FALSE IMPRESSIONS WERE DRAWN'

He has this knack of being able to make himself totally unobtrusive, quietly waiting for the band to wander out into the approaching dawn before settling down to an interview with more commitment than you'd dare expect at 4.30 am.

Springsteen emerged out of rhythm and blues and rock and roll and the whole legacy of Chuck Berry and people like Gary US Bonds. 'All those old R&B-type people – Bonds had a great feeling on all his records, a feeling that everyone was singing, you know, thirty guys all playing and singing in the studio at the same time on things like "Quarter To Three" and "School Is Out".'

This explains his obsession for a loose back-up band with a honking sax, and the same confusion, the same party chaos that he carries through so well in 'E Street Shuffle' and, more especially, 'Rosalita'. As a bar musician he had little use for lyrics that delved beyond the accepted demarcation lines of rhythm 'n' blues sentiment. 'I used to write straight rock stuff because the situation was such that whether we were playing in a bar or in a club the general conditions and PA were so bad you had to communicate on the most basic level you could and I was just never in a position to do more.

'But after that, the ten-piece band went down to seven-piece and then five-piece and then just me, so that's when I really started to write some different types of lyric. The thing is, I'd been fronting a band for nine years but when I walked to the record companies there was just me by myself with a guitar, and from that many false impressions were drawn.'

It's an important point and this fact, plus Columbia's dilatory behaviour in getting *Greetings From Asbury Park, N.J.* onto their schedules, resulted in Springsteen's debut being about half as auspicious as it might have been. 'The album was so old by the time it got released, and I write songs fast, so that I was doing all kinds of different material by the time it got released.

'I mean, I like to be doing new material but that record reflects the mood I was in at that particular time . . . you know, the fact of having to come into the city from where I was living, and I didn't have a band so it all contributed to that kind of down feel. But towards the end of the record I started pulling out of it with songs like "Spirit In The Night" which started to get into a whole different feel.'

Asbury Park was recorded at 914 Sound Studios, Blauvelt, New York, co-produced by Mike Appel (Springsteen's manager) and Jim Cretecos, featuring the collective talents of Vini Lopez, Clarence Clemons, Gary Tallent, David Sancious, Harold Wheeler and Richard Davis, of which the first four became regular members of the band and all but Lopez remain. That's the bare facts. The album, fronted by a picture postcard of Asbury Park, painted a sombre picture of city life and its victims – characters portrayed in the shadow of death. The production and some of the playing often leave room for improvement but it is impossible to deny the power and feeling which Springsteen's words and song structures exude, just as it's impossible to deny the presence and strength of his imagery even when it threatens to dictate or obscure a song rather than carry it along.

'I can rise to an occasion . . . like with that album. The rest of the time I'm kind of laid-back because there's too much going on to get excited about, too many people running around crazy. I just prefer to let it go.'

In New Jersey he prefers the incongruous . . . like water sports. He left the boardwalk life portrayed so vividly by Jack Nicholson in *The King Of Marvin Gardens* and misses the rundown environment of his adolescent period, living over a drugstore or whatever it was. The road is no place to write your new album; back in Asbury Park things were different.

'I see these situations happening when I sing them and I know the characters well. I use them in different songs and see them in shadows – they're probably based on people I know or else they're flashes that just appear there. There's a lot of

activity, a whole mess of people . . . it's like if you're walking
down the street, my songs are what you see, only distorted. A
lot of songs were written without any music at all, it's just
that I do like to sing the words.'

GREENWICH VILLAGE FOLK URCHIN

Springsteen's picture book of city street life is a nightmare
vision. 'My songs are supposed to be bigger than life,' he
claims, but he insists he has not been blessed with any greater
powers of insight than the next person.

'Jersey was so intense you couldn't even walk down the
street, so I used to go to New York and hang out in the Village
mostly, but also uptown a little bit. I was mostly by myself
with no particular place to go, but sometimes I'd hang out
with this other guy.'

So, paradoxically, when Springsteen made it with Columbia, it was as a Greenwich Village folk urchin. Totally out of
context. 'I'd written my first batch of songs, and if nothing
had come of it I'd probably have been back in the bars by
now,' he quipped at the time.

CBS went with 'Blinded By The Light' for the single,
Springsteen twisting as much distorted lyric into the metre
as possible and hanging a catchy chorus at the end of each
verse. A good ensemble legacy from his rock 'n' roll days.

> Yeah he was blinded by the light,
> Cut loose like a deuce, another runner in the night.
> Blinded by the light,
> He got down but the never got tight
> But he's gonna make it tonight . . . .

The best songs on that album, says Bruce, were those
written over a short period of time. Like the incredible suicide
ballad 'For You', which remains one of Springsteen's greatest

achievements as he recounts the final minutes of life drawing
back to the final chorus with its emotive cry.

> *I came for you, for you, I came for you,*
> *But you did not need my urgency.*
> *I came for you, for you, I came for you,*
> *But your life was one long emergency.*

'The Angel', says Springsteen, is one of his great favourites
– conceived, constructed and completed inside fifteen minutes. 'It's the most sophisticated thing I've done,' he said
referring to the sex-power-death trip of the Angel astride his
chopper.

> *The angel rides with hunchbacked children,*
> *Poison oozing from his engine,*
> *Wieldin' love as a lethal weapon,*
> *On his way to hubcap heaven . . .*

He hipped up the same theme in his trilogy of death in 'Lost In
The Flood', where he portrays death as a sort of macabre
disappearing point.

> *Well, that blaze and noise boy,*
> *He's gunning that bitch to blasting point*
> *He rides head first into a hurricane and disappears into*
> * a point*
> *And there's nothin' left where the body fell . . .*

More recently David Bowie pulled 'Growin' Up' and 'It's
Hard To Be A Saint In The City' from the same album to
record; one a pop song, the other perhaps a little too ambitious and expansive, but both pre-ordained for Bowie; in any
event, by the time Springsteen was set to record his second
album, *The Wild, The Innocent and the 'E' Street Shuffle*,
he'd ironed out all his problems. Same studio, same producers

but this time a band who had been knocked into shape on the road, largely through the experience of veteran horn player Clarence Clemons, who once worked with James Brown.

'The mistake,' Springsteen reflected, 'is in thinking that you *are* those songs,' in an obvious allusion to the self-destructive influence that the presence of his ego in those songs was having. 'To me a song is a vision, a flash, and what I see is characters in situations.

'I mean, I've stood around carnivals at nights when they're clearing up and I was scared ['Wild Billy's Circus Story', still one of the highlights of the show with Garry Tallent playing tuba and Danny Federici accordion]. As for Spanish Johnny's situation ['Incident On 57th Street'], well, I'd never get into that kind of situation, but I know people who have lived that life.'

You have to remember that it ain't easy to commute between Asbury Park and the Cafe Wha? down in the Village and hang onto your sanity. And it takes a lot of guts to blow your record advance on putting together a band – a band that Bruce calls 'a really spacey bunch of guys . . . but a pretty regular band'. There's been only one personnel change in two years, Ernest Boon Carter having replaced Vini Lopez on drums.

'Vini'd been around for years,' Bruce qualified vaguely. 'There'd been various pressures . . . it was a difficult decision to make.'

In truth, Asbury Park had a lot to do with the feel of the first album. 'Jersey's a dumpy joint,' Springsteen had said. 'I mean, it's OK, it's home, but every place is a dump.'

'EVERY SYLLABLE ADDS SOMETHING TO HIS ULTIMATE GOAL'

'Springsteen does it all. He's a rock 'n' roll punk, a Latin street poet, a ballet dancer, an actor, a poet joker, a bar band leader, hot-shit rhythm guitar player, extraordinary singer and a truly great rock 'n' roll composer. He leads a band like he's been doing it forever . . . Bruce Springsteen is a wonder to look at: skinny, dressed like a reject from Sha Na Na, he parades in front of his all star rhythm band like a cross between Chuck Berry, early Bob Dylan and Marlon Brando. Every gesture, every syllable adds something to his ultimate goal – to liberate our spirit while he liberates his by baring his soul through his music.' Another sizeable chunk from Jon Landau's *Rolling Stone* review that pretty much sums up the impact of a Springsteen show. But having looked at the lyrics, some qualifications of the musicians in the band.

Bruce looks like he's appeared out of thin air, but he's a regular old timer and he was just a straightforward rhythm guitarist in a band before coming out as a front man. He led a ten-piece in the bars and rough houses of New Jersey, and it was an experience that ultimately brought him down. But in the last and best bar band he had built up quite a following in the Southern States. 'Over about four years I played mostly down South – for some reason I got popular around Virginia, Tennessee and Carolina and I played in a lotta different towns with the ten-piece band.'

His band today may lack the sophistication of Van Morrison or Tim Buckley, but the versatility is indisputable. A long time admirer of Bruce's, watching the Georgetown gig and taking note of the amorphous nature of his songs, was moved to comment that he'd never heard Springsteen play or sing a song the same way twice. 'New York City Serenade' has changed beyond belief whilst 'Kitty's Back' (one of the best kinetic compositions) was stretched across a super-long embellished piano solo from David Sancious. 'There was more of the band in the second album and the songs were written more in the way I wanted to write, but I change the arrangements all the time in order to present the material best and to suit the style of the band. I just try to update the arrangements a bit to keep everyone interested. "Sandy", for instance, I like the way it is on the record, but it was entirely

different right up until the night I recorded it and then I
changed it.' For this next album Bruce plans to incorporate
chick singers and horns. He would do the same onstage but
for the economics of it all.

The road has really taken its toll on Springsteen's health.
When I'd seen him in Washington he'd been bemoaning the
lack of good food and swigging cough mixture from a bottle.
Some months later, talking to him on the phone to New
Jersey, he could find little cause for optimism. *The Wild, The
Innocent and the 'E' Street Shuffle*, far more of an energy/
band-participation album, he said, had generally been better
received and sold in larger quantities than the first album,
although Peter Philbin reckons the composition already
shows signs of him being sucked away from his native
environment. Technically it's a far better album, the tracks
are longer and go through more mood changes and yet it
doesn't reveal the same highs that the first had, though on
reflection I think it would have been impossible to paint as
vivid a picture as Springsteen had managed first time around.
In the light of this, the lyrics on the second album lack the
same monolithic grace as the first; no further qualification
necessary – just cop a listen to the finished product.

'I'm still fooling with the words for the new single, but I
think it'll be good,' said Springsteen, taking up the story once
again. 'I've written a lot of stuff for the new album but when I
get into the studio I'll have a clear picture – but it's a different
assortment of material and most of it relates pretty much not
to touring or playing in a band, because we haven't played
much at all this summer – but lately I've been getting a rush to
write new songs and I've got quite a few, some short and
some long.'

Mike Appel will again be producing. 'I haven't met anyone
else who understands the situation any better and he's very
involved; besides I don't like too many outside people involved, it just gets too impersonal, that's why I never pick
session musicians.'

He believes his band are improving and tightening all the time but as to whether his next album will outsell the previous two he's reluctant to say. 'I do sell records . . . but real slow and not many . . . about 500 or 1,000 each week. I don't think too many people listen to reviews and articles with regard to spending the bucks.'

He is particularly anxious to tour his current band in Britain before the line-up changes – and changes are very much on the cards. 'It's a very open situation right now. I'm definitely going to add people, possibly a horn section and people who can double on instruments like a violin and trumpet maybe.'

'RENTS ARE DUE AND ALIMONY AND WE JUST DON'T HAVE THE MONEY'

At last Bruce Springsteen realises he is on the verge of a breakthrough and by constant touring he has managed to 'erase false images that people have'.

But on a serious note he underlines his financial problem. 'I'd like to get out of this situation where I haven't paid the band for three weeks. Rents are due and alimony and we just don't have the money. At this stage of the game it's really a shame and I'd just like to get some income because in the last two years we've just managed to make ends meet and sometimes we don't; so we're at the lowest we've ever been right now and if we don't play every week we don't have money . . . it's as easy as that.'

But he clearly visualises the theme of his third album in the light of the first and second. 'Those were two very different albums,' he appraised. 'The second is more popular and it's sold more – I guess it's more musical, but the first one has a certain something for me. I tended to do two totally different things – the first album was a very radical album whereas the second wasn't quite so much. I'm surprised it didn't do better than it did because it sounded very commercial to me. This new album will possibly be something of a balance between the two – I'll try and hit somewhere between.'

There we have it, then. Bruce Springsteen, the city punk with a disparate bunch of bar boys he calls his band. Just a bunch of lost souls striving to recover and release theirs through the music, like a 'surfer boy stranded with city sand in my shoes', as Jimmy Spheeris once described his own urban paranoia.

But for all his shambolic appearance, and the weird stage drawl that makes him relatively unintelligible, Bruce Springsteen has used the legacy of the '50s more comprehensively than anyone, from his rough, tough R&B approach to the vivid documentation of his experiences. Maybe he is Bob Dylan, Jack Kerouac and James Dean all rolled into one, but if that's true then there's also a lotta James Brown and Gary Bonds tucked in there too.

Jon Savage

SOUNDS DIRTY: THE TRUTH ABOUT NIRVANA

the *Observer*, 15th August 1993

This feature occurred in unusual circumstances. The standard routine is that the act's PR approaches a magazine/newspaper's commissioning editor, who then assigns a writer to the story, or in turn the writer approaches the commissioning editor before the interview occurs. In this case, I had the interview before I had the outlet: Anton Brookes, Nirvana's dedicated press officer, had brokered an interview for me with the group on the basis of Kurt Cobain's enthusiasm for my book England's Dreaming. *I then sold the piece to Dylan Jones at the* Observer Magazine.

While flattering, there was a symmetry in this turn of events. When England's Dreaming *was first published, in late autumn 1991, I was obsessed with* Nevermind *– which I'd bought on the basis of a short, pre-release piece. It read like something I'd go for, and more than delivered on any expectation: I was particularly hypnotised by the circularity of* 'On A Plain', *which became the theme tune to a difficult book launch. As* Nevermind *became more than just a successful record, it seemed as though Punk Rock had finally conquered the American marketplace, fifteen or so years after its UK peak.*

*This interview was one of several conducted by the British music media to announce the release of Nirvana's first new post-*Nevermind *album,* In Utero. *We*

*all jetted into a situation that reminded me of the Sex
Pistols in summer 1977. In New York that July,
Nirvana were beyond a mere object of attention:
although the biggest US rock group, they had maintained a level of unpredictability that meant that no
one knew quite what was going to happen – not
a situation that the US music industry likes – and
the persistent stories that circulated about Cobain's
drug use and mental state combined with their already
established sociological import to create an intense
negative projection. Were they scapegoats for a
society's ills, revolutionaries, or both?*

*It was no problem talking to Chris Novoselic or
Dave Grohl: both were straight ahead and they just
got down and did it. Accompanied by Courtney Love,
Cobain was much trickier to pin down: after I managed to winkle them both out of a Melvins show, I sat
down with Cobain in my hotel room and began an
interview which I would now regard as the peak of my
life as a rock journalist. Time stood still as we reached
the state so well described by Paul Morley in* Ask: The
Chatter of Pop: *'Did you reach that uncanny, disorienting point where you float, right over edge of
a revealing all-round contemplation? Was it just a
cover-up? What appeared to be the trouble?'*

*Cobain was charming, occasionally sarcastic, sur-
prisingly quiet, and with a healthy interest in outsider
aesthetics – William Burroughs, Joy Division, Derek
Jarman. Despite his undeniable force, he did not look
well: although he was prepared to talk about his
heroin use, his statement that 'my whole mental and
physical state has improved almost 100 per cent' was
vitiated by the events of the next morning, when he
overdosed. Privy to this knowledge given in confiden-
tiality, I could not mention the overdose in the piece,
but it informed my conclusion, which was that*

Nirvana were walking a particularly precarious, high-stakes high-wire act. I still maintain that it could have gone either way, but maybe that's what I want to believe.

JS

SITUATED ON 51ST STREET and Broadway, in the heart of the old entertainment area, Roseland is a New York institution. In the 1920s it was the city's largest dance hall – 'the downtown headquarters for such urban dance steps as the Lindy and the Shag', according to a contemporary guide – but the formerly plush decor has been stripped and painted black for tonight's more brutal conditions of entertainment.

The dance floor is a war zone: a simulated war zone, to be sure, but still not for the faint-hearted. Hundreds of young men ricochet off each other at high speed in the moshpit, creating flows and eddies that take on a life of their own. And then, by a combination of individual effort and group will, one of them will crest on the surf of this human tide, splaying his body out in pure abandonment before disappearing again. It's a communal, physical release.

This is Nirvana's first New York show for almost two years. Expectation is high: this group arouse curiosity and passion like few others. Since their second album, *Nevermind*, went to the top of the US charts in January 1992, they have found themselves in a situation similar to that which the Sex Pistols experienced in 1977: to some, they are rock prophets, standard bearers for a generation; to others they are, as their drummer Dave Grohl dryly summaries, 'cynical slacker little fuckin' punk jerks'.

Although they are exceptionally successful, Nirvana are not quite as successful as some other artists on the *Billboard* chart. As *Nevermind* faded out of the top 200 in July this year, 13 acts had sold more records, including Garth Books, Kriss Kross, Michael Jackson, Boyz II Men and Michael Bolton – the country, R&B, rap and rock that are the staples of American pop. But *Nevermind* and its breakthrough single, 'Smell Like Teen Spirit', have come out of left field to create a culture and aesthetic impact that goes far beyond statistics.

Nirvana stir up deep emotions. Most obviously, *Nevermind* has changed American music: music media like MTV are now full of post-Nirvana groups like Pearl Jam, Soul Asylum and Stone Temple Pilots, who play that mixture of rock, metal and punk now known as 'alternative'. (Two years ago it would have been 'grunge', but following Perry Ellis's autumn 1991 collection, grunge has entered the language of fashion: the anti-fashion of sloppy T-shirts, flannel shirts and old Levi's that poverty-stricken bohemians and students have worn for years suddenly became high style.)

Nirvana have also been seen in sociological terms: as defining a new generation, the twentysomething 'slackers' who have retreated from life; as telling unattractive home truths about a country losing its empire and hit by recession as representing the final, delayed impact of British punk on America.

They have also shocked people by trashing male gender codes: kissing each other on the national network show *Saturday Night Live*, appearing in dresses in the video for their single 'In Bloom', doing pro-gay benefits. We may be more used to this in Britain, but America is a country with much more machismo in its popular culture. A sensational appearance on last year's globally broadcast MTV awards, where they smashed their equipment and mocked rock competitors Guns N' Roses, sealed their status as America's bad boys.

Nirvana have become an issue in America: they have attracted all the hospitality and scapegoating that goes with this territory. A September 1992 *Vanity Fair* article, which alleged that singer Kurt Cobain and his wife, Courtney Love, had taken heroin during Love's early pregnancy (an allegation hotly supported by the writer of the article, Lynn Hirschberg, and even more hotly denied by Love and Cobain), crystallized the couple's ascent, or rather descent, into celebrity. Suddenly, the stories were about Kurt 'n' Courtney – the twenty-something Sid Vicious and Nancy Spungen – rather than Nirvana the group. As Cobain now admits, 'it affected me to the point where I wanted to break up the band all the time.'

When American groups are successful, they tour constantly to keep their records in the charts. As *Nevermind* went on to sell 4 million copies in America (double platinum in the UK; 9 million world-wide), Nirvana withdrew. In the vacuum caused by their disappearance, the rumours flew: Cobain was dead; they were splitting up; they were recording a new album so unlistenable that no one would buy it. Kurt 'n' Courtney were hardly out of the news or the gossips columns: threatening unoffical biographers on the telephone and in person; being arrested for domestic unruliness in Seattle; fulfilling the media demands of punk couplehood.

By doing nothing, Nirvana have become mythic figures, a process that will be accelerated by three Nirvana-related books this autumn. This is a lot of baggage for anyone to carry, let alone three scruffs from the hinterlands of America. As they reappear in the public eye with an album called *In Utero* – 'in the womb' – the group are surrounded by an atmosphere of high tension, a magnetic charge that both attracts and repels.

Nirvana take the Roseland stage with everything to prove – straight into a sequence of crunching numbers: 'Serve the Servants', 'Come As You Are', 'Lithium', 'School'. Most alternate quiet, almost whispered verses with wild choruses which crackle like a power surge. The audience goes mad, cheering alike old favourites and new songs – the punning 'Penny Royal Tea' (named after a concoction used to induce abortions) or the pathologically personal 'Heart Shaped Box' ('I wish I could eat your cancer when you turn black . . .').

Nirvana are famed for leaping around on stage, even smashing their instruments, but tonight they don't do much except play hard and accurately. Bass player Chris Novoselic dominates stage left with all his six feet seven inches but, despite his lack of mobility, or in fact because of it, it is Cobain who holds your attention. He hunches into the microphone and croons, growls and then screams from the pit of his stomach. You might think this was just a teenage tantrum, but then you watch the group's control, you hear the Beatle-esque tunes and the smart, elliptical lyrics, and you realize that Nirvana are serious.

Just when you think that they're relaxing into the home run, something extraordinary occurs. Cobain leaves the stage for a couple of minutes. He reappears with a female cellist, who sits centre-stage, a dramatic contrast to all the boys moshing in front of her. The group start an acoustic song, 'Polly' – the story of a rape victim who outwitted and escaped her captor. It's a harrowing lyric, and Cobain sings it very quietly. Too quietly: the audience ignores him.

When it becomes clear that Nirvana are not going to rock, an abyss opens between the group and the audience: you can hear it as the buzz from the crowd threatens to drown out the acoustic instruments. Suddenly, Nirvana look vulnerable, but each song is more harrowing: 'Dumb', where sarcasm masks deep hurt; or 'Something in the Way', based on Cobain's experience of sleeping rough. Then they begin Leadbelly's 'Where You Gonna Sleep Tonight', which Cobain sings with all the keening notes of a Childe ballad, Appalachian-style.

'Where You Gonna Sleep Tonight' has that quality of desolation which haunts the most powerful American rock, from Leadbelly to Bob Dylan to Neil Young to R.E.M. As Cobain circles round the lyrical repetitions, his voice becomes more and more racked ('When you feel bad in America,' Cobain tells me, 'it's like losing your stomach'), and he pushes the words so hard it's as though he's trying to vomit them out. Then it's suddenly over: the group leave an audience non-plussed into an eerie silence. It takes a while before the calls for an encore become persistent.

Push me, pull you. Nirvana do encore, with 'Smell Like Teen Spirit', but follow it with several minutes of deliberate feedback by Cobain, who remains onstage long after Novoselic and Grohl have left, crouched in his own world. As an industry showcase, it's unprecedented; in America, success demands uniformity and repetition of what made you great. It's a total punk rock show: a bitter, dogged stand-off between the group's insistence on doing what they want and the audience's expectations of what they should do.

The sleeve of *Nevermind* shows a baby swimming under water towards a dollar bill on a fish hook. The intended meaning is clear: the loss of innocence, the Faustian contrast that usually comes with money. Take it, but if you do, you're hooked for life. It's a parable of Nirvana's current dilemma: they've taken the bait, but the contradictions of their success are threatening to tear them apart.

How can the members of Nirvana retain their integrity, which is very important to them, in a situation that demands constant compromise? How can they sing from the point of view of an outsider now that they're in a privileged position? How can they suffer relentless world-wide media exposure and still retain, in Grohl's words, 'the spontaneity and the energy of something fresh and new' that has marked their career?

Kurt Cobain materializes in the lobby of a smart midtown hotel. It's a quiet entrance, but an entrance nevertheless: for all his fragility, Cobain is very much the star when he needs to be. He is of medium height and painfully thin. His garb of baggy patched jeans, woman's acrylic cardigan and shredded red and black jumper – exactly like the one worn by the *Beano*'s Dennis the Menace – would cause him to be thrown out in any other circumstances.

It's the day before the Roseland concert. Dave Grohl and Chris Novoselic have already passed through on their way to the appointment for which Cobain is somewhat late. This is in character: Grohl is a straightahead 24-year-old, the son of an Irish/American family, who wears layers of ripped casual clothes and had the physique and stamina of the sportsman he was before punk took over his life at 15. 'Let's do it,' he says when we go to talk; he is the youngest of the three, and his precision and fire give Nirvana much of their attack. He would not be habitually late.

Nor would Novoselic, but for a different reason. A tall, rangy man, dressed in black, who handles his size with care, he is the bottom of the group – the bridge between Grohl's energy and Cobain's spaciness. The Los Angeles-born son of Croatian immigrants, he has the air of someone who has fought his demons: his teenage conversion to punk rock has matured into thoughtful application of his political beliefs. It was Novoselic who arranged Nirvana's last major show, a multi-artist benefit for Bosnian rape survivors, after visiting what had been his mother country.

If Grohl and Novoselic are definitely in the world, Cobain tunes in and out: 'You haven't been waiting for me, have you?' he asks the assembled company. 'If you have, shout at me.' But everybody is resigned to the fact that when you do anything with Kurt Cobain, you have to wait. This is partly due to the nocturnal time that many musicians keep, partly due to the fact that, like it or not, much of the pressure that surrounds Nirvana comes to rest on Cobain's frail shoulders.

His response, in public at least, is simultaneously to court and to flee attention. This is a quite understandable human trait and does not denote insincerity. At first, he mumbles and is vague. His straw-coloured hair is shoulder-length, centre-parted, and falls over his beard: together with the white 1950s sunglasses – the sort which people wore in the UK during the punk days – it means that you can hardly see his face. When you finally see his eyes, you understand why. They are of a startling blue sensitivity.

When you prise him away from the mania of his situation, Cobain is courteous, intelligent, quiet. Nirvana's success has meant validation for this German-Irish 26-year-old from

Aberdeen, 180 miles away from Seattle in America's North-West. Whereas once he might not speak for days, now thousands hang on his lyrics and public pronouncements; where once he was an outcast, attacked on his home streets, he can now flaunt his difference in the eyes of world, and be loved for it. He has also learned that if you're loved, you're hated, and that if you provoke, you get a backlash.

The three members of Nirvana were all born between 1965 and 1969, a fact reflected in their name, a sarcastic comment on hippie pieties: in some ways, they are acting out the freedoms and failures of that time. All three are the children of divorced families. 'A lot of people have this theory that we cling together because of that,' Dave Grohl says. 'We all basically grew up with our mothers, although Chris and Kurt went back and forth.'

Cobain was the youngest of the three at the time his parents divorced, and it hit him hard. 'It was when I was seven,' he says. 'I had a really good childhood and then all of a sudden my whole world changed, I remember feeling ashamed. I became antisocial and I started to understand the reality of my surroundings, which didn't have a lot to offer. It's such a small town that I couldn't find any friends who were compatible. I like to do artistic things, I like to listen to music. I could never find any friends like that.

'I felt so different and so crazy that people just left me alone. They were afraid. I always felt that they would vote me "Most Likely to Kill Everyone" at a high school dance. I could definitely see how a person's mental state could deteriorate to the point where they could do that. I've got to the point where I've fantasized about it, but I'd have always opted for killing myself first.'

The three were born into an environment where pop was the way of interacting the world. As the youngest, Dave Grohl was entranced by the first American response to English punk music: the new wave of groups like the B-52s and Devo.

Novoselic 'listened to hard rock radio like Judas Priest and Black Sabbath, then I wasted good years of my life listening to Ozzy Osbourne and Def Leppard.'

Cobain grew up with the Beatles, graduating to the American rock/pop of the day at high school: Cheap Trick, Led Zeppelin. 'My mother always tried to keep English culture in our family,' he says. 'We drank tea all the time.' Much later, he immersed himself in the English Gothic of Joy Division: 'I've always felt that there's that element of Gothic in Nirvana.'

Sometime in the mid-1980s, the Aberdeen outcasts met. 'I saw that Kurt was enlightened,' says Novoselic. 'I liked him because he was funny, he was an artist, he was always drawing stuff. He was always Bohemian, for sure, but always had trouble with rednecks. I think that was just his bad luck. One time this redneck just held him down and tortured him.'

'For a long time I had no male friends that I felt comfortable with,' says Cobain. 'I ended up by hanging out with girls a lot. I just always felt that they weren't treated with respect. Women are totally oppressed in small towns like Aberdeen. The words bitch and cunt were totally common; I mean, you'd hear them all the time. It took me years to realize that these were the things that were bothering me.

'I thought I was gay. I thought that might be the solution to my problems at one time during my school years. Although I never experimented, I had a gay friend, and that was the time I experienced real confrontation with people. I got beaten up. Then my mother wouldn't allow me to be friends with him any more, because she's homophobic. It was devastating, because finally I'd found a male friend who I actually hugged and was affectionate to. I was putting the pieces of the puzzle together, and he played a big role.'

All three were empowered by punk, as it slowly filtered from Britain through the US. Whereas in Britain punk groups were guaranteed major label attention until the mid-1980s, a network of independent labels and indeed national media attention, in America they were shut out after a disastrous Sex Pistols tour and the coincidental rise of disco: just after the Sex Pistols broke up on the West Coast in January 1978, the soundtrack to *Saturday Night Fever* went to the first of its 24 weeks at America's number one.

Punk's commercial twin, new wave, had limited but significant success in the early 1980s, but the pure stuff went underground, burrowing through America, city by city, like a termite. Each major city had its own scene: Washington, San Francisco, Los Angeles, Minneapolis. Few groups from this culture had any major label and clubs developed similar to the one that had fuelled the growth of rock 'n' roll in the 1950s.

Cobain had read reports of the Sex Pistols' US tour. 'I'd just fantasize about how amazing it would be to hear this music and be part of it. But I was 11; I couldn't. When I finally heard American punk groups like Flipper and Black Flag, I was completely blown away. I found my calling. There were so many things going on at once, because it expressed the way I felt socially, politically, emotionally. I cut my hair, and started trying to play my own style of punk rock and guitar: fast, with a lot of distortion.'

Cobain started Nirvana with Novoselic in 1986. He'd always written – thoughts, scraps of poetry – and they became lyrics. The group played locally in Seattle and Olympia, a college town that was home to a particularly thoughtful punk scene. This was based around the group Beat Happening, who ran their own club, set up their own label and recorded songs like 'Bad Seeds'. 'A new generation from the teenage nation', they sang: 'this time let's get it right'. In 1987, this generational rhetoric was charming but absurd: nobody thought like that any more. In 1992, it seemed like prophecy.

In the last years of the 19th century, Seattle had been an important transit point for the Klondike Gold Rush in Alaska. The city bore for many years the legacy of this boom-or-burst phenomenon. Nearly 100 years later, another gold rush occurred when the major record labels and national media descended on Seattle. What they found, and have since placed in the mainstream of American pop, was a form of music where, as Novoselic says, 'people had outgrown hard-core and were rediscovering rock – Blue Cheer, the Stooges.'

By 1987, two young college graduates, Bruce Pavitt and Jonathan Poneman, had a Seattle label up and running, Sub Pop, which released records by local groups like Mudhoney, Nirvana and Soundgarden. They were good at marketing books, slogans, and wanted a word to describe, half mock-ingly, half seriously, the noise that these groups made. It wasn't punk exactly, although it was steeped in punk attitude and politics; with the gut-wrenching downer pace of heavy metal and the tuneful tension of rock, it was . . . grunge.

Sub Pop released Nirvana's first single, 'Love Buzz', in 1988. Their first album, *Bleach*, was recorded a year later for just over $600. Dave Grohl joined in 1990 – the final focusing of the group. By this time, the American music industry was beginning to take up punk groups: the signing of New Yorkers Sonic Youth to DGC, a subsidiary of Geffen, had made waves, and it was DGC A&R man Gary Gersh who finally signed Nirvana in 1991. A bidding war put the advance up to £287,000, and the group went in to record *Nevermind* with producer Butch Vig.

By the time *Nevermind* was released, Nirvana were being handled by industry insiders: management by John Silva of Gold Mountain, record company by David Geffen – a highly privileged position. *Nevermind* made everything else the Seattle group had sound like a demo: although Cobain now disavows the record as 'too slick', Vig's production gave Nirvana a power and a clarity which enabled people to fully hear what was going on. Even with such a strong team and such a strong product, Nirvana were not expected to sell more than about 250,000 records: *Nevermind* sold over a million within six weeks of release.

Success brought Nirvana more problems than it solved. 'It

didn't anticipate at all,' says Novoselic. 'I didn't know how to deal with it.' 'We were touring constantly,' says Cobain, 'so I didn't realize what had happened until about three months after we'd become famous in America. It just scared me. I was frightened for about a year and a half: I wanted to quit. It's only after the birth of my child that I decided to crawl out of my shell and accept it.'

Nirvana should have been on top of the world but instead they freaked out. Part of the problem had to do with the culture from which they came, which had celebrated the outsider – 'Loser', read an early Sub Pop T-shirt slogan – and which was fiercely anti-major label, pro-independent. One of Nirvana's first acts on joining Geffen Records was to print a T-shirt that read 'Flower-stuffin' 'ketty-pettin' baby-kissin' corporate rock whores'.

The group's unnecessary agonizing about 'selling out' and 'corporate rock' ducks the more serious problem of how they can retain their strong ideals. Exposure to the mass market tends to iron out subtleties and ironies, as Nirvana have found to their cost. Nirvana are pro-gay, pro-feminist. Cobain's irritation at the attitudes of some of his new fans spilled over in the sleeve notes for the past-success compilation, *Incesticide*: 'I have a request for our fans,' he wrote. 'If any of you in any way hate homosexuals, people of different colour or women, please do this one favour for us – leave us the fuck alone! Don't come to our shows and don't buy our records.'

'As a defence, I'm neutered and spayed,' Cobain sings, and, indeed, he presents a view of men that runs against the macho self-image of a country where the ethic of youth, health and personal self-improvement is still strong. He presents himself, like Morrissey once did, as old, ugly, 'still ill'.

Rock requires personal authenticity, and Cobain embodies what he sings. 'My body is damaged from music in two ways,' he says. 'I have a red irritation in my stomach. It's psychosomatic, caused by all the anger and the screaming. I have scoliosis, where the curvature of your spine is bent, and the weight of my guitar has made it worse. I'm always in pain, and that adds to the anger in our music. I'm grateful to it, in a way.

'My stomach was so bad that there were times on our last tour where I just felt like a drug addict because I was starving. I went to all these different doctors but they couldn't find out what was wrong with me. I tried everything I could think of: change of diet, pills, stopped drinking, stopped smoking. Nothing worked, and I just decided that if I'm going to feel like a junkie every morning, vomiting every day, then I might as well take the substance that kills that pain. That's not the main reason why I took heroin, but it has more to do with it than most people think.'

Self-destruction haunts youth-culture aesthetics: the myth of 'Live fast, die young and have a good-looking corpse' that runs from Thomas Chatterton through to James Dean and Sid Vicious. The grunge generation was not immune: patterns of local drug supply meant that heroin was easily available and, cloaked in the loser ethic, many Seattle groups succumbed.

'I'd taken heroin for a year and a half,' Cobain says, 'but the addiction didn't get in the way until the band stopped touring about a year and a half ago. But now things have got better. Ever since I've been married and had a child, within the last year, my whole mental and physical state has improved almost 100 per cent. I'm really excited about touring again. I'm totally optimistic: I haven't felt this optimistic since my parents got divorced, you know.'

For the whole of the 20th century, America has thought of itself as, among other things, a young country. In this, the person of the child – from foetus to late adolescence (which, post-baby-boomer, can last until the mid-forties) – has become of prime importance. Out of this has come the youth culture which has colonized the world.

Now that America is in a crisis of recession, corruption and indeed social cohesion, the child and the teenager have become sites of struggle: the intense abortion battles, star revelations of child abuse, teen suicides, teen violence. Whether consciously or not, Nirvana have slipped into this national obsession, with their album concepts and messages from within the emotional front line.

Nirvana sing as traumatized children who have been empowered by the freedoms within popular culture. Their courage and talent have made them beacons for anyone who has felt the same way but have also placed them in the eye of the storm. Their growing pains are intense and are conducted in public: *In Utero* is a dark record, finely poised between self-destruction and optimism, and the Roseland show makes it quite clear just how much they are struggling.

Before the racked finale, however, Cobain does a wonderful thing: 'Ye-eh-eh-eh,' he shouts over five notes during 'Lithium', and, as the roaring crowd back him up all the way, the hairs on the back of your neck stand on end.

2
CLOSE ENCOUNTERS

Penny Valentine

THE SEEKER: JONI MITCHELL

Sounds, 3rd and 10th June 1972

This interview was much appreciated by Joni at the time. However, when Sounds *let some magazine I can't remember reprint it in America, she went nuts. Not surprisingly, as it turned out that what nobody knew at the time was that she had had an illegitimate daughter (I wish I'd bloody well known) and there was quite a bit about not having had kids and concentrating on being a musician.*

PV

PART ONE – 3RD JUNE 1972

THE LADY WHO walks on eggs is sitting in her hotel suite overlooking St. James' Park with her legs tucked up, her chin resting on her knees.

She is wearing a pair of jeans, a tiny printed shirt and a plain sweater over the top. Her feet are bare where she's kicked her clogs off, and her fine, fair hair trails across her shoulders almost hiding the silver hoops she wears in her ears. There is a tidy casualness about her appearance, a cleanliness and unrumpled freshness. And after the perfunctory look at you there's an acceptance that's surprisingly warm when you consider the image that has been built up around her over the years.

It was Richie Havens that called Joni Mitchell 'the lady that walks on eggs' some years back when we were discussing star

signs and environmental characteristics. And not knowing
her, it seemed from her music she was careful, delicate, going
through life frightened of breaking it. It was quite a capsuled
insight then – rightly capturing the fragility of a girl whose
relentless pursuit of happiness appeared destined to fail. And
yet, here and now, Joni Mitchell is a contradiction in terms
that shows almost before you speak to her.

That star syndrome, though, produces contradictions in
itself. The biggest with Joni is her metamorphosis on stage
and off. At the Festival Hall she was like a Hans Christian
Andersen snow queen, a throwback to her Scandinavian/
Canadian origins, the vocal pitched to hang like icicles on the
night air.

This Saturday, in a rainswept London, she is a comfortable
encounter, and – for all the outward initial purity – the bright
red painted toenails she wiggles while she talks make you
smile, simply because they are in themselves a contradiction
to the image.

After the Festival Hall she went to Europe for some
concerts and then came back to London on Thursday. That
night she took herself off to see Kurt Weill's *Threepenny
Opera*, found it had moved, tried to see *A Day in the Death of
Joe Egg*, found it had started. Undismayed, and she laughs
now telling it, she had gone back to the hotel, stuck her hair
up in a beret and prowled midnight Piccadilly alone with her
notebook of half-finished poems so that she could sketch
people in bars. On Friday she had taped an *In Concert* for
Stanley Dorfman and afterwards, at dinner, we'd talked
about her newly-completed house in Canada, and the plan
in her own mind that had never materialized: 'I thought I'd
lead a kind of *Heidi*-like existence, you know – with goats
and an orchard.'

The interview she has promised on Saturday is her first for
two years. She made a lot of decisions, back in 1970, one of
which was to give up working and travel around, the other
being to stop giving interviews. She'd had a rough time of it

mentally and physically, a whole wrong outlook on her life
and work. And to her, interviews were beginning to hurt: 'All
people seemed interested in was the music and the gossip – I
felt then that the music spoke for itself and the gossip was
unimportant.'

'I have in my time,' and she grins at the pseudodramatic air
in her voice, 'been very misunderstood.' But you can feel that
the constant intrusion into her private life got too much to
bear.

A lot of new songs have emerged from the two-year hiatus,
and in themselves are interesting insights into the change in
Joni's outlook: the loving humour of 'You Turn Me On (I'm a
Radio)', the pain in 'Cold Blue Steel and Sweet Fire', the
retrospective bitterness in 'Lesson in Survival'. But then there
is that feeling – haven't all her songs been directly autobiographical, total personal emotions?

'Well, some of them are, yes, directly personal and others
may seem to be because they're conglomerate feelings. Like,
remember we were talking before about the song for Beethoven and I was telling you that's written from the point of view
of his Muse talking to him. But that comes from an understanding that I thought I perceived. By reading books about
Beethoven I got a feeling which I felt was familiar, as I had felt
about people that are friends of mine. So that's from my own
experience, because it's my feeling for other people.'

And yet one had stuck particularly in my mind – 'Cactus
Tree' – the song about a girl who everyone loved and yet who
was 'too busy being free' to concentrate on returning that
feeling properly . . .

'I feel that's the song of *modern* woman. Yes, it has to do
with my experience, but I know a lot of girls like that . . . who
find that the world is full of lovely men but they're driven by
something else other than settling down to *frau*-duties.'

But then, I say, there is this impression she gives out –
someone on the move all the time, someone intent on having
freedom, even if it's a deceptive kind of freedom.

'Freedom *is* deceptive, though. It's like that line of [Kris] Kristofferson's: "Freedom's just another way of nothing left to lose" [*sic*]. Freedom implies a lot of loneliness, you know, a lot of unfulfilment. It implies always the search for fulfilment, which sometimes is more exciting than the fulfilment itself. I mean, so many times I've talked to friends of mine who are just searching for something and one day they come to you and they've FOUND IT! Then two weeks later you talk to them and they aren't satisfied. They won't allow themselves to think they've found it – because they've come to enjoy the quest so much. They've found it – then what?

'I think there's a new thing to discover in the development of fulfilment. I don't think it necessarily means trading the search, which is more exciting than the actual fulfilment. I still have this dream that you can come to a place where there's a different kind of medium – a more subtle kind of exploration to do of one thing or one place or one person. Like, drifting through lives quickly and cities quickly, you know, you never really get to understand a person or a place very deeply. Like, you can be in a place until you feel completely familiar with it, or stay with a person until you may feel very bored. You feel you've explored it all. Then, all of a sudden, if you're there long enough, it'll just open up and flash you all over again. But so many people who are searching and travelling come to that point where it's stealing out on them and they just can't handle that and have to move on.'

We talk about the time she spent travelling and how – although songs came out of it and so it was a productive experience – there was an innate disappointment. A sense – and this came out in her spoken intros at the Festival Hall – of disillusionment that what she had believed would be magical somehow never turned out that way. She was affected by that too, she admits, and yet after a thought she smiles at her own naïveté in expecting places to be untouched, in expecting to be totally absorbed into them and accepted.

'You tailor-make your dreams to "it'll be this way" and

when it isn't . . . like, if you have a preconceived idea of anything, then inevitably it can't live up to your hopes. Hawaii had so many really beautiful parts to it, and the island of Kawai is agricultural. I guess I had thought of [Hawaii] from all those *Occa Occa* movies I had seen – sacrificing the maidens to the volcano, rivers running with blood and lava, guava trees and,' she laughs, 'Esther Williams, you know, swimming through the lagoon. And you get there and have to sort through the stucco and the pink hotels. Crete was for the most part pretty virgin, and if you walked to the market you'd find farmers with *burros* and oranges on the side; it was wonderful. Matela was full of kids from all over the world who were seeking the same kind of thing I was, but they couldn't get away from, ummm – I mean, they may as well have been in an apartment in Berkeley as in a cave there, because the lifestyle continued the same wherever they were. And the odd thing to me was that after my initial plans to be accepted into the home of a Greek family fell apart, we came to this very scene – the very scene we were trying to escape from – and it seemed very attractive to us. There were so many contradictions, so much I noticed about life generally on those trips. Like, the kids couldn't get used to seeing all the slaughtered meat hanging in the shops – they'd only ever seen bits of meat wrapped in cellophane, and to see it there on its frame turned their stomachs. Most people have that reaction – look at last night over dinner when we started to complain because people were talking about eating birds. We got so upset, and yet at the same time we were eating chicken by the mouthful without even thinking. I go on vegetarian things every so often – well, fruitarian really. In California it's easy because it's warm most of the time. I think you need meat in winter. I have this friend who's a vegetarian and helped me build my house in Canada. We lived on fruit all summer, and he was a fanatical vegetarian – sneering at me when I looked at sirloin – but as winter approached he got colder and colder and I said "Look, you've got to eat some meat if we're going to finish this house." I had visions of him collapsing. He actually did break down finally and have a steak, and I felt really terrible corrupting, breaking down a man's principles, like that.'

I wonder if the house in Canada is a permanent move, whether she's had enough of the California scene and is moving back to her roots.

'Not really – moving back is like burning your bridges behind you. For one thing, I don't want to lose my alien registration card, because that enables me to work in the States. So I have a house in California – not the one in Laurel Canyon I used to have – for an address. The house in Canada is just a solitary station. I mean, it's by the sea and it has enough physical beauty and change of mood so that I can spend two or three weeks there alone.

'The land has a rich melancholy about it. Not in the summer, because it's usually very clear, but in the spring and winter it's very brooding and it's conducive to a certain kind of thinking. But I can't spend a lot of time up there. Socially I have old school friends around Vancouver, Victoria and some of the islands, but I need the stimulation of the scene in Los Angeles. So I really find myself down there almost as much now as when I lived there – because then I was on the road most of the time anyway. I'm so transient now that, even though I have the house in Canada, I really don't feel like I have a home – well, it's home when I'm there, you know, but then so is the Holiday Inn in its own weird way.'

We get on to the two-year break and I wonder how she'll take the intrusion into her reasons and her personal kick-back. But she's relaxed and forthright and I somehow sense it's a question she feels right in answering now that it's in the past.

'The first year I travelled, the second year I built my house and – in the process of building it and being alone up there when it was completed – I had written a lot of new songs. And it seemed to me that [they weren't] like a completed art until they were tried in front of a live audience. Well, not "tried", but there's a need to share them. I kept calling people in the bar of this lodge and saying, "Listen, want to hear a song?" and they say, "That's really nice – know any Gordon Lightfoot?" No, that's not really true – but I really did want to play in front of people, which was a strange feeling for me to get because two years ago when I retired I felt I never really wanted to do it again – ever.

'Like, I gained a strange perspective on performing. I had a bad attitude about it, you know. I felt like what I was writing was too personal to be applauded. I even thought that maybe the thing to do was to present the songs in some different way – like a play or a classical performance where you play everything and then run off stage and let them do whatever they want, applaud or walk out. I was too close to my own work. Now I've gained a perspective, a distance on most of my songs. So that now I can feel them when I perform them, but I do have a certain detachment from the reality of the story.

'I was too close to my own work. Now I've gained a perspective, a distance on most of my songs. So that now I can feel them when I perform them, but I do have a certain detachment from the reality of the story.'

Did it help her in that troubled time to get her feelings out on paper?

'Yes, it does, you know, it translates your mood. You can be in a really melancholic, depressive mood, feeling downright bad, and you want to know why. So you sit down and think "Why?" You ask yourself a lot of questions. I find if I just sit around and meditate and mope about it all, then there's no release at all, I just get deeper and deeper into it. Whereas in the act of creating – when the song is born and you've made something beautiful – it's a release valve. And I always try and look for some optimism, you know, no matter how cynical my mood may be. I always try to find that little

crevice of light peeking through. Whatever I've made –
whether it's a painting, a song, or even a sweater – it changes
my mood. I'm pleased with myself that I've made something.'

PART TWO – 10TH JUNE 1972

Last week Joni Mitchell spoke for the first time in over two
years about why she virtually 'retired' from the music scene
during a period of searching and self-exploration. How her
writing had become a therapy for her to overcome something
of a real crisis in her career and in her outlook.

In her London hotel, happily chain-smoking her way
through the afternoon, she continues our discussion of her
life and attitudes . . .

For Joni, then, the emotional release to her problems came
through her artistic involvement, her sense of achievement.
But the subject brings up theories on psychiatrists and
whether the ordinary person, who perhaps does not have
the artistic satisfaction of creating, is ever helped through
times of stress by them.

Surprisingly, it turns out, that despite her own forms of
release, Joni did once visit a psychiatrist herself just before she
made the decision to come off the road.

'A couple of years ago I got very depressed – to the point
where I thought it was no longer a problem for burdening my
friends with. But I needed to talk to someone who was very
indifferent, so I though I'd pay this guy to listen to me. I had
done a lot of thinking beforehand as to what was eating me,
so there wasn't a great deal of uncovering to do. I went to see
him and said, "Okay, blah blah blah" and just started to rap
from the time I came through the door – which turned out to
be 40 minutes of everything I thought was bothering me.
Which included a description of myself as being a person who
never spoke, which naturally he found hard to understand!
But it was true that in day-to-day life I was practically

catatonic. There were moments when I thought I had nothing pertinent to say, but there I was, blabbing my mouth off to him.

'So in the end he looked at me and said, "Well, do you ever feel suicidal?" and I said, "Sometimes I feel very bad, but I have to make another record . . ." telling him I had all these things to live for. So he just handed me his card and said, "Listen – call me again sometime when you feel suicidal." And I went out into the street – I'd come in completely deadpan, my face immobile even when I talked – and I just felt this grin breaking over my face at the irony of it all. At the thought that this man was going to help me at all. I don't see that [psychiatrists] really do much good. The idea that you disclose all these things to a person who remains totally anonymous seems not very helpful.'

But isn't that why people go [to therapy] – that they are anonymous beings?

'Oh sure – that is why people talk to strangers on trains and buses, for a release. But I wanted more than a release. I wanted some wisdom, some kind of council and direction. He didn't know. He only knew the way to his office in the morning and the way to the bar afterwards.'

Well, some people use them like a priest – almost as a confessional . . .

'True, but . . . did you read Hermann Hesse's book *Narcissus and Goldmund*? In reading that book – and I have never had any Catholic experience – but at the end when Narcissus the priest gives Goldmund a mantra to repeat over and over again, not reproaching him for his life, but just giving him a focus because he's so spaced out, kind of 'You're out of focus – get yourself in focus', I thought that was so brilliant; so many priests and psychiatrists miss the whole point of getting right to the heart of the person. Giving him rehabilitation and setting up a solution. Hesse is certainly my favourite author – although I must admit I hardly ever read. As a result, I find difficulty in expressing myself – suddenly I find how limited my vocabulary is. I never was a reader, I always was a doer. To me, reading was a vicarious experience. But I have a hunger now; there are times when I am among my friends and I feel like an illiterate.

'It's like I came through the school systems completely unscathed in a way, and completely unlearned in another way. Which makes me feel terribly ignorant. I find now that the most common phrase in my vocabulary is,' she lowers her voice sternly, 'I DON'T KNOW, I just don't know.'

Sadly, it's a common link between us – something we have to laugh at but knowing it's only a cover-up in exactly the same way that an excuse for scholarly learning is that 'living is more important.'

'Oh well, I think that both those sides are true. I think that a lot of people who [are] glued into books can only learn from books. Like, one thing I love is the exploration of learning. I love teaching myself things. In a way that handicaps me, because when someone tries to instruct me, I can't be instructed. This is particularly painful to me in my music, because someone will say, "Oh, I like the way you play piano, will you play these key changes C to E?" And I can't do it. The only way I could is if they play the tapes and let me wander around and choose my own chords.

'I was constantly rapped on the knuckles at piano classes because I'd listen to what the teacher played and I'd remember it. So I never learned to sight read properly and she'd bust me on it. I'd fake it – like, I'd read the music and it wouldn't be quite right, there was a certain amount of improvisation in it. And she'd say, "Those notes aren't in there". That kind of killed my interest in piano for a good 15 years or so. From the beginning I really wanted to mess around and create, find the colours the piano had buried in it. You know, I always feel like such an irresponsible creature.'

We move back to the songs. At the Festival Hall she debuted 'Lesson in Survival', which now, having discussed the two years away from the business, seems even more pertinent than it did that evening. She apologized for it on stage, saying she didn't necessarily feel that way now, but obviously it was a very bitter time.

'Yes, that was when I came off the road. I had a friend at that time I was very close to and who was on the verge of tremendous success. I was watching his career and I was thinking that, as his woman at that time, I should be able to support him. And yet it seemed to me that I could see the change in his future would remove things from his life. I felt like having come through, having had a small taste of success, and having seen the consequences of what it gives you and what it takes away in terms of what you *think* it's going to give you – well, I just felt I was in no position to help. I knew what he needed was someone to support him and say it was all wonderful. But everything I saw him going through I thought was ludicrous, because I'd thought it was ludicrous when I'd done it.

'It was a very difficult time, and the song was actually written for that person: "In the office sits a poet and he trembles as he sings/And he asks some guy to circulate his soul . . . okay on your mark red ribbon runner." Like, go after it, but remember the days when you sat and made up tunes for yourself and played in small clubs where there was still some contact and when people came up and said – maybe they did before, but you didn't care, you know? Ummm, well, I've got to clarify that – it is appreciated when someone says it and genuinely means it and you can see it's moved them, maybe changed them a little. Like, I've been really moved by some performances and I've been unable to tell them from my side of it because I know what it's like to receive praise. It's a very difficult thing to give sincerely and communicate that sincerity.'

Having gone through all those feelings, didn't she find it hard to come back to concerts and get involved in it all again – knowing what she knew and how she'd reacted to knowing it?

'Well, that part of the song I apologized for the most was the bitterness, I had felt so pressurized. I don't feel pressurized by it now, mainly because I intent to express myself in more than one medium, so if I go dry in one, I'll move into something else.

'You come to dry periods as an artist, and you get real panicky. I've known people that haven't written for maybe a year, and they're chewing their fingernails right down to the wrist. And I've known people who maybe haven't put out such a good fourth record and they feel they're on some sort of decline. Either they feel it personally or they're led to believe it. Their record company is beginning to withdraw from them, the spark is going out. Or maybe it's the fact that at 17 they were so pretty and all of a sudden in the morning they have bags under their eyes.

'But now I feel personally unaffected by all that, in that I feel my creativity in one form or another is very strong and will continue. I may, of course, just dry up all around some sort of . . . hey, I may become the whole Gobi desert next year! You know, I always say to Elliot (Roberts, her manager), "Oh, I haven't written anything for three weeks," and he's always laughing at me because I'm very prolific. But I'm also very lonely – which is one of the dues you pay. I don't have a large circle of friends. I have a few very close friends, and then there's a whole lot of people I'm sort of indifferent to. And I sometimes think that maybe that's not so good, that maybe I should go out of my way and be nice to everyone, you know?'

But it must be difficult for her – the star system is a trap where it's hard to work out who is a friend for simply what you represent and who for the person you really are.

'I used to see that as a problem, but there was also this thing where I'd be nice to anyone who was nice to me – that I had this obligation to be nice back. But that's a discrimination I've learned. I'm older and wiser now.'

The rain had stopped outside and the last rays of a 7:00

p.m. sun are filtering across the trees in the park. Joni plays a
little piano, eats a little butterscotch, and we move on to the
new album – her first for Asylum, the label that her co-
mangers Elliot and David Geffen started and which she joined
as a friend to lend her support to.

'Well, I've started on it. I've been into the studio to cut a
publisher's dub, when the songs were very new. I just cut
most of them by myself. For 'Cold Blue Steel' I got in James
Burton, who's really a great guitarist. Like, that song is a real
paranoid city song – stalking the streets looking for a dealer. I
originally thought it needed a sliding steel, but we tried that
and it didn't work. Finally I ended up with James playing
really great wah-wah – a furtive kind of sound. It's a nice
track, but in the meantime the bass line and the drums didn't
work solidly, so I have to recut that. I have a take of "Lesson
in Survival" which is really magical, the feeling is there, and I
don't think I'll do it again – so I have that cut and finished.

'Then I tried to do "You Turn Me On (I'm a Radio)". I've
never had a hit record in America, so I got together with some
friends and we decided we were going to make this hit –
conjure up this bit of magic for AM radio, destined to appeal
to DJs. Graham [Nash] and David [Crosby] came and Neil
[Young] lent me his band, and he came and played some
guitar and somehow it didn't work. There were too many
chefs, you know. We had a terrific evening, a lot of fun, and
the track is nice, but it's just . . . it's like when you do a movie
with a cast of thousands. Somehow I prefer movies with
unknowns. So I'm going to start looking for people who are
untried, who have a different kind of enthusiasm that comes
from wanting to support the artist.

'Like, Miles Davis always has a band that [is] really great,
but [the musicians] are cushions for him, you know. That
sounds very egotistical, that I should want that, but this time I
really want to do something different. Like, the music is
already a growth, a progression from *Blue*, the approach
is stronger and melodically it's stronger, I think that will be

noticeable whether I make a sparse record as I did with *Blue* or not. But I feel I want to go in all directions right now, like a mad thing right! I'd think, "This is really rock and roll, this song, isn't it?" and I see it with French horns and everything and I really have to hold myself back, or I'll just have a monstrosity on my hands. No, I don't feel trapped in this held-back careful image. I could sing much stronger than I do, you know, especially on the low register. I've got a voice I haven't used yet and haven't developed, which is very deep and strong and could carry over a loud band. And I'm very tempted to go in that direction experimentally.

'But rushing ahead of ideas is bad. An idea must grow at its own pace. If you push it and it's not ready, it'll just fall apart.'

Editor's note: *Tragically, Penny succumbed to cancer as* The Sound and the Fury *was being completed. She will be deeply missed.*

Cliff White

MARVIN GAYE: EARTHLY FIGHTS & MYSTIC FLIGHTS

New Musical Express, 9th October 1976

Freelancing for New Musical Express *from 1975 to 1979, my remit was to cover vintage rock'n'roll, R&B and soul and to provide a window on contemporary happenings in US black music ('What the funk is this?') to a predominantly white, 'rock' readership.* NME *was then a reasonably eclectic organ: non-rock correspondents had their submissions published regularly but we never expected to hit the front page.*

In 1976 it was announced that Marvin Gaye was to perform in concert in the UK, his first visit to Britain since 1964 when he was a lesser star in the Motown galaxy and had only, and uncomfortably, fulfilled some 'getting to know you' press engagements and a TV appearance. In the meantime, principally because of his 1971 album What's Going On, *his troubled life and his rebellious attitude to the Motown corporation, Marvin had become one of the foremost black American soul men to spark big time interest with the UK rock press since Otis Redding, although I don't think he realised it until he stepped off the plane.*

Unexpectedly it was me, rather than one of the hot core of NME *staffers, who was detailed to interview the enigmatic Mr Gaye. I guess I should have dressed for the occasion: my appointment was repeatedly deferred over two and a half days while I enjoyed room service in an expensive hotel where I could barely move or break wind because I'd turned up in denim. No matter, it wasn't my tab. And we finally got it on.*

During our dialogue, Marvin pointed out that he'd read my unfavourable review of his I Want You *album, released earlier that year, and he thought I'd been very unfair to him. This I duly reported. When* NME *ran my piece as a cover story a few days later, a typically exasperating typo had me quoting Marvin as saying it was a* fair *review!*

That evening I bumped into Marvin again at some promotional bash. 'I read what you wrote about me,' he murmured, not unkindly. For a split second I considered launching into a self-defensive rant about incompetent typesetters, thought better of it, nodded humbly and scuttled off. Twenty-six years later I can perhaps rest easy again.

CW

'HOW ARE YOU? I must say you have the patience of Job.'

Thus was I immediately disarmed by Mr Marvin Gaye at 5 p.m. on Tuesday September 28, 1976 after dogging his shadow since 9 a.m. the previous Sunday.

Or more precisely . . . because, as you may know by now, he didn't actually set foot on British concrete until 22.20 of that same day . . . waiting for the green light from any one of numerous representatives of a) his tour promoters; b) his PR company; c) his personal management; or d) the British office of his record company – no one faction of which seemed to know what the others were deciding . . .

And when I finally got to meet the man, the first thing he did was lay this observation about Job on me, when all I knew about Job was that they're the nearest competitors to Rizla for the cigarette paper concession of Britain.

Hmmm, I observe, feeling quite buoyant now that I'm

finally in the presence of the legendary Marvin Gaye: You're harder to meet than James Brown.

'Is he hard?'

He certainly was.

So now that I'm here and he's here too, I shuffle around this 14th floor suite of a reasonably plush Knightsbridge hotel looking for a suitable vantage point from which to talk to Marvin, who is secure behind a small, round table wedged between the television set and the ceiling-to-floor picture window. Behind him is a vase of flowers; before him on the table is a glass of red wine, presumably not the first and certainly not the last of many 'cause I'm only one of several scheduled interviewers that afternoon, and rapping with the press is thirsty work. If fact it doesn't take long to realise that Marvin's either naturally on a different plane from the rest of us or else he's drunk, stoned, or both, a state of mind he later describes as 'I'm really bombed here', which you can interpret any way you like. I finally decide to squat on the corner of a desk opposite Marvin's table, plonking myself dangerously close to a selection of family portraits.

'Can I perch here?'

'Sure you can perch there. Those are pictures of my children. I always feel better when they're close to me.'

I handle them delicately, passing them across the table while I ensure that the mic of my cassette recorder is close enough to Marvin to compete with the TV and background conversation. Precious stuff this – Gaye's notorious for either not giving interviews or spouting seemingly ridiculous waffle along the lines of 'The only thing between Beethoven and me is time.' As a Marvin Gaye fan who rarely has occasion to consider the talents of Beethoven and is sceptical about the myth of 'classical' composers I don't find that much-quoted line as outrageous as some. However it does lead me to believe that this isn't going to be a regular interview.

It wasn't.

But before I get into it, rapid mental revision reminds me of
one or two of the most salient facts of his career prior to this
visit.

For instance: Marvin Gaye hasn't been to Britain since the
mid-'60s, when he flew over to meet the press and guest on
Ready, Steady, Go.

At the time he was second-stringer in the Motown scale of
priorities, having been produced on a succession of fair-sized
American hits by William Stevenson ('Stubborn kind of
Fellow', 'Hitch Hike', 'Pride And Joy', and duets with Mary
Wells, 'What's The Matter With You Baby', and Kim Wes-
ton, 'What Good Am I Without You'); Brian Holland &
Lamont Dozier ('Can I Get A Witness', 'You're A Wonderful
One', 'Baby Don't You Do It', 'How Sweet It Is'); and his
brother-in-law, the boss, Berry Gordy ('Try It Baby').

Born in Washington in April 1939, the son of a minister,
Gaye arrived in Detroit and on the Tamla label via an
association with Harvey Fuqua, another brother-in-law to
Gordy. Fuqua had used a little-known group called the
Marquees (including Gaye) to replace his original Moon-
glows, one of the most popular R&B-cum-doowop groups of
the '50s. By 1962, most of the group had become the original
(Detroit) Spinners, Fuqua had married Gwen Gordy and
joined the burgeoning Motown set-up, and Gaye strung
along with him, marrying Gwen's younger sister Anna in
the process.

Yes, folks, 'twas truly a family affair. Around the time of
his brief trip to Britain in 1964 his career was boosted by two
fine Smokey Robinson productions ('I'll Be Doggone', 'Ain't
That Peculiar') that gave him No.1 soul hits and Top 10 pop
placings in America. From thereon in he has never scored less
from than top 20 soul/Top 40 pop, a track record that puts
him among the most consistently successful recording artists
of the last 20 years.

Until 1970 he was not generally considered as anything
more than one of the best of the Motown stalwarts (in fact he

was hardly considered at all by the mass media, who tended to concentrate on Diana Ross & the Supremes, Smokey Robinson & the Miracles etc), and his records were corporation productions, the best-loved of which were his duets with Tammi Terrell ('Ain't Nothing Like The Real Thing', 'You're All I Need To Get By') and a couple of superb Norman Whitfield creations ('I Heard It Through The Grapevine', 'Too Busy Thinking About My Baby').

However, with the turn of the decade came a dramatic change in Gaye's music in the form of his *What's Going On* album, the self-produced and largely self-composed masterpiece that was the first outward sign that Marvin Gaye was far more than just a corporation stooge with a flair for interpreting ready-made hits.

Now I'm not going to get into an analytical discussion of *What's Going On* and his subsequent releases, because I want to introduce you to the man himself . . . and anyway the message is in the music.

But I would just note that, aside from his music, certain other events have conspired to transform Gaye from a two-dimensional Mr Average to a much discussed legend-in-his-own-time, among them a series of loose outspoken interviews of the kind not normally given by Motown artists, in which he has revealed the running battle he's had with The Corp to establish himself as a major artist, the disintegration of his marriage, the heartbreaking death of Tammi Terrell (who apparently collapsed in his arms during a show), controversial opinions about drugs, sex, women, and his own talent . . . well, you name it, Marvin'll probably talk about it; providing you can corner him for an interview in the first place.

Not least of the notches in his growing reputation has been the publication of Elaine Jesmer's *Number One With A Bullet*, a fictional account of the cut and thrust within a black-owned record corporation that's not unlike Motown, featuring a hero called Daniel Stone who's generally assumed to be based on Marvin Gaye. Whether Stone is based on Gaye is largely irrelevant. The fact that most people seem to think he is, and that it's a very sympathetic portrayal in a nasty set of circumstances, has not done the real man any harm at all.

So, what with one thing and another, after many years of being generally ignored – especially here in Britain where he's never sold particularly well (none of his '70s records have made the charts) – in the last couple of years Marvin's reputation has blossomed enormously. Oh yes, could be it's also due to no new recording being released for over two years, which always helps the mystique if you're already big enough not to be forgotten in the meantime. With the booming of Gaye's reputation, British promoters began sparring for the right to bring him over. Jeffrey Kruger won the contest, the deal was signed, and that brings us back to a hotel suite in Knightsbridge where I'm poised opposite a handsome, fit-looking individual wearing a blue and gold knee-length robe.

Also in the room is Pennie Smith, our trusty photographer, who's come to know the name Marvin Gaye like it's burnt on her forearm, due to the fact that she's spent three days whizzing back and forth desperately trying to keep tabs on whether I've been awarded an interview; Angela the PR lady, a lovely Jamaican lady who I believe is Marvin's manager's daughter-in-law; and – last but by no means least – a bulky black gent called Wally Cox, currently one of Marvin's backup singers but previously a solo artist who, much to his amazement, is one of the hundreds of obscure recording artists with some sort of reputation in northern discos. Pennie and I are quick to conclude that he's also doubling as Marvin's personal heavy.

Marvin is . . . er . . . spaced out. He spends a lot of time gazing absently across the rooftops while he speaks, perhaps focusing on the distant chimneys of Battersea Power Station, radiating the aura of a guru who's about to wax mysterious and levitate himself sideways out of the window. At other times he turns inward, on the room and on himself, sitting with head bowed, playing idly with the stem of his wine glass or slowly smoothing the creases in the table-cloth, giving me the impression of a haunted victim or a condemned man.

There's undeniably an unreal, slow-motion atmosphere pervading the whole conversation. His speech is not slurred; on the contrary, he has a clear, precise voice, higher than I'd anticipated – but the conversation is erratic. Slow, measured thoughts are nudged by a sudden tumble of words, either emphasising or expanding what he's already said or occasionally contradicting himself, so that in equal time spans he might manage one, short, disjointed sentence or a whole string of overlapping variations on the same thought.

Having agreed to be interviewed, it seemed he wanted to answer almost everything as deeply and thoughtfully as possible – and when he didn't want to talk about something, instead of giving half an answer he just evaded the subject altogether. I break the ice with a routine question about this being his first tour for many moons . . .

'Major European tour, yes, but I've been touring quite a bit in the States the last two and a half years. Well, not as much as most American artists do, but I have been doing some touring because . . . I was very disappointed with my last tour . . . some of the dates in the States . . . But for the most part I've been pretty happy and I've been able to make a living.'

The sentences float about. What was disappointing? The crowd response; your own performance; the venues?

'No, the crowd response has been . . . I'm happy to see that the response is or has been what it is because in my early years as a performer I never quite got . . . I was never as visual a performer during the years of James Brown, Jackie Wilson, Sam Cooke. I was a struggling performer in the '60s, I didn't feel that audience reaction. Now it seems to be at the level that I can appreciate it as an artist. Perhaps I'm putting out a little more now than I did because I'm a lot more confident and that would make a difference.'

You don't get keyed up anymore?

'Well, I get keyed up, but in a totally . . . I get totally disconcerned with all the things that make a performer nervous before a show. My thoughts drift to other, non-attached things such as nature and animals and birds, and I nearly forget about the performance until I'm about to go on. Then all of a sudden a surge of energy comes through me five or ten minutes before, and I'm ready. Then all of the problems that haunt a performer, that make him nervous, give him butterflies, make him forget or not tune into his music, they're gone.'

During a short break when Marvin is called aside by one of his aides, the conversation strays to transatlantic business, and it transpires that Marvin Gaye reads his reviews – even the British ones. Ever the innocent, I bring up the subject of his latest album *I Want You* because, a) I didn't like it very much, and said so in these very pages, and b) I wanted to know the circumstances behind the recording. It seemed to me that a lot of it might have been recorded around the same time as *Let's Get It On* . . .

'I'd like to talk about that,' says Marvin, looking me straight in the eye for the first time in the interview, 'because I haven't been getting very good reviews on that album, especially here in England. The reviews that filtered back to the States were very . . . they weren't good reviews at all. There was one, I had a bald head, the guy put a picture of me in with my bald head . . .'

Oh gorblimey, I do believe he's referring to my review. Shall I leave now or blame it all on Neil 'The Guvnor' Spencer [*NME* Editor]? You're not going to believe this, I tell him . . .

'You did it!?'

Wellll . . . carry on, what did it say?

'I thought it was a horrible review! Did you write that?'

Marvin's Bedroom Technique Disappoints?

'Yeah, was that you?'

Yes, I must confess it was. Am I now going to be thrown

out? I ask half-jokingly, although you can never be too sure these days. Just ask the journalist who crossed swords with Barry White. Anyway, no panic, Marvin is a gentleman.

'No I'm not the type. I'm not vindictive. But I must tell you in all honesty I thought it was a very unfair review . . . because you see, many times when you hear . . . when you're writing a review you have to figure that although an artist may be disappointing, think of the work behind it.

'For some artists, music is good enough . . . and perhaps my *What's Going On* album was good enough that I could have followed it up with something similar and people would have still enjoyed it. And maybe my *Let's Get It On* album was good enough that, had I followed in its footsteps a little more closely, or stayed within the guidelines of it a little more musically, you would have enjoyed it.

'But I don't like to do that because I am so creative, and there are so many things to write about and sing about, that although *I Want You* bore the flavour of *Let's Get It On*, and though the subject matter is most profound and paramount in life – I feel that to expound on it again with a different set of songs and a different writer – I didn't write the songs; well I wrote some of them but most of them Leon Ware did – different music and everything, I felt that with those combinations and by adding my production ideas to it, it would make a viable, buyable product that people could understand.

'I went to great lengths, holding up the cover even – because as part of the package one has to consider the cover, one that will be interesting, because I like to bring something to people's lives. I don't like . . . suppose I'd just used a photo or something? I went to greatest lengths to buy a painting.'

Here I should point out that Marvin has a light, throwaway style of delivery when he's talking about how good he is or how clever he's been; not to mention a subtle sense of humour. He's not the sort of person whose eyes twinkle, but if he was, they would. I mean he believes in himself alright

– although I don't think he is quite so self-confident as he is sometimes made out to be – but he is not intense about it. You get tossed these seemingly conceited opinions en route to an overall explanation of what he is trying to achieve or how he has gone about something. I haven't seen that made clear in previous interviews, which is probably why he has had oddball quotes taken out of context. End of message.

'The picture was right, it had pretty good connotations and it was ethnic and it is something that people who are not coloureds can really check out; and those who are coloured, or black, can look at it and say, "Well, here is a study of us. That's really us." And I mean I go through all these things and then I read a review that really makes me sad because I don't think you really understood where I was coming from.

'Now perhaps it's boring to know that the message is the same. You feel that I'm not creative enough to go somewhere else, but that wasn't it. It's just that I wasn't doing anything. You have to think about that.

'You didn't know it but I didn't intend to do anything. I would have not been here now had I not done this, and I wasn't gonna do it, but Berry came and said, "Listen, man, dammit, you gotta do something, you been fooling around here for years. Now here's some stuff that Leon Ware went into the studio and cut. Look, I'm getting ready to let so-and-so cut it, but see if you like it. The stuff is you man, it's you."

'So he talked me into it, right? So I'm listening to it and saying, "Well, gee, that 'I Want You' track is not bad, Berry. 'After The Dance' wasn't bad, and a few other things. "Weelll, gee, I kinda like that music, you know." But then I said, "I don't know, damn, I'm not going to do anything, I'm sorry." So he calls me back a couple of times, says, "Come and do this album", you know, and I thought, well, I do like it so I'll go and do it.

'But I had no plans to produce anything on it myself because ninety per cent of the time, when I get mad I get very unproductive. And they keep me mad at them all the time by not treating me properly. I'm like a fine racehorse, but they won't treat me like a racehorse. At least a racehorse gets a rubdown after a race, I don't even get that. So anyway, at least if you're not going to pay me my European royalties, treat me right, you know what I mean? It's stuff like that I get angry about.'

I feel a distinct prickling in the small of my back as we start to slide into a danger zone. I drag the subject back to the album. I have thought about the album since my review, I tell him . . .

'Listen, let me say that you don't have to justify your review, for this reason. I feel very strange now. I thought that if I ever met you I'd be angrier with you than I am, but I think the reason is because . . . um . . . I must tell you that because I think I overdid it in some respects . . .'

'There are three very good songs on it – "Come Live With Me, Angel", "I Want You" and "After The Dance" – and I think to have three very good songs in an album – I would have to label it a success. Four songs, a very good album. And that's what I base it on, commercially speaking, I wouldn't do an album that didn't have at least three strong songs; I'd never cut it. And this is the kind of excellence that I think all artists should strive for, but it's impossible because they're mostly produced and they don't have the perception to do this.

'When people are controlling them they can't say, "Hey, what's happening?", they have to go by, "Y'all really think it's a hit?" "Yeah, I hope it is", and it might turn out that the producer is not as great as the artist's faith in him, and they might only have one decent song on the album. So everybody says "Oh, it's O.K." But when you have the perception . . . and most true artists have an idea, even when they're young, and they should be listened to more.'

Even more than *Let's Get It On*, *I Want You* was a woman's album – I mean you were talking directly to girls.

'I was, but I also thought that, in doing the product,

although I was speaking directly to women, it would be an aid to men.'

Wally breaks into ecstatic cries of 'Yes! Yes!' from his position on the couch. So he guarantees it works, can he?

'Oh yes. Really.' He confirms the aphrodisiac powers of Marvin's album with an enthusiastic nod of the head. 'I had fun doing it too. It just killed me.' 'Well, you know,' offers Marvin, 'if you don't think it works, try it some time when you got a difficult one on your hands. Really. Put it on and see if it helps. One time don't use it, and then the next time you have her just put the album on and really just see if it works. I'll bet you anything she'll be nice; she'll come around a lot nicer than the first time.'

O.K. fellas, this is where you come in. Progress reports please to Mr Gaye c/o Motown Corp. And if you suddenly see a new, appreciative review of the album you'll know it's worked for me.

The fact that you were more or less persuaded to record *I Want You*, does that mean you don't really see yourself as a recording artist with the need to record all the time?

'No, that's the only thing I see myself as. I don't see myself as anything other than a recording artist.'

So didn't you have either the inspiration or opportunity to do anything else of your own between *Let's Get It On* and *I Want You*?

'The business that I'm engaged in, outside the artistry of it, has not afforded me the opportunity to do any more albums than I've done. I have done work . . . I have so many albums in me and so many ideas that I can do stuff on just about anything and make a product of it, a complete statement . . . I have that gift (he rolls his collar in mock pride, and everyone laughs). But I won't give these innovations away for nothing. Because that's how our society is constructed, and although I don't believe in it, I'm not a fool either. So I'd rather do nothing.'

Marvin smiles again and looks as if to say, 'I trust you

understand what I'm talking about, because that's about all I've got to say on the subject.' Following the train of thought, I wonder what prompted him to come to Europe at this particular time. With the pound plummeting to an all-time low it can't be the cash. And he hasn't got a hit record here.

The enquiry provokes nothing but a twelve-second silence (I counted; you could hear a pin drop on the pile carpet) while Marvin stares fixedly out of the window. Try again.

Was it suggested to you, or did you say you'd like to do the tour?

Deep sigh. 'Well . . . I could always say all the things that would make all the English fans love me more, couldn't I? But it may not be the truth. However, now that I am here, and having done the two performances last night, the truth is I didn't believe the reception, the true, honest vibes and feelings, and I got something way more than I ever expected or dared dream to get from English fans.

'I didn't realise. Because I don't get paid a lot of money in American royalties for English record sales and I'm shocked to find . . . of course, I'll be told that it doesn't make any difference, the fact that I'm sold out on most of my performances has nothing to do with the fact that I don't sell any records in England.

'I'll be told something like that by my record company when I go back and naturally I'll probably say, "Yeah, you're probably right", and they'll go on not paying me my English royalties, then I'll be happy, you know, like dumb artists are supposed to be.'

Ironically, Marvin doesn't seem to sell records over here, unless the majority of his fans are so keen they rush out and buy imports before the British release. However, if not many people buy the new recordings, there are plenty more who are fanatical about his oldies, particularly 'I Heard It Through The Grapevine', and many were distraught that he didn't perform more than a verse or two of it at the Albert Hall.

'Right, well, what I'll do as a result of that information, I'll do a much longer version of it when I play the Palladium.' (He did, too.)

'You see, I only got a list of songs from the promoter. He told me all the songs that were popular over here and I just put them in a medley form for a few minutes because I haven't done them in years. In fact, when I sing them in America people go for pop and hot dogs.'

Yes, other artists have told me that in America they're only as hot as their last record – that the people have got very short memories.

'Very short patience with an old record. They are not at all thrilled with old records. The only way you can perform an old record in America is if you are very animated with it. So instead of appreciating the memory or anything . . . that might be a very psychological thing for me to consider about Americans too. I'll think about that later. They don't want memories. They're not a nostalgic people. It's strange that you should say that.'

Perhaps because America is still an energetic country whereas Britain, as you can see from today's headlines (CRISIS DOOM GLOOM etc.), is rapidly grinding to a standstill, so we want to look back all the time.

'Oh I don't think England has any problems. The only problem England has is the one that all countries have, it's that people don't have a true understanding of government, the really finer workings, the inner workings, the powerful circle of their government and those who are in power, and how they control and manipulate things.

'You're being manipulated very handily right now, and most English people can't realise what's going on. But one who really understands government knows. I don't think the country's in any trouble, as you will see in a few months; it'll all come back to normal the way it's supposed to.

'In America they have their problems too, but there is so much more going on, a broader scope of activity, so there's very little time to reminisce and be nostalgic. Actually, I don't consider that living. I think that's existing in a world where things are put at your disposal because you're supposed to want to afford recreation. And what the recreation is supposed to do is bring you back so that you may serve the system more efficiently.

'But it's all done with a sort of freedom facade to it, and you accept it because it was accepted by your parents and their parents and so on, it even becomes more acceptable as generations pass, and you're locked into this thing and it gets worse and worse and worse. They you go back and serve the system for a few hours and then you take your recreation. It's all very strange.

'American audiences are sometimes a bit nostalgia-minded, but only at certain times of the year, I find, around Christmas and holidays. For the most part they don't want to hear a bunch of old material, they want to think very progressively. We're a very progressive-minded society, if not aggressive-minded society. We don't have lot of time to think about the past because we're trained that way basically, and regimented like that.'

Are you the same? I'm speaking particularly about your own musical career. Do those old hits mean anything to you or are they just so much history? . . . [another lengthy silence] . . . Did you not enjoy performing them last night, knowing that the British audiences like to hear them?

'I can understand why British audiences would like to hear them, but to me they are very painful.'

Because of associated memories? 'Yes. Exactly. Especially with Tammi Terrell. Is there any more wine?'

We savour our refilled glasses of wine while Marvin explains that his lady, Jan, is at that very moment spending all his money 'at that famous department store that's right around the corner.'

Ah yes. Harrods. The most expensive store in London.

'Yeah, well, she knew that immediately upon looking in the window. She went, "Ahh, oooohh", and every time she did that my pocket shrunk. Did you ask me a question?'

If you don't perform regularly, and if you record erratically, what do you do with your time? Do you just like to stay outside of the business, writing and enjoying life as it comes?

'No. What I do with my time, my friend, is I concentrate on people's minds. And that takes a lot of time, so I'm using my time productively.' (You will gather that Marvin is waxing mysterious again.)

But to make that stimulating, surely you've got to be meeting new people all the time?

'Nooo. No, I only concentrate on those minds I want to concentrate on.'

So you spend your time concentrating on certain people's minds. Is that just to understand them better?

'No. That's for me to come out victorious.'

So life is a battle?

'Life is a tremendous battle, yes. You are battling with Mother Nature and with men, that's the battle. And with women. And that's the battle. Basically, if you only had Mother Nature to battle that would be hard enough. To try to live to be a hundred, which isn't very old.'

Of nature, men, and women, which do you find the hardest battle?

'Well, as I grow older I understand I'll find the battle with Mother Nature, who wants us back, the hardest. But it's unfortunate that most people come across that realisation when they're at the wrong time to fight. When they're the weakest – and that's when they're older.'

Every person reaches a point in their life when they realise that instead of growing they are dying, I say. Have you reached that point? Does it bother you?

'I think that any man who is not an impeccable warrior would have to say that death bothers him. But outside the impeccable warrior, and I use that term . . . and if you don't know what I mean, that's a whole 'nother subject . . .'

Is that a quote from something? (Always the dumbo, that's me.)

'That's a quote from Carlos Castaneda's teachings of Don Juan, who was a sorcerer, either in mythology or in reality, as you choose to believe. And his idea of impeccableness was one who has conquered most of life's fears and . . . desires, but ego as well – there's a word but I can't think of it. One who's conquered all the material things that man thirsts and hungers for. And once he's conquered those roads then he has to conquer the inner man. Those things are mostly fears, which is man's greatest enemy, which causes man to really die anguished deaths.

'Fear is a horrible thing we are faced with, but to overcome and conquer all fear is very dangerous as well as beautiful. It can cause your death because you become reckless. So it takes a very wise man to conquer these things and then to exist. A very impeccable warrior who has aids and allies and who calls upon the strong forces that are here on earth. And there are forces that can aid man, which become his ally to protect him because he's gained control over some of his mortal enemies.

'Well, I am nowhere near that, I am just explaining where I think I should be. And the thing is, I do believe that you can do this.

'You have to be afraid until you understand what death is, but once you get a pretty good realisation of what death is and why it is necessary . . . death need not be a fearful or horrible thing to those that have come to that point. Like the Buddhist monks who are able to burn themselves without flinching or protesting, they are not in their bodies, they are outside viewing the body. We do know that happens, so why don't we try to emulate or get close to that knowledge?

'To me it's stupid that we are fooling around doing all these ridiculous things when the problem is knowing oneself, finding out about oneself, becoming more Godlike as a result of finding out what your true Godlike qualities are. And if these people can master it, then all humans can have a better understanding, better tolerances. It's happening. Slowly, but it is happening. People are beginning to realise this.

'And therefore, to answer your question, death isn't a great problem. One who has enough power to master his body has no fear at all of death, he understands that death is another trip to somewhere else because his mind has been prepared and the body, the shell means nothing. All that is important is the mind.

'Nobody's done a death album yet, or an album about death. That's something I wouldn't mind doing. The only problem is that I feel death is as big a force as life. You cannot play with death. You must be careful when dealing or even talking abut death, as you have to be careful how you feel about love and about life. I feel that all these things are powers, and that earth is put together with many powers and some of them until they are sprung up.'

Marvin begins to demonstrate his belief by cupping his hands, with fingers pointing downwards towards the table-top, shuffling them to and fro like a street-spiv playing the three-card trick on an upturned suitcase . . .

'One side of the thing, the power, that makes up life is primarily dormant, and the other side is the side we all live in. The one side is where we go when we sleep, I feel the second side is where we wake up. The one side is when we're hypnotised, the second side is where we come back to when we're snapped out of it. The one side is peaceful and adheres to strict laws and you cannot survive on that side if you dare break any of the laws of nature and God. This side you can survive because it's looser.'

And this side is the one we recognise as reality?

'Right. But there's another world that we refuse to get into. We are afraid of it. I'm afraid when I sleep, I hate to go to sleep. When the moment of sleep finally comes I fight. Every day of my life since I've fought that last drop off into sleep because I don't want to be there. I don't know anything about it. But that is where I should want to be.'

What else are you afraid of?

'Well . . . I am terrified of flight. I am terrified of spiders and scorpions and insects. *But* . . . my terror is not panic. It's inborn, and I think that all of us are terrified of something or some things. As we grow up there is something that triggers this sort of response in our adulthood, and it happens in my case to be spiders and flight.'

Is that why you chose to travel to England by Concorde, because it was a shorter flight?

'No. I chose Concorde because it is basically still an experimental plane and I don't run away from my fears. I attack my fears, and when I attack my fears it makes me stronger. I have ridden an aeroplane every time I was booked, but I don't get on them for fun, if you know where I'm coming from. Because, although I'm terrified of flight, I face it. It's like being at war. A good warrior will get out of the trench and march towards the enemy although he's terrified. But the man who's a coward will stay in the trench.'

And all these personal thoughts and fears and beliefs that you're discussing with me, are these some of the things that you've expressed in your music that hasn't been released?

'Yes, some of it. I have an album that I think is very strong and I'm going to . . . the only reason I've held it back is because I have not been able to use the music I want. I have not been able to find the particular kind of sound that I want to accompany what I've already recorded. When I am close to that, if politically I am able to go about my work in a positive manner with Motown, then I'll finish the album.'

Suddenly it was time to go. Such is the way with pack-'em-in interview sessions. One minute you're heavily engrossed in conversation – or perhaps interrogation – and the next you are politely but firmly being made aware that your time is up. Come in, no. 9.

I was already in the hotel lobby before I realised that I hadn't even got around to asking him how much of himself he recognised in Daniel Stone. Maybe it's as well that I didn't. Marvin Gaye is undoubtedly a maverick in the Motown stable. A unique talent who seems to have survived fifteen

years with The Corp on the basis of 'If you can put up with
me, I can put up with you'. It is to be hoped that, with a bit
more understanding on both sides, he'll soon see his way clear
to record and release further examples of his own compositions and productions.

Meanwhile I'm rushing home to listen to his available work
with renewed interest. Maybe I'll even strike lucky with *I
Want You* tonight.

Richard Cook

WHEN DOES A DINOSAUR CUT OFF ITS TAIL? A CONVERSATION WITH NEIL YOUNG

New Musical Express, 9th October 1982

If you pressed me to remember much about most of the interviews I did during this period, I'd probably draw a blank. But for some reason I recall this one quite well. NME *had been trying to set up an interview with Young for some time, and the only opportunity was to try and nail him after a gig in Birmingham. There were some shambolic elements to the concert and Neil was apparently rather grouchy afterwards. His manager, Elliot Roberts, also on hand, told me gloomily that he doubted if Neil wanted to do it. I cooled my heels backstage and put up with various roadies making useful remarks like 'get out of the way'. Anton Corbijn had taken Neil's picture before- hand and had been allowed at least three minutes to get the job done. But in the end, Roberts came out of Young's dressing room, shrugged and said, 'We're on for tonight.' So we talked on the band bus going back to town.*

Something I left out of the interview text was a moment where Neil was excitedly telling me about a plan to make a record where he redid lots of old '60s hits in the all-electronic style which he'd tried on the Trans *album. When I told him that a group called the Silicon Teens (actually Daniel Miller of Mute) had already done it, he looked perplexed . . . and imme-*

*diately dismissed the idea from his future plans. My
negative contribution to the Neil Young discography!
He didn't even get on to the cover of* NME *that week:
Musical Youth, whose records have perhaps not en-
dured quite so well, were deemed to be a better bet.*

RC

OUT OF ALL THE absurd figures created and cherished by
rock'n'roll, there is none quite like Neil Young. He may
one day turn out to be The Last Rock Star. A few years ago he
made a record, *Rust Never Sleeps*, that catalogued a phase of
rock stretching from its folk roots to its dishevelled, feed-
backed afterlife – a kind of hello/goodbye gesture which has
since settled into a respectful slot in a long career of work.

It is still there, its power intact though ironically asleep; and
with a characteristic shrug Young has ambled on, leafing
through his American sketchbook and pursuing a personal
course fuelled and maintained by a loyalty rare among the
fandoms of the megastar. He's a lucky man.

The ambivalence of Young's position is so odd it's some
small miracle that he's kept his footing. On one level he's
behaved and performed with a disregard for the public, the
press and the business that might have had all three turning
on him; on another he's written a torrent of bankable music,
cut a great welter of records and mischieviously filtered out
actions and projects that suggest an operator so artful it's like
every risk and eccentricity has been checked over and honed
down first. For every *Rust Never Sleeps* there's a placid and
pastoral *Comes A Time*; every time Young tempts the abyss
he steps back from the brink again. He's a smart man.

Even with the safety net, Young has pulled stunts no other
American rock veteran would dare consider. For him to have
made a record as scruffily violent and personal as last year's
Re*ac*tor, after a dozen or more years in the rarified top
bracket of dollar rock, is exactly the sort of liberty the
American gods have forgotten to take with their careers;

for him to persist in playing with a forearm bar band like
Crazy Horse instead of the customary pedigree stable of
session bores only freezes further the aghast expressions of
his contemporaries.

At this distance it might seem like nothing more than an old
Canuck busker refusing to act his age and settle into a sleepy
middle life of pretty hums and regular reunions. There's
something appealing and amusing about the way Young
has not so much fought corporate pressure as strolled along
a different path, unaware that he's not supposed to go that
way.

Neil Young grew into an old rebel because he forgot to
watch where the rest of the parade went. Of course, the
parched bones and raw wires in Young's rock'n'roll are
tempered by a sentimental streak close to a mile wide. Even
as that inimitably frazzled guitar cuts lesions in the song you
can hear the romantic heartbeat pumping through – a childlike faith in the healing graces of love. His interest in the
flowering of the new wave could only ever be confined to its
outward spirit: Young has no interest in fatalism or despair.
He loves his rock'n'roll.

So, I guess Mr Young has both kept and eaten his cake.
Having clothed his folkie's frame in altogether tougher garb
he can travel when and where he pleases. He's found his old
audience has mostly stayed the course and he still plays
'Cinnamon Girl' and 'Old Man' for them; he's institutiona-
lised his modest rebel music while retaining enough of the
spitfire delivery to keep it breathing; and now he's looking for
something new again.

At 37, Young doesn't want to stay still.

'How are things at the New *Musical Express?*' he asks me.
'I don't read that much unless I'm actually doing something. I
like to see a little feedback because it's hard to tell what you
did when you're gone.' Does he read his record reviews?
'Depends what I'm doing. I do if I'm not too busy.'

He gives me an interrogative grin. It seems like he's worked a long time on that expression: in a face little marked by age a grin will spread out, the eyes widening, the brow wrinkling up, a gentle merriment always dozing somewhere in the recesses. The rascally beam of the *Comes A Time* cover seems so uncontrived, simple, amiable in person. I look for the wiseacre in the eyes but it doesn't seem to be there. Just a big, shambling, guitar-strumming Canadian.

Young's return to England at a mid-point on an enormous European tour is his first visit in six years. If any of the faithful have grown tired in the long wait it doesn't show at the Birmingham gig, his first over here.

A walkway extension of the stage enables the leader to move towards the audience like Larry Parks in *The Jolson Story*, except the way he stomps down it is more like Frankenstein's monster. With the homesteader's formal dress, old pug's haircut and set jawline the resemblance doesn't exactly end there. And always somewhere nearby is the eternally diminutive Nils Lofgren.

Lofgren's presence in this particular rock'n'roll circus is finally no big deal. I listened quite carefully but could hardly hear his guitar with Young's being amped up so loud. His usual gymnastic leaps and trailing scarves looked at odds with a diligent blue-collar band like Crazy Horse. We began to forget he was there.

The motorway unrolls outside our window. It's not very easy to get to Neil Young. After several rendezvous earlier in the continent fell through, we are face to face in his touring coach, something akin to a luxury cruiser with wheels.

Mr Young is pleased to talk. Like on how happy he is to be here.

'It's the truth! I'm really happy to be playing anywhere. I haven't toured in so long and this is what I was raised to do, what I trained to do in my whole life. The thing is it just got so big . . .

'Not to use your gifts in the right way is so abusive. I see a lot of people who are my contemporaries – who *were* my contemporaries in the '60s and '70s – who, uh, just haven't tried to continue what they were doing in the first place. They've tried to recreate what they already did thinking that's what success is – do it again and they'll like it again. What they really did first was to do something *new* that people liked – so they should try and do something new again.'

The sort of healthy outlook which might be expected from Young's modern half. But I feel it a duty to remind him of what he's just been playing – acoustic bleatings like 'I Am A Child' and frowsy old rockers of the 'Cinnamon Girl' ilk, aged entries from his balmiest days. The temptation to rely on proven familiars is disappointing.

'I don't believe in doing my old songs in a new way. I'd rather do new songs. The new stuff that I want to do has to be introduced chronologically. But I like shock value too. To see the expressions on faces.'

The sense of communal rite is still inescapable. How does he feel when he hears cheers of remembrance on the last line of a pale little tragedy like 'The Needle And The Damage Done'?

'I *know*, it blows my mind,' he murmurs, oblivious. 'I don't know what they're doing! I guess they just get off on it. They're reacting to seeing me doing it rather than to what I'm actually saying. Sometimes it gets to that point.'

Then he could rectify it by not doing that song.

'I suppose I could – I probably will, eventually. But that song means something to me. There's so many old songs that I won't do because I don't feel anything for them. "Southern Man's" on the edge for me – when we started the tour I could do it but now it's a little forced. When it starts feeling like that I don't wanna do it.'

Why is there so little material from his last few records, the hardest and most detailed music he's ever made? Nothing at all off *Re*ac*tor* or *Hawks and Doves*, one off *Rust Never Sleeps* . . .

'The band isn't right for them,' is the bemusing reply. 'I had these people I wanted to play with and then I tried to figure out the best songs they could do. It might seem obvious to you, but to me it's like, 20 albums of material and it's all there.' What does he think when he looks back at that huge body of work? 'It's really hard to get a grip on it,' he says, shaking his head. 'I can take one song at a time, one period at a time, but the whole picture – it's big. Like Panavision.'

'There's a lot of songs I haven't performed, ever. That are only on records. I only did them once, period. That was like, use take one for the record and that's it! I never sang them again. They have to jump out at me. I don't go through the album covers and decide which one I'll do.'

He might have changed direction in the past, but Young's newest offerings are a complete departure, arguably the most telling acknowledgement so far of the drift of electronic pop from a member of the senior rock hierarchy. The coming album, *Trans*, is Young grasping at the edges of liberating technology.

Amid some of his most ingenuous sounding anthems ('Little Thing Called Love', 'If You Got Love'), a frankly bizarre respray on 'Mr Soul' and a new raddled epic in 'Like An Inca' are five excursions into alien territory – the clean soar of synth-pop allied to the ugly sores of Young's scorched rock music. Voices are vocoded into abstraction, guitars dogfight with sequencers . . . it's a strange sound.

What motivated this interest?

'Well, I spend most of my time trying to remain open to new things. They reflect the fact that I've got so interested in electronics and machines. I've always loved machines. I feel that with all the new digital and computerised equipment I can get my hands on now, I can do things I could never do before!' His eyes widen still further, like a hayseed agape at a new tractor.

'I know this is just the beginning for me. I've been Neil Young for years and I could stay where I am and be a period piece, but as I look around everything's so *organised*. Everything's running on digital time. The new music with its kind of perfection is reassuring for me – you know the beat's going to be there all the time and it's never going to break down. That's fascinating and I think it's still soulful. The *manipulation* of machines can be very soulful.

'The song "Transformer Man" is one I wrote for my son with all this, and to me that's probably the best song I've written in the last ten years. It's based on the freedom to be able to assume different voices and characters.

'I'm in a very primitive stage of development with all this stuff, but the things I can do . . . like I could take your voice singing a note, compute that into a keyboard and have four octaves from you singing that note. Or I could vocode it and sing with your voice. Or anybody's voice. Bing Crosby's off one of his old records.

'You can still be creative – it's still my melodies, my enunciation, my feeling. It just lifts a restriction – why should I have to sing with my own voice in 1982, when I can stretch out in different directions?' Young almost evanesces with enthusiasm for his machines, and seeing that involvement from such a figure does give fresh heart in its way.

But there's also a threat of loss: Neil Young is one of the handful to actually raise a response from the puckered old flesh of folk-based rock'n'roll. The thread that runs through Young's last half-dozen records winds through a reinvented rural America, detail brushed in across scores of songs with the casual eye of films like *Two-Lane Blacktop* or *Rafferty and the Gold Dust Twins,* a giant landscape not so much reduced as fragmented inside the microcosm of a lyric. If he turns to the machine print-outs of Modern Man, won't that dustbowl vision blow away for good?

'I think that might be other people's view more than mine. I feel I need to do something that first turns me on – that's why I'm taking this course. It won't *replace* my voice and acoustic guitar.

'I don't know if I can be classed as a contemporary songwriter. I'm like a dinosaur with a large tail – I'm so big I have to keep eating all the time. I look around, there's not many dinosaurs left, just a lot of smaller animals moving very fast. And it's their vibrant energy that I need to stay alive. Sometimes I think I might have to cut off my tail because I can't afford to keep feeding myself.'

Mr Young is amused at the metaphor. How does he keep a perspective on himself as an icon in his kingdom?

'I put the perspective on rock'n'roll because that's what I owe it to. For my spirit it's a healing force and I give everything I have when I play it. If I didn't do that I'd just be a museum, ancient history up close. Maybe I am that anyway.'

The disregard for expectation hasn't been confined to a purely musical setting. The devious implants in Young's writing have wrought an overview on mythical America that reads out like a windblown panorama of tumbleweeds and the assorted debris of small-town living.

Recurrent echoes of the Civil War, the pioneer waggoners and the blueblood heroes of idealised North American legend litter Young's later work as frequently as his loner's yearnings for a lover's satisfaction. Faded emblems and yellowing narratives haunt the precincts of 'The Old Homestead', 'Powderfinger' and 'Captain Kennedy' like ghostly ancestors in ancient prints. In updating those spirits with the colours of the rock'n'roll song, Young has forged anew a rusted link with a popular mythology.

'Those songs are like a landscape. I don't *think* with those songs – I get myself to a certain place, open up and they just come to me. I wrote "Homestead" all in one shot, never looking at the previous line until it was finished. They might be polished a little but they first come *through* me – I never think, Oh, I'll write a song with three birds, a guy and a horse in it.

'North America's my home, I've been all over it. I don't write down all the things I see, I just watch and watch until something comes out. Really I don't have a personal view on

America as a whole. They're just disparate ideas that come together.'

What's the worst thing about America today?

'Nobody's thought of a replacement for gasoline yet. Yankee ingenuity – it's on the ropes.' Neil permits himself a wry chuckle. 'The Yankees'd like to be able to come up with the big answer. Everyone would. I think it's less discouraging there now than it was three or four years ago. People are becoming proud to be a part of it again, on the grandest scale. I think there's a lot of creative force there – a lot of loudmouthed bullshit too – but it's like all countries, America is different all over.'

What is his favourite place to be in America?

'I like to be in the forest. Near my ranch, in California. It's like a natural cathedral, you can walk in and come out cleansed. America's still so geographically immense and beautiful. Europe has been manicured over centuries, but America is a huge expanse of God's work.'

Is he of a religious persuasion?

'Not so much towards one story. There's a lot of stories – Jesus, Krishna, Buddha – same story, different imagery. I mean, you could have a religion on the atom. I believe in the universe, in sizes and relationships. It's too big for me – just too big! It goes on forever. Jesus Christ couldn't have walked all that distance.'

One thing Neil Young hasn't looked into is the support of the No Nukes movement. When a lot of those contemporaries of his have bolstered appearances with a bunch of benefits, Young has stayed adamantly clear of agitprop. He likes nuclear power.

'We don't have it down, and we don't know what to do with the waste. But how are we going to get to other planets? We need nuclear power to discover what's out there and discover another power source. A coal-burning rocket won't get there. I'd like to go to another planet. I'd go now if I could!'

Shouldn't we concentrate on saving this beleaguered one first?

'We should do both. We'll need an alternative if we don't save this one. It's a responsible thing to do – there's more and more people here, more waste, more threat of war . . .'

Young waves a hand towards the limitless sky, out through the window of the bus. For a moment the stars seem to beckon . . . I blink hard. If he's so concerned about these Vital Issues, what sort of contribution to any debate does he feel compelled to make?

'My contribution?' He growls the words like a wily old Congressman. 'It's ethereal, I guess. I put out all the time and if anyone wants to take me to space I'm ready to go. I'd like to take my family too. We have to go somewhere else eventually.'

Down to Earth – let's talk movies. After *Journey Through The Past,* a project long abandoned to celluloid limbo, Young returned to filmmaking with the graceless if entertaining concert record of *Rust Never Sleeps.*

'It didn't take much money,' he admits. 'Film isn't something that comes naturally to me. I tried to paint but I can't do that. I know I'm not a great filmmaker but I have a lot of fun trying.

'The concept was like a daydream. You know the way dreams jumble up things that you've seen that day, maybe with people you knew five or ten years ago at some place you think, you sort of know? That's how *Rust Never Sleeps* came out. It put the music in a different perspective.'

What did he think of Dennis Hopper's *Out Of The Blue,* a bleakly realised extension of Young's 'Better To Burn Out Than Fade Away' proverb?

'I thought it was brilliant, but I wouldn't recommend it for an evening's entertainment. It's so fucking repulsive. Doesn't it make your stomach turn, seeing what those people are doing to each other?'

What's his kind of film?

'I liked *E.T., Star Wars.* I *love Star Wars.* It's like a bible for kids – the force! What message could be better for kids than, if I believe I can do it, I can do it!'

Young has completed a new film, *Human Highway*, now in search of a distributor.

'It's about a, um, gas station at an intersection of the country – power plant next door – city in the background – people living there, sort of in the future, a little in the past. A little Laurel and Hardy.

'Music in films is so limiting – everybody knows the picture and the music goes together. Film music is locked into the film. Music by itself is fuckin' *huge*, it can be anything. Movies are so straightforward. Film is a little more vulnerable – it's easier to take a shot at it than it is with music.'

The Business is prepared to put up with Young's shenanigans – nixing whole albums just prior to release, playing the wilful child when it comes to the routine of rock-world procedures – because when it comes down to it he is the most mild and passive of outsiders. He never looks for trouble. We talk over the trends in American music, the disappointing new pretenders to the FM thrones and the smug refusal of the US mainstream to open up its ears.

'What keeps music alive is the small things which aren't even noticed on a grand scale. The new thing always has to start little.'

But what about – and I start on Asia, Robert Plant, the new orthodoxy and more before Young says, 'You're asking the same questions I'm asking. That's why it's difficult for me to answer! I feel the same discontent and I know that in a lot of ways I'm just like those people. That makes me even madder. That's why I should cut my tail off.'

He has a good stock of dinosaur anecdotes too.

'I remember when I was living at Zuma I told Carole King, you gotta come down and listen to my new album [*Zuma*]. It's the cleanest album you've ever heard. She came down and listened and [falsetto], this isn't a *stoodio* album! What are

you *talking* about! and James Taylor on "Heart Of Gold", –
C'mon, Neil, why don't you make a *real record!*'

Would he, this Last American Rock Star, like to make The
Last Rock Record?

'No, I hope nobody does. I think there'll be rock'n'roll on
other planets. Maybe there is now.'

And he looks again at the sky. London territory is in view –
Cricklewood, Kilburn. He finishes another anecdote with a
familiar line – *'back in those old folkie days'*, *a* personal
history diffidently rifled through every time he takes a stage.

'When I was in school, I was called into the principal's
office – I was always getting into trouble – and he asked me
what I wanted to do when I left. I said I wanted to be a
musician and play in bars and clubs. He said, OK, but what
do you want to do *then*? Like I had to stop sometime. I've
never forgotten that. It's like I've always been kicking against
it – like I have to carry on . . .'

Mick Brown

BOB DYLAN: 'JESUS, WHO'S GOT TIME TO KEEP UP WITH THE TIMES?'

the *Sunday Times*, 1st July 1984

Like everything that happens in newspapers, this inter-view was very much a last-minute thing. As I recall, the decision to write something about Dylan was made on a Tuesday morning and I was on a plane to Madrid that same afternoon without an interview having been arranged.

I managed to track down Bill Graham, who was promoting the tour and looking after Dylan's affairs. He was sceptical. Bob wasn't doing interviews. But just in case, how big would the story be, where would it run? And what had I written myself? 'Bob would want to read some stuff.' Reviews of the earlier shows in the tour had appeared already in London papers. 'Bob would want to read those too.' Bob was evidently some reader.

I telephoned the office and asked them to fax a selection of pieces and reviews and delivered them to Graham. (When, eventually, we met it was obvious that Bob, of course, had not read them, not read anything, was completely unaware that the pieces had been requested; furthermore seemed to be una-ware even of which newspaper I was writing for, and not the least bit interested in finding out.)

For the next twenty-four hours I was put on hold. I

was told to stay in my room and await a call which might or might not come. I was due to leave the next morning. At the moment when it finally became clear that I would not be interviewing Dylan, the telephone rang. I was told to be at the Café Alcazar (the name has remained lodged in my memory) at 7.30. It was now 7.00. I gathered my things, caught a taxi and arrived ten minutes late. Obviously he had come and gone (I have no idea what made me think, absurdly, that Dylan would be as fastidious a time-keeper as I am). Forty minutes later he walked through the door, no minders, no flunkies, no ceremony. We spoke for more than an hour before he left, as unobtrusively as he had arrived.

Reading the piece again, I'm reminded of Dylan's candour, good humour and grace – the complete opposite, in fact, of most of the descriptions I have read of him before or since. My impressions are the ones I prefer to believe.

MB

BOB DYLAN TUGGED at a cigarette, stroked the beginnings of an untidy beard and gazed pensively at the stream of traffic passing down the Madrid street. 'What you gotta understand,' he said at length, 'is that I do something because I feel like doing it. If people can relate to it, that's great; if they can't, that's fine too. But I don't think I'm gonna be really understood until maybe 100 years from now. What I've done, what I'm doing, nobody else does or has done.'

The messianic tone grew more intense. 'When I'm dead and gone, maybe people will realise that and then figure it out. I don't think anything I've done has been even mildly hinted at. There's all these interpreters around, but they're not interpreting anything except their own ideas. Nobody's come close.'

But a lot of people, it seems, still want to. Bob Dylan may no longer sell records in the consistently enormous quantities he once did – a fact to which he will allow a tinge of regret – but his capacity to hold his audience in thrall seems undiminished.

By the time Bob Dylan arrives in Britain this week for performances at St. James' Park, Newcastle, on Tuesday and Wembley Stadium on Saturday, he will already have performed to almost half a million throughout Europe – half a million people singing the chorus of 'Blowin' In The Wind', an esperanto that's as much a testament to Dylan's abiding influence and charisma as it is to the insatiable interest of the world's press in his activities.

This interest is equalled only by Dylan's determination to keep his own counsel whenever possible. As Bill Graham, the tour's garrulous American promoter and Dylan's closest adviser, keeps reminding you, 'Bob is not your everyday folk singer.'

All the German magazine *Stern* had wanted to do was touch base for five minutes in return for a front cover. Dylan declined. The press conference that he had been persuaded to hold in Verona, attended by 150 excitable European journalists, had been a fiasco: photographers barred, and the first question from the floor – 'What are your religious views nowadays?' – met by Dylan irritably brushing the table in front of him, as if to sweep aside that and all other questions to follow.

'I mean, nobody cares what Billy Joel's religious views are, right?' he tells me with a wry smile. 'What does it matter to people what Bob Dylan is? But it seems to, right? I'd honestly like to know why it's important to them.'

One expects many things of Bob Dylan, but such playful ingenuousness is not one of them.

Dylan protects himself well, not with bodyguards but by a smokescreen of privacy and elusiveness of the sort that encourages speculation and myth. Meeting him involves penetrating a frustrating maze of 'perhapses' and 'maybes', of cautions and briefings – suggestive of dealing with fine porcelain – culminating in a telephone call summoning you to an anonymous cafeteria filled with Spanish families who give not a second glance to the figure in a Hawaiian shirt and straw hat who at last comes ambling through the door.

He is surprisingly genial, youthful for his 43 years, lean, interested and alert, a man who treats the business of being Bob Dylan with an engagingly aw-shucks kind of bemusement.

It was in striking contrast to the apparition Dylan had presented the previous night, on stage in front of 25,000 people in a Madrid football stadium, his black smock coat, high boots and hawkish profile suggesting some avenging backwoods preacher.

The emphasis in his performance has shifted from the overtly evangelical songs heard in Dylan's last visit to Britain three years ago. Now it spans every phase of his 21-year career. The themes of social protest, personal love and religious faith have never been more of a piece. Dylan remains what he has always been, an uncompromising moralist. And to hear songs such as 'Masters of War', 'A Hard Rain's A-Gonna Fall' (about nuclear war) and 'Maggie's Farm' (about rebellious labour) invested with fresh nuances of meaning, not to say vitriol, is to realise that, while the sentiments may have become unfashionable in popular music, they are no less pertinent. Nobody else is writing songs like Bob Dylan. Nobody ever did.

'For me, none of the songs I've written had really dated,' he says. 'They captured something I've never been able to improve on, whatever their statement is. A song like "Maggie's Farm" – I could feel like that just the other day, and I could feel the same tomorrow. People say they're "nostalgia", but I don't know what that means really. *A Tale of Two Cities* was written 100 years ago; is that nostalgia? This term "nostalgic", it's just another way people have of dealing with you and putting you some place they think they understand. It's just another label.'

Labels exercise Bob Dylan greatly. People have been trying to put them on him since he started, he says, 'and not one of them has ever made any sense.'

The furore about his religious beliefs puzzled him most of all, 'like I was running for Pope or something'. When the word first spread that he had eschewed Judaism and embraced Christianity, and he toured America in 1979 singing overtly religious songs, the most hostile reception came not from rock audiences but when he played university campuses, 'and the so-called intellectual students showed their true monstrous selves'.

'Born-again Christians' is just another label, he says. He had attended Bible school in California for three months, and the book was never far from his side, but the idea that faith was a matter of passing through one swing door and back out of another one struck him as ridiculous. 'I live by a strict disciplinary code, you know, but I don't know how moral that is or even where it comes from, really. These things just become part of your skin after a while; you get to know what line not to step over – usually because you stepped over it before and were lucky to get back.'

Was he an ascetic? Dylan lit another cigarette and asked what the word meant. 'I don't think so. I still have desires, you know, that lead me around once in a while. I don't do things in excess, but everybody goes through those times. They either kill you, or make you a better person.'

By this time in the conversation it did not seem awkward to ask: did he believe in evil?

'Sure I believe in it. I believe that ever since Adam and Eve got thrown out of the garden that the whole nature of the planet has been heading in one direction – towards apocalypse. It's all there in the *Book of Revelation*, but it's difficult talking about these things, because most people don't know what you're talking about anyway, or don't want to listen.

'What it comes down to is that there's a lot of different gods in the world against the God – that's what it's all about.

There's a lot of different gods that people are subjects of. There's the god of Mammon. Corporations are gods. Governments? No, governments don't have much to do with it anymore, I don't think. Politics is a hoax. The politicians don't have any real power. They feed you all this stuff in the newspapers about what's going on, but that's not what really going on.

'But then again, I don't think that makes me a pessimistic person. I'm a realist. Or maybe a surrealist. But you can't beat your head against the wall forever.'

He had never, he said, been a utopian: that was always a foreign term to him, something to do with moving to the country, living communally and growing rice and beans. 'I mean, I wanted to grow my own rice and beans – still do – but I never felt part of that movement.'

But he could still look back on the 1960s with something approaching affection. 'I mean, the Kennedys were great-looking people, man; they had style,' he smiles. 'America is not like that any more. But what happened, happened so fast that people are still trying to figure it out. The TV media wasn't so big then. It's like the only thing people knew was what they knew; then suddenly people were being told what to think, how to behave. There's too much information.

'It just got suffocated. Like Woodstock – that wasn't about anything. It was just a whole new market for tie-dyed t-shirts. It was about clothes. All those people are in computers now.'

This was beyond him. He had never been good with numbers, and had no desire to stare at a screen. 'I don't feel obliged to keep up with the times. I'm not going to be here that long anyway. So I keep up with these times, then I gotta keep up with the '90s. Jesus, who's got the time to keep up with the times?'

It is at moments such as this that Dylan – once, misleadingly perhaps, characterised as a radical – reveals himself as much of a traditionalist; an adherent of biblical truths; a firm believer in the family and the institutions of marriage –

despite his own divorce from his wife, Sara; a man disenchanted with many of the totems and values of modern life, mass communications, the vulgarity of popular culture, the 'sameness' of everything. Did he read contemporary literature? 'Oh yeah, I read a detective story, but I can't remember what it was called.'

'At least in the 1960s it seemed there was room to be different. For me, my particular scene, I came along at just the right time, and I understood the times I was in. If I was starting out right now I don't know where I'd get the inspiration from, because you need to breathe the right air to make that creative process work. I don't worry about it so much for me; I've done it; I can't complain. But the people coming up, the artists and writers, what are they gonna do, because these are the people who change the world.'

Nowadays, he admits, he finds songwriting harder than ever. A song like 'Masters of War' he would despatch in 15 minutes and move on to the next one without a second thought. 'If I wrote a song like that now, I wouldn't feel I'd have to write another one for two weeks. There's still things I want to write about, but the process is harder. The old records I used to make, by the time they came out I wouldn't even want them released because I was already so far beyond them.'

Much of the time nowadays is spent travelling. He was in Jerusalem last autumn for his son Jesse's bar mitzvah – 'his grandmother's idea,' he smiles. Israel interests him from 'a biblical point of view', but he had never felt that atavistic Jewish sense of homecoming. In fact, he lives principally on his farm in Minnesota, not far from the town of Hibbing where he spent his adolescence. Then there is his doomed house in Malibu, California, originally built to accommodate his five children – good schools nearby, he says – but which he has seldom used since his divorce, and a 63ft sailing boat in which he cruises the Caribbean 'when I can't think of anything else to do'.

He had never contemplated retirement: the need to make

money was not a factor – he is a wealthy man – but the impulse to continue writing was. 'There's never really been any glory in it for me,' he says. 'Being seen in the places and having everybody put their arm around you, I never cared about any of that. I don't care what people think. For me, the fulfilment was always in just doing it. That's all that really matters.'

As the conversation had progressed, more and more people had realised who the man in the straw hat was. A steady stream had made their way to his table, scraps of paper in hand. Dylan had signed them all, with a surprisingly careful deliberation – almost as if he was practising – but his discomfort at being on view was becoming more apparent. As peremptorily as he had arrived, Bob Dylan made his excuses and left.

Glenn O'Brien

MADONNA'S BLOND AMBITION

Interview, 1990

I interviewed Madonna a number of times; I couldn't tell you the actual number. We met in her youth, and my late youth, when she was going out with my friend Jean-Michel Basquiat and he brought her to my home for Thanksgiving dinner. He was having his first big success as a painter and she was on the verge of releasing her first record. I had never heard of her, but I liked her immediately. Somehow I got the idea she was black, because she had dark hair in dreads and, apparently, one of the only tans of her life. Shortly after that I saw her perform on the roof of Danceteria and became convinced that she was going places.

We became friends, I suppose after I wrote something nice about her first album, and we encountered one another frequently for several years and had a lot of mutual friends. A few years after this I worked closely with her as her editor on the SEX book, which sold about a million copies and ruined her career several times. That was really fun. Madonna is very sassy and loves to crack wise, and I never had a bad time in her company. I never worked with anybody who was sitting on my lap before. Later I worked with her on the Girly Show *tour* book, which I did for peanuts. She said she owed me a big one, but I never got it, and now that she's married . . . I mean, and now *that* I'm *married . . . Actually, I think she should have simply given me that white 450 SEL that she was driving. She knew it was my favourite car and what are friends for. I have always been a great friend. My lips are sealed.*

Anyway, I always thought she was extremely cute and sexy and I loved the fact that she was going out with Warren Beatty at this time, who was even older than I. Madonna is also a genius, in both an under- and an overstated way, although I still think she should have become a lounge singer ten years ago when I told her to. I think her real genius is in flirting and being endearingly rude, although she has many genuine talents. I really miss having sassy chats like this with her. I always considered her a real friend. But she should have invited me to her wedding. I'm very famous in Korea.

This was a cover story in Interview, *after Andy Warhol died, and a couple of issues into the short-lived collaboration between myself, Fabien Baron, the great designer and another Madonna pal, and Ingrid Sischy whom Andy Warhol once referred to as 'that dyke from* Artforum.' *Shortly after this, Fabien and I left* Interview *and it was history. I mean, the rest is history.*

GO'B

I INTERVIEWED MADONNA at the Disney Studios, of all places, where she was rehearsing her *Blond Ambition* tour. It's not really so odd that she should work at Disney, since that studio produces her latest film, *Dick Tracy*, which also stars its director, Warren Beatty, but I half-expected Goofy and Donald to appear onstage with her dancers at any minute. I watched some of the rehearsal.

Madonna looked like a billion bucks in a Gaultier sheath with dangerous-looking silver nipples. The music and dancing were great, but there was a lot of trouble with the trap doors that day, and things were run through over and over. She and her choreographer, Vince Paterson, ran the rehearsal with a lot of good humour tempering their perfectionist frustration.

That evening, Burbank was being aerially sprayed for killer fruit flies, and Madonna said we should get out of town or our cars' finishes would be ruined. I was driving a crummy rental, but Madonna was driving her Benzo, so I followed her car into Hollywood, which wasn't easy. She's as exciting a driver as she is an entertainer. On the way to the restaurant she got into a screaming match with a huge guy driving a 'big foot'-type truck who almost backed over her.

When we got to the restaurant she said, 'He called me a dick. That's the first time anybody ever called me a dick.' I wondered if he had known it was Madonna he had called a dick. I wondered if it had anything to do with *Dick Tracy*. We'll never know. But I did have fun with Madonna, who is lovely, charming, and witty, even when she's making fun of you or giving you the third degree.

GLENN O'BRIEN: *The first time we met, I thought you were black. You had black hair and dreadlocks and a tan.*

MADONNA: I had a tan! How unusual. Oh, I think I had been to the Bahamas with Jellybean [Benitez]. That was the second tan in my whole life. Yeah, I came to your house for Thanksgiving dinner with Jean-Michel [Basquiat] . . .

To my dumpy apartment.

I can assure you that my apartment was dumpier. Anyway, I remember being hungry, but you guys just wanted to roll joints. I met your wife at Thanksgiving dinner. We're always eating together. So let's talk about your marriage.

No, let's talk about your show.

Let's not. Today was a horrible day. That was the worst rehearsal.

Well, I liked it, but I haven't seen it when you thought it was good. I loved the number where you're lying on the piano singing a torch song.

You saw only one segment of the show. I've created five different worlds, and the set is all based on hydraulics. One is going down and another is coming up. The world changes completely. I think of it more as a musical than as a rock concert. There is a straightforward *Metropolis* section, like my 'Express Yourself' video – that set with all the gears and machinery; it's very hard and metallic. That's the heavy-duty dance music. Then the set changes and it's like a church. We call it the temple ruins. It's all these columns, trays of votive candles, a cross. I do 'Like a Virgin' on a bed, but we changed the arrangement, so it sounds Indian. Then I'm being punished for masturbation on this bed, which is, as you know, what happens. Then we do the more serious, religious-type material – 'Like a Prayer', 'Papa Don't Preach' . . . Then it changes to what you saw, this Art Deco '50s-musical set. That's when we do three songs from *Dick Tracy*, and then after that we do what I call the camp section. Then it gets really serious again and we go into our *Clockwork Orange* cabaret set.

What's that?

It's a very sparse set with a backdrop of an orgy of naked people. The paintings are like Tamara de Lempicka – Cubist-like nudes – no pornography, no genitals. You just see people having fun.

How long have you been working on this? It's so elaborate.

Since September. Designing the stage, hiring people, firing people, hiring more people, designing the costumes with Gaultier, going over the music, changing the arrangements, picking the talent.

It's a big operation.

There are seven dancers, two singers, eight musicians, me, about a zillion tech guys just to take care of the musicians, and then all the crew guys underneath the stage working everything. There are a lot of people. Probably seventy-five to a hundred. And a lot of trucks.

I heard you fired yourself today.

Yeah. It's a running joke. I fire someone every day, every time something goes wrong. I fire Lenny everyday. He's the guy who opens the trap doors, and he's always doing it at the wrong time and almost killing me.

I was sitting near your dancers; they were really funny. They were talking to your piano player, who had on a new suit. The pants were short, and one of the dancers said, 'Your shoes should give a party so your pants can drop on down.'

The dancers are really funny. They keep me going. They're real pranksters.

I love it when they become mermen. You seem to have a thing for merpersons.

Mermen, yeah. I like to switch everything around. People like mermaids; I like mermen. I like the idea of men with tails on. I like the idea of men being the objects of desire, the sirens that entrap women, instead of the other way around. Some people would say that I hate men and that I like to do things to take power away from them, but you don't have to get that analytical.

I don't think putting men in flimsy, marabou-trimmed negligees is taking power away from them.

I think it's funny. Anyway, it's just a takeoff. Do you think it's offensive?

Not at all.

Well, a lot of people would. You're a really evolved guy. I can assure you that people in Michigan are going to throw tomatoes at me or something because I have guys in fish tails and negligees. But I like wearing men's suits, and I grab my crotch a lot.

But can you even tell if the audience is offended?

No. I just know from feedback afterward. But when I did the MTV awards and I was smoking, I could hear people booing. I'm sure I offend people when I grab my crotch, but I really don't care. That's bound to happen. And I know I offend people with my videos. But I don't hear it. I just get feedback later.

Do you ever get critical mail?

No. People that don't like me aren't going to take the time to write to me.

Really? I get mail about things I've written. Of course, those letters are usually from guys in jail.

I get letters from guys in jail all the time too, but they just want to have a date with me. Most people that don't like me are people that are fanatically religious.

Have you ever been censored?

I get censored all the time. You wouldn't believe the stuff that I'd like to do that never gets done.

But you've never had a video rejected.

No, but there was the whole Pepsi thing. They wouldn't play my commercial because I wouldn't take my 'Like a Prayer' video off the air.

Is that why you're drinking a Diet Coke right now?

I just like it. I thought MTV might not play my 'Vogue' video. You can see my breasts through my dress.

Is that really a first? I mean, there are an awful lot of erect nipples under spandex on MTV as it is. I guess as long as you can't see the dark aureole, or whatever it's called, that's O.K.

I don't know. I thought it might get censored.

You could put little animated black bars over your nipples, sort of like digital pasties.

Well, every time I do a video they say they're not going to show it. When I did 'Oh, Father', they said, 'We're not going to show the scene with the lips sewn up.' And I said, 'Fuck you.' And then they showed it. In 'Express Yourself' they weren't going to show me with a chain around my neck. I don't get their rules. I don't know what they find offensive. Then I don't know what's going to happen with the videos of songs I wrote for the *Dick Tracy* soundtrack. I had to change lyrics in the songs because the soundtrack is part of a Disney movie. I had to change things that had anything to do with sodomy, intercourse, or masturbation.

Is the movie sexy?

Yeah, but in a really '50s way. It's a really clean movie. People kiss, but they don't have sex or go the bathroom.

So tell us about Breathless Mahoney, your character in Dick Tracy. *Do you play yourself?*

Glenn! Do I play myself?! No! Am I a cartoon character?!

I don't know anything about Dick Tracy.

No one can ever just play themselves in a movie. That's ridiculous. Obviously there can be a lot of things in the character that are like you, but you've got to be a little bit inventor-imaginative. I mean, there are certain things in the character that I can relate to, but I'm not playing myself, for God's sake!

I'm glad we cleared that up.

Breathless is the queen of the one-liners. She's always cracking wise. I'm not always that way.

Beatty doesn't have that jaw, does he?

He's got the jaw he was born with. It's a pretty nice one.

All I remember about Dick Tracy *was that he had that right-angle jaw.*

Well, Warren didn't have any prosthetics. Me and Warren and Glenne Headly didn't have prosthetics. Everybody else did – all the bad people and some of the good people.

On the record you play in your show, is Warren singing with you?

Yeah.

He's surprisingly good. How come he never sang before?

Nobody ever asked him. I think he doesn't think of himself as very musical. But he's a very good piano player. He wanted to be a concert pianist when he was little.

You're always playing pretty loveable characters. Would you ever want to play a villain?

Yeah, but I've never been offered one. It would also be nice to play some unsympathetic characters. God knows, I have my bad side.

How about playing a mom?

Oh, yeah, sure. I'm down for that.

Are you down for being a mom in real life?
I knew that was the next question.
I wasn't planning it; it just popped into my head.
Yeah. I am. I don't know when, but I'm down.
Who are your heroes?
Mother Theresa. Isn't Gorbachev a hero?
I'd say so.
What about Havel, from Czechoslovakia? He's a hero.
*He's also totally into Frank Zappa and Captain Beefheart.
I think he's put Zappa on the Czech payroll as some kind of
cultural consultant.*
That's heroic. But it's hard to think of heroes, because not a
lot of people take risks these days. I'll probably get in trouble
for saying this, but I think those guys in Public Enemy are
heroes. They're not afraid to say things.
*I think that's the case with the better rap artists in general. I
think they are just about the only people who are really
contributing anything on a cultural level these days.*
Do you think Spike Lee is a hero?
Yeah, I do.
Me too.
Do you think, How can I push things to the limit?
I'm sort of naturally a pain in the ass. I naturally like to do
things that rub people the wrong way. No, that's wrong. Let
me rephrase that. I just like being controversial, I guess. Even
that doesn't sound right. But somehow it happens that way.
It's more like 'Hey, well, you know how they always say
things are this way? Well, they're not! Or they don't have to
be.'
Do you write songs that way?
I'm starting to. Especially on my last album. And when you
hear the *Dick Tracy* soundtrack, then you'll know.
Is it political?
Yeah. I think my 'Express Yourself' video is political too. It
depends on what you mean by political. When I think of
controversy, I never really think people are going to be half as

shocked as they are at what I do. I really couldn't believe how out of control the whole Pepsi thing got.

Maybe that's just the nature of bureaucracy. They're huge multinational corporations with many thousands of stockholders, and you're an entrepreneur with no stockholders. I was having breakfast this morning next to this record-company goon who was explaining to a management goon about the alternative charts and alternative radio and alternative acts. I thought it was funny that he said Lou Reed and Elvis Costello were alternative acts. I was wondering just where they draw the line. What do you think is alternative music?

I guess it's music that's not popular. I mean, alternative to what? I guess it's supposed to be music that makes you think, as an alternative to music that doesn't.

So what makes Elvis Costello considered alternative?

The fact that he's not popular.

He isn't?

He's popular in colleges, in a cult way. He's not popular like Milli Vanilli, right?

I guess. I'm not really sure who Milli Vanilli are.

You lie, Glenn! You know who they are!

I saw them on MTV once.

Don't tell me that crap. Look, you know who they are.

They have a lot of hair, right?

Do you think I'm going to fall for that? I didn't say you had to like them, but you know who they are. Now, they are alternative music.

Were you ever alternative? Were you ever on the college-radio chart?

I don't think so. If there's an underground disco chart, I've been on it.

O.K., what else should we talk about?

Oh please! You're the interviewer!

People always talk about what they want to talk about anyway. Come on, help me out.

Help you out! Gimme a break! I've been working all day,
honey.

Listen, it's after midnight New York time.

I've been working all day. I've been working all week.

*Why don't you just tell me some good lies that can be
picked up by the tabloids? Tell me about your lesbian affairs.*

That's old tabloid news.

It started with the nuns, right?

No way am I saying that. The lesbian stuff is old. I'll have
to lie about something else.

How about art? There's a lot on your art collection in the
Vanity Fair *article about you. When did you start collecting
art?*

As soon as I had the bread.

What's the first thing you bought?

A Robert Smithson painting.

Really?

You probably don't even know who that is.

Are you kidding? I just didn't know he did paintings.

The one I have is a beautiful, sort of abstract painting. But
you can make out the figure of an angel in it. So I call it my
guardian angel. It's hanging over my bed in New York.

Do you believe in guardian angels?

I believe that someone is protecting me. Otherwise I'd be
dead. Otherwise the guy tonight would have gotten out of his
car and beaten the shit out of me. Believe me, it would have
happened if I weren't protected, because I can't resist mouthing off to people when they curse at me. One time a guy did
that to me and I said, 'Fuck you, motherfucker!' I wasn't in
my car; I was standing on the curb giving directions to my
girlfriend. And this guy got out of his car. It was in the Valley.
It always happens in the Valley. This big guy got out of his car
and walked over to me, and I was thinking, Oh, my God, he's
going to beat the shit out of me. I was cowering. And I turned
into a person I've never been in my life. I said, 'I am so sorry! I
am truly sorry!' So I do think someone is protecting me. I

don't know if it's an angel. It could be the Devil. He could have his own hidden agenda.

Do you believe in psychics?

Yeah. I believe that there are real ones and there are fake ones.

Do you have any psychic power?

Yeah, I do. I think most sensitive people do. I think a lot of innate psychic power has to do with just being really observant.

How does your psychic power show up?

In dreams. Or in knowing when people are going to call, or what people are going to say, or what they are doing to do next.

Did you ever dream about being an entertainer when you were a kid?

No, I just had dreams about being murdered all the time. The only remotely entertainment-oriented dream I ever had was one where I dreamed I kissed Robert Redford. I was in the sixth grade. And it has not come true.

Have you met him?

No. I don't really want to kiss him. It was weird. I don't think I ever really had any fixation on him. But the dream was so vivid. I was really turned on.

So what sign are you?

Guess. It's so obvious.

Uh. Uh. Uh.

What do I do for a living?

Uh, you sing and dance. You entertain people. O.K., let's see . . . Leo.

Yes. That's right. Should I guess what sign you are?

Yeah. It's fairly obvious.

Are you a Virgo?

No.

It's obvious?

Well, it's not that hard. Think about when we first met.

I thought you didn't like me.

That happens all the time. I'm awful.

Let's see. What's an awful sign? Scorpio?

Stop! I'm a Pisces. You were close with Virgo. That's my opposite sign. I'm always working with them and marrying them.

I don't know that much about Pisces. I've never really known any Pisces. What are their characteristics?

A lot of writers are Pisces.

Do you have nice feet?

No, I have big feet.

Don't Pisces have nice feet?

No, they have influential feet.

Do they have foot fetishes?

Some do, I heard. I am attracted by a nice pair of feet.

You know how you have a body spot that's sensitive or powerful? There's one for each sign. Mine is my back. I have a great back. It's beautiful. I can say that.

Has there been any astrological pattern to your love life? Do you tend to fall for one certain sign?

Fire signs. I married a Leo. A lot of people in my family are Leos. My mother had a lot of us in the same month. She kept getting pregnant at the same time every year. I had my chart done once. I remember only two things from it. One was that I should eat more cooked vegetables. The other was that I was going to meet an older man who was going to be a great influence on me. And then I met Warren Beatty.

Has he been a great influence on you?

Yes. But I haven't been eating many cooked vegetables. I do eat a lot of raw vegetables. How come you use two tape recorders? Are you superstitious?

No, I'm really bad at doing interviews. I recently interviewed someone for an hour and a half and the tape recorder was on 'play', not 'record'.

He must have been a loser. Who was this person?

He's a professor of popular culture at Notre Dame University.

Snoresville.

Not at all. It was very interesting to hear someone speak in complete paragraphs.

I'm not doing that?

No you're not.

I am so. For instance, the way I'm talking now, I'm just going to keep going on and on in a never-ending sentence and keep going on and on and then put a period on the end of it. Is that a paragraph?

No. You have to speak in complete blocks of thought.

I don't know too many people like that. Warren Beatty is like that. He's very intellectual.

Articulate?

Extremely. He doesn't talk a lot but when he does it comes out in paragraphs.

Is he a scholar?

I'd say that. He's a scholar of humanity.

And you?

Am I a scholar? No. I'm not a scholar, I'm a sponge. I just soak things up.

You just study the videotapes of your rehearsals.

That's so fucking funny! No, I don't just study my video-tapes. Yeah, yeah. That's all I study.

I know you have a hard job.

I read. I'll tell you one thing I don't do: I don't watch TV.

Really?

Never. And I have four televisions. I used to read to lot more than I do now, I'm sorry to say. I just don't have time. There, I've said it again.

Well, what do you do on the plane?

I read magazines. I love reading magazines. It's my vice. Junk. Not like the *Enquirer* . . .

Woman's Day?

Vogue. Tatler. Details. Spy. The usual. I like *Vanity Fair.* It's high-gloss gossip.

Don't you think it's a little negative?

I guess.

Usually Vanity Fair *just likes English people or aristocratic felons.*

They weren't mean to me.

No, but you're one of the exceptions.

Maybe because everyone shits on me so much they felt sorry for me.

Everybody shits on you so much? Give me a break!

Come on, I get a lot of bad press.

You get so much good press.

Yeah, but I get a lot of bad press too. I get ripped to shreds. I've got everybody waiting to tear me down.

Who gives you bad press? What's the worst thing anybody ever wrote about you?

You know, I'm a good-for-nothing, no-talent has-been, and they can't wait until I drop dead.

That sounds like the alternative press.

Oh, they hate me. People who listen to Elvis Costello hate me.

But do they write lies about you?

Every magazine in the world writes lies about me.

What are the biggest lies that have been written about you?

It's not the big lies, it's the little titbits. I read about people that I'm dating that I've never met.

You should provide your own lies. Maybe there's something you'd like to tell out readers.

Well, I am really obese right now.

Really. How much do you weigh?

I weigh more than Roseanne Barr. Hey, you know what? Vince Paterson, who is choreographing the show now, his mother called him from Florida and said, 'Vince, is everything all right?' Vince said, 'Yeah, what are you talking about?' She said, 'Well, I know you're working for Madonna now. Is she O.K.?' He said, 'Yeah, she is fine. Why?' 'What's wrong?' She said, 'Well, I just read that she gained fifty pounds and she's having a really hard time working it off. She can't do the dance steps . . .' It's the silliest stuff. I must have been pregnant three hundred times in the last five years. I was dating Rob Lowe.

I was too. Are you the jealous type?

Are you?

No.

If your ex-girlfriend was dating someone, you wouldn't be jealous?

I don't think so.

Lie! Yes, you would! Everybody is.

Are you jealous of all your exes if they're dating somebody?

I have a little twinge of jealousy behind my knee. I secretly want to kill them. You get really territorial over people you spent years of your life with. You don't want anybody else to have them.

Going how far back?

Going as far back as I can remember. I mean, the idea that the first guy I ever slept with, my lover when I was fifteen, is married and has kids really breaks me up. I wonder if he still loves me. He probably does.

Maybe you just want to keep them all.

That would be nice.

I always used to think that would be ideal.

Do you think anybody would stand for that shit?

No, of course not.

But in an ideal world, where you were president, you could make it work that way.

I think Donald Trump is campaigning to be president now, carrying on.

With Marla? But he can't be president if he's had sex. That's the rule.

No, no. It's all cyclical. He wants to be like Kennedy, and he has to prove that he's a womanizer.

It's not cool to be like Kennedy anymore. Look at Gary Hart.

*No, Gary Hart just didn't have it. He didn't have that aura
of power.*

You mean Donald Trump is powerful? He's a wimp. Oh,
don't print that. I want tickets to the next Tyson fight.

*I do think it's all cyclical. You go through periods where
the country wants a real solid family man, and then you go
through periods where the country wants –*

A guy with a dick?

A potentate. And then he probably gets assassinated.

Ow! But Donald Trump? Isn't there anyone else? Couldn't
we get someone more handsome?

Have you ever considered running for public office?

I think I've had a fantasy about it. I'd have to hone up on a
few factual things if I did that. Maybe I'm too self-centered.

But there hasn't been a woman yet.

Give it time. Kim Basinger could become the mayor of that
town she bought in Georgia.

That could be a conflict of interest.

That's true.

But you don't have any ambitions like that.

I make jokes sometimes that I'm going to run for president
someday.

I think that's a good idea. In fact, I think I thought of that.

That you would run for president?

*No, that you would. Didn't I write that once? Didn't I
write 'Madonna For President' once? It sure rings a bell. I
think it was my idea. You just have to wait till you're 35.*

What are you writing down?

*That line that one of your dancers said: 'Your shoes should
throw a party so your pants can drop on down.'*

Is that your head, or did your neck just throw up? Do you
want to know my measurements or anything?

Yeah. What are they? What size hat do you wear?

I don't know.

O.K., what about your other measurements?

33-24-34.

Really?

Pretty good, huh?

I guess so. I always thought that ideally there was a supposed to be ten inches' difference.

34 when I'm having my period.

Do you find that all the women you work with have their periods at the same time?

That always happens. It pisses me off.

Why?

Because we're all on the rag at the same time.

It's a tribal thing.

What happens is that it screws things up. If you haven't been with that group of people for a while, and all of a sudden you're with them, you start your period earlier. It totally fucks up your cycle.

When you yelled at that guy in the car tonight, I think he didn't recognize you. You seem to be able not to be recognized.

I got recognized about twenty times on the way over there. People just wave.

So what's that like?

It's good and bad. It means you've made it.

You must like it. Otherwise you'd wear a hat in the car, right?

Right. Sometimes it bugs me when I'm in a bad mood and I'm driving my car and I look over and there's a car full of guys and they start following me wherever I go. That's a pain in the ass. But I could think of worse things that could happen to me. [Madonna pulls out a large bag of candy.] Do you want a piece of candy?

No, thanks.

I love candy, as you can see. I'm a sugar junkie. It's because I was deprived of love as a child.

But you have a big family. Don't they love you?

Yeah, I'm just kidding. I wasn't deprived. But I wasn't allowed to eat candy. That's really their reason. I've been gorging ever since I moved out of the house.

Your brother paints Madonnas, right?

He paints religious figures. Religion's been a major influence in our life.

Did you have a super-religious upbringing, or just the average Catholic home?

Super. I wasn't allowed to wear tampons until I married. My stepmother said it was like intercourse. I wasn't allowed to wear pants for a really long time.

What about your brothers?

You know how religion is. Guys get to do everything. They get to be altar boys. They get to stay out late. Take their shirts off in the summer. They get to pee standing up. They get to fuck a lot of girls and not worry about getting pregnant. Although that doesn't have anything to do with being religious.

Did you ever go through an atheist period?

No.

You just went from Catholic to pagan.

Do you think I'm a pagan? That means I worship false gods.

What gods are false?

That's the definition of a pagan.

That's the Catholic definition of a pagan. I mean, I believe in the main god, the big one, and I believe in Jesus, but I believe in all the other ones too.

I guess I am a pagan in the eyes of Catholicism.

Do people ever ask you out on dates?

All the time. You bet!

Besides prisoners from jail. Do you like it?

Sure. It's flattering.

What's a good pickup line?

'Haven't I seen you somewhere before?'

Does that work?

It depends on what they look like. But I really don't remember anyone giving me a pickup line. Usually only jerks have pickup lines.

In your Vanity Fair *article you called Oliver Stone and Andrew Lloyd Webber 'fabulous misogynists'. What's a fabulous misogynist?*

I just like putting a nice word with a bad word. It means they're grand in their misogyny. It's like calling someone a charming creep.

Are there a lot of misogynists in . . .

In Hollywood? They're everywhere, babe.

Is it as bad as it ever was? No improvement?

It doesn't seem like it. It seems racism is as bad as it ever was, misogyny is as bad as it ever was, homophobia is as bad as it ever was. You know.

You've been in business ten years. I've been in business twenty years. I think some things have gotten better.

You have a different perspective than I have. You're older. Like about a couple hundred years.

Yeah? I'm not as old as your boyfriend.

No comment.

Robert Gordon

ICE CUBE LETS OFF STEAM

Creem, 1991

Rap seemed so dangerous then. One of the most effective elements of John Singleton's Boyz N the Hood, *which Ice Cube had just starred in, was the constant off-screen presence of helicopters circling. South Central LA was like a war zone. Ice Cube had emerged, not just as a soldier, but as a leader, a communications officer for the troops.*

Since this interview in the early 1990s, rap has been fully co-opted by other cultures, achieving the pinnacle of assimilation: TV advertising usage. However, I don't believe rap – gangsta rap – has become any less dangerous. When I pull up next to a car full of people mouthing every word of a blaring song about hatred and killing, I believe that person's mind is being poisoned. It's beyond Hollywood shoot-'em-ups, beyond action picture violence. Gangsta rap supports gangsta thoughts, and it numbs minds to violence. You know what? I don't want my kids listening to it. Which probably means they'll play it really, really loud.

Re-reading this interview, I don't remember the tension in the hotel room as thick as it appears in print. I think we both felt invigorated afterwards; our conversation was full of sparring, neither of us changing – much. We disagreed, but there was a mutual respect.

RG

BETWEEN THE RECENT gubernatorial election in Louisiana and the release of Ice Cube's second solo album, the media has been busy hunting. No sooner than former Klansman David Duke lost that race, political journalists loaned their traps to music writers, who set out to interview the rapper and see if his rhetoric was as sturdy as his music.

Like Duke, Ice Cube speaks boldly and firmly about controversial topics. Both have been able to escape ensnarement by denying their meaning is what it appears to be. In the course of our discussion, Ice Cube was quick to free himself of the responsibility of his statements, contending that my opinions were founded in a culture different than his: 'You don't know where we're coming from or where we're going so it's hard for you to comprehend.'

Ice Cube is uncomfortable with his position as an artist, vacillating between being simply a cog in the wheel and a man of power. He has built a concept into his new album *Death Certificate* – a death side, 'a mirrored image of where we are today', and a life side, 'a vison of where we need to go' – which allows him couch his accusations and assertions in being a medium for life on the street, or to claim them as his own criticism of what is or belief in what could be.

Is the man who says the following a racist? From 'Black Korea': 'Oriental one-penny countin' motherfuckers' and 'chop-suey ass', ending with the lines 'So pay respect to the black fist/or we'll burn down your store right down to a crisp'; from 'No Vaseline': 'Get rid of that devil real simple/ put a bullet in his temple/'cause you can't be a nigger for life crew [N.W.A.]/with a white Jew tellin' you what to do'; from 'Horny Lil'Devil': 'True niggas aren't gay'.

I met Ice Cube in Memphis, where he was finishing the first stage of shooting Walter Hill's action film, *The Looters*. He was relaxed and affable, unlike the tone of his music. Throughout our discussion, he kept a member of his security force – Tommy, a large homey from the 'hood – at his side. This imposing gentleman listened quietly, making his presence known only by answering the phone on the first ring and speaking in a surprisingly quiet whisper.

Monitoring the David Duke interviews provided some guidance on how to talk to Ice Cube (ne O'Shea Jackson). Both claim to be spokespeople for a group whom they say the government is not for, by or of. Both control their interviews by advancing inarguably good statements like 'I am anti-poor' in Ice Cube's case, or Duke's claim to represent the working man, statements so inarguable that they are meaningless. Ice Cube deflects tough questions, turning to 'solid' anti-poor ground or lashing out against easy targets.

The heavy attention Ice Cube is getting has established him as a spokesperson. While it's revealed a man with some perceptive ideas about society, it's also revealed some misguided, ill-reasoned statements. This is Ice Cube's adolescent record, the flexing of his muscles. When he returns, this continuous probing of his ideas may produce a precise speaker with a definite, refined platform. If that record comes out next year, he'll be 23.

Tell me about this film you're working on.

It's a movie by Walter Hill. If you follow his movies, they're kind of like nothing nice, dark action movies. And this is a movie about two white guys from Arkansas finding out that there's some gold in St. Louis in a factory, hid under the floor of this building. So they go and try to get the gold and try to sneak in there and sneak out since the factory's abandoned. But then, man, our gang comes up and we got this guy we're going to scare like we going to blow him off the roof, and he ends up falling off the roof for real. And then the two white guys see us do it, so we go down there to handle them because they're witnesses. And they end up getting our leader's brother and snatch him into the room. Now, the predicament is, how are they going to get out without getting killed, and ours is how we going to kill them without getting our friend killed. So, my role is Savon, I'm like the bad guy's bad guy, because I want to overthrow King James, our gang leader who is Ice T, because I don't think he's running the group right. I think he's worrying about his brother instead of worrying about the group. So it's all kind of things – we find out there's gold there, and that throws another monkey wrench into the program. It's a real suspenseful action-type movie.

With the release of this second full album you've become a spokesperson. Was that your intention or a product of the media?

I wanted to speak. I like to get to kids' frustrations and put 'em on wax because the only outlet for doing that is rap music. We don't have any networks or anything like that, so the only way we can get our information out is through rap music.

This film sounds like an action film, and action films tend to be exploitative. Does that conflict with any message you want to have as a rap spokesperson?

No, not at all, because this movie in particular is about how scandalous people can get for money. It's that type of tip, it's not exploiting anything. I'm just trying to get more black faces on the silver screen.

To get black faces on the screen, would you take a role in blaxploitation films?

Oh, no. This is far from that. These are substantial roles in films. Film is just fiction, know what I'm saying?

If you're in a film pushing someone off the roof, how far apart is that character from the blaxploitation films?

Well, they're real far apart. I mean, you're entitled to your opinion, but the simple fact is that the US Army is the most violent of anybody. So you can't come down on the lower level until you go to the higher level. They've killed thousands and thousands of people. And they can blow up the whole front in one whop. How can you call Saddam Hussein an aggressor and not call yourself an aggressor because the United States aggressed in Panama and took over. You know what I'm saying? Don't be a hypocrite.

I agree. But what can you do about Iraq? What can I do? We can make our voices heard or we can state our opinion, try and sway other people, and that's exactly what I mean about taking a role in an action film. You're condoning violence.

This is a violent society, period. It's a thing like this – I have a son that I have to feed every day, too. If I'm in Rome I'm going to pretty much do as the Romans do until I have the power or the resources to change that. I mean, we can't do nothing until we can economically match or beat the structure that's doing it. So until I can economically beat the producer of this movie right here, then I have to use that as a stepping stone for people to adjust to seeing black faces on the screen. I'm using *Looters* as a stepping stone so I can write my own movie.

Is there a script that you're working on?

Yeah, it's called *America Eats Its Young*. I can't really go into it, but that's the title. Whenever I can get to my computer, I work on it, and it's coming along really good.

Switching to Death Certificate, *let's talk about some of the messages, like black separatism. What about the black-on-black crimes that ravage the black community?*

I'll say it like this: We have two lions and you teach them to love meat. But then you only throw them scraps. You can't really expect the lions to get along for those scraps, you expect them to fight over the scraps. That same effect is happening in the black community. We're taught to want, to want, to want. You can have, you can be rich, you can do this, you can do that. But they're just throwing scraps of economic avenues. Plus the gangs exist, so what you have is the lions fighting over the scraps. You have people fighting to get rich, and they'll fight each other.

But not all whites are rich.

Well, most white people know who they are and love themselves. Most black people are in a position of we don't know who we are, we don't know our history. We weren't taught to read or write for 436 years. You have black people who want to be anything but black. You're told white is right and black is not. If you want to tell a lie, tell a *white* lie. Subconsciously this affects the black people. Even if they show you a devil's food cake and an angel's food cake – those are things that are planted in the back of your mind, and they affect the way you live.

Knowing that for 436 years blacks were deprived of basic rights, how can you dis women the way you do?

Well, I dis black women for trying to be white women. That's what I dis, because it's a thing where you gotta be yourself.

So what should black women be?

Okay, a black woman sits home and she watches television and she wants the things that every woman wants. Chanel comes out with a purse, black woman wants the purse. And black woman should deserve to want that purse. But don't put the economic strain on the black man to get that purse, because the black man can't just work overtime to get these things. So it results into crime. If I gotta drive a Benz to get women in the community, I'll do anything I can to get a Benz. What I'm trying to do is break down this attitude.

I hear you cussing out women.

What I do, it's teaching, but it's teaching in our own way. I can't go out to the people out here and start speaking Chinese to teach them, because Chinese is a nicer way to teach them. I gotta talk exactly how the kids talk in the street or the message won't come across. It's hard for you to comprehend as well as a 17-year-old black young lady or a 17-year-old black male who is going through this every day. All this crime, this crack-selling – all this is a result of the opposite sex. Now, I take a position from the male's point of view, but I also produce a female named YoYo who takes it from the back end. Say okay, we don't want you for your money, just don't want us for what we got between our legs. And through those two ways of hitting it, hopefully we'll come up with understanding. I mean, this is my formula. Your formula might be different. This is the way I choose to do it and if I was doing the wrong thing I don't think I'd be at 1.1 million records right now.

You can't justify yourself with numbers. Look at Bush. What he's doing isn't right, and look how many votes he got.

Bush is just a part of big business. Bush is not coming from the heart. I still live with the people. I still live in South-central Los Angeles. I see what's going on, and I see why it's going on, and rap music is the only way we can communicate. If we had the TV, even radio – if we had any other kind of ways to get this same message across, then that can be an avenue. We don't have control over films as much as we do over our lyrics. I know John [Singleton] had to fight the film company to get certain things in *Boyz N the Hood*. If they wanted it out, it would have been out. We only have one tool, which is the records. That's the only thing we can put out uncensored and unedited and you know we ain't got to go through nobody to get the message. It's our network. Let's take Bush and get in his head and do a record just off his thoughts and see what he thinks. You'll see that the way people think is much, much more outrageous than Ice Cube could ever be.

Just like with John Singleton, the record company's censor-ship button may be a looser button, but if you put something on it that they don't want to put out, they're not going to put it out. It's not a free game the way you're saying it.

It's the freest one! Because, for one thing, these record companies know that they can't rap, but they know that they can make money. If they knew that they could rap, or find people that's as good as the rappers to do a different type of music, don't you think they would? Why should they leave us on there if they can find their people to do the same thing? And keep it all in the family.

If you've got rappers who can rap, why would you want to replace them with someone else? Who's in the family? I don't understand.

What I'm saying is this. I know that Bryan Turner, the president of Priority Records, can't rap. And I know he makes a lot of money offa me rapping. So that gives me a lot of pull, because if I don't make no records, he don't make no money. I'll get money. I've been poor before. I know how to handle it.

Well, let's talk about your treatment of women, because to me it seems there's a parallel between the treatment of women and the treatment of blacks. They've both been oppressed by the power group, so I don't see why one oppressed group would attack another.

It's not attack.

Let's use an example from the disc. The girl with VD in 'Look Who's Burnin''. You're telling her she's never going to be wanted again.

No, no. You can't look at the record song for song for song, you gotta look at the side! It's a death side and a life side.

Okay, but why is the girl who's got VD never going to be wanted again, but the guy who's got VD is going to go back out and he'll still be a part of society?

I never said a guy had VD. The guy is there to get some rubbers. That's why the guy is there. He sees a girl that said to him before, 'Oh, you're too rowdy to talk to.' She started messing around with some college dude and ended up catching it. That's what the record is about. The record is about saying, hey, you overlooked me and you still got burned.

But it doesn't stop there, it goes, You overlook me and you got burnt and now –

Now, nobody in the neighborhood is gonna wanna mess with you. And that's just the truth! That's just a sign-of-the-times song. I'm just holding a mirror up to how we living today. That's why I don't want to drop no singles off the album, because you can't look at the album song for song, you gotta look at the concept of each side.

So what's the new way of thinking about 'Horny Lil' Devil'?

'Horny Lil'Devil' is a song saying that this country's not going to rape our women like they did in the past, or rape our manhood like it's doing in the present. And not going to break us down to the point where we hate ourselves and are feeding on ourselves. That's over with, and that's done with.

Does that include black gay people?

No, I'm talking about a mental thing. I'm talking of a rape of our manhood. When we're not given the economical avenues to provide for our family, so our women are forced to work and forced to do these things while the man sits at home. You go in any corporation out here and you'll see the black woman working but you won't see the black man. The black man will be a janitor or anything. A black man can go to college but in most cases in the corporation you will see the black woman and not the black man. What I'm saying is cut the establishment off, help yourself. Love yourself. Unity is the key. Black people are not united like we should be.

So how can you say that and hang Eazy-E from a tree?

Eazy-E? That's a battle rap. How can Eazy-E say when they catch me they going to cut my head off and fuck me with a broomstick? How can they say that? He comes out at me, so I come out at him.

But that just spirals right along. If you're doing that, you're ignoring everything that you just told me.

Not at all, not at all. Because sometimes you gotta. And he's a spy, you gotta get rid of the spy before you can do any kind of mission. Same thing. You gotta get rid of the sellouts before we can accomplish anything. Because if we don't get rid of the spies before we move, the enemy is going to know our movement before we even get going. So we got to get rid of the hypocrites. There's no room for hypocrites.

But you just were talking black unity and you gotta stick together and then talking about 'I gotta get rid of this guy.' And I can go talk to him and he can say the same thing about you, right? All I'm saying is if you start playing God and saying these people are okay and these people are not –

I'm not playing God. I just give my opinion. Some people think my opinion is not relevant. But 1.1 million people think my opinion is relevant. And hopefully 1.1 million people are willing to listen to the ideas to make them a reality. Just like, say, Martin Luther King. One man with an idea. But he could do nothing unless the masses of people agreed with the idea, and are willing to make that idea a reality. Ice Cube. One man with an idea. I can do nothing unless people agree with my idea and are willing to make that idea a reality.

I'll tell you what sounds frightening about the scenario. It's that then you can say okay, we're all together. But I think this guy's a spy, get rid of him. And I think this guy's a spy, get rid of him. And all of a sudden, people who may or may not be spies or innocent or guilty or – you're pointing 'em out and getting rid of 'em.

Well, what about Bush? He says, 'I think Saddam is a spy!'

What about Bush? You're right! Why be like him?

No, because I don't think like Bush thinks. Know what I'm saying? But he's a person that, I mean, if you're the power then you're going to use your power the best way you can to what you think is right. What's scary, if you're accused of a crime and you're innocent, you shouldn't worry about the punishment. But if you're accused of a crime and you're guilty, that's when you worry about the punishment. Now, Americans gotta look theyself in the face and ask are they guilty of the crime? And if they are, they gotta take their punishment.

What does that have to do with you picking out people? How does that reconcile –

I'm gonna tell you what Eazy-E did.

Let's not do Eazy-E. Let's do –

Well, who have I picked out besides him?

Seems like you dis gay black males.

No, not at all.

In 'Horny Lil' Devil' you say, 'True niggers aren't gay.'

Yeah, and I say in that song you ain't gonna fuck me outta

my land and my manhood. That's what I'm saying.

So why is a gay black man not a true black man?

No, what I'm saying is a true black man would not allow hisself to get fucked out of his manhood, regardless of if he is gay or straight. This is talking about the power structure.

What is his manhood?

His manhood is being able to provide for his family. Being able to run the household. Being able to get respect from his family.

Did you play the dozens when you were growing up?

Of course. That's all that record about N.W.A. is, the dozens. You think I'm going to go get Eazy-E and hang him from a tree and burn him? All I have to live for and to go for? You think when they catch me they going to fuck me with a broomstick? Those are dozens, man. You can go back farther, you can go back to '81 and '82 to rap music when 'Roxanne' came out and then 'Roxanne's Revenge' and then LL versus Kool Moe D, and boom, boom, boom. It's a part of the music. Everybody plays the dozens. You got mud-slinging in fucking political campaigns. David Duke is this, or such and such is that. And I mean it's a part of life. The biggest of the big play the dozens. So, I mean, by us playing the dozens how are we at any kind of fault?

I'll tell you. Because this setup of society right now is fucked up. And if you just invert it, it stays as fucked up as it ever was, it's just inverted. Society has to be improved, and that doesn't mean just taking blacks and making them do what the whites do and whites and making them do what the blacks do. And men do what women do, and vice verse. That ain't gonna solve anything. It's short-sighted, and I think that to justify playing the dozens by saying the highest of the high play the dozens doesn't justify it.

No, I'm not, I'm sayin that it's a part of life and it's a part of the community. Everybody do it. I look worse to my fans if I don't respond than if I do.

What would happen if y'all went out on stage, you as Ice

Cube and them as N.W.A., and said, you know, peace?

Well, that could be done too, if they're willing to do it. I'm not against that at all.

I've read your responses in other interviews about attacking the Koreans and citing Jews –

I don't cite Jews. I cited a Jewish man. [From 'True To The Game': 'Whites and Jews/Who are they to be equal to?']

Cited him as a Jewish man.

He is a Jewish man. He's a Jewish person, he's done me wrong. And I just explained to the people that he done me wrong. It's just a fact. If he was green, I'd do the same. It doesn't matter that he's Jewish. I mean, I work with so many Jewish people in the industry it doesn't make sense for me to say anything that's anti-Semitic, about Jewish people as a whole. You can't say all of nothing and make it true, unless you say all human beings are going to die.

Let me tell you where the explanation doesn't work for me. I'm gonna leap for a second. When you talk about not being anti-white but pro-black, the thing that that rings of, and echoes of, is exactly what David Duke says. The inverse.

What does David Duke say?

'I'm not anti-black, I'm just pro-white.'

Okay. I agree. You ain't gotta be –

But Duke is obviously –

He was in the Klan!

Right. He's fucked up, man.

He was in the Klan, and they kill black people. But being pro-black, we've never killed white people. We've never put white people on slave ships, we've never put them in the hulls of ships. Man, this country has got their foot on our neck. You can't put me in the same position as David Duke.

But you're putting yourself there.

I'm not. I'm pro-black. Just because I'm pro – I'm anti-poor. And black people are who is poor and black people are who I come from, so of course I must speak on their behalf. In certain situations.

But when you go attack –
Attack who's oppressing us?
Are the Koreans oppressing you?
I'm saying this. Just pass respect. I'm doing no more than what Spike Lee did in *Do The Right Thing*. All the kids wanted was respect, okay? You're in our neighbourhood, which is cool, because until we get our act together, somebody has to make the money. But, while you're in our neighbourhoods, pay respect to the people that come in and put your kids through college. That get you your cars. That spend their money in your shop and do this thing. That's all the subject of that song is.
But at the beginning of that song you have the Korean voice asking how many or something and you have a black voice responding, 'Twenty, motherfucker!' Respect has to be mutual.
Of course. I got that insert off of *Do The Right Thing*. In most cases that concern me, I been walking in the store with ten people that was with me, and five of y'all have to wait outside because they ain't enough people to watch the other five. Hurry us up. You buy, you go. That type of stuff is not even called for. And it's showing us total disrespect. And we can't sit back and tolerate it. Koreans been there twenty, thirty years. What have they given back to the people that has given and spent with them? I'm not advocating nothing against nobody, I'm just saying pay respect. Because if you don't, black people get fed up. In L.A., a Korean lady shoots some black girl in the back of the head. On a video camera. Six months probation. Now, months before that, a black guy shoots a white lady's dog, and gets six months in prison. So look at the message. A dog in this case is worth more than this black little girl's life. We're getting fed up. To say that we ain't is a lie. And to not express our frustrations and our anger when we had a chance to is wrong for the black community, because then when it gets to a boiling point and no discussions can be made, people from the Korean community can't

say, 'We didn't know, nobody told us.'

But I'm saying that someone has to be the one to initiate good will. If you go in and say treat me right or I'm gonna burn your store down –

Man, let me tell you this. Talk about good will. I saw my family, well I didn't see but I saw pictures of my family in the streets with picket signs – 'Nonviolent Movement' – getting beat and getting wet with a water hose and getting lynched. Now, a nonviolent movement, that's as peaceful as you can get and this country did that to them. People don't know how on the edge black people are – to the point where there's no return, there's no talking, we don't want to hear what you gotta say. I can't lollygag, there ain't no nice way to say pay us respect. We've been in the dirt for so long and we're so tired, our lives seem to be nothing to nobody. Not even ourselves. You can ask a middle-class man if he feels that way and he's going to say no, everything's fine.

Middle-class people on the record get dissed too.

Of course.

Tell me why the ones who are trying to make a change –

Make a change for who? Make a change for yourself, trying to make a change for the people? I mean –

You said people don't respect themselves.

You gotta teach them how to respect themselves.

But are they imitating whites in their opinion or in your opinion, or is there a way that they can be middle-class and not imitate whites?

Yes.

What would that be?

The way to do that is to, when you get a certain position, take a look back. Who can you help, what can you do. I mean, I help people all the time. People work in my company. If you don't look back and you just try to fit in, then you done sold us out. You done sold all that blood that was on the streets of Memphis, and on the West Coast, too. And the North! Everywhere around this country.

What do you think of the Wiesenthal Institute's call for a ban?

My philosophy is this, and my position is this. I'm not anti-Semitic, that's on the record, whether they believe it or not. That's what I meant. I'm pro-black. I'm not anti-anything but anti-poor. And that's my belief on that.

Do you have any intention of sitting down with the people at the Center, like Chuck D. did, to resolve your differences?

No, because I'm not going to tell them any more than what I just told you. They have their opinion, they have their attitudes and their feelings. I been on TV, I've been to the press. I don't have to lie. If I was anti-Semitic, I wouldn't be scared to say it. I don't fear nobody but God, that's the only one I fear. I don't fear Rabbi Cooper or Simon Wiesenthal.

Why don't you print your lyrics?

Because a lot of people will try to use that against me. A lot of people wouldn't take the time to listen or try to understand where I'm coming from. A lot of people read the headlines but not the story, a lot of people would take the record for face value but would not study the record like the kids do. The kids listen to the records every day. They know them back and forth, they know exactly what I'm talking about, exactly what I mean. People doing articles, they don't look, they listen one or two times, they take it at face value, they hear a couple of 'motherfucks' and shit and they say it's just a terrible record. That's why I don't print my lyrics. Because if you want to know what I'm saying you'll listen to it hopefully at least more than once.

Did you meet Jacqueline Smith, the woman protesting the exploitation of the Lorraine Motel where King was assassinated?

Yeah, I went by there. That's a damn shame. The man died here and then they going to build a Civil Rights Museum but nothing is going back to the people. That's just showing you how they could give a fuck and you ain't nothing but a dollar and if you ain't helping them make a dollar you're no good to

them. That's how the country is. They'll embrace you as long
as you're making a dollar, man, but if you say look I'm going
to start my own thing, they'll say whoah whoah.

Did you go to Graceland while you were in town?
No, I'm not interested.

Reprinted with kind permission of Creem *magazine*

Will Self

MORRISSEY: THE KING OF BEDSIT ANGST GROWS UP

the *Observer*, December 1995

I'd been doing occasional pieces for Life, *the* Observer *newspaper's magazine supplement, when the opportunity to interview Morrissey came up in November 1995. I remember the exact date (unlike so many others in my life), because I'd just moved back to London after more or less four years out of town.*

I was living at the less fashionable end of Notting Hill at the time and I kept running into a friend who had a small studio on the Portobello Road. This friend had done quite a bit of work with Morrissey and I knew he knew him well, but for reasons of nerdishness and probity (an odd combination), I decided not to ask this guy if he could give me the inside edge before the interview.

I say nerdishness because I was a BIG fan of Morrissey (in as much as I've ever been a big fan of anyone). I'd bought most of his work over the years, both with the Smiths and solo, and knew a lot of the lyrics by heart. I didn't want to be completely disabused about the man before I met him, and I suspected my friend would do just that. I say probity because I did (and still do) believe that a responsible interviewer should trust to his own impression of his subject. I've never interviewed anyone looking to publish gossip about them (whether substantiated or not). I expect people to take me as they find me (something I confess they seldom do), and I do my best to honour others in the same way.

In truth the experience of actually meeting Morrissey was intimidating. He was big, he looked fit, he clearly didn't suffer fools at all. I felt seedy and small and foolish. Nevertheless, I thought we got on fairly well, and at the end of the interview he suggested that I ask for him after the Wembley gig and perhaps come backstage. When it came to the gig I committed the unspeakable solecism (at least that's how I like to see it) of taking my then girlfriend. After the gig Morrissey's PA came out to the backstage bar area, spoke with me, then retreated, only to return a few minutes later to say that Stephen had decided to go home immediately. I was gutted.

After I'd filed the piece I asked my musician friend about his time working with Morrissey. He told me things that were disturbing and libellous in equal measure. For once I regretted my decision not to ask around about an interview subject in advance of meeting them.

WS

HEAVEN KNOWS HE was miserable then. Morrissey was the archetypal mixed-up young man: anti-fun, seemingly tortured by his sexuality, with a detached and ironic worldview. His peculiarly English brand of Ortonesque camp has made him a national treasure. We find Morrissey in mature mode. Has the boy outsider become an adult and joined the rest of the human race?

It's a well-known fact about Morrissey that his record contracts stipulate various wacky, star-like things. One of them is the presence of certain, very particular kinds of snack food during any interview. So it is that the first thing that meets my eye when I enter the penthouse boardroom of RCA

Records is a table; laid out on it are plates of crisps (plain, or so I've read) and some KitKats; to one side are bottles of pop.

At the outset, Morrissey is drinking a cup of coffee, and during our discussion he occasionally elides his way out of anything remotely resembling an impasse by alluding to these eatables: 'This is such great coffee,' he pronounces at one point, and when I ask him what's on his mind he replies: 'This KitKat.'

These are just the sort of tropes Morrissey comes up with from minute to minute, turning phrases as he does, like rotating signs outside petrol stations. Morrissey is for many people irredeemably associated with the 1980s – and even to say this brings that decade into sharper focus. In the 1980s a particular kind of male adolescent angst and self-pity infused the zeitgeist, and Morrissey was its avatar. He was the first male pop star to address a whole generation of boys who were growing up with feminism, a heavy underscoring to a period of natural inadequacy and uselessness.

His miserablism came from that archetypally grim, ravaged provincial city, Manchester. Cut off from a supporting popular culture with any remotely intellectual element, or political undercurrent, Morrissey forged the Smiths, the pop band who were to be spokesmen for the Miserablists, and penned their national anthem 'Heaven Knows I'm Miserable Now'.

Morrissey's hipness and artistry was always wedded to an exquisite taste for the most subtle kitsch of the recent English past, and slathered in Yank worship. But mixed in with all this came his ambiguous campery.

Among the trainspotters of the music press, his break with Johnny Marr, his songwriting partner in the Smiths, has been insistently viewed as a creative death for him. Yet some of the solo material he has recorded is just as strong as anything they ever did together – and by the same token, who outside the music press has heard much about Johnny Marr in the past five years?

Suited darkly, booted sturdily and wearing one of those

jersey-esque shirts that almost define the retro-committed, Morrissey is very attractive in the flesh. The deeply-set blue eyes coruscate from beneath a high, intelligent brow, and given his self-professed celibacy, one of the first things any conscientious interviewer does is to try to assess the quality of his physical presence, his essential heft.

Is this a man tortured by his own sexuality and that of others? Is this a man about whom lingers a faint scent of fleshy revulsion? No, on both counts. His handshake is firm, warm even. His body language is far from craven. Indeed, there is something quite affectingly embodied about him. At one point in our conversation he commented on my face: 'You've actually got the face of a criminal that I've met . . . a very strong face. A very determined face.' Setting aside the content of this remark, it stuck me that this was not the sort of thing that someone intent on denying corporeality would be likely to say.

And of course, while his well-publicised encouragement of the excessive and physical devotion of his fans has a double-edged quality about it (you can touch, but only in this contrived, aberrant way), in person he lampoons his own self-created shibboleths, again and again and again. When I suggest to him that stage invasions puncture the surface of stardom and confront him with fans who are 98 per cent water, he replies: 'Let it be punctured, let it be punctured, that's my motto.'

The following week at Wembley Arena, the star goes so far towards puncturing that he almost bodily hauls a would-be stage invader through the arms of bouncers, past the rank of monitors and into his arms. He receives kisses on both cheeks as no more than his due. He also bends down into the thicket of arms waving towards him and as much takes as gives out the benediction.

There's a submerged incongruity here, but one that works in his favour. Perhaps one of the central ironies about this most ironic of performers is that he clearly seeks adulation from those most indisposed to give it – the Dagenham Daves and Rusholme Ruffians who people his landscapes – and eschews the advances of those who regard his talent as essentially poetic. When I ask him if he's ever been attracted to the world of the intelligentsia, he is emphatic: 'Absolutely not. In fact, scorn is perhaps all I really feel. I feel quite sad for such people. I think that everything there is to be lived is hanging round the gutter somewhere. I've always believed that and still do.'

Which rather begs the question: exactly how much hanging around the gutter is involved in researching his marvellously deadpan little word pictures? He mentions 'certain pubs around north and east London . . . but I'm not the sort of person you're likely to spot because I don't go about wanting to be noticed . . . I'm just slipping in and slipping out, and if you were looking for me you'd never find me.'

He tells me that performance for him represents 'exuberance', and when I tax him that this goes somewhat against his self-styled anti-fun posture, he grins and admits it. That being said, Morrissey's idea of post-gig kicks is not exactly what we expect from a pop star: 'Just pure silence.' I found this attitude refreshing, but it did act as a springboard for Morrissey to trot out some of his more passé attitudinising: 'Life's incredibly boring. I don't say that in an effort to seem vaguely amusing, but the secret of life is that there's no secret, it's just exceedingly boring.'

I got the feeling that these kinds of sallies are a form of bluff for Morrissey, and that he throws them out in much the way that aircraft in World War II dropped strips of metal to fool radar. If his interlocutors rise to such chaff, then they're not really worthy of consideration. But he's also an adept at sidestepping the conventional psychoanalytic thrusts of the interviewer.

When I mention the 'vexed question' of his sexuality, he replies: 'It doesn't vex me. I don't exactly think it vexes other people at all. People have their opinions and I don't mind what they are. I mean, there's a limit to what people can actually assume about sexuality, and at least I'm relieved by that. I don't think people assume anything anymore about me. I'm sort of classified in a non-sexual, asexual way, which is an air of dismissiveness that I quite like.'

The interesting thing about this speech is, of course, that the exact opposite is the truth: it does vex people, he does mind, there are no limits to what people can assume about sexuality (which is far from being a relief), and it is he himself who has struck the asexual attitude. It's worth remembering at this point that it was one of Morrissey's heroes, Oscar Wilde, who defined celibacy as 'the only known sexual perversion'.

Perhaps it would be too trite to suggest that the plaintive refrain of 'The Teachers Are Afraid Of The Pupils', the lead track on his latest album *Southpaw Grammar*, is in some way an echo of this posture: 'To be finished would be a relief,' the singer proclaims, again and again and again.

The sting really comes when I say: 'Do you think you've pulled that one off?' And with another smile he replies: 'Yeah. Quite well. I think the skill has paid off quite well. I've managed to slip through the net – whatever the net is.' Then there's a neat little bit of wordplay, analogous in the Morrissey idiolect to a boxer's centre-ring shuffle. I interject: 'But,' and he overrides me: 'I know you're about to say "but", but so am I. It's not really an issue, there's nothing to say, and there's nothing to ask, more to the point.'

He's right. Unless I choose to be a boor and attempt to crash into his private existence, there really is nothing to ask. This is the 'skill' that Morrissey has perfected and it's a skill that in anyone else would be described as maturity.

Yes, that's the only revelation I have to give you about Morrissey: he is, against all odds, a grown-up. How exactly he has managed this growing-up it's hard to tell. The lineaments of the biography give the impression of a direct transferral from air guitar in front of a suburban Manchester mirror, to air guitar in front of hysterical crowds at the Hacienda, followed by 13 years of – albeit anomalous – stardom. Where exactly did he find those normal interactions, normal relationships, necessary to affect maturation?

Of course, it's no secret in the business that his 'no-touch' persona bears little relation to a man who closely guards his close friendships; and quite clearly something is going on here. It was once said of Edward Heath that if he did have sex at all, it was only in a locked vault in the Bank Of England. I don't wish to speculate about whether or not Morrissey has sex, but if he does I think it's fairly safe to assume that the 'locked vault' is a function of two things: an unswerving dedication to maintaining a genuine private life, and a capability for generating immense personal loyalty – a loyalty vault, if you will.

When we discuss the issue of camp, which informs so much of his artistic sensibility, right down to the title of one of his solo albums, *Bona Drag* ('bona' meaning attractive or sexy in gay argot), he veers off into the Kenneth Williams diaries: 'It was quite gruesome, quite gruesome. I've read it a couple of times and each time it's been like a hammer on the head. An astonishingly depressing book. It's incredibly witty and well done, but the hollow ring it has throughout is murderous, absolutely murderous. I think he was always depressed, because the diaries spread over a 40-year period and even at the beginning of them he was saying, "Why am I alive, what's the point?" And this was 1952. It's astonishing that he lasted so long.'

I tax him that some people might view his life as being a bit like that, and he replies 'it's not, it definitely isn't,' with a deeply-felt emphasis. So deep that I'm moved to put to him the most extreme contrast to Williams's life of emotional and sexual barrenness: 'Have you ever considered having children?' 'Yeah,' he says flatly, in his burring Mancunian voice. When we tease out this issue it becomes apparent that what bothers him about having kids is to do with his quite legitimate fear of over-identification with them: 'I wonder what they'd do. I mean, what do they do when they're 11? What would they do when they were 17? What happens when your child turns round and says: "Look, I don't like this world. Why did you bring me into it? I don't want to be part of it. I'm not leaving home. I'm staying here, I refuse to grow up"?'

But if there are shades of his own (allegedly) willed infantility here, there are also discernible the lineaments of grown-up Morrissey, Morrissey whose 'skill' has served him well. He seems to understand only too well the impact of the ambiguous image he has created.

Morrissey, it became apparent to me, is someone who finds his love for other people painful and overpowering. In this he is, of course, like all of us, but perhaps more so. He has given up on his favourite soap, *Coronation Street*, but when discussing its replacement in his affections, *EastEnders*, he lets slip a yearning for a very populated, very unmiserable arcadia: 'I think people wish that life really was like that, that we couldn't avoid seeing 40 people every day that we spoke to, that knew everything about us, and that we couldn't avoid being caught up in these relationships all the time, and that there was somebody standing on the doorstep throughout the day. I think that's how we'd all secretly like to live. Within *EastEnders*, within *Coronation Street*, there are no age barriers. Senior citizens, young children, they all blend, and they all like one another and they all have a great deal to say, which isn't how life is.'

Perhaps here the complex mask of ritual, signs, signals and cultural references that Morrissey has devised to obliterate the very non-contrived human character beneath, slips a little. But I'd be wary of pushing it. To me he said: 'I wish somebody would get it right. I don't mind if they hate me, as long as they get it right.' And yet 'getting it right' would be wholly destructive for the image, if liberating for the man.

Throughout the solo career there has been a strenuous

conflation of the notion of 'Englishness' with that of a camp, Ortonesque liking for 'rough lads'. Was Morrissey, like William Burroughs, I wondered, possessed of an eternal faith in the 'goodness' of these rough lads? Was this atmosphere, so vividly captured in *Southpaw Grammar*, one he saw as an arcadia or merely one of nostalgia?'

'It's pure nostalgia, really, and there's very little truth in it. I'm well aware of that. I know that it's all pure fantasy really, and 50 per cent drivel. Everybody has their problems and there is no way of being that is absolutely free and fun loving and without horrific responsibilities. It just isn't true. And I think I've had the best of it personally. I don't think I'm missing anything because I'm not a roofer from Ilford.'

Did we really expect anything else? Every alleged 'arcadian' image Morrissey produces is in reality shot through with irony. The eponymous hero of 'Boy Racer' is described thus: 'Stood at the urinal / He thinks he's got the whole world in his hands.' And as for poor 'Dagenham Dave', 'Head in a blouse / Everybody loves him / I see why.' Yes indeed! But then, by the same token: 'He'd love to touch, he's afraid he might self-combust / I could say more, but you get the general idea.'

The implication being one of what? Chronically repressed homosexuality? Or merely the singer's own *tedium vitae* in the face of the exhausted husk of English working-class culture? The rubric here is one of subversion, subversion and more subversion. This being most graphically shown when Morrissey, 37 and rising, comes on stage at Wembley Arena (where he is supporting David Bowie) with his somewhat younger fellow musicians. Either it's *Happy Days* with Morrissey as the Fonz and the vaguely bat-eared guitarist as Richie, or else something altogether more sinister.

The backcloth is a giant projection of the cover of *Southpaw Grammar*, the face of an obscure boxer that Morrissey himself plucked from the anonymity of an old copy of *The Ring*. There's a wheeze and a creak from the massive bunches of speakers dangling overhead, and Jerusalem starts up, being sung by some long-gone school choir. The effect, in tandem with the suited, cropped figures striding about the dark stage, is extremely unsettling. Is this the start of some weird fascist rally?

Then the band crashes into the opening chords of 'Reader Meet Author' and Morrissey begins to flail at the air with the cord of his microphone, pirouetting, hip-swivelling, for all the world like some camp version of Roy Rogers. He'd be run out of the British National Party in seconds if they caught him swishing about like this! Again he has subverted the political in a peculiarly personal way.

Later on in the set, Morrissey and the band perform the dark and extremely depressing song 'The Operation'. Like many of his songs this one is addressed to an unnamed person. Morrissey must be one of the few songwriters who uses the second person more than the first. 'You fight with your right hand,' he yodels, 'and caress with your left', and as he joins up the couplet he wipes the arse of the air with a limp hand. This is presumably what he means by *Southpaw Grammar*, and the manifest and ongoing preoccupation with 'the other' in his work is so antithetical to his posture of bedsit isolation that I wonder again just how truly protean a person this is? To me he said: 'I don't feel trapped in your tape recorder and on those CDs. I don't at all. I can do whatever I like and I can become whatever I like, and if next week I want to have 13 children and live in Barking, then I can and I will, and nobody will stop me.'

This is all very double-edged, very southpaw. On one reading it smacks of an arrested, adolescent will-to-omnipotentiality, but on another it's an indicator of great sanity, and a refusal to believe wholly in the image he has created. While in his first incarnation, as the taboo-busting frontman for the Smiths, Morrissey was prone to using his platform for issuing diktats on all manner of issues unrelated to popular music, his fame now appears to have been well worn in, like a favourite old overcoat.

He confirmed this when I asked him how he managed to keep such tight control over the empire he has created: 'I only manage it by repeatedly saying "no". And then the obvious reputation gathers around you that you are a problem, because you are awkward, you are difficult, and you don't really want to be famous. But I just don't want to be famous in any way other than that which naturally suits me.'

I wonder what's going to happen to Morrissey. My hunch is that he may well find iconic pop status an increasing drag. He is a very funny man to be with, but he keeps his wit well reined in. Just one example of this came when we dissected the 'vexed question' of my not having a television. 'Is that a political statement?' he asked me, and when I said it was he rejoined: 'Do all your neighbours know that you don't possess a television set?'

I think the wit is reined in because it's so destructive of the ironic edifice he has created. Stardom requires a certain kind of stupidity to sustain it, and Morrissey is far from being a stupid man. He is responsible – among other things – for encapsulating 200 years of philosophical speculation in a single line: 'Does the body rule the mind or does the mind rule the body? I dunno.'

His ambitions as an artist clearly don't require him to feed the Moloch of celebrity with more creative babies. He once memorably sang, castigating yet another of his numinous others for their sexual peccadilloes, 'On the day that your mentality / Catches up with your biology.' But I think the comparable day of reckoning for Morrissey will come when he allows his sense of humour to catch up with his irony.

Even at Wembley Arena it looked as if the band had invited their uncle to come along and do a turn with them. Morrissey has too acute a view of himself – one hopes – to become one of those granddads of pop, perambulating around the stage in support hose, permanently marooned in some hormonal stretch limo. He told me he could 'do anything', I certainly hope he does. England needs him.

3
ON THE SCENE

Paul Williams

THE GOLDEN ROAD:
A REPORT ON SAN FRANCISCO

Crawdaddy!, June 1967

I had just turned nineteen when I wrote this piece in early June 1967. I was living in New York City and editing a rock magazine, Crawdaddy!, *which I'd founded the previous year. The magazine's assistant editor, Tim Jurgens, was from the San Francisco area, and when I'd visited California (for the first time in my life) in December, he'd directed me to some rock ballroom shows. I saw Moby Grape at the Avalon, Big Brother & the Holding Company at the Ark, Jefferson Airplane at the Matrix and the Airplane and the Grateful Dead at the Fillmore.*

While on that December '66 visit to California, I'd gotten stoned (high on marijuana) for the first time while interviewing Brian Wilson in a tent in the living room of his mansion. In March 1967, I'd been invited to help organise the first 'Be-In' in New York City. So I was very ready to be excited and impressed by what I encountered in the Haight-Ashbury on my return visit to San Francisco in May. There were no 'objective' observers of the scene at that time. Just listening to the records, and going to the shows, you immediately wanted to be part of this community, this social/cultural/political movement. As the teenage editor of a rock'n'roll magazine, I had the opportunity to participate by spreading the good news. 'Listen to this album, man, it'll change your life!!'

In many cases, that turned out to be true.

PW

SITTING IN THE window. Sixth Avenue, Greenwich Village, flirting with the girls going by, the Grateful Dead very loud on 4X speakers somewhere in the room behind me; 92 degrees, a week short of summer, a week back from the Coast, San Francisco. Now, three thousand miles away, what do those words mean? Was I ever anywhere but here?

The geography of rock. There are a half-dozen LPs sitting by my New York City phonograph, at least two from San Francisco: *Moby Grape* and *Grateful Dead*. Rock Scully, a Dead manager, just walked by; the Grateful Dead are at the Café Au Go Go, two blocks from here. The Moby Grape are midtown, playing at the Scene.

We speak of a San Francisco Sound because these groups *developed* there. They may not come from there (Skip Spence is a Canadian, the Steve Miller Blues Band got together in Chicago); they may not even live there (Moby Grape is technically a Marin County group; Country Joe are #1 in Berkeley, but half a dozen local bands get better billing in San Francisco). But San Francisco – the Fillmore, the Avalon, the Trips Festivals, the Diggers, Owsley's acid, Haight Street and Ashbury and Masonic and Golden Gate Park, the Straight Theatre, Herb Caen, the *Barb*, the communication company – these have been and are and will be the environment and influences that have shaped the music of many of the best bands in America.

More specifically, the several aspects and influences of the San Francisco area have created a community; out of this community has come a feeling, an attitude; and it is this attitude that has imparted a unity to the music coming out of the Bay Area. It is this attitude that is most commonly reflected in the San Francisco Sound.

There is a geography of rock; San Francisco *is* different from New York musically, different because the music made by the Grateful Dead would be different if they had developed in New York, playing the Night Owl or Action City, trying to get a master sold, living on East 7th Street and maybe dealing meth for rent money, padlocking their front door and freezing in the winter and worrying about the air and not having children till they can afford the suburbs, reading the *New York Times* and having maybe two dozen friends that they see once every two months or so, never considering that they might find a manager who wasn't just an adversary, never thinking that there was much more to it than making the charts, never wondering about the empty girls with too much make-up and an unshakeable confidence in this best of all possible nothings . . . probably hating each other after a while and wondering why people shat on them for doing just what everyone else does.

New York is New York, and it's very good for some things. The energy it generates is second to none; nowhere in the world is there as much activity to dive into every time you turn around. Some people thrive on that. I do, much of the time, and that's why I stay here; but I don't think it's a place to make music. San Francisco is.

The trolleys run along Haight Street pretty often; the tourists snarl up the traffic a bit, but still you can get from the *Oracle* office to Fillmore Street, change, and arrive at the Fillmore or Winterland in less than twenty minutes. At fifteen cents for the entire journey, that's not bad at all. The Avalon is a little further away, but just as accessible, and nowadays often more worthwhile.

But the ballrooms have lost their importance. They were vital once; without Bill Graham, and the hard work and business know-how he threw into the Fillmore when the scene was starting, there might never have been an SF Sound to talk about. Give him credit, and give Ralph Gleason credit too – without his enthusiastic columns in the *SF Chronicle* the city would have no doubt shut down those psychedelic superstructures before you could say 'building inspector'. And Ken Kesey, the man whose Trips Festivals irrevocably tied together rock'n'roll and light shows and the head community, The Family Dog, illuminator Bill Ham, the Charlatans, the Matrix, and Jefferson Airplane, all those originators who now cling to their place in history with alarming awareness that, after two years, the past is buried in the dust of centuries.

The ballrooms have given way to environments even more closely knit into the community. The great outdoors, for one; the Panhandle is only two blocks down from Haight Street, and on an average weekend you'll hear everything from Big Brother & the Holding Company down to the local teen group playing top 40 hits off-key. And it's all free, free not just from admission charges but from walls and stuffy air and hassles about coming and going; free so that the music is as much a part of your life as a tree in blossom. You can stop and embrace it, or pass on by.

The Panhandle is the San Francisco Sound today: the music of the street, the music of the people who live there. The ballrooms, obsolete in terms of the community, have been turned into induction centers – the teenyboppers, the college students, the curious adults come down to the Fillmore to see what's going on, and they do see, and pretty soon they're part of it. They may not go directly to Haight Street with flowers in their hair (though many of them do), but they change, they shift their points of view, their minds drop out of Roger Williams and into the Grateful Dead.

Back on the Street something is happening that may be even more important than the music in the park. The Straight Theatre, long a cherished vision, has burst into reality. The Straight is an ancient movie house, an imposing structure capable of taking some 1700 people out of the center of Haight Street and into whatever it feels like presenting. The property includes a theater, which will be used for concerts, gatherings, poetry readings, etc., a dance workshop, another smaller theater for experimental drama, a photographic studio and darkroom, various storefronts, a backyard mall, and more, all of which is being lovingly shaped by devoted hippie artisans into what should be the model for future art centres all over the country.

And in the air, another major change: KMPX-FM, not just radio for heads but rock radio for rock heads, a station that totally ignores the top 20 (because you can hear that stuff any time you want on seven other frequencies) and just plays what it feels like playing. KMPX is run something like a college radio station; the people in charge know much more about rock and roll than they do about radio programming, how to talk jock, how to sell an audience, or any of that other crap. They make mistakes – records go on the turntable at the wrong speed, careless comments go out over the air – and everyone loves them. There are no mistakes, because they can do no wrong. They're human, and they love the music – and that's what's been missing in radio till now.

If you examine San Francisco closely, you'll find major changes taking place in almost every aspect of city life. New attitudes towards jobs, towards education, towards entertainment and the arts. Basic shifts in the relationships between man and his environment, shifts that have affected every facet of that environment, changes that best can be communicated not in words but in music: Big Brother & the Holding Company, Jefferson Airplane, Moby Grape, Steve Miller Blues Band, Country Joe & the Fish, Quicksilver Messenger Service, the Grateful Dead.

Consider the albums. The Airplane was first – and second, too, for that matter. The San Francisco Sound on records begins with those first two notes of 'Blues from an Airplane', and a more noble beginning would not have been possible. Regardless of how many better albums have been recorded since *Jefferson Airplane Takes Off,* that album still glows with the beauty of the first trip, the birth cry of a new era in music. *Between the Buttons* was the definitive last statement of an earlier age; *JA Takes Off* is the first of a new generation of rock albums, of which *Sgt Pepper* is only the latest and best.

Tim Jurgens, Ralph Gleason and Marty Balin all used the word 'love' in their attempts to pin down what made that first Airplane album different. It is much easier now to understand what they were getting at. Jefferson Airplane Loves You, with what has been disdainfully referred to as 'potato love' – the indiscriminate love for all people simply because they *are* people. This attitude enriches their music. Compare *Revolver* with *Sgt Pepper*: do you really think the Beatles loved you when they recorded the earlier album?

Surrealistic Pillow, the Airplane's second, is a definite bringdown; certainly the worst LP to come out of the current Bay Area scene (not considering such piffle as the Sopwith Camel, who ceased to be an SF group when they met Erik Jacobsen). The problem with *Pillow* is mostly that it's not an album; it's a collection of tracks that neither feel good nor sound comfortable together. The Airplane, of course, were the first SF group to record a second album, and it is likely that at least one other good Bay Area group will flounder on their second try. And *Pillow*, despite its disunity, has half a dozen fine tracks that prove that the group is better, even if their LP is worse. Sometimes progress is not reflected in quality – and this is often the fault of fate and the A&R man more than the group.

At any rate, the Airplane's first LP is easily as good, in context, as that of any other Bay Area group so far; and how well other groups do on *their* second albums remains to be seen. It's always kind of lonely to be first in line.

The Grateful Dead's first try is pure energy flow. West Coast kineticism has developed into a fine art; the first side of this album rolls with a motion so natural that one suspects the musicians have never listened to the Who or the Kinks or even the Four Tops – they have developed their own kinetic techniques without reference to the masters in the field. With one exception: this album has so much in common with *The Rolling Stones, Now!* as to be almost a sequel.

Of course, I'm not complaining. *Now!* will always stand as one of the great rock albums, and by giving us the New World, sun-rising-over-the-Pacific-Ocean version of that album the Dead have unquestionably added to the quantity of joy around. And the Dead's LP is much more first-hand: where the Stones glorified the mythical American South rock joint in 'Down the Road Apiece', the Dead give you the feeling that that kind of wonderful abandon is a part of their daily scene ('Golden Road').

The Stones assume the persona of Chuck Berry driving down the New Jersey Turnpike (which they've probably never been on!) to convey their personal energies in 'You Can't Catch Me'; the Dead do a song with almost identical impact ('Good Morning, Little Schoolgirl') but they don't need to think of themselves as Sonny Boy Williamson – the song goes out direct to every teenybopper in the audience, and by the time they start into the fourth minute or so, every member of the band really feels every word that Pigpen says. Musically, the Stones' performance is as good (in fact, better) than the Dead's; but where the Stones confront a mythical highway cop, the Dead confront the actual members of their audience. Hence the *Grateful Dead* LP, though not quite as good as *Now!*, is at times even more effective.

(The Stones do, of course, confront their audience in 'Everybody Needs Somebody to Love', but it's not emotional confrontation. It's great showmanship, posturing – similar to the Dead's terrific posturing when they 'do' the whole Kingston Trio era and its approach, in 'Cold Rain and Snow'. I'm comparing the Dead to the Stones not to show a preference for either, but to point out the fascinating similarities in the impact of their music and in the music itself – play 'Schoolgirl' after listening to 'You Can't Catch Me' to appreciate the extent to which the Dead resemble the Stones in their concept of what music is and how a rock band should perform.)

The first side of the Dead album is one song, unrolling its varied but equivalent delights at top speed. 'Beat It On Down the Line' ('That's where I'm going to make my happy home') moves into the certainty of 'Good Morning, Little Schoolgirl' with the ease and impact of Jean-Luc Godard. Garcia smiles, Pigpen squints, and you're on your way. And you can't turn back. 'See that girl? . . . Well, she's coming down the stair – and I don't worry, I'm sitting on top of the world.' (Appropriate J. Garcia guitar run here.) Breathless.

The flip is something else: introspective, more like a journey than a joyride. 'Morning Dew' conjures loneliness, pain, uncertainty, courage; pleads, asks, questions, denies; and finally, 'I guess it doesn't matter anyway.' Apocalyptic. Or just resigned. 'I thought I heard . . .'? And whatever it was, you'll find it in the song. Beautiful, with a kind of intense detachment. San Francisco isn't known for its vocalists, but this song could change all that.

'New, New Minglewood Blues' serves as a sort of bridge in the context of the album, which is not at all the nature of the song in live performance . . . and no doubt this is one of the many things about this LP that disappoints fans of the live Dead. The more you've grown to love Grateful Dead live performances over the years the more difficult it must be to accept an album which is – though very beautiful – something completely different. Only 'Viola Lee Blues' has any of the fantastic 'this is happening *now*!' quality of, a good Dead performance; only 'Viola Lee Blues' takes you away as far as the longtime Dead fan has grown accustomed to being taken. It's an escape song – a prisoner for life dreams his way to the dim edges of space and time – and if you don't think you're a prisoner, surrender to 'Viola Lee' and see what happens.

When the *Country Joe* album arrived at the *Crawdaddy!* office, it was immediately inscribed, 'This record is to be played on special occasions only,' and certain factions suggested that it would be in poor taste to even review such a sacred work. Sacred or not, this album does seem distantly removed from anything that has been previously associated with rock and roll. Indeed, the staunchest hard rock supporter on our staff can find no redeeming musical value in it at all. He's wrong, of course; or, to be more accurate, he's somewhere else. For many people, this album is so exactly where we are, it's frightening. To be played on special occasions only.

Words should be applied to this album with extreme caution. Like a kaleidoscope, it's easy *not* to appreciate – all you have to do is stare *at* the toy instead of into it – but if you do dig it, you may suddenly find it very hard to decide which of the sliding multicoloured worlds all around you is your own. It's perfectly fair of me to especially dig 'Flying High' because I'm a long-time hitchhiker; but when I decide that 'Section 43' is without question a midsummer thundershower, and then realise that the storm is outside the window and not in my head, perhaps I'm too involved in the music.

Background music is an old concept; this album, at last, is in the foreground. It is Joe MacDonald's world, and you are invited in. Does it seem strange that the introduction to 'Flying High' has nothing to do with the song, or that Lorraine's first name is really Martha? Not at all – remember, we are guests here. This is Berkeley 1967, Fish Street, residence of Country Joe – we are invited to see, hear, feel, smell, but not participate. 'Grace' – that's not a singalong. This is music at its most sensuous and least analysable – sounds, unidentifiable, flash at you, words evoke pictures but no meaning, you never hear the same thing twice. But you always feel the state of grace.

'Death Sound' ('I see the minutes chasin' the hours'), that homicidal tambourine, schizophrenic lead guitars. It's all in the impact; if it doesn't scare you, I can't talk you into fright. 'Section 43' – simply the most satisfying, evocative piece of music I know; I could wander its paths forever. It's a concert performance – no individual virtuosity can be found and praised; each person did his job precisely and flawlessly, up to (and especially) the feedback and few tinkling notes at the end. The brilliance is in the composition; and in a subtle way we should consider this whole LP a composed rather than a performed work, because every note seems to have been firmly in place in every song long before the actual recording of the album. On 'Love', a mistake is met with 'Aw, come on,' as if nothing could be more ridiculous at this point than doing something wrong. Indeed, a perfect Fish album: it *had to* be this way.

'Masked Marauder' is utterly delightful; an instant movie soundtrack for whatever is going on around you. (Theme music, not background stuff.) 'Superbird' would be instant #1 if radio stations weren't so sensitive. It's the only rock and roll song on the album, and of course it's perfect. 'Drop your guns, baby . . .' Wow!

Everything on the album is one-of-a-kind, as a matter of fact; like *Sgt Pepper*, the only thing linking these songs is that they like to be heard together. 'Sad & Lonely Times' is a ballad, very simple, very warm – pretty. 'Not So Sweet Martha Lorraine' is a totally different type of ballad: Berkeley Gothick, cynical, respectful, overpowering. Even affectionate; few people who've heard this album could really describe this song, but every one of them could describe Lorraine. And though every description would be different, each would be thoroughly respectful, thoroughly correct. David Cohen (organist) is magnificent.

And 'Bass Strings' is the invocation of the Muse. 'Hey, partner, won't you pass that reefer 'round? . . . I think I'll go to the desert . . . Just one more trip now, and I know I'll stay high all the time.' If you want to understand the Bay Area, 'Bass Strings' will give you a fair start.

Well, it took me a long time, but I finally figured out who Moby Grape remind me of: the Everly Brothers. Also Buddy Holly, Buffalo Springfield, middle-Beatles, Byrds, New Lost City Ramblers, the Weavers, Youngbloods, the Daily Flash and everybody else. Above all, the Grape give off this very pleasant sense of *déjà vu*. Rock has become so eclectic you can't even pick out influences – you just sense their presence. I don't really know *why* the Grape remind me of the Everly Brothers. But it's a nice feeling.

Moby Grape is one of those beautifully inextricable groups with four guitarists (including bass), five vocalists, five song-writers, and about twelve distinct personalities (Skip Spence alone accounts for five of them). The Grape is unusual for an SF group in that it does not have an overall, easily-identifiable personality. It is without question schizophrenic – which is nothing bad, because the group is extremely tight and they simply shift personality from song to song. Their music is always unified; it's their album as a whole that's schizoid. In fact, much as I like it, I enjoy the songs even more one at a time (for your convenience, Columbia has issued almost the entire album on singles – which is particularly nice because the mono mix is far better than the stereo, which must have been done too fast).

Skip Spence's two songs make it clear that he's the most talented – though not the most prolific – songwriter in the group. 'Omaha', to my tastes the toughest cut on the album, is one of the finest recorded examples of the wall-of-sound approach in rock. It surges and roars like a tidal wave restrained by a sea-wall. Moby Grape is a particularly violent group – not in the sense that they want to do harm to anyone (it is a huge misunderstanding to think violence is inherently evil, or that it necessarily causes harm – there is violent joy, and this album is proof of that), but in the sense that almost every song is attacked with great force and abandon. Moby Grape assault their audience, bathing them in almost unavoidable joy. Jamming it down their throats, in fact. The other Skip Spence song on the LP, 'Indifference', is another screamer, a well-constructed, brilliantly-executed shuffle number, to be sung on the street, loud, early in the morning, or listened to in the afternoon with your fist pounding the table.

Peter Lewis is second in the hierarchy of Grape writers, and
probably the most sensitive. He shares with the other Grape
members the ability to create extremely appealing melody
phrases, chorus lines, and rhythm riffs; this ability, combined
with the resultant concentration on structure, tightness and
brevity, is what makes all the Moby Grape songs sound like
good singles. Lewis, in 'Fall on You', puts together a number
of catchy little themes into a very nice, very fluid song,
vaguely reminiscent of 'One More Try'. In 'Sitting by the
Window', he waxes almost eloquent, with just enough restraint to make the song both illuminating and unassuming.
The guitar-work is really excellent; the three Grape guitarists
work together with exceptional taste throughout the LP.

But describing each song is not really the way to write
about Moby Grape. They are elusive; you detect a thousand
moods and changes, but you never quite hear the words,
never know who's singing, never are certain who's playing
lead. You can't pin them down, can't get too close; you learn
to forget, learn to absorb their music, learn to stop trying,
submit to it – and sooner or later it all comes clear. Country
Joe and the Dead are very clean; this group never lacks for
tightness, but they get fuzzy round the edges. They aren't
involving, but you dig the changes; they aren't involving, but
you listen for the words; they aren't involving, but there's
something going on here – and slowly but surely the depth in
this music (which at first attacked you but seemed so unin-
volving) swallows you up, and you feel the complexities it
invokes.

Moby Grape is an almost ideal example of a 'rock and roll'
group, and their emergence now, as the historical concept of
rock and roll seems on the verge of disappearing into a music
too complexly-based to fit a general description, is both
surprising and quite pleasing. The Grape play short, melodic
songs, complex but straightforward, tightly structured with
careful drumming and rhythm, experimental (but not 'far
out') bass, exciting, well-thought-out lead guitar (no fooling

around) and early Beatles- or Everlys-style group vocals. A given song ('Mr Blues') might draw on C&W and blues traditions, Otis Redding phrasing, Keith Richard restrained lead guitar, 'Captain Soul' rhythm progressions, etc. And every note is proper, polite. It's enough to make you nostalgic; nothing is more refreshing than the unexpectedly familiar.

These are the major rock albums to come out of the Bay Area thus far. However, there is a very important, very good album recorded by a San Francisco group in the new vein *prior* to the Airplane's first LP. I haven't mentioned it because the group is not generally thought of as a rock group. They are classified under jazz, which is fine; but I think at this time we can also add John Handy's *Live at Monterey* album to the list of great SF rock LPs. Listen to it, study its structure and its changes, and I think you'll understand why.

Rock is not a term that can be or that wants to be defined. San Francisco rock is an even more elusive concept, particularly when one removes the obvious geographical limitation and includes the Who's 'Happy Jack' and *Sergeant Pepper's Lonely Hearts Club Band*. One specifically San Francisco, or New World, trait is the inclusion of open acts of kindness toward the listener within the body of the album. Throughout *Sergeant Pepper* you feel that the Beatles are with you and understand where you're at ('we'd love to take you home with us'). The Who in their comic operetta 'A Quick One' bathe the listener in the repeated assurance that 'you're forgiven.' For everything. And the gentle applause at the end of each side of the John Handy album is a subtler application of the same effect.

Geographically, the San Francisco groups have the common heritage of the Bay Area '65–'67, and all the influences present there; most specifically, they have all been reared by the same audience, the Fillmore/Avalon crowd, the first good rock audience in America. This audience is responsible for, in addition to the Airplane, Handy, the Grape, Country Joe, and the Dead, at least three other fine groups as-yet-unrecorded: Big Brother & the Holding Company, Quicksilver Messenger Service, and the Steve Miller Blues Band.

Big Brother is in many ways the most exciting group in the Bay Area; and though they are all white, Sandy Pearlman has correctly called them 'the best spade band in the country.' Their arrangements, their control of what they're doing, their material all indicate that under the right conditions they could produce the best SF rock album yet.

Steve Miller is the most creative of American white blues bands at present, which says a lot for the San Francisco influence. Quicksilver is a fine example of a group that would have gone nowhere were it not for the SF audience egging them on; they're still in the growing stage, and not yet ready to record, but there's good reason to believe that the moments of brilliance they now enjoy will soon become hours of brilliance. Outside of San Francisco they wouldn't have bothered getting better because they wouldn't have needed to.

Above all, the San Francisco Sound is the musical expression of what's going down, a new attitude toward the world which is commonly attributed to 'hippies,' but which could more accurately be laid at the feet of a non-subculture called People, earth people, all persons who have managed to transcend the superstructures they live in. People who have responded to the reality of the industrial revolution by requiring that they run the system and benefit from it rather than be made part of it. In very small print between the lines of 'Naked If I Want To', 'Grace', and 'Cream Puff War' is written the following message: There is a man, me, and there are Men. These two forces will and must interact as smoothly as possible. Everything else – concepts, objects, systems, machines – must only be tools for me and mankind to employ. If I, or Men, respect a system or a pattern more than ourselves, we are in the wrong and must be set free. 'Nothing to say but it's okay . . .'

Miles

NEW YORK DOLLED UP: GLITTERMANIA IN GOTHAM

International Times, 1972

This article was written for IT, *the London under-ground newspaper that John Hopkins and I founded back in October 1966. The point of the underground press was that, unlike* NME *or the other British music papers of the '70s, you could write about anything you wanted, including sex and drugs, and use four-letter words if you felt inclined.*

This article could not have appeared in anything other than an underground paper in Britain at that time. It was written in February 1972, when I was living in New York City at the Chelsea Hotel, writing for Fusion, Crawdaddy *and various other legendary but now defunct magazines. The downtown art scene was just blossoming, though the punk scene had not yet started. The back room at Max's was going strong, and there was a definite sense of something about to happen, but no one really knew what. As the reader will immediately detect, I had not heard of any of the bands I was writing about. None of them had yet recorded, or even played very many gigs. I went to the event with Denise Felieu, who had been to some of the Dolls' previous gigs at the Mercer Arts Center – where they had a residency – and who really rated them highly.*

The New York Dolls were not in fact gay, though some of them were bi – and David Johansen once

declared himself tri – but they gave a pretty persuasive
imitation of a bunch of Christopher Street drag queens
and certainly convinced me. The Dolls, and the other
acts at the Mercer that night, were part of a typical
American overreaction to what they thought was
going on in London with David Bowie and the
glam-rock scene. By overdoing it they came out the
other side and created a new thing of their own.

This piece was written more than thirty years ago
and uses language that I would not use now. However,
it would be a pity to change it – it has a certain
poignancy. It's a snapshot of the innocent, pre-AIDS
downtown scene in New York, like an entry in an old
journal, half-remembered.

M

NEW YORK: An endless Valentine's Day all-night party, Feb
11th, 10 pm till dawn, featuring the New York Dolls and
their revue.

Scene: The Mercer Arts Center in Greenwich Village (well,
nearly), where an audience looking like the cast of *Satyricon*
is assembling, not even the below-freezing wind brings a glow
to their deadly white faces as they totter in on their 3″
platform shoes. At least 15% of the men wear heavy makeup,
and almost all the women do (plain white with thick vivid
lipstick), though the odd problem arises where some of the
women I thought were men turn out to be women after all.
Oh, you have to be on your toes in New York these days.

I go along with Denise and Wendy from the Women's Rock
Group Grapevine (for protection?). The audience is mostly
teenage or early twenties. A Chinese-American wearing a
diamond necklace and brooch, Fu-Manchu moustache and
long robe greets a girlfriend and they begin to talk quite ordi-
narily about school and what a drag their teacher is. 'Come over
to my house, man, and we'll blow some grass, listen to some
R&B and ball.' If only things were like that when *I* was at school.

Backstage, Ruby and the Rednecks are getting ready: The Rednecks all wear little white satin majorette dresses, and – were it not for the sinister look in their eyes – would even be called 'cute'. Ruby is shrieking with laughter: someone has used up all her quaaludes, she learns. She flaps her arms hysterically, knocking over her portable dressing table and giggling out of control. 'Get me,' she stammers, 'another large tequila. I've gotta get this together.' Her hair is a giant orange back-combed balloon, like an extra-terrestrial plant form.

A girl on high silver platforms, a green lurex jumpsuit and orange lipstick approaches: 'Sorry, Wayne, I couldn't get the dildos you wanted.' 'Oh, that's alright, darling! I'll get by!' Wayne beams archly at everyone. Actually, he's the only gay person in the band known as Queen Elizabeth Featuring Wayne County. They are representative of a new wave of New York groups who've picked up on Marc Bolan, Slade, Elton John, David Bowie in a big way and combined them with such historical figures as the Fugs, the early Mothers and the very much present-day Lou Reed . . . together with such groups as the Children of Light and the Cockettes (famous for flashing cock on stage), who represent the West Coast branch of all this.

This being post-Rolling Stones New York faggot-rock, the kids in fun city seem to polarize between goodie-goodie rock such as Crosby-Stills-Nash-whatsit-Taylor-Joni etc . . . and the heavy stuff featuring the 1000-watt beat that would move a 40-ton meat truck. It's a fact that LA soft-rock has been stomped on by glittering lurid day-glo platform shoes worn by a female-impersonating posturing hard-rock singer.

There are three separate performance areas at the Mercer, and as three groups are therefore performing at once I don't get to see them all. Queen Elizabeth features Wayne County. Wayne looks like a drag queen, even doing a strip during his act. Sporting a huge Afro-wig sprayed vivid green and pink, along with a black neck-ribbon and diamond necklace, he postures and flaps his skinny bare arms in frustrated gestures.

He wears black tights that exaggerate his thin thighs and hips, and over these sports a Seven Veils outfit. The overdone lipstick and weird snarling expressions show that it is not the glamorous plastic *Playboy* woman he is impersonating but some other tortuous image of a woman he has (his mother? He sings about her, as I'll describe). He totters about on outrageous high platforms being as gratuitously obscene as possible.

Behind Wayne a right greasy drummer in T-shirt and over-lubed Duck's Ass kicks out a strong beat and is really tight and loud like a movie from the '50s projected on that part of the floor. The bass player is resplendent in leather and studs, glittering metallic green pants and sparkle make-up, and often seems to be in the midst of some private orgasm as he stumbles about, eyes closed, reinforcing the beat with huge bass chords. Two little guitarists from Brooklyn – brothers, like two chubby Bob Dylans in Rupert trousers, teased hair and makeup – jump and sing together like a pair of hopped-up bunnies, strange expressions shining through all the glitter dust on their faces. ('Was it those pills?'). While in front of all this Wayne performs his 'cleaned-up act'.

He seems to be sniffing coke right there on stage from a little tube he wears round his neck. The audience loves it. He is singing a song about 'Down At Max's' (Kansas City), and he dedicates 'Stuck On You' to the Dave Clark Five and does an awkward strip, finishing up in a pair of flesh-coloured tights with imitation pubic hairs stuck on front which he combs and thrusts at the audience. By now he has broken through and animated them (accurate word), and has every-body laughing.

Triumphant he straps on an artificial vagina: 'I'm ready any time you are!' and goes down on the silver sprayed legs of a mannequin during a song called 'Dead Hot Mamma' which concerns someone's incestuous relationship with his mother's corpse. This actually managed to shock some people, the female photographer in front of me actually cracking up in rather hysterical laughter. The song wouldn't get BBC airplay.

Wayne rips off his Afro wig to reveal his own matted locks sprayed with day-glo pink and green. By now he is drooling a bit and his lipstick is smeared. He puts his bra back again and continues with 'It Takes A Man Like Me To Fuck A Woman Like Me', a hand-clapping hard-stomping number in which he plays maracas, eventually fucking himself with one in his artificial cunt and waving the other above his head as he jumps about the stage in some kind of awful climax. But no, there is more . . .

A rather touching little number called 'I'm So Confused' is followed by 'I'm Your Wonder Woman', in which Wayne confronts himself with a huge double-ended limp rubber penis which he sucks, drools over, swings like a baton while strutting across the stage, stuffs between his legs, leers at the audience with and beats on the floor. A number of the high-school girls in the audience become quite hysterical at this, and even the group falters in their heavy backing as they miss notes through laughing.

The audience could well be in the group, a woman with black lipstick looks dead – a very weird scene. Many men wear full drag, a man near me with a full beard also desports a floor-length red ball gown and ethereal smile. Some couples wear unisex makeup and are hard to distinguish from each other in the welter of day-glo, lurex, tinsel, glitter dust on flesh, and clothes, studs, satin, silk and leather, lurid reds, pink angora tops, green boas and totally transparent blouses. And of course everyone has gained at least 3″ in their multi-coloured platforms.

The total effect is quite sinister after London, which still tends more towards the warmth and friendliness of lace and velvet, Gary Glitter notwithstanding. New York is cold and distant in silk and satin, the faces remote in dead white makeup like wandering ghosts of a lost humanity.

OK, here come the NY Dolls. The lead singer looks like

Jagger, same big mouth and everything. The lead guitarist
looks a bit like Keith. They've modelled themselves on the
Stones, a terrible *alter ego* Rolling Stones, come to haunt
Mick'n Keith and the boys with a direct expression of all that
camping on stage. A hard rock, camp, prissy 100% homo-
sexual group in black tights posturing and imitating all of
Mick's stage gestures and leaps. It's terrific! The lead singer
wears a tank-top, diamonds and diamond rings, while the one
who models himself on Keith has a Rod Stewart hairdo, only
overdone and worn with a red satin Marc Bolan jacket. The
second guitarist is very weird, with pale white makeup and
straggling curly hair: he darts about the stage in tights, a mini
skirt, toy gun and holster and a transparent top. The bass
player is large, looks like Richard Brautigan with straw hair
and a fetching white dress, and seems very much out of it. The
drummer is also in a white top and makeup, with all five
balanced precariously atop outrageous platforms.

They are a heavy group, sounding a bit like the Move did in
the old days, and just as loud but more soft and floppy. When
fans gleefully throw chocolate kisses at them, they all fussily
run and hide on the far side of the stage area leaving only the
lead singer to get all hot and bothered trying to protect
himself from the harmless sweeties, pleased at the attention
but scared of his hair getting mussed-up as well. He pouted
'Bbbbbrrrrr . . .' down the scale, then, hand on hip, turns his
cute little nose up at someone in the audience who laughs.

It's hard to imagine what the Stones did to deserve all this.
An eerie sense of golems or doubles from a Gothic novel is
present. These preening, posturing musicians actually play
some pretty heavy rock, and a number like 'Jet Boy' really
takes off. Not a bunch of harpies, though they simper at
times; they're not flaunting their homosexuality in the way
Wayne County does, they're actually *like* that (though friends
of Wayne say that *he* is actually like that as well). So Faggot-
rock emerges from out the closet and nothing could get it
back in again by the look of it.

A strange sight are all the high-school girls who sing along and dance to the Dolls. They know all the words, and the Dolls are as normal to them as Arthur Brown was to the UFO crowd in '67. Imagine having fond memories of your teenage years as a fan of the New York Dolls! True, they play good rock and that's a lot.

The vaudeville aspect is present most in Eric Emerson and the Magic Tramps, who feature, apart from Eric, an electric violinist with a touch of the gypsy in him. Eric looks like he just arrived from Muscle Beach, covered with gold glitter dust and flexing his muscles to make little bits pop off while he gives naughty looks to the boys in the audience. He is a combination witch doctor and Captain America in a white feather head-dress and white tights with sort of gold lead jock-strap.

Waving bunches of feathers, he leaps in the air shrieking, coming down in a cloud of fluff and little feathers. He rocks with 'Great Balls Of Fire' but can't stop his huge grin and limp-wrist action, so it becomes a sort of hard-rock French cabaret act. Other notable numbers included the music from *Can-Can*, in which Eric wore a delightful red flamenco dress. The act ended with the theme from *The Lone Ranger*!

I missed Alan Suicide, who I'm told has a spectacular act (!), and caught fragments of acts with other sequinned, glitter-dusted performers. The entire thing is almost some outrageous parody of the 1930s American glamour concept. It's hard to believe that Hollywood was ever that tacky, until one goes there. No, all this is real, as a nation coming out from under 10 years of unpopular war, a history of puritanism and genocide, greets four more years of Nixon with its most potent weapon, Faggot Rock, the music of total drop-out!

Vivien Goldman

THE ROAD TO WIGAN CASINO: NORTHERN SOUL

New Musical Express, 11th October 1975

Re-reading this article after so long was like breaking the lock to a long-lost treasure box and finding photos that it takes a moment to recognise are YOU. Who knew, back then, that, along with all-night raves at Ladbroke Grove shebeens and after-hours sessions with Jah Shaka's sound system, those endless North-ern Soul nights that nonetheless seemed to speeeeeed by would remain the permanent template for How To Rave, not just for me, but for a global nation?

The Big Bang happened when the outlaw spirit of the pioneering shebeen operators, who seized their fun and profit when and where they could, combined with Northern Soul's ferocious need to belong to a tribe and find a wider identity by devouring specific dance music and drugs in communion with your peers. Result: the rave movements documented by Simon Reynolds' Energy Flash *(aka* Generation Ecstasy*), a startling number of whose interviewees were Northern Soul alumni. Now the hyper-speed and adrenaline fever of Northern Soul, so like hi-energy garage, is taking its place in the timeless pantheon of Mental Musical Movements, always liable to be unleashed again.*

At Wigan's arch-rival, the Blackpool Mecca, twirls, backspins, leg-splits and Nureyev kicks, the canon of pre-breakdance moves, exploded all over the dance floor, and midnight ravers huddled over their hold-alls in the lobby, selling gold-dust 45s by long-lost, one-hit soul men. DJ Ian Levine presided with partner Colin Curtis over the totally tartan Highland Room, that still gets my vote for best club décor. Soap-opera vendettas devoured DJs like Ian and Wigan's Russ Winstanley, and scenemakers like battling editors Dave Godin of Blues & Soul *and* Black Music's *Tony Cummings. Self-appointed guardians and cultural gatekeepers of the scene, they had the power. A power, anyway; as the all-too-human backdrop to the dancers' transcendental communication, they were transformed each week from dead-end kids to emperors of their esoteric universe.*

I was also a kid when I wrote this, but I knew one thing: 'The spirit of Northern Soul was to be found on a few feet of parquet flooring,' the drum on which flying feet could beat their own rhythm of eternity.

VG

THE YOUNG BOY sitting cross-legged on the edge of the stage looked as if he was about to throw up.

It was 4:30 a.m. at the Wigan Casino. He looked as if he should have been in bed hours ago, but here he was, gazing plaintively up at slick cabaret master Tommy Hunt, as if the suavely dressed black man held the answer to all of adolescence's traumas.

You see, the jam-packed Edwardian-style venue that is the Wigan Casino has seen many, many events in its time, but nothing as strange as the weirdo phenomenon of Northern Soul. Wherein many youngsters, mostly of Anglo-Saxon origin, assemble at 12.30 on a Saturday night/Sunday morning, intent on forgetting the frowstiness of an existence which in weekdays consists of a boring dead-end job, or no job and no money.

They forget it all, submerge their sorrows in a whirlpool of high-energy activity, dancing the night away to singles long

since forgotten by everyone except possibly the artists concerned. Singles which, good or bad, are the losers of the
record world.

They are resurrected from the mouldering vaults of ware-
houses in Chicago or junk shops in Bury, Lancs., to live again
as the focal point in the lives of thousands of Northern
working-class kids.

And the Wigan Casino is the temple of the hopes and
desires of this race who seem (at least to this outsider) to find
little or no satisfaction outside the steaming world of the
dance floor.

It all begins in the fish and chip shop next door to the
Casino, facing the Wigan ABC – probably the only chippy in
the country to open up for custom at 11.30 and shut again at
2.00 a.m. It's crammed full of youthful Wigan-ites, and the
atmosphere is electric over the Hall's meat and potato pies.
Also served is that peculiarly Northern delicacy, squashed
processed peas in gravy. Even in the interests of journalistic
science I didn't bring myself to have a bash at the peas. But the
peas are good.

There's a small fortune to be made for some enterprising
bag manufacturer wanting to break into the Northern Soul
market. Everyone, but *everyone*, lugs around hefty portman-
teaus emblazoned with badges and stickers with mottoes like
'Major Lance – The Torch Lives' and other cryptic codes.
You need them if you've hitched from Huddersfield or Reading, if not for a change of undies, then for the singles you hope
to sell, swap, or merely hear blasting over the speakers in a
glow of possession.

All the fans are extremely smartly-dressed, no matter how
far the journey or how uncomfortable the pilgrimage. Fellas
are invariably kitted out with a singlet to sweat through, a
pully to put on to prevent double pneumonia when you leave
the Casino dripping hot into the nippy Wigan morn, and,
judging from the traditional aroma, at least three spray cans
of Brut.

Tonight, the excitement is particularly intense. Two years ago to the day, the first ever Wigan all-nighter was held, designed to fill the gap left by the closure of the all-nighters at the legendary Torch in Stoke, and the equally legendary Twisted Wheel in Manchester.

The fact that the Casino took off with a bang is borne out tonight by the number of punters prepared to queue for hours in a remorseless drizzle on the off-chance of getting one of the 500 tickets left for door sales – the other 1,500 sold out a fortnight before.

The representative from Spark Records (one of the only companies geared wholly to Northern Soul, and proud possessors of Wigan's Ovation), himself a Northern singles producer, said with awe: 'They murder each other trying to get in.'

A comment like that is like a red flag to a bull for an ace cub reporter, isn't it? I immediately charged for the entrance, only to be pushed back by a solid horde of lads who, once out of the rain, were in no way going to be manoeuvred in the direction of the street. A surly bouncer gave me the once-over – 'An' wot do you think you're doing?' etcetera – so playing safe I nabbed an unsuspecting youth.

'So tell me, what's it like out there?' I ask conversationally. 'Are they murdering each other to get in?'

'Not at all, nothing like that', responds the fresh-faced lad. Then, suspiciously – 'Are you a journalist?'

I'm forced to concede. And he produces an N.U.J. card of his own. Would you believe, a journalist who's also a Northern Soul fan! Who actually lives the life! In the company of my new-found guide I check out the upstairs cloakroom, a secluded spot where a steady stream of bedraggled Young England is forcing its way in to the Casino free of charge via the roof, in a spirit of adventure worthy of Biggles himself.

Got to admire the initiative of these young people. They all seemed to be suffering mild abrasions of one sort or another, but spirits rode high despite all.

'Well, you don't want to *pay* do ya?' explains a well-turned-out youth. 'I've been coming here ever since it first opened. Stopped coming here, mind, when all those journalists from London came down and it all got commercialised. And look at them now (gesturing at a hapless youngster) – he ought to be home in bed! Can't be more than fourteen!' The inference appears to be that he knows everyone has to be fourteen once, but this is ridiculous.

Back on the dance floor, a steadily shifting mosaic of dancers is already glowing and blossoming strangely in the ultra-violet light. Each dancer is moving in a private pattern of his/her own, staring fixedly at the stage where a top Wigan DJ like Russ Winstanley or Richard Searling is spreading the word. Basically, tonight is like every soul night at the Wigan Casino. As soon as the last rock fan from the evening rock session (featuring heavy English rock) has filed out, an army of cleaners descends and makes all pristine for the 12.30 invasion. And then the kids seethe in. And then they dance.

That's the regular pattern of the evening, and that's what it's like tonight but more so. 'Cos there's gonna be surprise appearances. 'Y' know, like the peas!' as some wag roguishly exclaimed. Who is it to be? Those in the know are confidently anticipating the Chi-Lites dropping in on their way home from a nearby gig. Well, I was waiting for the Chi-Lites more than eight hours, and they weren't there when I was, that's for sure.

But there was a goodly number of people there that night who couldn't have cared less, either way. Among them were the 'VIPs' safely ensconced in the VIP Room with lots of booze, lots of nosh, and generally lots of room for a fascinating display of the noisome infighting, bitchiness and back-biting that the individuals who consider themselves to be controllers or guides of 'the Northern Scene' love to indulge in.

This particular night saw tensions in that cosy room which led to near fisticuffs. Producers, journalists, deejays, music biz types, all circled each other warily, occasionally lunging in for a quick snap and then retreating to eye one another and lick their wounds. This intriguing parade of human behaviour took place quite independently of the spirit of Northern Soul, which as we all know is to be found on a few feet of parquet flooring.

It's refreshing to pop back and forth between the two environments. The main dancing body of the enormous Casino building is divided into three main parts: The most important is the central dance section, with its stage and gilded balcony running right round. Walking into this central section has the same kind of impact as strolling into the tropical rain forest from an air-conditioned limo.

H-O-T. And W-E-T.

The actual walls are sweating, great drops of condensation beading every surface, backstage as well. Every move is a struggle, and attempting to cross from one side of the Casino to the other means an exhausting and dangerous voyage, comparable to circumnavigating Piccadilly Circus tube station at the height of the rush hour in a sweltering heatwave. For six hours.

Section the second is Mr M's. That's where I spent the first part of the evening under exceptionally bizarre circumstances.

My colleagues and I were ushered into this slightly smaller dance area, also with a balcony complete with tables. This was when the regular patrons of the Casino were indulging in their Saturday night knees-up. As we walked in, a burly Wigan-ite was laying into an ugly looking bouncer – '. . . paid my money and now they won't even serve me at the bar!' With surprising patience the bouncer explained that there was only waitress service, and two peroxide beauties led the placated Blunt Northerner to his plush chair.

If you diverted your attention from this real-life drama, your attention was bound to be caught by a personage exchanging risqué banter from the dais with the assembled

Wigan punters. This was a performer in the great British tradition, a drag artiste. And a dirty drag artiste. Quite frankly, there was such a crush in the hall, that it took me five minutes to decipher from whence came those naughty wise cracks. By the time I adjusted my vision to peering through people's elbows and slightly to the left of their beehive hairdos, the Drag Queen was slowly beginning to go through the motions of a strip. Off comes the long glove, to delirious shouts of 'Get 'em off!' . . .

Cut to the same room, two hours later.

Every figure in the room appears to be straining to dance in the face of opposition of sheer numbers. The room is now 'Mr M's', the oldies area of the discotheque, where by popular demand DJs like Davie Evison spin 'oldies'; faves on labels like OKeh, Ric-Tic and Mirwood – now-defunct labels that specialised in a quasi-early-Motown sound.

Oldies DJ's have a tendency to regard themselves in a rather pompous light, as educators of the youth of the Casino, with a sacred trust to turn them on to the grand old 'oldies' and open their eyes to the inadequacies of modern manufactured Northern Soul sounds such as Simon Soussan's Moog instrumentals (Soussan is a big name in the Northern Soul. A former major bootlegger, he now produces artists like the Sharonettes, released on the Black Magic label).

One advantage of being an 'oldies' DJ is financial. Most DJs simply couldn't afford to emulate Blackpool's Ian Levine – who comes from a wealthy family and may be said to have independent means – and make regular trips to the States, so they dig out their own fresh new Northern Soul sounds.

Mr M's keeps itself to itself, and the fact of the second anniversary doesn't seem to make much difference to the oldies freaks, except there is more of 'em.

And now, on the third sector of the Casino, the area backstage. This isn't like a concert-hall backstage; it's another regular meeting-place for the DJs and the more long-standing fans.

It was there that I met the gentleman who proved to be the only live entertainment of the soiree.

It must be a surprise to Northern Soul freaks of long standing that it was Tommy Hunt who appeared on that momentous anniversary, because Tommy has never yet had a Northern Soul biggie. Hunt is most commonly known for having sung the original version of Bacharach's 'I Just Don't Know What To Do With Myself'. He also sang in the Flamingos, who cut a classic version of 'I Only Have Eyes For You' (currently riding high in the charts once more by A. Garfunkel).

Since those hits, Hunt has, in this country at least, been a fine performer on the cabaret circuit, where he was singled out by Mike Walker, manager of the Wigan Casino and associate of Wigan's Ovation, and Barry Kingston, the producer of Spark Records. Hunt has a single released on Spark, a re-recording of a big Northern Sound by the late Roy Hamilton, 'Crackin' Up'. It is definitely among the more mediocre Northern singles.

Tommy Hunt is a skinny, superhip dude with a neat, if familiar line in argot, 'You from the *NME*? Groovy! This sure is a groovy place' et al. As soon as he hits the stage, he does a couple of neat backdrops, a few flips and contortions here and there, just to show the kids he knows where he is.

And that's when I noticed the fat little boy on the edge of the stage. He seemed to me to sum up so much of the mood of the Wigan Casino that night; a surfeit of energy, just waves and waves of untrammelled force aimed at the stage. For this lad in particular, the emotion seemed to be more than he could comfortably handle. So he looked as if all this energy was going to churn and churn inside, till it found the most convenient way of expelling itself from his body – through the mouth.

Tommy's set wasn't designed to do this boy's digestion any favours. It was one of those wham-bam-thank-you-ladies-and-gennulmen acts that doesn't leave you room to think.

The relentlessness of its flow was geared to match the metabolic rates (mostly artificially induced) of his audience.

With lots of encouraging asides to his excellent band, e.g. 'This is it brothers give me a hand and we're gonna tear this place up', Tommy galloped his way through everybody's favourite black music standards – 'Walk On By', 'Get Ready', 'My Girl', 'Hang On In There Baby', and so on. The musicians moved as if wired up to an invisible metronome. The crowd was utterly, uncritically receptive as The Man delivered what sounded as if it was his regular cabaret act speeded up.

The feeling of the show was very different from the last live spot I saw there, when Herb and Brenda Rooney – the Exciters – were on; the sense of mutual adoration on that occasion was almost insufferably intense. It was more like visiting Lourdes than going to a soul nite.

Meanwhile, Tommy has discarded as many layers of clothing as complies with decency ('Now I feel cool!'), has flattered the audience ('This is where it's all at!') and delivered 'Never Can Say Goodbye' (Esther Phillips' current Northern hit) in fine voice.

Then – a shock.

Hunt sang an exquisite 'Help Me Make It Through The Night'. He actually apologised before starting – 'I know you kids like the fast songs, but let me do one slow one and then I'll get back to your favourites.' All of a sudden, here was a SOUL singer. The difference was alarming. It made me feel sad that such a talented performer should be scoring financially through the more second-rate aspect of his talents – Hunt's gift is more suited to bringing out the depth in a ballad-style, emotional number than to injecting expression into a fast Northern stomper.

When the ecstatic audience finally let Hunt leave the stage, he staggered on his knees towards his buddies, the Fantastics, waiting for him in the dressing room. Jesting (I trust), he gasped, 'I shoulda stayed in cabaret!!'

The next and final high point of the evening's entertainment (apart from the touching moment when various feuding
soul bigwigs gathered on the stage, temporarily reunited, to
cut the cake decorated with 'Heart Of Soul') was the DANCE
COMPETITION!

This took me back to my youthful days watching *Ready
Steady Go,* when the best and brightest of the Cromwellian
would challenge their equivalents from some other hip nit-
erie. In this instance, the winner was such a foregone conclusion it was ridiculous – a dryad-like slip of a lad with curly
blond hair and a gamin expression. Rather like the *Death In
Venice* youngster, this budding heart-throb instinctively upstaged everyone by hogging the front of the stage with his
startling, gravity-defying twirls and spins.

Instead of just being very quick and accurate as they all
were, he managed to combine that incredible speed with lots
of expression and feeling. His stylised fluttering hand movements alone marked him out instantly. (Hey, any of you out
there *Come Dancing* fanatics too?)

THE WINNER!

This prodigy, in case any of you wish to seek him out (and I
wouldn't blame you in the slightest), is named Danny Daniels. He asked me not to reveal his age, and he works in an
engineering firm, which he thinks is 'Great'. Did he expect to
win?

'No, not at all,' replied the boy with heart-wringing mod-
esty. This lad could go far.

And that, with special mention to Dave Duncan for doing
well, is that.

By now, it was 8.00 a.m. On a regular night, the Casino
would be packing up, but today, the festivities were to
continue till 10.00. But for those of us with a journey to
London ahead, enough was sufficient.

Quite a few fans had complained to me that they reckoned
a lot of people there that night came just to say they'd been
THERE. Well, so what, really . . . it was a massive, hot,

steaming event. A celebration of two years of staying up late, grooving all night long, and keeping the soul flag flying up there in the freezing North. All I can say is MAZEL-TOV, which translated from the Yiddish means, roughly, Jolly Good Show.

Caroline Coon

REBELS WITHOUT A PAUSE: THE PUNK ROCK EXPLOSION

Melody Maker, 7th August 1976

For young people with no money or power, the early
'70s was a time of grim political betrayal. Today I can
say, without embarrassment at my naïveté, that I was
aghast and shocked when a majority of the '60s 'street-
fighting' white rock rebels became millionaires and –
instead of continuing to support protest groups and
castigate the Establishment – sold out. Like millions of
music fans, I felt personally let down and outraged.
But I was also curious. What would happen next?
How would the next generation react?

I first heard the Sex Pistols at their first Nashville gig
in March 1976. I went to that gig because the band's
name seemed tough and hard, perfect for the moment,
unlike other bands who were exhorting me to check
them out with names with Jim Custard Pie.

Although I was dismayed to be confronted by the
antithesis of 'peace and love' idealism, I understood a
group of young people expressing their anomie as
'hate and war' anarchism, because I knew the anger
was justified. I got the point of the Sex Pistols immediately: they were continuing the tradition of popular protest song, the music medium every generation
can use as an effective retort to the ruling class and the
sold-out cynicism of bland corporate rock.

But would I, a girl, be allowed to tell their story? I

knew I would have to battle against the dumb, and ultimately fatal, commercial music media resistance to anything political or radically progressive – not to mention the sexism. It took me four months of persistence in editorial meetings, and the confidence to know I was right about the incredible exploding punk scene, to finally get the OK.

When this scene-setting essay appeared in Melody Maker, *I remember feeling that intense professional thrill of being first to spread the word. But it was a personal triumph, too.*

CC

JOHNNY ROTTEN LOOKS bored. The emphasis is on the word 'looks' rather than, as Johnny would have you believe, on the word 'bored'. His clothes, held together by safety pins, fall around his slack body in calculated disarray. His face is an undernourished grey. Not a muscle moves. His lips echo the downward slope of his wiry, coat-hanger shoulders. Only his eyes register the faintest trace of life.

Johnny works very hard at looking bored. Leaning against a bar; at a sound check; after a gig; making an entrance to a party; onstage; when he's with women. No, actually, *then* he's inclined to look quite interested.

Why is Johnny bored? Well, that's the story.

This malevolent third-generation child of rock'n'roll is the Sex Pistols' lead singer. The band play exciting, hard, basic punk rock. But more than that, Johnny is the elected *generalissimo* of a new cultural movement scything through the grassroots disenchantment with the present state of mainstream rock. You need look no further than the letters pages of any *Melody Maker* to see that fans no longer silently accept the disdain with which their heroes, the rock giants, treat them.

They feel deserted. Millionaire rock stars are no longer part of the brotherly rock fraternity that helped create them in the first place. Rock was meant to be a joyous celebration; the inability to see the stars, or to play the music of those you can see, is making a whole generation of rock fans feel depressingly inadequate.

Enter Johnny Rotten. Not content to feel frustrated, bored and betrayed, he and the Sex Pistols – Glen Matlock (bass), Paul Cook (drums) and Steve Jones (guitar) – have decided to ignore what they believe to be the elitist pretensions of their heroes, who no longer play the music they want to hear. The Pistols are playing the music they want to hear. They are the tip of an iceberg.

Since January, when the Sex Pistols played their first gig, there has been a slow but steady increase in the number of musicians who feel the same way – bands like the Clash, the Jam, Buzzcocks, the Damned, the Suburban Sect and Slaughter and the Dogs. The music they play is loud, raucous and beyond considerations of taste and finesse. As Mick Jones of the Clash says: 'It's wonderfully vital.'

These bands' punk music and stance is so outrageous that, like the Rolling Stones in the good old days, they have trouble getting gigs. But they play regularly at the 100 Club, which is rapidly becoming the venue at which these bands cut their teeth.

The musicians and their audience reflect each other's street-cheap, ripped-apart, pinned-together style of dress. Their attitude is classic punk: icy-cool with a permanent sneer. The kids are arrogant, aggressive, rebellious. The last thing any of these bands make their audience feel is inadequate. Once again there is the feeling, the exhilarating buzz, that it's possible to be and play like the bands onstage.

It's no coincidence that the week the Stones were at Earls Court, the Sex Pistols were playing to their ever-increasing following at London's 100 Club. The Pistols are the personification of the emerging British punk rock scene, a positive reaction to the complex equipment, technological sophistication and jaded alienation which has formed a barrier between fans and stars.

Punk rock sounds simple and callow. It's meant to. The equipment is minimal, usually cheap. It's played faster than the speed of light. If the musicians play a ballad, it's the fastest ballad on earth. The chords are basic, numbers rarely last longer than three minutes, in keeping with the clipped, biting cynicism of the lyrics. There are no solos. No indulgent improvisations.

It's a fallacy to believe that punk rockers like the Sex Pistols can't play dynamic music. They power through sets. They are never less than hard, rough and edgy. They are the quintessence of a raging, primal rock-scream.

The atmosphere among the punky bands on the circuit at the moment is positively cut-throat. Not only are they vying with each other, but they all secretly aspire to take Johnny Rotten down a peg or two. They use him as a pivot against which they can assess their own credibility.

It's the BSP/ASP Syndrome. The Before or After Sex Pistols debate which wrangles thus: 'We saw Johnny Rotten and he CHANGED our attitude to music' (the Clash, Buzzcocks) or 'We played like this AGES before the Sex Pistols' (Slaughter and the Dogs) or 'We are MILES better than the Sex Pistols' (the Damned). They are very aware that they are part of a new movement and each one wants to feel that he played a part in starting it.

All doubts that the British punk scene was well under way were blitzed two weeks ago in Manchester, when the Sex Pistols headlined a triple third-generation punk rock concert before an ecstatic capacity audience.

Participation is the operative word. The audiences are revelling in the idea that any one of them could get up on stage and do just as well, if not better, than the bands already up there. Which is, after all, what rock and roll is all about.

When, for months, you've been feeling that it would take ten years to play as well as Hendrix, Clapton, Richard (insert favourite rock star's name), there's nothing more gratifying than the thought, 'Jesus, I could get a band together and blow this lot off the stage.'

The growing punk rock audiences are seething with angry young dreamers who want to put the boot in and play music, regardless. And the more people feel that 'I can do that too', the more there is a rush on to that stage, the more cheap instruments are bought, fingered and flayed in front rooms, the more likely it is there will be the rock revival we've all been crying out for.

There's every chance (although it's early days yet) that out of the gloriously raucous, uninhibited *melée* of British Punk Rock – which even at its worst is more vital than much of the music perfected by the Platinum Disc Brigade – will emerge the musicians to inspire a fourth generation of rockers.

The arrogant, aggressive, rebellious stance that characterises the musicians who have played the most vital rock and roll has always been glamorised. In the '50s it was the rebel without a cause exemplified by Elvis and Gene Vincent, the Marlon Brando and James Dean of rock. In the '60s it was the Rock'n'Roll Gypsy Outlaw image of Mick Jagger, Keith Richard and Jimi Hendrix. In the '70s the word 'rebel' has been superseded by the word 'punk'. Although initially derogatory, it now contains all the glamorous connotations once implied by the overused word 'rebel'.

Punk rock was initially coined, about six years ago, to describe the American rock bands of 1965–68 who sprung up as a result of hearing the Yardbirds, the Who, Them, the Stones. Ability was not as important as mad enthusiasm, but the bands usually dissipated all their talent in one or two splendid singles which rarely transcended local hit status. Some of the songs, however, like 'Wooly Bully', '96 Tears', 'Psychotic Reaction', 'Pushin' Too Hard', have become rock classics.

In Britain, as 'punk rock' has been increasingly used to categorise the livid, exciting energy of bands like the Sex Pistols, there has been an attempt to redefine the term. There's an age difference, too. New York punks are mostly in their mid-twenties. The members of the new British punk bands squirm if they have to tell you that they are over 18. Johnny Rotten's favourite sneer is 'You're Too Old'. He's 20.

The British punk rock garb is developing independently, too. It's an ingenious hodgepodge of jumble sale cast-offs, safety-pinned around one of the choice risqué T-shirts especially made for the Kings Road shop, Sex.

Selling an intriguing line of arcane '50s cruise-ware, fantasy glamour ware and the odd rubber suit, this unique boutique is owned by Malcolm McLaren, ex-manager of the New York Dolls, now the Sex Pistols' manager.

His shop has a mysterious atmosphere which made it the ideal meeting place for a loose crowd of truant, disaffected teenagers. Three of them were aspiring musicians who, last October, persuaded McLaren to take them on. They wanted to play rock'n'roll. They weren't to know what they were about to start and even now no one is sure where it will lead. All Steve, Glenn and Paul needed, then, was a lead singer.

A few weeks later Johnny Rotten strayed into the same murky interior. He was first spotted leaning over the jukebox . . . looking bored.

Mick Farren

LIVE FROM NASHVILLE: A LIMEY AT LARGE IN MUSIC CITY USA

New Musical Express, 13th November 1976

Back in the glory days at NME, *I used to love to go places, and the infinitely corruptible record companies were all too ready to pay for me to go to Paris, New York, or even Los Angeles to be wined, dined, and generally maintained in a manner to which I could have easily become accustomed if it meant ink for their latest hype. Once the mandatory observation of the hype was dispatched, I'd scuttle off about my own business to see what was up with the international trash aesthetic at CBGB or the Whisky. My visit to Nashville was a little different, in that I brokered my own corruption. Over a bunch of Soho lunches, I cut a deal whereby I would travel to Nashville and be lodged in a Holiday or Ramada Inn on the corporate tab, without any hype-act as a focal excuse. I'd just run around and interview as many of their country stars as I could shake a cassette at while I did a story that was essentially 'Farren drinks his way through the downhome heartland'. My real ambition was to do 'fear and loathing in Nashville', but even* NME *wasn't ready to run my complete and full-blown blue-yodel hallucination horrors.*

Although my first motivation to do the story was an illogical rerun romance – exactly during the first flowering of punk – with Johnny Cash, Patsy Cline,

*and Hank Williams, the autumn of 1976 was also a
neatly historic moment to be visiting Tennessee. The
South was in the process of rising again. Marijuana
and long hair had finally been incorporated into
country culture, and 'outlaw' was the new word being
bandied about. Southern liberal Jimmy Carter was
being elected president, but the Reagan right was
mobilising for its successful 1980 power play. This
same post-Vietnam cultural and political polarisation
had been amply demonstrated just a few months earlier in the classic Robert Altman movie* Nashville, *if I
needed confirmation that it was a proverbially interesting time to be doing what I did.*

MF

PART ONE

THERE ARE THREE waitresses in the dining room of the hotel.
One is one-time curvy-cute but now running to fat. She must
be in her early forties. Her hair is dyed red in an elaborately
casual Ann-Margaret construction. The second waitress is
maybe a couple of years younger. She is thin to the point of
emaciation. Her hair is sculpted, whipped-cream, white-
blonde, piled on top of her head. It's similar to Tammy
Wynette's, only Tammy's coif job is always expensive while
the waitress' is strictly budget and it shows.

The third waitress is a gawky black girl in her late teens.
She seems to have no trouble at all about the way she looks.

All three of them wear red nylon uniforms. The skirts are
way too short, It doesn't do a thing for any of them.

The thin one has been bringing me breakfast. I've tried to
read *The Tennessean*, one of the Nashville morning papers.
There's very little out-of-state news, and virtually none about
anything outside the USA. You feel that if India sank into the
sea it would rate about two inches at the bottom of page 17.

The only familiar things are *Peanuts* and the face of Jimmy Carter, which seems to crop up quite often.

The thin waitress flashes a set of dazzling white bridgework, asks solicitously if I want some more coffee. I decline. I've had two cups already. I sign the check and write in a tip. Again the dazzling smile.

'It's sure been a pleasure to serve you.'

In the face of Southern hospitality first thing in the morning, all a poor London boy can do is try to be David Niven charming.

'Thank you.'

'You're real welcome. You have a nice day, and come again, y'hear?'

I am, in fact, going to come again for a whole week. Each time it's the same ritual. The phrase 'Come again, y'all' is like a kind of secular blessing.

You might be wondering why you have just been treated to a blow-by-blow account of your humble correspondent's first breakfast in the city of Nashville, Tennessee. It may seem kind of irrelevant, but it somehow seemed to sum up the city. The hospitality was phony, plastic and yet perfectly genuine. It was my first contradiction in a city of contradictions.

You come across them just about every minute of the day. For instance, on one hand, everyone will tell you that the old South, the bigoted, gun-toting, Bull Connors, redneck South, has gone. They'll demonstrate quite clearly that there is new, enlightened, progressive, economically-booming South. You only have to drive around to see that this is all true. The new president is a Southerner.

And yet people talk about the Civil War as though it was just yesterday.

The city of Nashville is proud of its high-speed urban development. It's also proud of its funky, small-town, good-old-boy traditions.

Hell, even the stars present you with the same anomalies. Around town the big names of country music are treated like they were some kind of royalty. They seem like aloof figures cocooned in rhinestones and palatial mansions. Most of them aren't above making a buck on the side, though.

George Jones operates a tour coach line and runs an amusement park. Faron Young and maybe a dozen more top-liners own bars that bear their names. Even the great Johnny Cash has a roadside attraction where tourists can buy junk souvenirs.

During that first breakfast I was seeing everything with the slightly disorientated, but unnervingly clear vision that can only be produced by a bad hangover in a strange city. It's an extreme form of culture shock, in which even using lifts can be confusing.

The night before, around 7.30 Nashville time, or 1.30 a.m. London time (my brain was somewhere between the two), I'd been met at Nashville airport by my two record company contacts. These two gentlemen were to be my guides and mentors for the next six days.

It was the same Nashville airport you saw in the Robert Altman movie. A small, funky airport where they don't have those unpleasant telescopic tubes that run to the plane. You just walk down the aluminium steps and across the tarmac carrying your flight bag, coat, camera, whatever. Just like a Beatle or a goddamn president.

They don't get all that many Englishmen in Nashville. My friends the record company men are set up to get their money's worth. For the next six days, I'm going to be run off my feet by non-stop Southern hospitality.

The man from CBS takes me from the airport into town. On the drive I get my first lesson on the new South, its booming economy and political hopes. It's come a long way from *Easy Rider*, baby.

On first glimpse, the city is much like any other small American town, overhead wires, neon signs, wide streets, empty sidewalks and low buildings except for a clutch of high rise making the downtown business section.

There is nothing so unique about the Nashville Skyline.

Except for one thing: we drive past a floodlit, full-size replica of the Parthenon. It's the same one where Barbara Jean is gunned down in Altman's movie.

We reach the hotel and find that the RCA press chief has got me for the evening. Everything is mapped out. There's no time for rest and recuperation. I dump my luggage, climb into the RCA man's pale green Chevy and we're off for my first night in town.

The first stop is a place called the Pickin' Parlour. It's a fairly new place done out in Peckinpah-cantina-style old wood. It's an outlaw-orientated joint and most of the customers are longhairs.

The verb *to pick* and the adjective *outlaw* are heard a lot in Nashville. Everyone seems to pick. Even drummers. But outlaw is by far the word of the year.

On this particular night the featured attraction is Steve Young and his band. Young is very definitely outlaw. You may not have heard of him yet, but if RCA have their way, you probably will. Right now he's being given the same treatment previously handed to Guy Clark.

Steve Young has immaculate outlaw credentials. He wrote 'Lonesome, On'ry And Mean' for Waylon Jennings and is something of a Jennings protégé. It would seem by rights that he ought to be in Austin, Texas, but he has come to Nashville for the big push.

Relations between Austin and Nashville are, to say the least, delicate. The Willie Nelson/Waylon Jennings axis that started the whole outlaw cult originally antagonised the Nashville establishment by cutting through a lot of the clichéd, rhinestone-encrusted bullshit. Nelson and Jennings left 'Music City USA' in disgust and based their operation in Texas.

At that point Nashville, who saw the outlaws as part hippies and part bums, was pleased to see them go. Now Austin gets written up in *Playboy*, makes the national charts and all but threatens to eclipse Nashville as the country music fountainhead. The Nashville establishment is being forced both to mass produce its own outlaws and bribe the existing ones with superior promo machinery.

Outlaws? It's like Jesse James getting a bank loan for some new guns. Bah!

But behave like a whore, Mickey, the record company is paying the bill.

I'm introduced to Steve Young. I think it's supposed to be a brief pre-gig interview but I'm too tired and jetlagged to be intelligent. And there's another problem. People don't understand my accent. Here in the South, they no spikka da cockney.

Steve Young is shortish, stockyish and sincereish. He has sideburns and a Zapata moustache. He is wearing the standard outlaw suit: tattered jeans, Levi shirt, black leather vest and a Stetson hat. Across the back of the vest are embroidered the words 'Renegade Picker' and a Confederate flag. 'Renegade Picker' is the title of Young's first RCA album.

In a spasmodic conversation that keeps drifting into disorientated silence, I find out that, although 'file under outlaw' seems to be the way to commercial success, establishment Nashville still calls Willie Nelson a sonofabitch behind his back. Although Willie and Waylon are now unstoppable, obstacles still get in the way of the up-and-coming rebel cowboy.

When Young gets on the stage, one thing becomes clear. Whatever the hype may be, he's very, very good. His voice is clear and ringing in the manner of the Nelson/Jennings masters, and if he'd got up in Dingwalls, his guitar playing would be phenomenal. In Nashville, it's high average.

The songs are fairly predictable: Merle Haggard, Willie Nelson, Dylan, a bunch of his own tunes, 'The Night They Drove Old Dixie Down' (remember the South hasn't forgotten the Civil War). The set is split into two parts. During the first, he is mournfully alone with his guitar. For the second, the band comes on and starts to kick out some rock and roll. This is the main advantage about so-called outlaws. They're not afraid to get down and rock.

Unfortunately, even when the rock and roll is under way, I'm still feeling mournfully alone. It must be breakfast time in London. I begin to sink into my beer. The lady at the table orders me a black coffee and gives me three little pills. After a while I start to feel better. It's not only physiochemical but metaphysical. Haven't country music and pill-poppin' gone hand in hand since Hank Williams?

From the Pickin' Parlour, the RCA man and I move on. The next stop is the legendary (I'm informed) Printers Alley. I'm in a kind of alert daze.

Once upon a time, Printers Alley was Nashville's red light district, overflowing with razor fights, shootings, drunken cowboys, crazy fiddle players and golden-hearted whores. Today it's been relatively tamed. (Why have red light districts always been tamed by the time I get to them? The last one was apparently Bangkok, and now even *that's* going down to the communists.)

Today all Printers Alley has to offer is topless bars, strip joints, and country night-spots where hopefuls in the Tammy/Dolly/Johnny school are trying to make a name. It's the kind of place where you get the feeling that if a girl don't make it fronting a band she'll probably slide down to stripping or cut-price, executive-special, happy-hour relief massage.

That is, it's safe but sleazy – like the punters want.

We go into a place called Ronnie Prophet's. There's a sign outside announcing Boots Randolph, but he's not on till next week. Tonight we have Ronnie Prophet himself.

So who the hell *is* Ronnie Prophet?

The crowd – if you can call it such, the place is only half full – are tourists in polyester suits and Tammy Wynette dresses. Two Vietnam veterans are drinking morosely at the bar. The support act is in full flight. They wear matching burgundy cowboy suits. The lead singer is called Darlene or Charlene or something of that ilk. She has red hair, a good figure, a forgettable voice and a low cut green dress that goes well with the burgundy suits.

She performs the distaff side of the C&W hit parade like an air hostess pretending to be a country star. I later learn that her ma and pa are in the club to see her get her first break. They'll probably save her from the massage parlour.

As she goes into 'Stand By Your Man', a large Jack Daniels is put into my hand and I'm escorted to Ronnie Prophet's dressing room.

So who the hell is Ronnie Prophet?

Ronnie Prophet is a stand-up comedian-cum-guitar player. He plays in a kind of sub-Les-Paul mode with lots of electronic gadgets. The humour is sophisticated good-ol'-boy, with lots and lots of impressions and a frog routine that I presume must have been a hit in the South at sometime or another.

He is a fast-talking, well-groomed, archetypal Dixie figure. In other lives and other ages he could have been an auctioneer, a con man, a preacher, a bible salesman or even the roving gambler. He also looks enough like Merle Haggard to be his brother.

Although none of you have ever heard of the guy, he does pretty damn well for himself. Aside from a part share in the night club, he has a syndicated TV show that goes out in the South and, of all places, Canada.

Ronnie Prophet, I guess, is the lower echelon of the Nashville empire. He is the traditional entertainer/hustler. His line goes straight back to the singing cowboys who sold patent medicine and to Ma Everly, who baked cookies to sell mail order over the family radio show. Prophet has four albums out on his own label. He sells them direct mail on his TV show.

He is the total opposite side of the coin from Steve Young and the outlaws. He may also be scuffling to make it, but he's doing it the Nashville way and scuffling in comfort.

He comes on and does his spot. I am the stooge for a bunch

of terrible cockney dialect jokes. I am also fed a good quantity of Jack Daniels. Both whiskey and humour are a practised blend of mashed-up corn.

After the show, Prophet takes me out to see the rest of Printers Alley. We go into a place called The Black Poodle. This joint is old shit-kicking Nashville almost being a parody of itself.

The polyester count is way down, this is a place of Stetsons and Johnny Cash suits, a place where sessionmen drink and, at the same time, put themselves on display to the tourists. Somebody tells me Charlie McCoy has just left.

Ronnie Prophet is greeted the way a good old boy should be. We rate a table on a raised dais overlooking the band. The band work on a stage that is actually behind the bar, strip-joint-style. The bartenders work in what looks like a minia-ture orchestra pit in front of them.

The band are getting down and getting funky. They have a 20-stone pedal-steel player. Prophet tells me his name – Joe Vest – adding that he's renowned round town for both his pickin' and his eatin'.

The band are fronted by a diminutive lady with a blond pageboy haircut and tits like Dolly Parton's. What she lacks in size she makes up for in energy. She is squeezed into a short, tight, buckskin Minnie Ha-Ha outfit, all beads and fringes.

The 'Pickers Welcome' sign is hung from the bandstand with a vengeance. A brilliant but anonymous harp player gets up. Back at the table I'm being introduced to a series of cowboys. I seem to be shaking hands with half the club.

'From England, huh?'

'That's right.'

'Hear things are pretty bad over there right now?'

'The money's all gone and it ain't rained since March.'

'That's rough.'

I'm learning to communicate. The only trouble is, the more you communicate the more the Southern hospitality quotient goes up. Everyone who sits down at the table insists I try another brand of whiskey. I have been through Beam, Daniels, Old Crow, Old Forester, Old Granddad, Wild Turkey and Rebel Yell. Rebel Yell tastes like petrol and burns your gums.

Ronnie Prophet, after a little persuasion, has got up on stage and is doing his act all over again. For this crowd, the jokes are a whole lot raunchier than they were in his own place. The lady from the band comes and sits at my table. I think someone's told her that I'm an English writer who might help her career. She talks. I try to answer. It's impossible. I'm too tired and drunk to know whether I'm drunk or tired. The waitress (she's in a short black dress and fishnet stockings) brings me yet another drink.

Faron Young comes into the place. I'm introduced to him. There's a lot of country hee-haw about how his first name's the same as my last and 'Goddamn, they're spelled different.'

After a lot of repartee and backchat, Faron gets on stage and sings. From where I am, the night has taken on an unreal dreamlike quality. There's a black wrought-iron rail beside the table. I find my hand is holding on to it for dear life. If I should let go, I know I'll float clear away over the heads of the crowd.

I'm surrounded by cowboys. It's my last chance. Of what, I'm not sure. I beckon to the waitress.

'You have any Remy Martin?'

She holds a conference with the bartender. He dusts off a neglected brandy bottle. She brings back Remys all round. It's the first time I've been allowed to spend money all night. The cowboys are mildly suspicious. They look, sniff, taste, swallow.

'This here drinkin' brandy's okay by me.'

I think I've made friends.

Prophet gives me a ride back to the hotel in a small black star-ship that passes for a car. It has automatic roof, seats, windows, stereo, and more softly-lit green dials than a 747.

'You should come over the house and eat dinner, y'hear?'

I fall into my hotel bed. The bed is as wide as it's long. I'm on my own. Maybe these are the roots of all that country angst.

I'm back in the open top MG with the man from CBS. His name is Jim Kemp. He is telling me that the biggest industries in Nashville are Bible printing, insurance, country music and distilling whisky. We're on our way to the country home of Lynn Anderson.

Lynn Anderson's main claim to fame in the outside world is the single 'I Never Promised You A Rose Garden'. She has, however, had a string of other hits that never saw the light of day outside the country charts. She came up in Nashville at almost the same time as Dolly Parton, Tammy Wynette and Loretta Lynn. Where the first two have emerged in the world of general entertainment, Lynn Anderson has stayed strictly country.

The drive to her home takes half an hour. It's through the lush green vegetation of the Tennessee hills. The freeway dwindles down to a two-lane blacktop and finally an impossible switchback of a dirt road.

We swing through the gates and two huge snarling dogs hurl themselves at the car. We've already been warned about the dogs. They are attack-trained. These isolated expensive homes in the hills apparently suffer from prowlers. Tammy Wynette's house has already been robbed, vandalised and set fire to. The two of us sit perfectly still as the dogs snap around the car. We don't move a muscle. I'm praying that they don't jump over the windshield.

A lady comes out of the house. She turns out to be Lynn Anderson's secretary-cum-home-help. At a word from her, the dogs become tail-wagging house pets.

We're conducted inside. The house is nothing like I expected. On her publicity pictures, Lynn Anderson is the archetypal rhinestone cowgirl in Nudie outfit and Stetson. There's none of this tasteless gaudiness about the huge living room. It is furnished with European antiques, there are modern original oils on the walls, and dozens of horse show trophies. Breeding Tennessee quarter horses is Lynn Anderson's main interest, after music.

Lynn herself was different to what I might have expected. No Stetson, no fringes, no rhinestones. In fact she was wearing blue jeans and a T-shirt. Her blonde hair was scraped back. She looked like an efficient, affluent housewife on the Mary Tyler Moore pattern. With her is her five-year-old daughter, who sits and listens through most of the interview.

We're given Cokes all round. The conversation starts with the stereotype of Nashville and country music.

It seems that the rest of the world has an image of Nashville being entirely populated by cocktail waitresses and truck drivers. This cracks Lynn up.

'Isn't it?'

Lynn explains how country music has really only started to break out of its narrow confined following. 'It's people like Tammy, Dolly and Bobbie Gentry who took the music across to the pop audience.'

As she talks it becomes clear that Lynn is an intelligent woman with a sharp, alert mind. She's a long way from the gushing, brainless Southern belle that is the popular picture of the female country star.

She goes on to explain just how narrow the C&W field can be. 'A lot of people think the only thing I've ever done is "Rose Garden". In fact, I've had eight number ones in the country charts.'

But country music is spreading. It is one of the fastest growing areas of music. I point out to Lynn that the majority of people who'll be reading the interview have come to country music via rock and roll. They're more likely to be listening to the Eagles than Roy Acuff.

'I think the Eagles, and people like Loggins and Messina, are terrific. The standards of writing and musicianship they're bringing to country music can do nothing but improve the music. Of course, there are a lot of people who'd disagree. There's a strong conservative element in Nashville who think the music should be kept within narrow confines. I suppose I shouldn't be singing it either. I was born up in North Dakota.

'I don't believe in drawing a line and saying, that's country and that isn't. You can't really compare someone like Waylon Jennings with, say, Earl Scruggs, but they're both playing country.'

So what *is* country?

'It was the lyrics that first attracted me to it. They're lyrics that just about everyone can identify with. There's no one, no woman, that is, who can listen to "Stand By Your Man" without knowing what it's about.'

A kind of white working-class Southern music?

'You could say that.'

The word 'white' brings us to the first difficult subject, the race situation in the South. As I'm asking about it, I wonder if I've gone in too deep too soon. I don't want to be bounced out of the trip's very first interview. Lynn, however, is quite willing to talk about it. I ask just how much the traditional redneck racist is really a thing of the past.

'You have to realise that, until really quite recently, it was socially acceptable to be a racist. It was part of the South's history, part of its aura. Now it's no longer being flashed up on the TV screen that it's chic to be a racist, things are starting to change. People are beginning to realise which way they should go.

'A lot of negative feelings are being swept under the carpet. They still exist, only they're now being hidden. Frankly, there's a lot of people about with some very animalistic feelings. Racism provided a very easy vent for their frustrations.'

Lynn grinned. 'It'll be interesting to see who they kick in the teeth next year.'

Having jumped straight in on one delicate area, I decided that the only thing to do is to trample on to another one.

Doesn't country music sell a very conservative, conformist stereotype to its audience? Lynn moves in on this one kind of obliquely.

'People want simple stereotypes.'

Country music as the great soap opera in the key of G?

'What can get difficult is that they expect the artists' offstage life to be like the characters in their songs. Sometime it can get really uncomfortable. They want a Tammy to be standing by her man in real life. If a girl's singing truck-driving cheating songs, everyone assumes she's an easy pick-up.'

This isn't, however, quite what I was getting at. Wasn't country's stock-in-trade of family, country, God and apple pie just a mite restricting to the spirit of '76?

'I got to confess that I don't sing those kind of songs. I sing pretty vanilla lyrics. I think I'd probably rather have it that way. Any entertainer seems to have an amazing power over the people. People really do believe what you say. Presidential candidates realise this, and ad men realise this. That's why our present presidential candidates were so busy wooing . . . Robert Redford.

'I got in a bind with politics. During the last election I was asked to do some things for a candidate. I told them no. I didn't want to lend my name or my image to something I don't really understand, or want to. They went ahead and did it anyway, without my permission.'

Would you like to say who they were?

'It was the Democratic Party.' It's all starting to sound too much like the Altman movie.

What did you do about it?

Lynn laughs. 'I went out and did some things for the other guys, the Republicans. The whole incident got me thinking very seriously about what I said on stage. If the White House is aware of that kind of power, it's something you have to be very careful about.

'I think that's the trouble with politics today. It's all become entertainment. Running the country hardly comes into it. The guy who wins is the one who conducts the best circus. Did you see the drawing in the *National Lampoon* of Charley Pride putting on blackface?'

This pulls us neatly out of politics, and with some skill Lynn steers the conversation into a more conventional interview. A lot of facts emerge. Lynn Anderson's mother was a songwriter and Lynn, who had done some back-up work on Mom's demos, was offered a recording contract while majoring in journalism at college. She is married to Glyn Sutton, who also produces and writes for Tammy Wynette.

'Glyn would come home with new songs, songs like "I Don't Want To Play House" and I'd say, can I have that, and he'd tell me no, that one's for Tammy.'

We begin to drift into more serious waters. This time, it's the position of women in the world of country music. The question of sex and the exploitation of sex naturally rears its ugly head. It's natural in any conversation about the role of women in entertainment. The trouble is, you can't just come out and ask this pleasant, cultured lady, 'How much dick does the average lady singer have to manipulate in order to get on in Nashville?' Instead I hedge around the point.

The legends, and more recently the movie *Nashville*, suggest that for a girl to make it in Nashville is more a matter of whom you know and whom you sleep with than what you can do.

'You mean the casting couch?'

That's right.

Lynn doesn't object to the question, but she makes one thing quite clear. 'I was never introduced to anything like that. Of course you hear rumours, rotten stories, but I ignore anything I don't know for sure is true. I may have been sheltered. I always had people to help me, first my mother, then my husband.

'I think the kind of ladies who audition on the casting couch don't really have anything else to offer. I don't think any worthwhile producer would want a girl with talent to do anything but sign her name on a contract. Women have as much to offer as men. I don't think a producer or manager would jeopardise that by pushing for something more.

'I get asked this question quite a lot on the road. Mama with her little girl by the hand wants to know, should I take my child to Nashville? I always tell them, send a tape, there are always people willing to take advantage. It's not just sexually, but also on the financial end. It's not just in the music business. There are people willing to take advantage in the gas station business or in the grocery business. Every business has its manipulators and its pushers.'

From Lynn Anderson's country retreat we head back into Nashville and make for Music Square. The early afternoon temperature is in the 90s, and the air-conditioned record company offices are a glacial haven.

Music Square is modern efficiency. Slab-sided concrete buildings contain people who talk about product, potential and shipping units. The main thing that tells you they're selling country music and not computers is that they still have cowboy boots under their neatly pressed Levi's. Although even *that* is hardly a sign. In Nashville it's possible that even computer salesmen wear cowboy boots.

My pre-packaged afternoon consists of a tour of some of the studios. This is due to start around three o'clock and it's only 1.45. I have just over an hour to kill.

On the corner of Music Square is the new building, a modern concrete ranch house that houses the Country Music Hall of Fame. I wander over there through the heat. I'm about the only person walking on a street where cars pass in a constant stream.

Outside the Hall of Fame, tour buses are unloading their mainly geriatric cargoes of tourists. I'm suddenly caught in a surging crowd of blue hair, double knit, polyester casual senior citizens. I fight down panic and make a run for the desk marked Information. I ask for the PR person, who conducts me inside. This way I don't have to join the line of pushing, shoving old folks.

The Country Music Hall of Fame is something of a disappointment. It mainly consists of glass cases full of hats, boots, instruments and other bits and pieces belonging to country stars who've been dead so long that only the senior citizens have ever heard of them.

The place is only half built and the few exhibits they currently have on show are tastefully arranged so they lead you straight to the souvenir shop. Here you can buy a guitar-shaped version of just about any common household object.

Artefacts of Jimmie Rodgers and Hank Williams are mildly interesting, and so is some of the antique recording equipment. It's pretty easy to keep moving, though. Something in the guitar exhibit stops me dead in my tracks.

Standing in a case is a Martin D-18. The serial number is 80221. Stick-on gold plastic letters, the kind you can buy in Woolworth's, spell out E VIS. The L has at some point in time dropped off. A card by the guitar informs me that it was 'a guitar used by Elvis on his early tours and Sun Records recordings. The back is scored with deep scratches. They have obviously been made by Presley's belt buckle.'

I stand looking at the guitar for quite a while. I know it qualifies as a Unique Experience, but I'm not quite sure what to do with it. I go to the bar next door to think about it.

PART TWO

The Earl Scruggs Revue is recording in CBS studio B. For those who don't already know, ol' Earl's Revue consists of his three sons Gary, Randy and Steve, plus Jody Maphis and Jim Murphy. He seems to have acted on the maxim: If you can't find the perfect band you can always breed it – given time.

They are working on an uptempo track called 'Tall Texas Woman', a rocking saga of one of those well-known demonic

Southern women who can turn a man into a shadow of his former self. They are such a common legend, and yet so impossible to meet, that they've got to rank with Bigfoot or the Yeti.

Although the song is strong on whiskey-drinkin' and good times, there isn't too much of that going on during the session. Recording in Nashville is a serious business. In fact, it's more like a prayer meeting than a London session.

Chairs are pulled up in a tight circle. Everyone sits very relaxed, legs folded, backs to their amps, instruments cradled on their knees. Only the drummer is isolated in his own baffled-off box. Earl relights his pipe between takes.

Earl is very slow-moving. I'm kind of surprised. A year ago, when the Revue was playing the Starwood and the likes of Alvin Lee and Roger McGuinn were getting up to jam, Earl had looked more than sprightly for a guy with grown-up sons. This time he seems stiff and stooped. Later someone tells me that he was only just recovering from a serious crack-up in his private plane.

At the best of times, a journalist at a recording session, unless it's a band he knows really well, is a definite spare part. Although Earl has given me an affable welcome, the session is so quietly intense that it's like intruding on a family's serious Sunday afternoon.

After about a half-hour, I split. And on the way out, someone tells me that this is the studio where *Blonde On Blonde* was recorded. I'm hit on the head by another Unique Experience. I've just been lolling around on hallowed ground. The fan that lurks within is close to boiling point.

Back in the heat again, I walk the single block from CBS to RCA and meet up with Paul Randall, their head of publicity. He takes me down to the oldest studio. Ronnie Milsap is in there, rehearsing for a live album he's due to record at the Opryland Auditorium the next day.

As we go into the studio, I'm zapped by yet another U.E. This is the studio where Elvis Presley recorded things like

'Don't Be Cruel' and 'Hound Dog'. It's almost more than the sublimated fan can stand. It threatens to kick its way out and terminally blow my cool.

The Milsap session is much more what you'd expect from a Nashville session. The small studio is packed with people. There is Milsap entrenched behind a Bechstein grand. The guitar player and bassman are penned off by sound baffles. The drummer is contained in a dinky little sound booth, tarted up to look like a fake log cabin. Over on the far side of the round studio are three back-up singers nearing middle age. In another corner are two fiddle players. Jammed in the rest of the space are a pedal steel player and a guy playing vibes.

I later discover that he is the legendary Charlie McCoy. McCoy worked on *Highway 61* (the guitar on 'Desolation Row'), *Blonde on Blonde* and just about everything Elvis Presley has done in the last eight years.

There are a lot of Stetsons in evidence, and the studio is decorated with glue-on western decor. It's like a Ponderosa steak house, the roadside eatery chain owned by old man Cartwright from *Bonanza*.

Ronnie Milsap's drummer is black – the first and the last black musician I see working in Nashville.

The control room is crowded, not only by engineers and tape ops but by a number of clean-cut young men in executive casuals. They are avidly watching the session. One is the producer, I can't figure out the function of the rest of them.

Both here and at the Earl Scruggs session, I notice that the producer plays a much more autocratic role than anywhere I've ever been before. He calls all the shots and seems a virtual dictator. Later, Charlie Daniels is to explain more about this uniquely Nashville system.

From the Milsap session, we go down into the sub-basement. This is the RCA deluxe, numero uno studio. No cowboy tack here. This is the grounded-starship-style studio that I'm used to. Here Chet Atkins is doing a mix.

If Chet Atkins isn't the king of Nashville, he must certainly be the Talleyrand of Music City, USA. He is white-haired, exquisitely middle-aged and exudes dignity like lesser mortals exude sweat. I'm introduced to him. His handshake is courtly. I have to admit: in the presence of this country aristocrat I am overawed.

Chet doesn't feel like talking. He has work to do. His luxury, custom-built Gretsch is hooked into the board by direct injection. He is adding discreet single notes to an otherwise finished cut. Beside him, a short balding guy of about the same age is underlaying discreet tones with a mini synthesiser. The two musicians and the engineer work with the ease of grand masters who have been together for maybe a score of years.

All this effort is going into a bouncy lament by a chick singer. I imagine it is destined for a fast climb on the country charts. Why else should she be getting the best?

Paul Randall drives me back to the hotel. I go up to my room with every intention of going out and exploring the city on my own. I call room service and have a meal sent up, then I step into the shower. I turn on the TV and sit on the bed to dry my hair, while a middle-aged black guy who's been holding four people hostage in an office building in Cleveland kills himself in tight close-up on *Eyewitness News*. Shortly afterwards the jetlag gets me and I pass out. I have only been in Nashville for 24 hours.

I wake up about 9:30. The Republican convention is in full cry on the TV. The Reagan delegates are howling and blowing their noisemakers. The close-ups of political mutants covered in badges, funny hats and rosettes are almost as horrific as the earlier suicide. I drift off to sleep again.

The next time I wake up it's 3 a.m. *Mary Hartman, Mary Hartman* is on. This is the soap opera to end soap operas. Mary has retired to bed with a nervous breakdown. Her friends and neighbours, oblivious to Mary's condition, keep dropping in to tell her their troubles. Mary, unable to cope, keeps eating Valium and wondering how many it takes to overdose.

Suddenly it's eight o'clock and William F. Buckley Jr. and J.K. Galbraith are debating the convention. I decide to get up and make an early start. Even taking time over breakfast, the start is still two hours too early. I have to sit through an hour of *Bugs Bunny, Sesame Street* and *The Dinah Shore Show* before Paul Randall picks me up to take me out to Opryland.

Declaring Opryland open was one of Richard Nixon's last public duties before he resigned. As a PR exercise for Nixon, Opryland was a disaster. Roy Acuff handed him a yo-yo. Nixon was unable to get it to come back up the string even once. Who needs a president who can't even work a yo-yo? Afterwards he played the piano, proving beyond doubt that he was a better yo-yo player than a pianist.

For Nashville, Opryland has been an unqualified success. It's a Disneyland-style amusement park with an overall country music theme that draws in millions of tourists every year. The large, acoustically superb auditorium has replaced the old cramped downtown Opry house.

Ronnie Milsap's live recording is set for lunchtime. Even at that early hour there are enough visitors to Opryland to fill the 4,000-seat hall. They are ushered to their seats by a team of Dolly Parton look-alikes in short orange uniforms, and watched over by the somewhat sinister Opryland police in white Stetsons and dark grey cop suits. I make a mental note not to lose my backstage pass. I don't want to hassle with these guys.

Before Ronnie Milsap even gets on the stage, a very professional M.C. rehearses the audience to get the required level of applause.

The curtains open, and there are the same people I saw at the rehearsal yesterday. Only now they're decked out in their very best spangled suits.

The Milsap show is MOR country with a vengeance. There are the usual ingredients: cheating ballads, heartbreak ballads and the odd uptempo number. After each song the crowd go wild. I am frankly not impressed.

During a break, Milsap gets out from behind the piano and comes to the front of the stage. He makes a lot of lame jokes about falling into the pit. Is he telling us he's drunk or something? It's only then that the penny drops. He's blind. That's why he wears black wraparound shades and his personal roadie hangs on to his arm all the time.

There's something slightly distasteful about the blind schtick.

They finish up with, of all things, 'Honky Tonk Women'. The Stones turn a parody of MOR country into a rock and roll classic. Milsap turns it right back into MOR country again. I'm not sorry that it's time to go.

Charlie Daniels opens a can of Pabst Blue Ribbon. 'We tied one on last night. We was watchin' the convention.'

One of the people round the table laughs.

'Watching the farce.' Charlie grins. 'Yeah, watching the farce.'

The Pabst seems like a tonic to Charlie, but then again, Charlie Daniels is the kind of individual who looks at home with a beer in his hand. Built like a Mack truck, Charlie could just as easily be straddling a chopped-down Harley Davidson Duoglide or driving Texas longhorns up the Chissum Trail.

From all this you'll probably realise that Charlie Daniels definitely drops into the outlaw category. It's not just his Stetson, turquoise jewellery and funky ranch hand clothes. Charlie has gone his own way and, in consequence, had his ups and downs with the country establishment.

The setting for the conversation is hardly outlaw, however. We're sitting on the patio of a luxury reproduction ranch house, looking down at the swimming pool. It's the same place where the elderly country singer had the party for Elliott Gould in the *Nashville* movie. Charlie has rented it as a rehearsal studio.

So what problems has Charlie had with the Nashville music business?

'I guess I just don't play the same kind of music. I'm not a

Nashville musician. We're not a country band. It's got a country base but we play R&B and we play rock and roll.'

Did Charlie feel that Nashville resisted change?

'Yeah, I think that's true. It's all the same people doing it. It kind of makes for a oneness. I think a lot of it's the producers. They run things in Nashville. This is the last place where they've got record company staff producers. It makes for a Tin Pan Alley situation.'

I thought back to the authoritarian executive figures I had seen producing the sessions the previous day.

You think this kills off creativity?

'I think it runs off creativity. The music business is a lot more than the people in Nashville. Hell, let everyone pick.'

One of Charlie's first claims to fame was doing sessions for Dylan in Nashville. He worked on *Nashville Skyline*, *Self Portrait* and *New Morning*.

'I was supposed to do just one session, but Bob Johnston and Dylan liked it and I stayed on to do all of them.'

So what was it like working with Dylan?

'I noticed that people from Britain really hold Dylan in awe, much more than we even do here in America. Hell, he's just a man like anyone else. He was a perfect gentleman to work with. I really enjoyed those sessions. They were loose, I mean, there was a very loose attitude. Although we really worked hard. The *Nashville Skyline* album was recorded really quickly. I think there were 18 sessions booked, and we finished in six.'

It emerges that the country standards on *Self Portrait* were recorded at the same sessions as *Nashville Skyline*. How did Nashville react to Dylan's, to say the least, unique versions of these hillbilly classics? Charlie grins.

'When they got released, a bunch of people made money out of it. Money can change people's minds about most things.'

Daniels' relationship with Bob Johnston was a long and productive one. With Johnson producing, Charlie has worked with, among others, Al Kooper, Leonard Cohen and Marty Robbins. He has also had one of his tunes, 'It Hurts Me', picked by Elvis Presley for a single.

'That kept me in change for a while, although the money did seem to get whittled down a bit before it got to me.'

From session work Charlie has moved on to taking his band out on the road.

'We're working about 250 days in the year.'

Doesn't that drive you crazy?

'Hell, no. The only thing drives me crazy is being away from my wife and boy. I hate these prissy mothers who say, 'Oh god, I can't stand being on the road, I can't stand planes.' I say, put that mother in a field and let him follow a mule's tail, pushing a plough, for three, four, five hours, or load hay, or work in a factory. Then put him on the road and see how he likes it.'

Charlie warms to a subject that is obviously close to his heart.

'The reason people go crazy on the road is because they drink too much liquor and take too many drugs and don't get enough sleep. The road's easy now. I was on the road when it was really hard. I ain't got no sympathy for people who don't want to work. That's bullshit.

'I hear these pussy-mouthed musicians talking about identity crises. I guess I've never got educated enough to have an identity crisis.'

There's just no way you can help liking Charlie Daniels. Right now he is in Nashville recording a sequel to his *Saddle Tramp* album. The title is *High Lonesome*.

With the band's schedule, doesn't recording constitute something of a rest?

'Yes and no. It's a holiday in so far as everyone gets to go home and see mom and the baby. But we work pretty hard. We work maybe three hours, come out here, take a break and have a beer and then get back to it.

After a digression into comparing western movies, we get

away from Charlie Daniels and on to the South in general. I
ask him what happened to the old nigger-lynching, hippie-
baiting redneck image. Charlie bursts out laughing.

'You been listening to Yankees. The movie *Easy Rider*
came out and just about scared everyone to death.'

So it was a myth?

'Hell, no. I lived all my life in the South. I can remember the
Jim Crow laws, the back of the bus. I thought that was the
way things were supposed to be. I never knew any different.

'When they passed the equal rights law, it made me mad. I
really thought black people were inferior to me. That was the
way I was brought up and I didn't know any better. It's only
when a man gets up and starts thinking for himself that he
sees things are different.'

What really changed things in the South?

'Communication, television, people travelling. Anything
that happens in the world, you get to hear about it in two
hours. With all that going on, you can't hold on to your
prejudices.

'The unions got the wages. Of course, the unions ain't
perfect, but where once people used to work their asses off to
make a living, now they can travel and see things as they
really are.'

The South is obviously another subject close to Charlie's
heart. The South is what's happening. The South and the
West are where the growth is going on. It's both – the
economy and the population. There's a steady drain of people
drifting south. It's warm and you can breathe the air.

'Old line politicians used to ignore the South, and now the
next president will be from Georgia. Everyone's going to have
to admit that we don't have horns, we don't want to kill all
the niggers, and we don't burn down synagogues.'

Charlie Daniels is one of the people whom Jimmy Carter
lists as being among his rock and roll friends. Charlie is
obviously a staunch supporter.

'What do people think of Carter over in Britain?'

'He's had a good press. People aren't half as nervous as they were when Nixon was elected. I was scared when they gave that dingbat the button to play with.'

There's another of Charlie's earthshaking chuckles. 'We were pretty damn nervous over here, I can tell you. You can tell everyone in Britain they don't have to worry about Jimmy Carter. He's got it covered.'

The political lecture gets side-tracked into how the USA ought to make friends with Cuba so Charlie can get some good cigars for a change.

'I mean, who cares if Fidel Castro makes a little money?'

Back at the hotel, I've got the TV on again. The lead news item is about Loretta Lynn. The second is about a local hero, Joe Gilliam, who was busted for cocaine and a gun. Because he copped a plea, the cocaine was changed to marijuana and the gun forgotten.

In between items are two fascinating commercials. One is the C.W. McCall Kearns Bread ad that was the inspiration for 'Convoy'. The other is an anti-litter spot that has the slogan 'There ain't no lower class than Tennessee trash.'

I go out on the town at night. This time it's an off duty trip with Jim Kemp from CBS. After a magnificent steak and a bottle of Beaujolais that tastes like Ribena, we start the Nashville tour, and that means a tour of the bars.

We make a start on South Broadway. This is decayed inner city. South Broadway was once the hub of the Nashville music industry, before it moved to the air-conditioned concrete boxes out on Music Square. Now it's run down, seedy and lethargic, surviving on the tail end tourist viewing the corpse of better days.

Tootsie's Orchid Lounge is a place of legend. In the old days it was the first place that the fabled kid, getting off the Greyhound bus with his guitar, headed for. Now the only people in there are a couple of glum truckers hunched over the bar and a guy in a cowboy hat playing pinball.

Across the street is Ernest Tubb's record store. There isn't all that much life there, except on a Friday night. That's when there's the long-running *Midnight Jamboree* broadcast that goes out live on radio station WSM. This is a long-standing Nashville tradition that attracts stars ranging from Willie Nelson to Bill Munroe.

Saturday also cooks in its own way. That's when they stage *WNAH Music City Gospel Time*. In Nashville, religion is never very far away.

For that matter, booze isn't very far away either. Tonight it seems to be 100% proof Wild Turkey that's being set up in front of me. It looks as though the evening is building up to be another Pearl Harbor for my liver.

We walk down the street and past a place called The Safari. In their window they have a display of outrageous, rhinestone-studded jumpsuits, supposedly made for Elvis Presley.

As I'm walking away, a lime-green mid-'60s Chevy pulls up beside me. A black guy in dark glasses leans out. Inside, behind the tinted windows, are three more brothers. The first brother wants to know if I'd like to buy a diamond ring for 20 dollars. When I tell him that I don't, he starts to hustle me for a couple of bucks for gas.

I decide not to pull out my wallet and head for the car at a very fast saunter. As we're pulling away, an N.P.D. car makes a U turn with the perfect *Police Story* four-wheel skid. The brothers burn rubber in the opposite direction.

We leave the South Broadway area and head for the Church Square neighbourhood. This is the current entertainment spot, without the hustlers and winos we found on Broadway. Here the drunks have credit cards and drive Mustangs.

We hit a number of bars. The clientele seem surprisingly young. There is a fair sprinkling of teenagers who must be using phony IDs in order to drink. The recorded music is the usual Eagles/disco mixture that you could just as easily find in Amsterdam or Cleveland.

We finally wind up in the Exit Inn watching Doc Watson.

The Wild Turkey is reaching out for my brain, and I have to get a firm grip to take in Watson's immaculate picking.

They've started promising me stars. So far I've been around and looked at Nashville going about its daily doings, and talked to some of the eminent, but I have yet to come in actual contact with a genuine living legend.

This causes the various press offices with whom I'm dealing a number of headaches. Living legends are not only hard to come by, but when they reach that level they seem to shun the public gaze with the same tenacity as the Loch Ness monster. The first few phone calls make this very clear.

Johnny Cash is out of town working in L.A. on his Sunday night TV special that has replaced the Cher show in the prime CBS family entertainment slot. Even if he was in town he'd be unlikely to talk.

George Jones is out of town, as is Porter Wagoner. Waylon Jennings categorically doesn't give interviews. Neither does Willie Nelson.

Tammy Wynette likes to give interviews, but right at this moment she has some problems of her own. The first is that she's been in and out of hospital with an infection of the inner ear, brought on by bronchitis. The second is that she is in the middle of what is to her short-lived marriage with real estate developer Michael Tomlin. It doesn't appear that Tammy will be able to manage a press interview.

My best bet seems to be Dolly Parton. She is quite happy to talk to me. The only problem is, when. Nobody is very clear about that. It'll be when Dolly decides to 'drop by'.

This involves me in a lot of hanging about, particularly around the RCA building. It's not entirely fruitless. I do meet a number of other happenings Nashville people. There's Dickey Lee, who reminisces about working with Sam Phillip's Sun label shortly after Presley, Cash and Jerry Lee Lewis had moved on to better things.

Dickey Lee is an established Nashville songwriter. His big breakthrough was 'I Saw Linda Yesterday'. Another million seller was the doom-laden 'Patches'. One of his songs is at present scheduled as Elvis Presley's next single.

And now Dolly Parton.

'If you think of Dolly Parton you think of the big hairdos, the rhinestones, the glitter, the over-exaggerated this, the over-exaggerated that, but at least when you think of me, you get a *picture* of me.'

Thus spake Dolly, giving the picture of herself better than any introductory paragraph. Dolly is a star and she knows it. Not only does she know it, but she loves it. When you're used to so much world-weary rock and roll angst, she positively lights up the room with the childlike delight she seems to take in herself, her success, the big-breasted bundle of dynamite image.

'I'm like a cartoon character that everyone can recognise.'

Doesn't that bother you sometimes?

'No, I love it.'

Talking to Dolly is almost like riding the rapids. She uses fifteen words where one would do. She's usually one, if not two or three jumps ahead of you. She also exudes at least ten times the raw energy given off by the average blood-spitting, fire-breathing rock and roll axeman.

'I love the glitter and the rhinestones and all of that. The new underground people in country music, they wear the patches, the faded denim. I wore that when I was a kid. I had nothing else then. I had eleven brothers and sisters and we were as poor as you can be and live to tell about it, so now I like the bright clothes and the makeup and all.

'Emmylou Harris is a dear friend. She dresses real plain, in denim and all, and she looks really good in it. I guess we just switched. I'm just a gypsy who likes shiny things. I think Emmylou had more when she was a kid. I'm just like a child dressing up in her mother's clothes.

'I'm not made up where it counts, though. I don't have no rhinestones in my soul.'

Dolly's childhood figures large in her conversation. She comes from a huge family who attempted to eke out a living in the mountains of East Tennessee. This was the archetypal hillbilly world of moonshine, farming, fundamental religion and abject poverty. This background, plus the act of breaking out of it, seems to have given her a strength and resilience that don't come to many. It's also given her an appreciation of success that is almost unique.

'You have to have the luxury of hard times to appreciate the good times.'

The breakaway from the hard times came in 1964 (Dolly still pronounces it 'nineteen and sixty four') when she, in the company of her uncle, came to Nashville looking to make a career in music.

'We were poor folks with nothing but a lot of dreams. We knocked on just about every door on Music Row until someone took notice of us.'

She was originally signed to a songwriting deal, and then a recording contract. In 1967 she hitched up with Porter Wagoner as a traditional country duo, and then eventually went out on her own. This was the time of the big breakthrough by the women in Nashville.

'Patsy Cline and Kitty Wells, they were really the first. They pioneered the way for me and Tammy and Loretta. People used to think that women should stay home, have babies and sing in church or around the house. Then a few brave women got brave enough to try something. They proved to everyone that they could hack it just like the men.'

Songwriting seems almost as important to Dolly as her singing. She is unashamedly proud of her writing ability.

'I think writing helped me a lot in Britain. Emmylou recorded some of my songs and told people about me. I don't think it was until I came over to Wembley that people in Britain started to think of me as a performer.'

If you wanted to be unkind you could say that Dolly is a walking cliché. Even her street clothes are lime-green and skin-tight. The confectionary hairdo is immaculate and her makeup looks as though it was done by Rembrandt.

The thing is that you'd never want to be unkind to Dolly Parton. She just gushes love. It's almost indiscriminate. You get the impression that she just loves doggies, kitties, folks, God and America. In anyone else it would be cloying to the point of suffocation, but there's so much obvious strength in her character that you can't help liking her.

Her conversation constantly comes back to her poor white farm-girl roots. These roots are a mixture of a huge, close family, simple religion and hard times.

'You can't grow a beautiful flower if you don't have strong sound roots.'

Her upbringing seems to have toughened her, and yet done it without leaving scars. Even now she's a star she seems to have a knack of holding on to that hillbilly upbringing.

'I think I keep in touch because of the way I was raised. If I see a working man, I think of my daddy. If I see a woman struggling to bring up a bunch of kids on nothing, I think of my mama. All of this is the experience and feeling I put into my songs. If I see kids I think of my brothers or my sisters or myself.

'I don't think I'll ever change. I know what it is to be without, and now I've got something, not to share it or to be humble about it, I'd be a fool.

'Nobody's that big they can't be brought down. I get down sometimes, but I sure get up again pretty quick. I might bend; but I know I'm never going to break.'

The thoughts of Dolly come in rapid-fire homilies a lot of the time. Like Charlie Daniels, she subscribes to the idea of 'not having enough education to have an identity crisis.'

'I've got enough good common sense to know what I don't know.'

She keeps returning to the Bible, love, family and positive thinking.

'A lot of people would do a lot more if they could get the negative out of their minds for long enough.'

Dolly, however, is also a realist.

'Sure, we all love sex and men, or women, or what your kick is.'

This led us squarely into the truth about the Nashville casting couch. Dolly is the frankest lady on the subject that I've met on the whole trip.

'You'd be amazed at the people here who've had to do that kind of thing in order to get started. I have to say that I didn't. I had the talent and I made it on that. I didn't have to sell my body. When I got to that point I'd already started and I didn't have to make that decision.

'I truthfully don't know what I would have done if I'd been faced with it. I love music more than anything. I don't know how much it meant to me.

'When you tell the folks at home you're going out to make it in the music industry, you can't go back. You can't go home and say you failed. You can get so far down you grab at anything.

'There's a lot of people who are something today who went that route. The saddest thing is the people who went that route and still didn't make it.'

No conversation with Dolly Parton can end on a down note, though. She apologises that she has to stop talking because she's got a vocal session later in the day.

'I could go on talking for ever. I have so much energy. I think I'd make it at anything I did. If I had to work in a factory I'd be the best worker there. If I was in a restaurant I'd end up head waiter. I can be happy anywhere.

'People have got to learn the difference between success and being successful, and failing and being a failure.'

Someone signed me on for the bus tour of Nashville. At 8 a.m. on a Saturday morning, I hate them. The tour operator is yet another bouncing, energetic Nashville lady. At 8.15 I'm drinking orange juice and coffee, chain smoking and feeling sick. At 8.30 I'm on the bus.

It borders on the horrific. For a start, I'm the only person on the bus under 60. Because of a Nashville city ordinance, you can't smoke on buses. I'm seated next to a pleasant enough old gentleman, but communication is limited. I know I wanted to absorb the whole thing, but this is going too far. I want to go back to bed, but it's too late. The tour bus is already rolling.

The other occupants of the bus are on a senior citizens' lightning, cut price, 36-hour excursion from Akron, Ohio. They peer avidly out of the windows as we drive slowly through the down town area. Bleak-looking workers are waiting at bus stops.

We pass the original Grand Ol' Opry House. A drunk is stretched out on the sidewalk. We go down South Broadway, pass the world's largest Bible warehouse and then head out into the lush green suburbs.

This is the homes-of-the-stars part of the trip. Lines of synthetic *Gone with the Wind* mansions, each in its neatly manicured four or five acres. The guide's commentary was bright and jolly, but after a while I ceased either to know or care which house belonged to Marty, Jimmy or Tammy. All I wanted was a drink and a cigarette.

I at least got the cigarette at the House Of Cash. The House Of Cash is not in fact Johnny Cash's home, but a combined recording studio and 'Johnny Cash Museum' – the museum part, which is open to the public, is minimal. A few roped off photographs, paintings, Indian relics and gold discs lead you inexorably to the souvenir stand at which you *buy something*. Once you've *bought something*, you get back on the bus.

We circumnavigate the Cash estate. There's a herd of cows. They are all black. We're informed by the guide that, in keeping with his image, these are the only kind of cattle kept by Cash.

We come to the real Johnny Cash residence. It's a split-level built from fake antique stone, in the middle of a cluster of split levels. This is a neat piece of Cash real estate development. It is pretty and overlooks a medium sized lake. Other residents include Cash's mother, Roy Orbison and some successful Nashville businessmen.

The tour guide tells us how, soon after the Cash home was built, before his marriage to June Carter, Cash and Waylon Jennings moved into the empty house. Without even the benefit of furniture, they attempted unsuccessfully to come off booze and speed.

The ultimate destination for the coach tour is Opryland. There the senior citizens will spend their afternoon. I'm not going to share this pleasure. I'm catching a 6:30 plane to Los Angeles. The last attraction before we reach the amusement park is a long distance view of the spot where Jim Reeves' plane went down.

According to the guide, the freeway that we're travelling on wasn't built then. The land was raw forest. It took searchers three days to find the wreckage and the body.

I spend my last afternoon in Nashville just wandering about shopping for souvenirs. I discover a copy of Conway Twitty's greatest hits in Ernest Tubb's record shop. I also buy a lot of T-shirts and a trucker's licence plate that reads 'GOD IS MY CO-PILOT'.

With all this accomplished, I just walk. On an overpass that crosses the main highway, I stop and try to take stock of the jumble of images that have been thrown at me in the last week.

Beneath me is an eight-lane highway. A constant stream of huge semi trucks rumble past. In between them is the smaller fry of cars, campers and pick-ups. They are all moving through. They aren't stopping in Nashville. To the people on the road the city is just another point on the map.

I guess that this is one of the problems about Nashville. It may proclaim itself Music City, USA, but aside from the music, the Bibles and the booze, little else goes on there.

It's not a busy international port like Liverpool, New York or London. Neither is it a sprawling industrial wasteland like Detroit or Chicago. It's a small town, where the only new stimuli or information come from the passing truckers or trains, and farmers coming into town.

It makes for a kind of conservatism, a resistance to change that is one of the less fortunate cores of country music. It's the thing that drives talent to L.A. or Austin.

As you walk round the city, you're conscious that a lot of time is spent dwelling on the past. The tourists come to see the hallowed relics of country music; not its ongoing creative future.

Obviously country has a future, but whether it lies in Nashville or will be scattered through other centres all over America depends on how readily Nashville can take to change. Country music is on the move. The question is, can Nashville move with it?

John Mendelssohn

POISON THE HOOD: NIGGAZ WITH ATTITUDE

unpublished piece for *Playboy*, 1991

In 1991, when I was four and forty, I hooked up with a literary agent who purported to be enthusiastic about my fiction. While she sent my manuscripts out, said she, it would be good if I could provide a couple of nonfiction ideas she might try to sell too, just in case. Remembering the time he nearly tackled me outside the Troubadour to prevent my seeing Laura Nyro perform with a head cold, and mindful of his having just sold his record company to the Japanese for $150 billion or whatever it was, I casually speculated that a David Geffen biography might be fun.

Guess what she sold. I proceeded to spend the next six months phoning everyone who'd ever met the great man, and having him or her hang up on me, often after calling me a woeful so-and-so or worse. The Gefster, you see, hadn't liked the idea of my appointing myself his biographer (years later, he awarded the job to some gormless business writer who's unfit to wash my mouse pad), and had told everyone to stonewall me.

Mr Jerry Heller, once agent to a lot of Geffen-mentored singer-songwriters, was one of the very, very few who defied (or, possibly, hadn't gotten wind of) the edict. I found him very charming and quite the raconteur, and when I gazed into his extraordinary blue eyes I thought I could see my future. Months later, after Geffen had managed to persuade my might-

*have-been publisher not only not to publish my book
about him, which I had no recourse but to base on a
bunch of old magazine articles held together with
chewing gum, dental floss, and a lot of snide jokes,
but also to derogate my considerable skill as a writer in
gossip columns, I remembered how swimmingly Jerry
and I had gotten on, noted that the foulmouthed thugs
he managed had taken to selling tens of millions of
records, as we called them then, and proposed the
piece you're about to read to Playboy, for which I'd
always wanted to write because it pays so well.*

*A funny thing happened. When I phoned my won-
derful new friend Jerry to tell him the wonderful news,
he acted as though he'd just heard the Geffen edict.
No, he wouldn't be speaking to me. But I was damned
if I was going to let the recalcitrance of my principal
source slow me down, not with $45,000 at stake. (I
have added a zero for the sake of hyperbole.) In my
finest hour as a journalist, I tracked down and interviewed a large number of others with axes to grind and
got the story written – and how!*

*Along the way, I met a couple of interesting char-
acters. One of Heller's fellow middle-aged Caucasian
rap impresarios turned out to have been the composer
of the New York pimple-pop classic 'Barbara Ann'.
When one of his artists, a big scary convict type who
called himself Tweety Bird (because he could), turned
out to be a homophobic numbskull, I was amazed to
find myself getting right in his face, at no little personal
risk. He kept demanding if I were gay. I kept insisting
that it was his rampant stupidity, and not my sexuality, that was the issue.*

*The jazz trumpeter Wynton Marsalis has been
quoted as thinking of rap as the modern equivalent
of the minstrel show. It is one of the few things on
which Wyn and I agree. It seems to me that gangsta*

rap is essentially black persons (and the occasional Eminem) pretending to be subhuman for the entertainment of white people. I have no doubt whatever that life in the ghetto is horrific. I question whether those who live in it derive greater succour from the ugly rage of the gangsta rappers than their parents did from the transcendent beauty of the music of Smokey Robinson, say. Five bucks say they don't.

In the end, the piece wasn't published. Playboy had bought the rights to publish an excerpt from Ice T's autobiography. Once they'd done so, they felt all rapped out for a while. Their readership's loss is your gain, and my own.

JM

ON A SPRING EVENING in 1991, the late Eazy-E accepted the invitation of Dr Dre, his fellow member of the notorious 'gangsta' rap group NWA, to come hang with him at a recording studio in Hollywood not far from where their mutual dream had been born.

Eazy was well aware of Dre's growing dissatisfaction with his share of their record company's huge profits, but who could he trust if not the good doctor? Hadn't they clawed their way out of one of the West Coast's most nightmarish ghettos side by side? And since he'd bailed him out of jail way back when, after others had refused, hadn't Eazy made his friend richer than either would have dreamt of ever being only a few years before?

Once at Galaxy Studios, though, Eazy wasn't greeted by Dre, but by three huge guys in black who took him into a dark room and informed him that they were holding his Jewboy manager hostage outside in a van. They tapped lead pipes in their leather-encased palms. They revealed gun bulges under their shirts and produced some documents they wanted him to sign, documents that would release Dre from his contractual obligations to Eazy. They offered him a pen and tapped their lead pipes some more, a little less patiently. But Eazy hadn't prospered selling yay-o on the streets of the CPT (as the gangs called rock cocaine and Compton, respectively) by being easily cowed.

It turned out, though, that they didn't have just his Jewboy manager, but his mama too. And they were going to get his signature on their documents or kill the bitch.

Gimme the damn pen.

Half a decade before, Hollywood had been a long drive, an absolutely endless bus ride, and a world away. But with Reaganomics having wiped out all the youth programs, what better shot at getting out of Compton did a motherfucker have than cutting a rap record and hoping that it made him the new LL Cool J? And so, hearing the ads on KDAY, they swarmed by the carload to a little record pressing plant on Santa Monica Boulevard where, if he liked a fellow's tape, the old white dude proprietor, Don MacMillan, would press 500 12-inch singles for him for only $600. MacMillan would send a couple hundred to his distributors, whose salespeople would take them into stores and radio stations nationwide, and the kid would get $200 or $300 to take back to his neighborhood.

Compared to the South Central Los Angeles environs of his old record company, in which he'd become accustomed to witnessing shootouts on the way to work, his new stomping grounds impressed Don MacMillan as relatively tranquil, its gay teenage runaway hustlers and Hispanic gangs notwithstanding. But to the kids from Compton, the squalid sector of Hollywood in which Macola Records was based must have looked like Shangri-La. In the decades since George Bush lived there briefly as a fresh-out-of-Yale oil-bit salesman in the late '40s, Compton had turned into a war zone. Not an inch of its ten square miles wasn't claimed by at least one of its 40 street gangs; locals observed with a strange sort of pride that if you started running east on Rosecrans from Central, you could get gatted on – shot at – by seven different gangs by the time you reached Atlantic Boulevard less than two miles away. If you reached it.

At the high schools, 300-pound football players allowed skinny freshmen gang members to humiliate them at will, for to fight back would be to dodge bullets on the way home from practice in the afternoon. And that chirping sound wasn't crickets, but the beepers that summoned kids from class to close drug deals. By day, children were cut down by errant Crips, Bloods, and Pirus bullets on their schools' front lawns. And at night, the city really got dangerous, as the crackheads who'd been sold macadamia nuts rolled in Anbesol flew into rages and reached for their own gats.

Don MacMillan was struck by how a lot of the kids who hung out in the lobby of his pressing plant seemed slightly in awe of little Eric Wright, who called himself Eazy-E. Maybe it was that he was so bright. Or maybe it was the breadth of his ambition. As a product of Compton's infamous public school system, he had absolutely no idea where anything was – where San Francisco was, or Seattle – but he still openly aspired to presiding over his own recording empire.

Back in the 'hood, though, Eazy inspired considerably less admiration than in Macola's lobby. While it was known that he'd use his fists if he had to, it was equally well known that his girlfriend Joyce kept him on a very short leash, and wasn't averse to walloping him upside the head with a GI Joe lunchbox if, for instance, he neglected to beep her for too long at a stretch.

It was even more widely known that the reason he seemed always to have money in his socks was that he was a dope man. While a lot of Comptonites viewed drugs in general as a blight, who could come down that hard on an individual kid who retailed a little chronic or stress or even yay-o to make a buck or two? How else was a teenage father supposed to be able to give his girlfriend money to buy his babies food or get decent speakers in his lowered Chevy – by working at motherfucking McDonald's? And if he didn't sell the shit, somebody else surely would. And wasn't it a whole lot better than killing for money, as some boys in the 'hood were known to?

In the spring of 1986, Macola released Eazy's 'Boyz-N-the-Hood', an orgy of gangsta posturing written by a zealously malignant local teenager who called himself Ice Cube. Eazy's performance was almost comically inept – his inflection childish, his rhythm shaky – and at first it seemed as though the record might stiff. Promoting it, MacMillan's men didn't even approach radio at first, but instead hired a few brothers to tape posters up in the ghetto and hand out free cassettes on Crenshaw Boulevard, on which the young studs of South Central liked to drive back and forth glowering on a Saturday night in their six-fours, demonstrating their ability to survive bass levels that would have killed less manly men.

At first, one could buy the record only at the daily Compton Swap Meet in the old Sears building on Long Beach Boulevard, and in none of the big chain stores. But then the white kids of the San Fernando Valley discovered it, and it began to fly out of the Wherehouse in mostly white, suburban Northridge, out of Tower in mostly white, suburban Encino. It took fully eight months before the record finally took off nationally, but when it did, it was to the tune of 200,000 copies sold.

The bad news for Eric being that he had now to perform, the prospect of which scared him shitless. It was one thing to deal yay-o on the streets of Compton, apparently, and a similar one to cow the other boys in the lobby at Macola Records, but quite another to get up on stage in front of people. Seemingly to insulate himself, he assembled a 'posse' that included Andre Young – nicknamed Dr Dre because he idolized the Philadelphia 76ers' Dr J. Formerly one of the most bashful boys in the CPT (if the father of five children by three different girlfriends by age 23), Dre had turned down a drafting job at Northrop Aviation (no damn McDonald's for Dre!) in favor of club disk jockeying.

Converting dope money into turntables, the entrepreneurial Eazy had hired him to DJ at birthday parties for $30 a night. But it was as a member of the World Class Wreckin' Cru that Dre had gained his greatest local notoriety. Suave seducers who rapped seductively over techno music and moved in unison like the Temptations, the Cru posed for their Macola album cover in makeup and much purple, Dre in a white sequined bodysuit and the expression of one suspecting that he might be making a grievous mistake.

Behold, though, how passionately the Cru was loved in even the Spanish-speaking parts of the ghetto. 'One night me and Dre were riding around,' Cru kingpin Lonzo Williams remembers, 'when a Mexican in a Pinto hit the back of my car and broke these bands that hold the muffler on. I jump out talking shit. These ten cats along the wall drinking beer stand up when they see a black guy stepping to an older Mexican guy. Dre's sitting in the car scared shitless.

'When they see his Wreckin' Cru jacket, the Mexicans say, "Hey, man, where'd you get that from?" He says, "I'm Dr Dre, man." I'm in hardcore mini-Tijuana talking shit to drunk Mexicans, and I'm supposed to get my ass whupped. Instead, we have to sit there and drink beer and kick with them for about 20 minutes while they fix my muffler!'

Lonzo, in whose studio Dre's stepfather gave everyone in the Cru's circle karate lessons after Ice Cube was beaten up at Washington High, was like Dre's big brother. 'I bought him a car, which eventually went to the impound because he had a very bad habit of never paying his tickets; at one time he had $500 worth. I bailed him out of jail, but two months later, he had another stack of warrants. Wreckin' Cru wasn't working and money was getting tight; Dre was spending all of his on tennis shoes and motel rooms. So I told him, "Look, I'll go half with somebody, but I can't afford to keep doing this." Which was where Eazy stepped in with his drug money.'

It was Eazy who named his posse NWA, but it was the old white dude Don MacMillan who figured out what the letters stood for. 'I was in a meeting with a bunch of other black guys when he came in and said he wanted NWA on the record. He told me he saw it on a sign – I think it might have been for Northwest Airlines or something – and that it looked real good. I started laughing. He said, "What are you laughing at?" I said, "I figured it meant Niggers With an Attitude." A minute later I thought, "Oh, shit, what have I said?" But they all laughed.'

Realizing in time that everyone stood to come out ahead if his young customers were guided by experienced management, MacMillan invited the participation of another old white dude, a key early patron of white Chicago blues and the overseer-turned-owner of the record company for which MacMillan had worked in South Central. Morey Alexander, the very picture of a cigar-chomping, tsouris-exuding music biz sharpie, in turn phoned the middle-aged Jewish music biz veteran who'd booked the harmonica virtuoso Charlie Musselwhite for him thousands of years before, back near the beginning of both their careers.

Jerry Heller had been Creedence Clearwater Revival's agent in the late '60s, but hadn't gotten rich until the early '70s, when he represented most of David Geffen's biggest singer-songwriters. He helped launch Elton John in America and booked the tours that established Pink Floyd, drank prodigious amounts of cognac, snorted prodigious amounts of blow, and seduced prodigious numbers of starlets. By decade's end, he'd lost his credibility after representing a bunch of L.A. skinny tie acts on which everyone lost his shirt. By and by, the poor devil had resigned himself 'to being an also-ran the rest of my life, to living in a condo and making $200,000 a year.' Which rankled painfully, since 'I'm actually one of the brightest guys I've ever met'.

Having dutifully idolized John Kennedy while pursuing his MBA at USC, this son of Cleveland's most fashionable suburb somehow wasn't appalled by the young Comptonites' apparent sociopathy, by their hatred of women and avowed penchant for violence. Indeed, he managed to convince himself that it was the most important music he'd heard since 1965.

Conversely, the boys from the 'hood didn't mind Heller's being old (over 40), Jewish and white. Far from it, in fact, for wasn't a white boy manager exactly what a motherfucker needed really to get over? And it wasn't brothers one saw representing all the top athletes, the ones with shoes named in their honor, after all, but Jewboys. Whatever you had to give up was worth it – 20 percent of a fortune was still apt to buy a closetful of Air Jordans! Back in the hood, word got around that Eazy, knowing that he ought to bring something to the table, gave up a paper bag containing $40,000 at the meeting where he asked Heller to help him realize his dreams of empire.

Thinking more like the owner of a pressing plant than a great impresario, believing rap to be only a fad, Don Mac-Millan hadn't contractually tied up any of his unlikely new stars. Noticing which, his lieutenant Chuck Fassert – decades earlier the composer and lead singer of the Regents' 'Barbara Ann' – resolved to form his own label to distribute Eazy's coterie's stuff, and agreed with Heller on a deal for the NWA and the Posse album for $50,000 – and a $13,000 Rolex wristwatch for Eric. But while Fassert was on the road getting the money from his distributors, Heller jilted him.

The creation of a pair of escapees from K-Tel, of late-night TV hucksterism infamy, Priority Records was in a position to double Fassert's bid as a result of having recently sold a million and a half California Raisins albums. And Eazy and his homies, hard core gangsta niggaz though they loudly proclaimed themselves to be, continued to be managed, recorded, promoted, and distributed entirely by old white dudes – most of them with surprising connections and back-grounds. The uncle of John Phillips, who distributed NWA's records in the South, had discovered Elvis and founded Sun Records. Recording engineer Donovan Smith, who paled noticeably when Dre ensured that the bass was loud enough to rattle a six-four's windshield, was a lapsed surfer, Priority kingpin Bryan Turner a Winnipeg-born hockey fanatic.

The old white dudes behind the group soon saw much, much green. *Eazy-Duz-It*, his 1988 full-length debut, sold two million. So did NWA's *Straight Outta Compton*, whose tone Ice Cube set by warning that he 'should never [have] been let out of the penitentiary,' owing to his Charles Manson-ish criminal record. Never mind that he'd recently been an architecture student at college in Arizona, and before that, thanks to bussing, a senior at a salubrious suburban San Fernando Valley high school.

The fearsomeness about which Cube and his homies bragged was strangely at odds with the album's thank-you list, which started with God and 'our mothers and fathers'. Asked how his nurse mother (presumably neither a bitch nor a [w]ho[re], unlike any woman on their record) felt about NWA's records, the obtuse, personable DJ Yella would confide, 'It didn't bother her; she never listened to them. It was making money. Anything we said been said before. Everybody says bad words here and there.'

As though the group's vocabulary, rather than its ugly nihilism, were the issue! 'To me,' Eazy unashamedly confided on *Duz-It*, 'girls are female dogs.' In the world NWA's records described, all men were amoral brutes who 'think with [their] dingaling[s],' self-loathing thugs who revelled in getting drunk and murdering one another. Had virulent white supremacists ghostwritten their stuff for them, who'd have been able to tell the difference?

But who could be concerned about ugly nihilism in the face of the revenues the group was generating? 'All of a sudden,' Heller was heard to rhapsodize, 'these kids had come out of nowhere and made me important and rich again. I'm living in a mansion and driving big cars, doing all the things that I'd resigned myself never to doing anymore.'

Experts agreed that the real Niggaz' audience consisted substantially of white suburban teens who bought their records to experience danger vicariously. While white kids loved hearing self-described niggers threatening one another, though, at least one hip-hop journal observed that NWA had relatively few fans in the ghetto. Indeed, back in the 'hood, NWA's success inspired much disdainful grumbling. Eazy's former homeboys called him a gimmick, and said that if he were six feet tall – that is, not impish – he'd never have captured the public fancy. Motherfucker couldn't rap a damn Christmas present! They bitterly decried his having imported extras from neighborhoods other than the CPT for his videos, and this after they'd sold his damn tapes for him out of the trunks of their cars! His own little sister and his cousin Chris were both said to think him a dog.

The FBI didn't care for him either. Getting an earful of *Outta Compton*, its assistant director of public affairs sent Priority an indignant letter astutely observing that 'Fuck Tha Police' 'encourages . . . disrespect for the law enforcement officer.' Your tax dollars at work! Not to be outdone, the Fraternal Order of Police voted not to provide security at NWA concerts.

The group's 40-date national tour in mid-1989, during which Eazy wore a bulletproof vest onstage in spite of 80 percent white audiences (white kids love this shit!), was nonetheless without tragic incident – except for the group being torn apart from within. 'Eazy calls me from their hotel in Columbus, Ohio, to tell me they're having a fight about their white cocksucker manager,' Heller relates proudly. 'Ice Cube says, "It's either him or me." If Eazy lets him play his little black/white game, there's no more Ruthless Records [as Eazy had christened his empire]. But he tells him, "NWA is me, Dre, Yella . . . and Jerry Heller; here's your plane ticket home."'

Maybe, as Heller speculated, it was that the eternally scowling Cube couldn't endure being only the second most charismatic member of the group, after Eazy. Or maybe, as Eazy himself speculates, it was that NWA's ambitious publicist, Pat Charbonnet, had begun trying to sell the group on the idea that 'we should do these side deals somewhere else. She couldn't get me to do it, so she went to Ice Cube. She went from being a publicist to being Ice Cube's manager. Now she's running his record company. That's good for her, but I don't know if it's good for him.'

Back in Compton, there'd been widespread amazement at Dre's new image. 'Dre never gangbanged a day in his life,' according to Wreckin' Cru's Lonzo Williams. 'When we had fights, he was the last person to do any swinging. We had several situations when all we needed was manpower. But when me and [Cru rapper] Cli-N-Tel and the rest of the fellows would be out there, Dre was like, "Hey, I got to mix these records." It would take a hell of a lot to convince me that he's really the person he's claiming to be.'

Said 'hell of a lot' presumably being something other than what Dee Barnes, the petite host of Fox-TV's *Pump It Up*, alleges happened at West Hollywood's Speakeasy club on a late January evening in 1991. While his bodyguard kept might-have-been intervenors at bay, the good doctor yanked Barnes off the ground by her hair and ear and slammed her against a wall. Tiring of which, he tried to throw her down a flight of stairs but lost his grip. When she fell, he kicked her in the ribs and stomped on her hand. She ran into the ladies' room, but he was right behind her, punching her in the back of the head.

Not, it was crucial to understand, that he hadn't been abundantly provoked. A couple of months earlier, *Pump It Up* had inserted a segment featuring Yo-Yo, Ice Cube's sweetheart, into a program otherwise spotlighting NWA. Feeling his oats as a result of the platinum success of his *AmeriKKKa's Most Wanted* album and his extraordinary performance in *Boyz N the Hood* – the movie – Cube had eagerly seized the opportunity to express his great distaste for his former colleagues.

'Somebody fucks with me,' the once-slender, ever-heftier

Dre explained of his manhandling of the 105-pound Barnes, 'I'm going to fuck with them.' After failing to get him to agree to write and produce four tracks for her *Body and Soul* album without credit, Barnes filed a $22.7 million lawsuit against both Dre and those of his colleagues in NWA who assured the press that she'd gotten only what she'd had coming. Bitches not being shit and all.

So Dre's life had come to imitating his art, or at least that of his gigantic new mentor Marion (Suge) Knight, who, since failing to set the National Football League afire, had become one of the most dreaded goons in Los Angeles black music circles, the 'nasty motherfucker' in whose honour one-time NWA co-manager Morey Alexander keeps a loaded pistol in his desk drawer.

Terror, thy nickname is Suge. Not only violent, Suge also seemed a little crazy, and was absolutely implacable. At a benefit for a South Central charity organization at the Hollywood Palladium, for instance, he decided that he wouldn't let his artist, Michelle, go on until she was paid. Never mind that, because the whole thing was for charity, nobody was being paid, not Another Bad Creation, not even Boyz II Men. It took a while, but the KDAY DJ who was hosting the event finally made Suge understand.

A few days later, though, when he encountered the DJ in a restaurant, Suge got right back in his face – in front of the guy's family and a whole restaurant-full of comparably horrified diners. Pushing him against a wall, Suge loudly warned, 'This is going to be the last time I [ask] you [for the money],' presumably in the same tone in which he'd advised Morey, 'You could be dead too' when Morey tried to intervene in a dispute between Suge and Jerry Heller. It later came out that Michelle had gotten herself a black eye for going on stage without Suge's authorization.

NWA's second full-length album, *Efil4zaggin*, included a song soliciting calls to the group's 900 number and a coupon with which one could order official Niggaz 4 Life T-shirts and

posters, and thus was remarkable for its brazen exploitive-
ness. It was far more remarkable, though, for its blood-
curdling misogyny. 'Fellows, next time they try to tell a lie
that they never sucked a dick,' the rapper Ren urges at one
point, 'punch the bitch in the eye. And then the ho will fall to
the ground. Then you open up her mouth, put your dick in
and move the shit around. And she'll catch on and start doin'
it on her own.'

Elsewhere, explaining with jaw-dropping candor why he
refers to himself as a nigger, Dre brags about 'gettin' paid to
say this shit here, makin' more in a week than a doctor makes
in a year.' In 'Message to B.A.', he advises the faithless Cube
that 'when we see your ass, we're gonna cut your hair off and
fuck you with a broomstick,' if not put 'a motherfucking
bullet in your forehead.' White folks loved this shit; *Efil4-
zaggin* debuted at No. 2 and supplanted Paula Abdul's
Spellbound at No. 1 a week later.

On his own next album, the platinum *Death Certificate*,
Cube got right into the spirit of the thing, calling for 'a bullet
in the temple' of the white Jew 'devil' Heller – this when he
wasn't busy vilifying gays and Koreans and threatening the
latter with arson. White folks loved this shit, but a nationwide
boycott by 3000 Asian grocers forced the makers of St. Ides
(the malt liquor that hoped to supplant Olde English 800 as
the ghetto's cheap intoxicant of choice) to rescind its TV and
radio spots starring the community-minded Cube.

In England, *Efil4zaggin* inspired talk of toughening the
Obscene Publications Act. Even the mad Irish chanteuse
Sinead O'Connor fled the shrinking ranks of NWA's apolo-
gists. Life was good. But here came the rift that tore NWA
apart for keeps, as it dawned on Dre – scrupulously oblivious
to business since his Wreckin' Cru days – that Eazy seemed to
be getting a great deal richer than he even though Dre had
understood them to be 50/50 partners.

According to Heller, no less than the music business
colossus Sony was in the forefront of the conspiracy to turn

Dre against Eazy. 'They told him the kinds of things that these guys have historically told young black artists with white managers. He's not very bright, and when they offered him $15 million to leave us and go with them, he was ready to forsake his friends and his roots and morals.'

Within 24 hours of the Night of the Leather-Gloved Thugs – of Dre being released from his Ruthless contracts and Eazy's mama's not being killed – Heller's lawyers had filed a state court action to invalidate Dre's liberation on the ground that Eazy had acceded to it only under supreme duress. Heller further hired a couple of RICO (racketeer-influenced corrupt organization) aces to file a $248 million lawsuit against Suge and Dre and friends, corporate and other. Eazy cackled, 'Dre now works for a bodyguard that used to work for him for, like, $75 a night,' and someone broke into Heller's home in the gated west San Fernando Valley estate in which he, Eazy, and Dre all lived like robber barons to spraypaint 'Payback's a motherfucker, Jerry' on the mirrored closet doors in one of his bedrooms. And thus did the ghetto come to Calabasas.

It was painful to wonder how many Reaganomics-ruined youth programs could be restored in Compton for the fortune Heller and Eazy reconciled themselves to spending on Suge-sized bodyguards of their own each month. The most painful part being that, like Eazy's friendship with one of the LAPD defendants in the Rodney King case, the bodyguards might have been all for show, since Eazy, Dre, Ice Cube, and Ren were seen hanging out happily in different combinations at Roscoe's House of Chicken and Waffles in Hollywood. Could it be that their promises to sodomize one another with broomsticks without the benefit of lubricants consti-tuted one of the most egregiously cynical publicity ploys in the history of American entertainment?

Once their individual careers died down a little bit, friends speculated, you'd read about the forthcoming release of a third NWA album. Not that there was much sign of any of their careers dying down. Ren's characteristically conciliatory

Kizz My Black Azz EP reached No. 12, and was in the charts for 13 weeks. Just in time to make the season bright, Ice Cube's wantonly spiteful *The Predator* entered the charts at No. 1 in December 1992. And Dre's comparably malevolent *The Chronic*, released a couple of months later, was still in the Top 5 six months after release, with sales exceeding two million.

White folks continued to love to hear self-described niggaz threatening one another. Back in the CPT, though, nothing much seemed to have changed. Bored, jobless, and without prospects, the boys in the hood still guzzled 8-Ball on street corners and talked a lot of bullshit about how they would somehow claw their way out of the ghetto too. But you never heard one say he wanted to do it Dre's way. His shameless fronting, that gat-in-your-mouth shit of his! When push came to shove, it had turned out to be rich white Century City lawyers like John Branca, formerly Michael Jackson's main man, who fought Dre's battles for him. Here he was in the Top 10 and on MTV talking homeboy this and homeboy that, and he hadn't done shit for his homeboys, hadn't even hired one of his uncles to work for him. And right around the corner from where his grandmother still lived, boys were still selling yay-o to put a few bucks in their pockets.

There'd been a time, not so many years before, when they'd have done anything for the brother, would have taken a bullet for him. And now, they agreed, if Dre ever again dared to show his face in the 'hood, they'd steal his jewellery.

Or maybe put a bullet in the motherfucker themselves.

4
CONGREGATIONS

Michael Lydon

MONTEREY POPS! AN INTERNATIONAL POP FESTIVAL

unpublished piece for *Newsweek*, 20th June 1967

Tiny Tim was at Monterey. He didn't play on the big stage, but he sat back in the artist's lounge on a white folding chair, beaming smiles through the waves of brown hair falling over his face as he strummed his ukelele and sang old songs in his high-pitched voice. I didn't put Tiny Tim in my story – who would have believed me! – but there he was, nightly gathering a little circle of bemused and amazed listeners. Brian Jones thought Tiny Tim was 'brilliant'.

Reporting for Newsweek *took me to Monterey. I'd gone to work for* Newsweek *right out of college in 1965 – I was a reporter in the London bureau when* Rubber Soul *came out, Carnaby Street was jumping, and the Who were at the Marquee. In January '67, just as the '60s musical-social ball was bouncing westward,* Newsweek *moved me to San Francisco. I arrived in time for the Human Be-In and soon was hanging out at the Avalon and Fillmore, interviewing Jerry and Janis, and covering student demonstrations in Berkeley. In May I began to hear rumours of a huge hippie festival: all the best new bands were coming, this was going to be far-fucking out!!*

Monterey was far-fucking out. I drove back to San Francisco Monday morning, slept like a log, got up Tuesday and wrote the piece in one four-hour burst and sent it to New York, where the editors boiled it down to ten paragraphs. The full piece's splattered prose, I think, does capture some of the magic and the music of those three days, but just like I couldn't get Tiny Tim in, I couldn't get in a lot that happened at Monterey. Who could? Times like that weekend are so intense that we can only measure their impact as they echo in our lives down through the years.

Monterey still echoes for me as one of those signal events that set me on my adult path. Pennebaker's superb film Monterey Pop *has kept the festival's sound and images from fading in memory. This festival gave birth to generations of music festivals that blossom to this day. Many of Monterey's offspring much outgrew their mother, but none had her tentative innocence, her blushing first-time exuberance.*

ML

THE MONTEREY International Pop Festival is over, all over. And what was it? Was it one festival, many festivals, a festival at all? Does anything sum it up, did it mean anything, are there any themes? Was it just a collection of rock groups of varying levels of proficiency who did their bit for a crowd of thousand who got their fill of whatever pleasure or sensation they sought? Was it a real-life living of *Privilege*, the most significant meeting of an avant-garde since the Armoury show or some Dadaist happening in the '20s? Was it, as the stage banner said, 'Love, flowers, and music', or was it Jimi Hendrix playing his guitar like an enormous penis and then burning it, smashing it, and flicking its pieces like holy water into a baffled, berserk audience? Was it a hundred screaming freak kids with warranted faces howling and bashing turnover oil drums and trash cans like North African trance dancers, or was it the thousands of sweet hippies who wandered, sat, and slept on the grass with flutes and bongos, beads and bubbles, laughing and loving softly?

Was its spirit Simon and Garfunkel, singing like little-lost-lamb castrati, or was it Ravi Shankar rocking over his sitar and beating a bare foot while opening up a musical world to 7,000 listeners who, at his request, did not smoke for his three-hour concert? Rolling Stone Brian Jones was part of it, wandering for three days silent inside his blond hair and gossamer pink cape; so was a girl writhing on a bummer at the entrance to the press section. While no one helped, cameramen exhausted themselves recording her agony. Was it a nightmare and something beautiful existing together or a nightmare and many beautiful things existing side by side?

One is left only with questions that a mind besodden with sound and sound and sound and sound cannot answer. On Saturday night, Jerry Garcia of the Grateful Dead commented: 'There's a lot of heavy stuff going on.' Whether he meant music or acid or emotion or everything, he was right. Something very heavy happened at Monterey last weekend.

Those very odd three days began in Friday's coldest grey air as the first of the crowd began to circle through the booths of the fairground. The only word for it then was groove. A giant Buddha stood in one corner, banners decorated with astrology signs waved, and everything the hippie needs to make his life beautiful was on sale: paper dresses, pins, earrings, buttons, amulets, crosses, posters, balloons, sandals, macrobiotic food, and flowers. There was a soul food stand, the Monterey Kiwanis had fresh corn on the cob, the Congregation Beth El had pastrami sandwiches, and hippies with the munchies snapped their fingers to the popping of the popcorn stand. In the festival offices Mama Michelle of the Mamas and Papas was hard at work doing everything from typing to answering the phone. Papa John was keeping his cool in his grey fur hat which he never once took off in the frantic chaos.

Nothing but chaos could have been expected. The whole festival had been nothing more than an idea two months before in the head of publicist Derek Taylor, and in the rush of preparation had changed itself many times.

At first it was to be a commercial proposition; then Taylor, unable to raise the money needed to pay advances to the invited groups, had gone to Phillips and Dunhill producer Lou Adler for bankrolling. Why not make it a charity and get everyone to come for free, they suggested, and suddenly it became not a money-spinning operation but a happening generated by the groups themselves which hopefully would make some composite statement of pop music in June 1967.

The festival was incorporated with a board of governers that included Donovan, Mick Jagger, Andrew Oldham, Paul Simon, Phillips, Smokey Robinson, Jim McGuinn, Brian Wilson, and Paul McCartney. 'The Festival hopes to create an atmosphere wherein persons in the popular music field from all parts of the world will congregate, perform, and exchange ideas concerning popular music with each other and with the public at large,' said a release. The profits from ticket sales (seats ranged from $6.50 to $3.50; admission to the grounds without a seat was $1) after paying the entertainers' expenses was to go to charities and to fund fellowships in the pop field. Despite rumours that part of the money would go to the Diggers in both Los Angeles and San Francisco to help them cope with the 'hippie invasions,' so far, no decision has been made on where the money will go.

This vagueness and the high prices engendered charges of commercialism – 'Does anybody really know where these LA types are at?' asked one San Francisco rock musician. And when the list of performers was released there was more confusion. Where were the Negro stars, the people who began it all, asked some. Where were the Lovin' Spoonful, the Stones, the Motown groups; does a pop festival mean anything without Dylan, the Stones, and Beatles?

'Here they are trying to do something new,' said the Fillmore's Bill Graham, 'and they end up with group after group just like the jazz festivals. Will anybody have the chance to spread out if they feel like it?'

But as the festival unfolded it was clear that if not perfect the festival was as good as it could have been. The Spoonful could not come because of possible charges on a pot bust they had helped to engineer to avoid a possession charge against themselves; it was rumored, moreover, that John Sebastian wants to spend all his time writing and that they are breaking up as a group. Two of the Stones are facing pot charges of their own in England. Smokey Robinson and Berry Gordy were enthusiastic about the festival at first, John Phillips said, but 'then they never answered the phone. Smokey was completely inactive as a director. I think it might be a Crow Jim thing. A lot of people put Lou Rawls down for appearing. "You're going to a Whitey festival, man," was the line. There is tension between the white groups who are getting their own ideas and the Negroes who are just repeating theirs. The tension is lessening all the time, but it did crop up here, I am sure.'

Phillips also reported that Chuck Berry was invited. 'I told him on the phone, "Chuck, it's for charity," and he said to me, "Chuck Berry has only one charity and that's Chuck Berry. $2000." We couldn't make an exception.' Dylan is still keeping his isolation after the accident which broke his neck last summer, and, though rumors persisted up to the last minute Sunday night that the Beatles would appear – or at least were in Monterey – they decided to keep their 'no more appearances' vow. Dionne Warwick made a last minute bow-out with a bad throat, and the Beach Boys, whose Carl Wilson faced a draft evasion charge, decided to lay low.

Yet, as the sound poured out incessantly – the concerts, with nary an intermission, averaged five hours in length (can you imagine going to four uncut top volume *Hamlet*s in three days, or sitting in the Indianapolis pits while they re-ran the race eight times over a weekend?) – gaps were not noticed. One dealt with what was at hand, and what was there was very, very good indeed. There were a few disasters who can be written off from the start. Laura Nyro, a melodramtic singer accompanied by two dancing girls who pranced absurdly; Hugh Masekela, whose trumpet-playing is only slightly better than his voice (he did, however, do some nice backing for the Byrds on 'So You Want to Be a Rock 'n' Roll Star'), and Johnny Rivers, dressed like an LA hippie, who had the gall to sing the Beatles' 'Help' not once but twice.

Others, like the Association with their slick high-schooly humor, didn't fit in; still others like Canned Heat, an LA-based blues band, had bad days. But the majority rose to new heights for the concert. There was the feeling that this was the place, that the vibrations were right, that one was performing for one's peers and superiors. 'I saw a community form and live together for three days,' said Brian Jones Sunday night. 'It is so sad that it has to break up.'

That community was formed not only on the stage between the performers and the audience but backstage, at the artists' retreat behind the arena called the Hunt Club, and in the motel rooms where parties went on till dawn. There was little off-stage jamming (no motels had the space, proper wall thickness, or power) except for a four-hour blast between the Dead, the Airplane, and Jimi Hendrix that carried the members to breakfast Monday morning after everyone else had gone home, yet everyone talked, listened and grooved with everyone else. The variety of music was tremendous, blues to folk to rock to freak. There were big stars, old stars, comers, and groups who avoid the whole star bag. If one was good, in whatever bag, one was accepted. Music styles were not barriers; however disparate the criteria, there seemed to be some consensus on what was real music and what was not.

The festival had a sort of rhythm to it which was un-doubtedly coincidental – the organizers swore that there was no implicit ranking in the order of the acts – but which worked. Friday night was a mixed bag to get things moving, Saturday afternoon was blues, old and gutty, new and wild. Saturday night opened some of the new directions, then a return to peace with Shankar Sunday afternoon; and a final orgiastic freakout Sunday night.

The Association began it all in the cool grey of Friday night with a professional style and entertaining manner, doing a fine job on their sweetly raucous hit single 'Windy'. Then the Paupers, a four-man group from Toronto, provided the first surprise. The almost unknown group, managed by Albert Grossman, Dylan's grandmotherly and shrewd mentor, was able to get a screaming volume and a racy quality unmatched by some of the bigger groups. 'I found them at the Cafe au Go Go in New York,' Grossman said. 'They are cutting the Jefferson Airplane to pieces so I signed them up.' Only together seven months they are sure to get better. 'We are trying to create a total environment with sound alone,' said lead guitrist Chuck Beale. 'Sound is enough. We don't use lights or any gimmicks. When we record we never double-track or use any other instruments. What the four of us can do is the sound we make. That's all.'

Lou Rawls, the blues singer whose 'Dead End Street' is currently in the charts, came next and pulled the audience back to what he called 'rock 'n' soul'. Backed by a big band, he looked as if he'd have been more at home in a night club, but his fine funky voice and from-the-heart monologues about the nitty-gritty of Negro life were soulful indeed. To watch him was to be back at the Apollo where rock is flashy, stylish, and flamboyant, but still communicating with the kids high in the balcony. 'The blues,' he said as he came off exhilarated, 'is the way of the future. The fads come and go, but the blues remain. The blues is the music that makes a universal language.' Other music at the festival seemed also to speak to all, but Rawls, a solid member of the professional black school of music, hit one major thread: the new music is still close to the blues, and most of the far-out sounds in the three days were but new blues ideas. He also had his finger on another key truth: 'I'm trying to portray the facts as they stand. A few years ago rock was all facade, all doo-wah-diddy-diddy, all prettied up. I get the feeling that people now are trying their best to be where it's at.'

After Johnny Rivers stayed on too long, Eric Burdon, one of the best white blues singers around, romped through a half dozen numbers with his new Animals, the high point coming with 'Paint It Black', the Jagger-Richards masterpiece on which he, unbelievably, improved, particularly with the zany screechings of an electric violin. Brian Jones, sitting in the dirt of an aisle, applauded wildly.

Simon and Garfunkel finished off the night, and what can one say about them? 'Homeward Bound' brought back memories of the time when a sweet folk-rock seemed to be the new direction, but though the song sounded nice enough, they seemed sadly left behind. 'Benedictus' had them harmonizing like choirboys, and they did an encore, a funny new nonsense song, 'I Wish I Was a Kellogg Corn Flake'. When the last note floated out about 1:30 am, the first night was over and the peace was extraordinary, While the lucky (or unlucky?) few drove to their motels, the mass of the crowd drifted to the huge camping area near the arena and to the football field af Monterey Peninsula College nearby. There, with the sweet smell of pot drifting over sleeping bags, music continued in singing and talking and in just being.

In the bright hot sun of Saturday afternoon the serious blues shouting began. Canned Heat led off with an uninspired set, and then came one of the most fantastic events of the whole shebang: the voice of Janis Joplin, singer of Big Brother and the Holding Company, a SF group almost entirely unknown outside of the Bay Area. A former folk singer from Port Arthur, Texas, Janis was turned on a year ago by Otis Redding, and now she sings with equal energy and soul. In a gold knit pants suit with no bra underneath, Janis leapt, bent double, and screwed up her plain face as she sang like a demonic angel. It was the blues big mama style, tough, raw, and gutsy, and with an aching that few black singers reach. The group behind her drove her and fed from her, building the total volume sound that has become a SF trademark. The final number, '(Love is like a) Ball and Chain', which had

Janis singing (singing? – talking, crying, moaning, howling) long solo sections, had the audience on their feet for the first time. 'She is the best white blues singer I have ever heard,' commented *SF Examiner* jazz critic Phil Elwood.

Country Joe and the Fish, the acid-political group from Berkeley, came next, and while they did not reach their accustomed heights, their funny, satirical words and oddly dissonant music went over well. They did two of their political songs. 'Please Don't Drop that H-Bomb on Me, You Can Drop It On Yourself', whose title is the complete lyric, and 'Whoopie, We're All Going to Die', which contains the memorable line, 'Be the first on your block to have your boy come home in a box'. These were among the very few explicit protest songs at the Festival; nowadays rock musicians are musicians first and protestors a slow second. 'There are two parts to music,' said lead guitar and music writer for Country Joe, Barry Melton, 'the music and the lyrics. Music we have with everybody, but some say the lyrics shouldn't be political. Everybody agrees with us on the war, but we feel that in this society you have to make your stands clear. Others don't want to speak up in songs, be right up front. That's why we put politics in.'

Melton's songs, particularly 'Not So Sweet Martha Lorraine', a nightmarish song about a mysterious lady who 'hides on a shelf filled with volumes of literature based on herself' and who gets high with death, have been called 'pure acid,' but Melton says all music is psychedelic. 'One part of LSD is liberation, to do what you want to do. I feel I do that, do what I want to do. When I hear a sound that is groovy I use it. I try to find music all over the place. Listening to anything can give you musical ideas. That's freedom, and maybe that's psychedelic.' He spoke for most of the groups. It would be hard to find any of the musicians who has not taken LSD or at least smoked pot, but by now it has become so accepted that it's nothing to be remarked on by itself. Acid opened minds to new images, new sounds, and made them embrace a wild eclecticism, but rather than being 'acid' as such, it has become music.

Al Kooper, an organist who has often played vith Dylan, took a half an hour with some funky blues organ and vocal, but the action began again with the Paul Butterfield Blues Band, a newly-constituted version of the group which, more than any other, led the revival of white interest in blues bands. Led by Butterfield's fine voice and better harmonica, and with the strange melancholic whimsy of Elvin Bishop's guitar, the backup band of bass guitar, trumpet, sax, and drums rocketed through some very impressive work. They also returned for the Saturday night show, with Bishop showing off his odd voice on a gloomy blues, 'Have Mercy This Morning'.

The Butterfield group, which began years ago gigging with Muddy Waters in Chicago, knew, unlike the Quicksilver Messenger Service and the Steve Miller Blues Band who followed, precisely what it was doing. Without being uptight, Butterfield was precise. They swung deftly on a broad emotional range, but the strongest memory is the haunting, looping sound of Butterfield's harmonica as it broke a small solo of just a few notes into tiny bits and experimented with their regrouping.

The blues afternoon ended with a group that had no idea (apparently) what it was doing but did it with such a crazy yelping verve that it looked like in time it could do anything it wanted. Billed as the Electric Flag, it was the first time it had ever played together, and under that name it never will play again. Mike Bloomfield, its leader and lead guitarist, has been gradually building the band after leaving Butterfield's group a few months ago. Its name in the future will be 'Thee, Sound'. 'As in "dedicated to thee, sound",' says Bloomfield, 'the whole world of sound, not just music.' Its set was an astounding masterpiece of chaos with rapport. Drummer Buddy Miles, a big Negro with a wild 'do' who looks like a tough soul brother from Detroit and who is actually a prep-school-educated son of a well-to-do Omaha family, sings and plays with TNT energy, knocking over cymbals as he plays. Barry Goldberg controls the organ, and Nick 'the Greek' Gravenites writes the songs and does a lot of the singing. The group was, for the acts present as well as the audience, a smash success. The Byrds' David Crosby announced from the stage Saturday night that 'Man, if you didn't hear Mike Bloomfield's group, man, you are out of it, so far out of it.'

The afternoon concert rode out with the Electric Flag on a wave of excitement that faltered in the evening concert. There was a curious feeling around late Saturday; everything was still very groovy, but the sweetness was going. The excitement of the music was getting too high. That stalled Saturday night but the level did not diminish. San Francisco's Moby Grape led off the concert overshadowed by the rumor, fed by the ambiguous statements of the festival management, that the Beatles would appear for the record arena audience of 8,500. The Grape had a driving excitement and some very nice playing with the four guitars, but no particular impression stands out, Masekela was terrible but his conga player Big Black was brilliant, holding up his reputation as the best conga player in the business. The Byrds were disappointing. Considered by many to be America's Beatles, they were good, doing several new songs, but they lacked the excitement to get things moving. Butterfield was not as good as he had been in the afternoon and went on too long, and the evening hit bottom with Laura Nyro.

From there on out, things got better. The Jefferson Airplane were fantastically good. Backed with the light show put on by Headlights, who do the lights at the Fillmore, they created a special magic. Before they came on the question hung: are the Airplane as good as their reputation? They thoroughly proved themselves. As they played hundreds of artists, stagehands and hangers-on swarmed on to the stage dancing. Grace Slick, in a long light blue robe, sang as if possessed, her harshly fine voice filling the night. In a new song, 'Ballad of You and Me and Pooneil', they surpassed themselves. Playing largely in the dark, the light show loomed above them, its multicolored blobs shaping and reshaping, primeval molecules eating up tiny bubbles like food then splitting into shimmering atoms. The guitar sounds came from outer space and inner mind, and while everything was going – drums, guitar, and the feedback sounds of the amplifiers, Marty Balin shouted over and over the closing line, 'Will the moon still hang in the sky, when I die, when I die, when I die,' They were showered with orchids as they left the stage.

In no time Booker T and the MGs were on, rocking through some very dynamic blues, and suddenly Otis Redding was there, singing the way Jimmy Brown charged in football. 'Shake,' he shouted, 'Shake, everybody, shake,' shaking himself like a madman in his electric green suit. What was it like? I wrote at the time, 'ecstasy, madness, loss, total, screaming, fantastic.' It started to rain and Redding sang two songs that started slow, 'to bring the pace down a bit', he said, but in no time the energy was back up again. 'Try a Little Tenderness' he closed with, and by the end it reached a new orgiastic pitch. He finished and a standing screaming crowd brought him back and back and back.

Day two was over and Sunday came grey and cold, but the excitement was still there and growing. Could anyone believe what had happened, what might happen? Hours of noise had both deafened and opened thousands of minds. One had lived in sound for hours: the ears had come to dominate the senses. Ears rung as one slept; dreams were audible as well as visual.

Sunday afternoon was Shankar, and one felt a return to peace. And yet there was an excitement in his purity, as well as in his face and body, and that of the tabla player whose face matched Chaplin's in its expressive range. For three hours they played music, and after the first strangeness, it was not Indian music, but music, a particular realization of what music could be. It was all brilliant, but – in a long solo from the 16th century – Shankar had the whole audience, including all the musicians at the festival, rapt. Before he played, he spoke briefly. The work, he said, was a very spiritual one and he asked that no pictures be taken (the *paparazzi* lay down like lambs). He thanked everyone for not smoking, and said with feeling, 'I love all of you, and how grateful I am for your love of me. What am I doing at a pop festival when my music is classical? I knew I'd be meeting you all at one place, you to whom music means so much. This is not pop, but I am glad it is popular.' With that he began the long melancholic piece. To all appearances he had 7,000 people with him, and when he finished, he stood, bowed with his hands clasped to his forehead, and then, smiling, threw back to the crowd the flowers that had been showered on him.

Sunday night the festival reached its only logical conclusion. The passion, anticipation and adventure into sound had taken one as far as any could have thought possible, and yet it had to go further. Flowers and a groovy kind of love may be elements in the hippie world, but they have little place in hippie rock. The hippie liberation is there, so is a personal kindness, openness, and pleasantness that make new rock musicians easy to talk to, but in their music there is a feeling of a stringent demand on the senses, an experimenting with the techniques of assault, a toying with the idea of beautiful ugliness, the creativeness of destruction, and the loss of self into whatever may come,

One of the major elements in this open-mindedness is feedback. Feedback is nothing new: anyone who has played an electric guitar has experienced it. Simply, feedback happens when a note from a vibrating string comes out of the amplifier louder than it went in and re-reverberates the string. The new vibration adds to the old, and thus the note comes out of the amp louder still. Theoretically, the process could go on, the note getting louder and louder, until the amp blew out. In practice it can be controlled so that the continuing

note is held as with a piano's pedal. That means that behind
their strumming and picking, the musicians can build up a
level of pure electronic noise, which they can vary by turning
to face the amp of face away, moving toward it or moving
away. Feedback can tremendously increase a group's volume,
produce yelps, squeals, screams, pitches that rise and rise,
that squeak, blare, or yodel wildly. If nothing else, this festival
established feedback. One major test of each group was their
ability in using feedback, and though it has many uses and
effects, ovrerall it creates a musical equivalent of madness.
Every night featured feedback, but Sunday night was feedback night and a complete exploration of a new direction in
pop music.

The night was foreshadowed by the first group, The Blues
Project, the New York band which shares the new blues
limelight with Paul Butterfield. Their first song featured
electric flute in the hands of Andy Kolburg. It was part blues,
part Scottish air, part weird phrases that became images of
ambiguity. Big Brother and the Holding Company came back
and were weaker than they had been, but one short number,
'Hairy', was a minute composed of short bursts of utter
electronic blare, chopped up into John Cage-like silences.
A group too new to have a name – The Group with No Name
was their billing – were terrible and may well not last long
enough to get a name. Buffalo Springfield were totally professional but largely undistinguished, except for a closing
song, 'Bluebird', which alternated from the sweet sound to
the total sound.

And then came The Who. Long popular in England, where
they've achieved a notoriety for their wild acts at London's
Marquee Club, they had never been seen in America. They
were dressed in a wild magnificence, like dandies from the
17th, 19th, and 21st centuries. They opened with one of their
English hits, 'Substitute' ('I'm just a substitute for another
guy, I look pretty tall but my heels are high') with singer
Roger Daltrey swirling around the stage in gothic shawl

decorated with pink flowers, and Keith Moon defining the berserk at the drums – he broke three drum sticks in the first song and overturned one of his snares. They had a good, very close sound, excellent lyrics ('Lets have a kiss for an old engine driver' went one song), and the flashiest guitar presence of any group to appear.

Then John Entwhistle, bass guitar, stepped to the mike and said, 'This is where it all ends,' and they began 'My Generation', the song that made them famous. A violently arrogant demand for the supremacy of youth – 'things they say look awful cold/ Hope I die before I get old' – the song has Daltrey stammering on 'my g-g-g-generation' as if overcome by hatred or by drugs. After about four minutes of the song, Daltrey began to swing his handheld mic over his head, while Pete Townshend smashed his guitar strings against the pole of the mic before him, building up the feedback. Then he ran and played the guitar directly into his amp. The feedback went wild, and then he lit a smoke bomb before the amp so it looked like it had blown up, and smoke billowed on the stage. He lifted his guitar from his neck and smashed it on the stage again, again, again, and it broke, one piece sailing into the crowd. Moon went psychopathic at the drums, kicking them through with his feet, knocking them down, trampling on the mics. The noise continued from the guitar as everything fell and crashed in the smoke. Then they stopped playing and walked off unconcerned, leaving only the hum of an amp turned on at full volume.

It was known to be a planned act, but like the similar scene in the film *Blow Up* (inspired by the Who) had a fantastic dramatic intensity. And no meaning. No meaning whatever. There was no passion, no anger, just destruction. And it was over as it began. Stagehands came out and set up for the next act.

That was the Grateful Dead and they were beautiful. They did at top volume what Shankar had done softly. They played pure music, some of the best music of the concert. I have never

heard anything in music which could be said to be qualita-
tively better than the performance of the Dead on Sunday
night. The strangest of the San Francisco groups, the Dead
live together in a big house on Ashbury Street, and living
together seems to have made them totally together musically.
Jerry Garcia, lead guitar, and owner of the bushiest head at
the Festival, was the best guitarist of the whole show. The
Dead's songs lasted twenty minutes and more, each a masterpiece of five-man improvisation. Beside Garcia, there is Phil
Lesh on bass, Bob Weir on rhythm guitar, Bill Sommers on
drums, and Pig Pen (who seldom talks) on organ. Each man's
part was isolated, yet the sound was solid as a rock. It is
impossible to remember what it was like. I wrote down at the
time: 'Accumulated sound like wild honey on a moving plate
in gobs . . . three guitars together, music, music, pure, high
and fancy . . . in it all a meditation by Jerry Garcia on a
melancholic theme . . . the total in all parts . . . loud quiets as
they go on and on and on . . . sounds get there then hold
while new ones float up, Jerry to Pig Pen, then to drums, then
to Lesh, talking, playing, laughing, exulting.'

That sounds crazy now, but that's how it seemed. The
Dead built a driving, unshakeable rhythm that acted not just
as rhythm but as a wall of noise on which the solos were
etched. The solos were barely perceptible in the din, yet they
were there like fine scrolls on granite. At moments Garcia and
Weir played like one instrument, rocking toward each other.
Garcia could do anything. One moment he hunched over,
totally intent on his strings, then he would pull away and
prance with his fat ungainly body, then play directly to some
face he picked out in the crowd straining up to the stage. Phil
Lesh called to the audience as they began, 'Anybody who
wants to dance, dance, You're sitting on folding chairs, and
folding chairs are for folding up and dancing on,' but the
crowds were restrained by ushers, and those who danced on
stage were stopped by nervous stagehands. It was one of the
few times that the loose reins of the festival were tightened.

Was it necessary? Who knows? But without dancing the Dead didn't know how well they had done. Lesh was dripping with sweat and nervous as he came off, but each word of praise from onlookers opened him up. 'Man, it was impossible to know how we were doing without seeing people moving. We feed on that, we need it, but, oh, man, we did our thing, we did our thing.'

They certainly did. The Dead on Sunday night were the definition of virtuoso performance. Could anybody come on after the Dead? Could anyone or anything top them? Yes, one man: Jimi Hendrix, introduced by Brian Jones as 'the most exciting guitar player I've ever heard'. Hendrix is a strange-looking fellow. Very thin, with a big head and a protuberant jaw, Hendrix has a tremendous bush of hair held in place carelessly by an Apache headband. He is both curiously beautiful and as wildly grotesque as the proverbial Wild Man of Borneo. He wore scarlet pants and a scarlet boa, a pink jacket over a yellow and black vest over a white ruffled shirt. He played his guitar left-handed, if in Hendrix's hands it was still a guitar. It was, in symbolic fact, a weapon which he brandished, his own penis which he paraded before the crowd and masturbated; it was a woman whom he made love to by straddling and by eating it while playing the strings with his teeth, and in the end it was a torch that he destroyed. In a way, the heavily erotic feeling of his act was absurd. A guitarist of long experience with Little Richard, Ike and Tina Turner, and the like, Hendrix had learned most of his tricks from the masters in endless series of club gigs on the southern chitlin' circuit.

But, dressed as he was and playing with a savage wildness, how to describe it? I wrote at the time: 'total scream . . . I suppose there are people who enjoy bum trips . . . end of everything . . . decay . . . nothing louder exists, 2000 instruments (in fact there were three: guitar, bass, and drums) . . . five tons of glass falling over a cliff and landing on dynamite.' The act became more than an extension of Elvis' gyrations, it

became an extension of that to infinity, an orgy of noise so
wound up that I felt that the dynamo that powered it would
fail and fission into its primordial atomic state. Hendrix not
only picked the strings, he bashed them with the flat of his
hand, he ripped at them, rubbed them against the mic and
pushed them with his groin into his amplifier. And when he
knelt before the guitar as if it were a victim to be sacrificed,
sprayed it with lighter fluid, and ignited it, it was exactly a
sacrifice: the offering of the perfect, most beloved thing, so its
destruction could ennoble him further.

But what do you play when your instrument is burnt?
Where can you go next? 'I don't know, man,' said Hendrix
with a laugh after the show. 'I think this has gone about as far
as it can go.' 'In England they've reached a dead end in
destruction,' said Brian Jones. 'Groups like the Move and the
Creation are destroying whole cars on stage.' Asked what it
all meant, Andrew Loog Oldham, whose Rolling Stones have
pushed far into their own violence kick, said, 'If you enjoy it,
it's okay,' and the screaming, frightened but aroused audience
apparently enjoyed it very much.

After a short and only mildly recuperative silence, on came
the Mamas and the Papas, backed by vibes, drums, tympani,
piano, and John Phillips' guitar. They were great, everything
the Mamas and Papas should be. Mama Cass was in fine
form, joking, laughing, and hamming it up like a camp Queen
Victoria. Introducing 'California Dreamin'', she said, 'We're
gonna to this song because we like it and because it is
responsible for our great wealth.' When they finished a wave
of applause swept from the furthermost reaches of the crowd
up to the stage and the hundred of more musicians, stagehands, and hangers-on dancing and shouting in the wings.
'We're gonna have this Festival every year,' said Mama Cass,
'so you can stay if you want.' The roar of renewed applause
almost convinced me that the crowd would patiently wait
through the summer, fall and winter, never stirring until next
June.

Now that the Monterey Pop Festival is a day in the past, what did it prove about pop music? In a way, it proved little. Pop has few of the formal identifying qualities of jazz or folk, and so it did not prove that pop music is now here or there or anyplace. It did show that pop is still in a continuuum with the blues, still loves and gets inspiration from the blues. It also showed that LSD and the psychedelics have tremendously broadened the minds of the young people making the new music.

It also demonstrated the continuing influence of the Beatles. Dozens of the other Monterey performers owe their being there to the Beatles. John Phillips was a folk singer until he heard the Beatles. 'They were not so much a musical influence as an influence because they showed that intelligent people could work in rock and make their intelligence show.' Moreover, Monterey Pop ratified the shift away from folk music that has been going on for over two years. The Festival was, among other things, the largest collection of former folk singers and guitarists ever gathered in one place. Musicians trained in folk make up the bulk of the new rockers. This means that they came to rock 'n' roll, not as the only form, not the one they were trained in, but as an experiment, as a form they looked at first from the outside, and whose possibilities they rather distantly considered.

That sense of experiment makes rock so lively today. The years of folk training, in which the two marks of status were knowledge of esoterica and the quality of performance, mean that the new rockers feel a need to push further and further ahead, and also that they are excellent players. The general level of musical competence was extremely high, and the heights hit by Mike Bloomfield and Jerry Garcia were as high as those reached by Chuck Berry, Bo Diddley, Doc Watson and other immortal folk and rock guitarists.

In some ways it was surprising that there was little experimentation in some directions. No group went far afield from the basic instrumental line-up, staging, song lengths, and musical form. This indicates that rock is still rather traditional, that it is still a commercial art, that the public will not take leaps forward that are too wild, that the performers are still young and unsure of themselves, and that the rock revolution is still new.

This may all change, and if it does, the Festival will have played an important role. Brian Jones was right: for three days a community formed. Rock musicians, whatever their bag, came together, heard each other, praised each other, and saw that the scene was open enough for them to play as they liked and still get an audience. They will return to their own scenes refreshed and confident.

The whole rock-hippie scene was vindicated. Even the police thought it was groovy. Monterey police chief Frank Marinello was so ecstatic that Saturday afternoon he sent half his force home. 'I'm beginning to like these hippies,' he told reporters. 'When I go up to that Haight-Ashbury, I'm going to see a lot of friends.' The fairgrounds, which at times held 40,000 people, far more than any other time in its history, were utterly peaceful. The tacit arrangement that there would be no busts for anything less than a blatant pot orgy was respected by both sides. When Mama Cass introduced 'California Dreamin' at 12:30 Monday morning, she said, 'This whole weekend was a dream come true.'

The Monterey International Pop Festival was a dream come true. An odd, baffling, and at times threatening dream, but one whose main theme was the creation and further growth of rock 'n' roll music, a music as young, vital, and beautiful as any being made today.

David Dalton

ALTAMONT: AN EYEWITNESS ACCOUNT

Gadfly, November/December 1999

We'd been to all the rock festivals. We were true believers.

As the evening star radiated enigmatic pulses across the universe, my acid bride and I stood on the roof of our building on 31st Street and with eyes we'd not yet used looked north into the future. We saw old Gotham transmuted into something rich and strange. The phallic hypodermic of the Empire State Building looming over us metamorphed into a giant yellow #2 pencil; the metal and glass boxes of mid-town were now abandoned; Central Park had become a reservation for hashish-eating Indians. Western Civilisation had come to its senses at last.

Like Eleusis or Karnak, rock festivals and be-ins were the great religious festivals of the late '60s, tribal gatherings of the mutant children of the bourgeoisie where we hummed together in lysergic swarms to frequencies that would open the millennial gates of Paradise. O deluded ones! Or were we? Just because everybody decided to revert to the cult of the dark satanic mills doesn't mean it's a good thing.

The Monterey Pop Festival in the summer of '67: 'Bliss was it in that dawn to be alive,' said Wordsworth. 'But to be young was very heaven.' And that's the way it felt; Monterey's memory for me only slightly clouded by subsequent revelations of the scaly, be-

hind-the-scenes dealings of Lou Adler and other LA hustlers (see my Living with the Dead *for full details—or ask Zelma Redding, Otis's widow*).

Woodstock, to my mind, was an entirely phoney episode and horrible in every conceivable way. A bloated, soulless golem of a festival, the prey of opportunistic propagandists – an amorphous, meaningless event, whose very lack of substance and soul made it ideal for media manipulation and portentous pronouncements.

But now, in December of 1969, their Satanic Majesties were planning their own festival. Who among us could miss that? I'd been writing for the newly hatched Rolling Stone *since its second issue* – back then it seemed the true voice of the hippie ummah. In the casual way one travelled in those days, no arrangements were made beforehand as to where to stay. You just got on a plane and crashed at someone's pad (quaint words of yesteryear!) when you got there.

From the airport I called Jann Wenner. Jane (then Mrs Wenner) answered the phone and said, 'Of course, just come on over.' That night we all resolved to get up early and go, and I fell asleep on the living-room floor. By the next morning Jann was lugubriously pacing back and forth in the kitchen. He'd been watching the news on TV. It didn't look good. 'It's going to be a mess,' he said. (He was right about that!) He resolved not to go. I was stunned at his unreasonable spasm of common sense.

'What a lame reason that is,' I cajoled him. 'It's the Stones, man. Are you going to miss the apocalypse because it's inconvenient?' He looked at me ruefully. I stopped short of telling him about the anticipated alien presence at Altamont. We went down to the heliport (cue blues riff) and hitched a ride into the maelstrom.

Unlike Woodstock, Altamont was a real event – a

*little too real, as it turned out. A bunch of Leonard
Nimoy In Search Of blather was spouted about Altamont by Jerry Garcia & Co. – the Stones having
brought it on through what? Their pantomime,
aren't-I-evil lyrics? You're kidding me – call ASCAP
at once. Pure Valley-Girl-on-crack mumbo jumbo.
And too much nonsense has been written about
how Altamont was the end of the '60s (or was that
Charlie Manson?). But, O my brothers and sisters,
don't you know that the '60s never ended – that was
their problem (and ours). If you don't believe me, just
turn on your radio.*

DD

THE DEVIL WANTED his rock festival. After all that flim-flam at
Woodstock four months earlier he felt like rolling himself a
big fat joint and planning the thing down to the last scaly
detail. As it happened, his minions, the Rolling Stones, were
at that very moment on a tour of the States. Most excellent!
'But what about a little touch of irony, eh?' said the Devil to
himself. 'Why don't I put some bleachers out in the sun and
hold it, say, down on Highway 61? Yes, the very thing.' The
Devil, too, would have his day.

THE ROSY APOCALYPSE

Altamont, 6th December, 1969. The name itself is fraught
with menace – its flinty suggestive syllables (altar-mountain-
tumult) reinforcing biblical overtones. ('The devil taketh him
up into an exceeding high mountain and showeth him all the
kingdoms of the world . . .') Altamont has become infamous
as the apocalyptic moment known as the end of the '60s, the
moment when the termite-riddled walls of the New Jerusalem
finally came tumbling down.

If the seeds of Altamont started anywhere, it was in Keith

Richard's Moroccan-encrusted living room on Cheyne Walk, circa the fall of 1969. Rock Scully, manager of the Grateful Dead and minister of culture for Haight-Ashbury, had come as an emissary to the court of the Rolling Stones. Soon, overweening plans were afoot. We expect nothing less from the combined forces of the two most delusional and drug-drenched bands on the planet. The only contact with reality for this lot consisted of negotiations with their drug dealers and the occasional highly publicised bust. It was a combustible mix. Mass gatherings of their equally brain-scrambled flocks were bruited about – events that would be cosmic in scope. What it all meant would have to be deferred – it was just too boggling to sort out just then.

The Stones were quite pleased with their showing in the psychedelic sweepstakes. They had put on a free concert in Hyde Park on 5th July 1969, and it had been – *brilliant!* Mick in the flouncey dress that Mr Fish had designed for him, releasing butterflies and reading Shelley (it was ostensibly a memorial concert for Brian Jones, the Stones' guitarist who had died two days earlier). As security they'd used Hell's Angels. Well, er, *English* Hells Angels – the Stepney chapter. East End yobs playing at being in a motorcycle club. The Stones like to flirt with pantomime violence – always fun and decorative, isn't it? And hadn't these rough lads given the show just that bit of *Clockwork Orange frisson* that the afternoon needed?

The 1969 US tour had gone fantastically well for the self-styled Greatest Rock and Roll Band in the World. Of the '60s' big three (Beatles, Stones, Dylan), the Stones were now the only thing left, what with the breakup of the Beatles and Dylan having pointedly taken himself out of the running with *Self-Portrait*, his beer-drinking album of cover songs. The Stones, on the other hand, had moved on into new territory, a brooding neon-haunted Delta of their own imagining, with the myth-spinning albums *Beggars Banquet* and *Sticky Fingers*. And now they were touring to support the uncannily apocalyptic *Let It Bleed*.

However, there was one fly in the ointment: the Stones had been getting bad press about the price of their tickets, so Rock Scully (always up for the next folly) told them, 'Play for free, that's what the Dead do'. A free concert in Golden Gate Park!

The Parks Department granted use of the site on one condition: no announcements about where the event would take place until 24 hours before the concert. Should the promise be broken, the permit would be revoked.

Meanwhile, back in San Francisco, the local *hip-oisie* and biker riffraff had their own reasons for getting a free concert together. The idea was to try to bust the cycle of gang violence that had erupted in the last year in San Francisco. There was a mini-war going on between the Brown Berets, the Wah Ching and the other Chinese gangs, the black biker gangs, the Black Panthers, the Latino gangs and several different feuding biker factions: the Gypsy Jokers, the Hell's Angels and Sons of Hawaii. They were all violently clashing with each other in what was a pretty small turf (the population of San Francisco, the city itself, was only 750,000).

Perhaps a big powwow in Golden Gate Park involving all the different gangs would be just the thing. Get a budget from the Stones for beer, briquettes, beans, rice, burritos and so on. Gathering of the tribes, man!

Maybe it was because it was 'Sympathy For The Devil' time and the Stones weren't getting much sympathy, but one fine day Mick Jagger blurted out the plans for the free concert in Golden Gate Park. Result: they lose the permit. But the Stones weren't ready to abandon the idea that easily. To save face, they started looking for another location. There was another equally compelling reason to press on regardless: Albert and David Maysles were making a movie of the tour – the aptly named *Gimme Shelter* – and a big California-type concert with tepees, hookah-smoking hippies in tie-dyed tatterdemalion and bare-boobed dancing chicks would provide the perfect climax.

So the frantic search for a new location was on. Lawyer Melvin Belli and Woodstock promoter Michael Lang were flying around in helicopters and other such nonsense, and by now the whole world knew that there was going to be a free Rolling Stones concert. People were pouring into the San Francisco airport for the Big Event, the new location to be announced momentarily.

Once the site at the Altamont Speedway was chosen, the original plan of bringing everyone together was totally blown. How were Chicanos, blacks and Chinese expected to get the hell *out* there? Take the (nonexistent) bus?

The Stones had used Hell's Angels at their Hyde Park concert, but *English* Hell's Angels were a far cry from visigoths of the Oakland chapter. The Stones' infatuation with the heraldry of the Hell's Angels could be the beginning of a *big* problem, but attempting to explain this to Mick Jagger was fruitless.

'Listen, man,' Scully was trying to tell the Mick, 'you can't *hire* Hell's Angels. They're, uh, not for hire.'

Jagger quizzed him peevishly, 'Wot you saying then, exactly?' Surely, reasoned Sir Mick, the Hell's Angels would leap at the opportunity to act as the Praetorian Guard for the Stones, wouldn't they?

'Waaal, Mick, I dunno . . .'

Sam Cutler, the Stones' rowdy tour manager, was equally smitten. 'Oh, come off it, the Hell's Angels would be *perfect*. We used 'em in Hyde Park.'

'Uh, Sam, those kids, excuse me, were not Hell's Angels. They had 'Hell's Angels' *painted* on their jackets, for chrissakes! Like a costume party! These guys are red-and-white, real-time, Death's Head Angels! They went to Korea! Vietnam! They're fuckin' *killers*!'

Mick and Sam exchanged very noisy winks and soon decided to 'hire' the Hell's Angels for a truckload of, I'm not kidding, ice and beer.

DAY OF THE LOCUSTS

All day Friday, the Bay Area radio stations were telling people to stay away, that you wouldn't be able to get in anyway, but anybody who had ever been to a festival, lived in the area or was just plain determined knew that that couldn't be true and came anyway. I'd flown in from New York and was sleeping on Jann Wenner's couch.

By early Saturday morning when the gates were opened, the surrounding hills were covered with people, encampments and cars. Down on the highway, traffic was backed up six miles in either direction.

California. The desert (really just scrubland). You couldn't have a more apocalyptic theatre. Although from the air there seemed to be something ominous about such a massive gathering on these bald hills, the easiest thought that morning was that Altamont was going to be another Woodstock.

Woodstock, however, was a horse of a different colour. And it took place on the *East Coast*. Someone called it the most rehearsed event in the history of the world. But Californians are not generally inclined to rehearse these things, and some of the tension of the day that followed came from fans who gathered so desperately in the desert because they expected the Stones to create a totally *new* kind of theatre. They didn't realise that the Stones' image of America was a fantasyland barely thicker than an LP and that the Stones' theatre was one of re-enactment.

Whatever it was that drew us to this place, everybody wanted it. Everything about Altamont was *compulsive*. In retrospect, it seems incredible that everyone scrambled so fiercely to get there – walking, riding, hitching, flying into this reckless expedition in a state analogous to somnambulism. Once it had been announced, it had to happen even if a few details *had* to be forced to make it happen, like moving the entire site just twenty hours before the performance.

'Somehow,' said Keith, 'in America in '69 – I don't know

about now, and I never got it before – one got the feeling they really wanted to suck you out.' It was obvious why the fans wanted it so badly, but the Stones wanted it to happen just as much. The idea of a free concert in the City of Love appealed to them too much to let it slip away because of a few inconveniences.

Saturday morning I went down to the heliport where they were loading equipment for transport to the site. I ran into a couple of hulking Stones roadies who told the pilot that they couldn't possibly lift Keith's monitor – wink, wink – without my help.

From the air, the bleached-out hills around Altamont looked metallic in the haze and glare of the morning sun. Approaching the site, cars silted the base of the hills in crazy coloured splotches. People swarmed like fur around the spindly shanks of Chip Monck's stage, poised like a Dali-esque mantis. 'Once the kids started,' Bill Wyman said later, 'once the ants come down the hill make way watch out . . . they're going to eat you!'

And there was something swarming and ominous about this gathering – kinetic energy zinged through the air like psychic pellets. The place was a war zone. The state of the Altamont site was unimaginably appalling, a mini-Vietnam of garbage and old car wrecks. This, combined with the steep grade of the canyon slope, resulted in stoned people rolling downhill onto the stage.

'There is too much of something,' wrote Michael Lydon in *Ramparts*. 'Is it the people, the dope, the tension? Maybe it is the *wanting*, the concentration, not just of flesh, but of unfulfilled desire, of hope for (or is it fear of) deliverance . . . have we jammed ourselves together on these here hills miles from home hoping to find a way out of such masses? If that is our paradox, is Altamont our self-made trap? And yet . . . might we just be able by acting out the paradox so intensely to transcend it?'

Which is where the 'Motorpsycho Blues' entered the picture. The image of the Frisco and Oakland chapters flanking their Satanic Majesties on stage was just too tempting for the Stones to resist. But if the Angels were hired to *protect* the Stones, the question was: from *whom*? One Angel ridiculed the idea by saying that they had been hired to protect the Stones from ten thousand screaming chicks. Part of the problem was that the Stones thought of America in terms of past tours and Hollywood movies. As David Crosby said, 'the Rolling Stones are still a little bit in 1965 . . . to them an Angel is something between Peter Fonda and Dennis Hopper.'

The Stones put the Hell's Angels in charge of security, but most of the Angels didn't show up; the real dudes were at a big meeting of the entire Bay Area governing board of thieves and plunderers, deciding how to divide up the territory. This is the Yalta of the gang powwows, and, Stones concert or no Stones concert, the Angels are very turf-conscious, like a pack of wild boars in rutting season.

So that left 'prospects' as practically the only Angels at Altamont, young cats trying to prove themselves. What you had was East Bay rowdies on Ripple and ludes. Out of control with no one to rein them in. Pure gelignite.

THE FIRE IS SWEEPING MY VERY STREET TODAY

Everybody at Altamont *wanted* something, and the collision of exorbitant expectations could hardly have happened at a worse time, in a worse place or with a worse choice of participants. The Stones themselves were on a negative trajectory. 'Gimme Shelter' and 'Midnight Rambler' seemed almost like presentiments of the sweeping chaos and random violence to come.

By the time the Stones touched down on the speedway's asphalt pit in the late afternoon, the whole infernal machinery had already been set in motion. As Mick moved away from the helicopter, a kid punched him in the face. It was an omen, but so many other more practical warnings had been shunted aside to *get it on*, so why should an incident like this that could have happened anywhere . . . anyway it was already too late.

The girl who slipped up to the stage during Santana's set could have told them, not to mention the moon in Scorpio and God knows what else. With all the astrological preoccupations of San Francisco, no one had bothered to check. But by late afternoon no one needed to be told either. What was going on was obvious. Hell's Angels beating up Hell's Angels. A pledging Angel does a karate feint to a brother, who boots him in the groin. 'Don't pull any of that shit on me, bitch,' and he walks away.

The crowd that milled around the Stones' caravan was hardly unusual for a rock festival. Straight and stoned, drunk and floating freaks with college kids and super beings in their otherworldly robes – people who seemed to exist only for this kind of event. From time to time, Mick and Keith peeked out from the caravan door, drinking wine, eating sandwiches, and signing autographs, trying to bring the afternoon around. But nothing could change the prevailing mood, which was nasty and oppressive. Fights were breaking out everywhere, one hair-raising thing after another.

Jerry Garcia's old school bus became the Dead's dressing room. Jerry was shaking and huddling with Mountain Girl on the floor of the bus through the worst of the fighting – the Hell's Angels and guns and pool cues and all of that. They'd arrived fully-medicated – gummy opium, mescaline and half a key of rolled joints, but all the dope in the world wasn't going to help a bummer like this.

Phil Lesh, even more jittery than Garcia – if that's possible – was peeking out through the saggy curtains of the bus, giving us a running commentary on the savage sideshow outside. Grisly and violent images were replaced by others even more disturbing and incomprehensible.

'Jesus Christ, there's this three-hundred-pound naked guy, and – oh God! – the Angels are beating him to a pulp.'

'Phil, please, *no more.*'

Pigpen was huddled in the back of the bus, too numb to react. Night must fall.

Not until the Jefferson Airplane go on do Garcia and company venture out of the bus. Part way into the set, Marty Balin gets into a fight with an Angel named Animal wearing a grisly cowl made out of wolf fur. It's road-kill, essentially, that he has shaped to go over his head, complete with snout, teeth and whiskers. All that's missing from his outfit are horns. Animal proceeds to smack Marty Balin in the face and has to be pulled off the stage kicking and screaming, still trying to smash Marty in the face with his boot. It's a moment of pure terror. In the film *Gimme Shelter* there is something chilling about the shift in Grace Slick's voice from her opening comment, 'What the fuck is going (on?)' to her pleading, 'Everybody, please cool out,' as she realises that the command of the stage has been usurped and the Airplane are not invulnerable. After that, the Angels commandeer the stage. Jerry holds up both hands in an involuntary gesture of keeping back some unseen host of demons. He is petrified and runs straight back to the bus speechless and shaking like a leaf. He turns every shade of pale and whispers, 'Oh, maaaan, there is no way we're doing this. There is absolutely no way.' Jerry has a new plan: 'Go sort it out, man. Talk to the Angels or something.'

Oh, sure, Jerry. If somebody would only just *talk* to the Angels, the misunderstanding could get itself worked out.

Dan Healy, the Dead's sound guy, pokes his head into the bus: 'The Airplane are coming off stage, what do you guys want to do?'

Well, they *had* planned to go on just before the Stones, but things seem to be falling apart too quickly. It's essential, if more chaos is to be avoided, that the Stones play as soon as possible. Many more bands have shown up than anticipated,

the show is going on too long, and if the Stones go on after the
Dead they will go on *way* too late. It is already starting to get
dark, and there are no lights and no lit roads to find the way
out of his godforsaken place. Two hundred thousand people
in this demonic gully!

'Let the Stones go on, this is *their* madness,' says Phil.

'No way we're going to *play* good, anyway. Yeah,' says
Jerry (ever the pusillanimous philosopher-realist), 'we're just
gonna give our enemies more ammunition.' Our *enemies*?

They take off while the Stones are playing, happy to have
gotten the last helicopter out of Saigon.

GOD SAID TO ABRAHAM, KILL ME A SON

Night has fallen by the time the Stones hit the stage. It is so
cold that even the mass of arc lamps and the huge electric
heaters in front of the stage cannot keep the chill off. The
stage is very low and ringed in hierarchical layers with
Angels, film crew, friends and photographers who from time
to time get thrown off the stage. Everything is schizophrenic.
Nude chicks and guys slither over the sides of the platform
only to get booted trampled and lacerated with pool cues.
Their hair and faces matted with blood, they simply climb up
again. It's as if they *want* to be clobbered.

Not much time is wasted; Keith has already tuned up
backstage. Zip into 'Jumping Jack Flash', Mick's mythic
autobiography, and it could hardly have been more appropriate.

> *I was born in a crossfire hurricane,*
> *And I howled at my ma in the driving rain . . .*

Keith: 'It felt great and sounded great. Then there's a big
ruckus about one of the Angels' bikes being knocked over in
front of the stage. Oh dear, a bike's got knocked over. I'm not

used to bein' upstaged by Hell's Angels – over somebody's *motorbike*. Yes, I perfectly understand that your bike's got knocked over, can we carry on with the concert? But they're not like that. They have a whole thing going with their bikes, as we all know now.'

'Carol' is next, an old rocker, and the hogmasters can dig that too. A temporary pause. Then 'Sympathy For The Devil' brings on another outburst. Each discharge of violence in front of the stage causes the crowd to sweep back into the darkness behind them. It's hard to believe that it's possible to clear so much space under so much pressure in so little time. What makes it possible is total *fear*.

'Something always happens when we get into this number,' Mick says calmly. This time it's a nude chick who is freaking out in the front row. Six Angels jump on her. 'Now, fellows, I'm sure it doesn't take *all* of you to take care of this,' Mick says in high camp.

They're only into the third song, but already it's obvious that the riveting power of the music is not going to turn back the tide. 'Brothers and sisters,' Mick says a little tremulously, using apocalyptic words from 'Gimme Shelter', 'Why are we fighting? Who wants to fight?'

The Stones suddenly seem very fragile. Mick appears especially vulnerable; divested of his sensual reality, he is the butterfly prince, a delicate gossamer figure in the camp of the Huns. With the threat to the Stones, all our collective dreams seem to collapse and layers of illusions are ripped away.

We – Andy, my acid bride and I – followed the Stones onto the stage. We are now standing about ten feet from the Stones. The stage is ringed with Hell's Angels. To my alarm I see Andy – so skinny and frail that a gust of wind could blow her sideways – has ventured beyond the phalanx of Angels, with her 8mm camera, oblivious to the danger. She is drawn to the prancing Mick with magnetic traction. Closer and closer she moves, led on to the very rim of the volcano by the hypnotic dance of the butterfly prince. Too late I see an Angel reach out and grab her by the shoulder. In the slow motion of terror his arm doesn't just reach it s-t-r-e-t-c-h-e-s, like Plastic Man's. I know he'll break every bone in her body if he throws her off the stage so I now – in an act of desperation – put my hand on *his* shoulder. I'm probably going to lose a few teeth, but what the hell. The Angel turns menacing towards me – ah, but I have a flash of inspiration: in my best mucker cockney I say, 'It's awright, mate, ahm Mick's bruvver, Chris, and she's wif me.' Somehow in the dread-zone, time has accelerated for me so that the Angel's face now seems to move in grotesque stop-frame jerks. His mouth open, drooling, his eyes pinned and glazed regard me quizzically. He's drunk and stoned. I've overloaded his circuits and in a millisecond pause I grab Andy and pull her away.

Teeth-grinding amphetamine paranoia is rampant, and in that collective psychic storm Meredith Hunter, a young black man, gets pulled into the undertow. The stage is so low that it's hard to tell what is happening, and in one of the many random acts of violence, Hunter is knifed to death by two Hell's Angels. The chaos and terror are so pervasive that few people notice the murder; it's just another bone-crushing skirmish among a hundred others. The Angels pull his blood-soaked body underneath the Dead's stake bed truck.

In *Gimme Shelter*, we clearly see the silhouette of Hunter's gun as he pulls it out of his jacket. We witness Jagger's reaction as he watches the slow-motion frames of this chilling moment on the editing machine. Was Meredith Hunter going to shoot Jagger? Or was Hunter reacting to the relentless badgering by the two thugs who stabbed him, racist Angels who couldn't handle seeing a black man making out with a pretty white girl?

And there are no cops to be found anywhere. There's never a policeman when you need one! Hey, they're smart, they stayed away. Let the Hell's Angels kill the Hippies, what the fuck do we care? One of the interesting aspects of the Altamont 'experiment' was, of course, to see how feebly the counter-culture handled a crisis *without* the help of the customary social restraints – those very guardians of middle-class society that we had so loudly railed against. We had seen the future, and it was not exactly the utopian blueprint we'd had in mind.

YOU KNOW NEITHER THE DAY NOR THE HOUR

As we all drifted away from Altamont that night, everyone who was there knew it was the end of that kind of event for ever. We could no longer afford apocalypses. We had used up all the unreasonable cosmic-radical anticipations for another hundred years. But if it is the business of the future to be dangerous, Altamont is witness that to pull time in both directions is totally explosive.

Woodstock and Altamont, polar opposites in a mass media-generated parable, have collapsed in on one another as prequel and sequel of light and darkness in an ongoing passion play of the '60s. Woodstock is peace and love, the triumph of Woodstock Nation; Altamont is guns, drugs and the end of the world. But in reality they were just two ends of the same runaway train. The same fuck-ups, the same cast of characters.

Woodstock was no more peace and love than Altamont was. They were the result of the same disease: the bloating of mass bohemia in the late '60s. At that point, Mercury, the patron saint of merchants and thieves takes over, all hell breaks loose, and the Devil starts setting up his bleachers out on Highway 61.

The astonishing thing was that almost nobody saw it coming. The Dead at least should have read the writing on their *own* wall. A couple of days before Altamont, Emmett Grogan of the Diggers had left this message scrawled on the blackboard at the Dead offices at 710 Ashbury: 'CHARLIE

MANSON MEMORIAL LOVE DEATH CULT FESTIVAL.'

Garcia, in the cosmo-blather of the times, dopily blamed the Stones' songs for bringing on the disaster. Oh really, singing about the Devil can make him appear? As Marianne Faithfull, Jagger's girlfriend at the time, said of his supposed devotion to Satanism, 'A devotee of *satin*, perhaps'. Still, Altamont had a determining direction for the Rolling Stones, too. They went on to mock the earnest mayhem of rock's desperate adolescent expectations in 'It's Only Rock'n'Roll'. As Stanley Booth said, 'After Altamont, the Stones opted for comedy.'

The haunting possibility of narrowly averted onstage assassination – a recurrent paranoia of the late '60s – along with the brutal death of Meredith Hunter (and the concomitant demise of the counterculture) has always made Altamont seem to be the ideal marker for the end of the '60s. True, it conveniently took place in the last days of the decade, but, according to my memory, the '60s died many times before that: with the Summer of Love, with *Sgt Pepper,* with the Death of Hippie, with the election of Nixon, with Charles Manson (the Tate-LaBianca murders occurred just one weekend before Woodstock).

Or did the '60s, an exhausted behemoth in bell-bottoms and platform shoes, stumble on into the next decade, watching helplessly as its sacred hatchlings – Jimi Hendrix, Janis Joplin and Jim Morrison – met their fates one after another, and like some last phantom of our great expectations, unable to remember what it wanted, melt into the thin air of the '70s?

Simon Reynolds

LOLLAPALOOZA: A WOODSTOCK FOR THE LOST GENERATION

New York Times, 4th August 1991

This piece was written in the summer of 1991, at a time when alternative rock was very vital if fragmented, yet was still being denied access to the pop mainstream. Only a few months after the Lollapalooza tour – essentially a mobile alt-rock festival – had finished up, Nirvana smashed their way on to MTV and radio playlists, and the whole grunge explosion was under way. While there isn't a direct link between the two things, I definitely think that Lollapalooza created the sense of pent-up energy massing outside the barricades, and it made people in the music industry and media aware of the sheer demographic heft of the alt-rock generation.

There are also some parallels between Jane's Addiction and Nirvana. Both were mixing up metal and punk, albeit with different reference points: Jane's Addiction were something like a cross between Led Zeppelin and the Banshees (Perry Farrell had been in an LA Goth-rock band called Psi-Com), while Nirvana, coming more from a classic UK punk and US hardcore sensibility, were more visceral than ethereal, colliding Black Sabbath with Black Flag.

In the event, the goal of uniting punks and metal-kids was achieved on a much grander scale by Nirvana, but for a while Jane's Addiction were doing a similar kind of thing and were functioning as a focus for the disparate disaffected of the Bush years. Expanding on Jane's ability to gather different tribes together, Lollapalooza was an ambitious undertaking and a genuinely inspired idea. Then, as Lollapalooza continued over subsequent years, its development reflected the gradual decline of alt-rock into a new conformity; a disillusioned Farrell eventually gave up his involvement in the festivals. Back in the summer of 1991, though, the concept was informed by real idealism and a determination to make something happen.

                                                                    SR

THERE'S NO CONTEST: this summer's biggest tour is the aptly-titled Lollapalooza, a mobile rock festival featuring a bill of premier alternative bands – Siouxsie and the Banshees, Living Colour, Nine Inch Nails, Ice-T, Butthole Surfers and the Rollins Band – headlined by the critically-acclaimed Jane's Addiction. The tour is currently crisscrossing North America, doing 26 shows in 21 cities, including two New York-area dates at Waterloo Village in Stanhope, N.J., on Aug. 11 and 14. There may be other, bigger-grossing tours, but for fans disaffected with routine concerts, nothing can rival the sense of expectation and event that Lollapalooza has aroused.

The tour was the brainchild of Jane's Addiction's lead singer Perry Farrell, its drummer, Stephen Perkins, and Marc Geiger and Don Muller from Triad Artists, the group's booking agency. The idea was conceived after Jane's Addiction attended Britain's Reading Festival last year. The band was booked to play at the festival, an annual three-day event featuring top alternative bands, but pulled out because of illness. Instead, band members attended as spectators and, impressed by the atmosphere, soon began to wonder why there was nothing similar in the United States. Geiger and Muller, who had previously organised alternative rock tours of the United States, decided that a mobile festival was feasible, if logistically daunting.

From the start, Farrell wanted Lollapalooza to be not just a musical event but a cultural smorgasbord, with a diverse array of tents, booths and displays exploring a number of political, environmental, human rights and cultural issues. The idea, says Muller, is to bombard festival-goers with stimuli and data and 'raise as much public awareness in a single day as possible.' At each show, there is an 'art tent', displaying work by local artists personally selected by Farrell.

In this respect, Lollapalooza seems to be a conscious attempt to re-invoke the '60s sense of rock as counterculture, in defiance of today's perception of rock as a leisure industry. 'It's throwing a lot of issues into the public consciousness,' Farrell says. 'I want there to be a sense of confrontation. But I'm not declaring myself left-wing or right-wing, I'm actually bringing both sides into it.'

While planning the festival, he toyed with having National Rifle Association and armed forces stalls next to representatives from Greenpeace or animal rights organisations, to stimulate debate. 'It would be way too easy for me to take everything that's obviously politically correct and have this hip, left-wing event. But I don't want to make out I have the answers, all I want to do is pose the questions.'

The N.R.A. and the armed forces recruiters, however, proved to be gun-shy about the event; participants instead range from the League of Women Voters to Handgun Control Inc. to Body Manipulations, which will display body piercing.

The lineup of bands for Lollapalooza is just as varied. Each band represents a different faction of alternative rock: Siouxsie and the Banshees (goth, a mystical, morbid descendant of punk, whose fans look like Morticia from *The Addams Family*), Living Colour (black rock), Nine Inch Nails (electro-industrial), Ice-T (gangster rap), the Butthole Surfers (acid rock) and the Rollins Band (hardcore punk).

Jane's Addiction's music is itself a product of the fragmen-
tation and cultural overload that Farrell wants Lollapalooza
to mirror. Like Faith No More and Fishbone, Jane's Addiction belongs to the new hybrid genre that has been dubbed
'funk-and-roll', but the group takes musical miscegenation
further than any of its peers. Jane's Addiction emerged from
the same late-'80s Los Angeles metal scene that spawned
Guns N' Roses. But by its second and third albums, *Nothing's
Shocking* and *Ritual de lo Habitual*, it became clear that
'metal' was an inadequate tag for Jane's Addiction's exhilarating fusion of heavy rock, funk, reggae, ethnic influences,
tribal rhythms and art rock. 'Three Days', an epic, 10-minute
track off *Ritual*, covers the distance between the astral metal
of Led Zeppelin and the ethereal, ambient drift of the Cocteau
Twins. Some regard Jane's Addiction's departure from the
straight and narrow of populist rock as self-indulgent, others
as heroically pretentious. But for all its art-rock complexity,
the band seldom sacrifices the raw attack of pure rock and
roll.

At live shows, Jane's Addiction unites disparate subcul-
tures as successfully as it melds musical influences. Its audience is a bizarre coalition of metal fans, punks, college-radio
hipsters, goths, nouveau hippies and the unaligned and
curious. What attracts such a motley array of fans is that
the band has managed to bring back a sense of rock and roll
as an underground. There's a strong element of ritual and
ceremony to Jane's Addiction performances, heightened by
the group's stage backdrops: for the Lollapalooza tour, a
shrinelike construction is covered with icons, candles and
sculptures. 'Most of the stuff that we use at the moment is
taken out of my apartment,' says Farrell, who is something of
a jack of all trades (his sculptures appear on the covers of
both *Nothing's Shocking* and *Ritual de lo Habitual*).

Jane's Addiction also has an aura of danger and the
forbidden. Farrell's lyrics and life style are steeped in Romanticism's creed of impulse, instinct, living on the edge and

systematic derangement of the senses. His rock-and-roll forebears are Patti Smith, Iggy Pop of the Stooges and, above all, Jim Morrison. Farrell, who is 32, has revived many of Morrison's favorite riffs: the idea of 'reinvention of the self' (as a glamorous deviant), the notion of the rock singer as shaman, the Dionysian quest for oblivion through excess. Jane's Addiction is a heady confusion of *fin-de-siecle* decadence and back-to-nature primitivism. Is there a contradiction there?

'The only way I can see that excess is against nature is that maybe when you get intoxicated, you can get sick,' Farrell says. 'But both decadence and the back-to-nature impulse are about freedom. You feel free when you hit the great outdoors, and you feel free when you get intoxicated.'

Farrell is also interested in magic and syncretic Latin American forms of Catholicism that incorporate pagan rituals. The back of the *Ritual de lo Habitual* album depicts a medicine shelf packed with potions (plus a canister of Methadone, an allusion to the group's highly-publicised drug problems). On a recent trip to Mexico, Farrell married his girlfriend in a blood-mingling ceremony presided over by what he describes as 'a very serious witch'. Perhaps Farrell is attracted to paganism because it is sensual and earthy, whereas monotheistic religions like Christianity, Islam and Judaism tend to restrict the ways of the flesh.

'The problem that a lot of people have with me is that I'm having a good time,' says Farrell. 'It's not even that they disapprove of what I do, it's just that I'm doing it, and they're not. That's what I hate about those patriarchal religions: the guilt trip. I just don't feel guilt.'

Hence lyrics like 'ain't no wrong now, ain't no right, only pleasure and pain' – in essence, Nietzsche's *Beyond Good and Evil* rendered in rock and roll idiom. For Farrell, the only sins are self-denial, the deferment of gratification and boredom. 'The only time I feel guilty,' he says, 'is when I know I'm doing something that's really worthless, like watching TV,

when I'm belittling myself by allowing my time to be consumed by nothing.'

Farrell's creed is Romanticism's age-old quest to 'live now'.
Or as he puts it on 'Jane Says': 'I'm gonna kick tomorrow.'
Like Jim Morrison, Jane's Addiction's message to its fans is
not to 'waste the dawn', but to choose a life of insatiability
and restlessness.

'For a lot of the year, I'm usually in a different city every
day,' says Farrell. 'I simply can't fathom how people can bear
to stay in one place. I'm bored very easily.' His fear of stasis
and routine may have led to the decision to break up Jane's
Addiction after Lollapalooza and pursue other artistic ambitions. Farrell has directed and appeared in a feature-length
film, *Gift*, which has no release date. 'I told Warner Brothers
I'd give them five videos if they gave me $125,000 to make a
movie. And I went to Mexico and made a film. So basically I
got Warners to pay for my vacation. Mexico is wild. The
people are hot-blooded, the weather is hot, the food is hot.
The art is great, too.'

Farrell's decision to end Jane's Addiction may confound
the group's fans. The band is on the verge not just of major
commercial success, but of becoming a countercultural icon
for a disenfranchised generation. The singer is adamant,
however, that his future musical projects will not take place
under the name Jane's Addiction. The group is, however,
going out in a blaze of glory. Lollapalooza is a boon for the
twenty-something generation, a happening that may instil
pride in teenagers who have grown up under the shadow of
rock's mythic past. As 'Classic Girl', the last track on *Ritual
de lo Habitual*, puts it: 'They may say, "Those were the days"
. . . but in a way, you know for us *these* are the days . . .
Yeah, for us these are the days.'

5

LIVE AND DIRECT

Bill Millar

HIT THE ROAD STAX! OTIS REDDING AND FRIENDS IN FINSBURY PARK

unpublished piece for *Soul Music Monthly*, June 1967

Soul Music Monthly, *edited by Tony Cummings, was one of several fanzines which sprang up in order to review and interview the visiting deluge of mid-'60s soul singers. The previous twelve months had played host to (deep breath) Lee Dorsey, the Exciters, Clarence Henry, the Drifters, Irma Thomas, Patti LaBelle and the Belles, James Brown, Arthur Alexander, Don Covay, the Vibrations, Doris Troy, Ike & Tina Turner, Roy C., Ben E.King, Billy Stewart, Solomon Burke, Otis Redding (at Tiles Club in Oxford Street), Charlie & Inez Foxx, Maxine Brown, Alvin Cash & the Crawlers, the Dixie Cups, Robert Parker, the Mad Lads, the Spellbinders and Edwin Starr. And those are just the ones I saw.*

Most of these performers played tiny clubs. They were hired by former pop promoters who bought them for as little as £30 a night and put them up, sometimes two or three to a room, in the then unfashionable Notting Hill where I would knock on the door with pencil and notepad during my office lunch-hour. It was an unrepeatably fantastic time to be obsessed by black music.

Soul Music Monthly *ceased publication in April 1967. It was reactivated (as* Soul Music *and then* Shout*) later that year when my review of* The Otis Redding Show*, an uncharacteristically grand package*

*promoted by Arthur Howes in association with Phil
Walden, was no longer topical. But here it is now with
all its 36-year-old embarrassments. My own toes curl
at the references to 'sense of rhythm' and 'coloured
musician'. Moreover, Charlie Gillett, the renowned
author and broadcaster, told me I shouldn't use the
word 'negroid' – not if I wanted any black people to
read about my enthusiasms. Charlie also told me that I
needed to polish a style if I ever wanted to be paid for
this stuff. It was the best advice I ever received.*

BM

IT WAS PERFECTLY clear that every performer on the Stax
show was going to receive the most sympathetic applause
should he or she subsequently turn out to be thoroughly
excellent or near-mediocre. For the second house, the place
was packed to capacity and the curtains parted whilst many,
including myself, were still finding their seats. Consequently,
the repertoire of the MGs is none too clear but first off they
appeared to be playing 'Gimme Some Lovin'' – some may
prefer to think it was Homer Banks' 'A Lot Of Love'.

In lime-green suits and white shirts, the group followed with
'Red Beans and Rice', the puffy-faced Duck Dunn fronting the
combo on bass and leaping up and down like a renegade from
a red-hot rock group. In contrast, Steve Cropper, the most
popular MG, was very quiet and very much in the background. If he has a personality, he lets it retire behind his
instrument and performs with neither physical gesture nor
change of expression. On what I think must have been 'Hip
Hug-Her' his guitar sprang to life and amazing lengthy note-
bending solos echoed around the theatre.

Booker T., looking much older than his photographs,
concluded the MGs set with 'Green Onions'. What rapport!
The subtle interchange between Cropper's superb, anguished
guitar phrases and Booker's blue organ riffs delighted us all.
The crowd stood up and cheered.

The rhythm section was augmented by three horns to give the fans a taste of the Mar-Keys sound. In royal-blue suits, Wayne Jackson on trumpet, newcomer Andrew Love on tenor (a coloured musician) and Bob Snyder on baritone, the full band led off with 'Philly Dog' and finished with a marathon 'Last Night'. Quaint to observe white man Wayne Jackson step up to the microphone to offer the classic 'Oooh Last Night' in a negroid accent. The Mar-Keys' spot was excellent but all too short. In fact, the whole two-hour show seemed to flash by in a matter of moments, possibly because every performer was an unknown quantity stage-wise and was obviously worth watching, whereas normally on a theatre date one sits bored to death by a motley crew of British groups long before the star performer can do his stuff.

One could tell the lay-out of the programme had been thought of before Percy Sledge dropped out of the package. As a result, Arthur Conley received bigger billing than everybody except Otis!!! This slight but long-limbed young man received a huge round of perhaps undeserved applause. In a blue suit, he grabbed the hand-microphone for 'Midnight Hour' and threw his jacket into the wings for 'Sweet Soul Music', a song that is, in fact, a corruption of Sam Cooke's 'Yeah Man'. Arthur proved to be tremendously popular. Certainly a sharp mover and a buoyant, if diminutive, personality. After a very brief 'Land of 1000 Dances' he made a spectacular exit sliding from one side of the stage to the other on one foot à la James Brown.

In a brilliant, long gold lamé gown and short, cropped hair, Carla Thomas took the spotlight for 'Let Me Be Good To You'. A nice, tight, swinging rendition with nifty drumming from Al Jackson all the way. 'Yesterday' – a number recorded by 'a London [sic] group', said Carla – was a surprise. It was delivered in a big-ballad voice. 'B.A.B.Y.' concluded Carla's set and regrettably she was off almost as soon as she was on. A pity – she should return for a club tour.

I was not overawed by Eddie Floyd's performance. One

becomes a little blasé about the never-ending succession of soul-singing gentlemen whose over-riding talent is to see how many times it is possible to cram 'Lemme Hear You Say Yeah!' into three songs. Eddie was one of those and really he was not sufficiently distinctive to score well. Many disagreed, however, and he gained a rousing reception. 'If I Had A Hammer' came first; performed many times better on innumerable occasions. 'Knock On Wood' – an excellent tune – got the loudest applause, and, after removing his jacket, Eddie swung into a few bars of his latest 'Raise Your Hand'. The audience went overboard, but I'm afraid I was singularly unimpressed. Eddie also made the ghastly technical error of singing 'Long Live Your Queen'. Enough said!

God bless Sam and Dave for reminding us what soul music really is all about. In dapper black suits and white shirts the duo opened with 'You Don't Know Like I Know', searing through a climax that became wilder and wilder. The impact, after Eddie Floyd, was simply too much. 'When Something Is Wrong With My Baby' stole the show for everyone. Sheer undiluted emotion. The crashing beat and the slow wailing lyrical harmony of Sam and Dave was a tonic for us all. This number alone was well worth the price of the ticket. The Sam Cooke/Simms Twins song 'Soothe Me' also received an enjoyable workout with doses of solo chanting and standout bass-playing from Duck Dunn. Sam and Dave removed their jackets to dance, sing and shout their way through 'Hold On, I'm Coming'. Double dynamite to be sure. Footstompin', handclappin' excitement gained the pair the standing ovation they deserved.

Otis walked smartly on in a black, double-breasted suit and opened with 'Shake'. As with other up-tempo numbers it seemed to be speeded up but fortunately the Mar-Keys gave out with an accompaniment that was more proficient than that of Otis' own band. At Tiles, last September, everything Otis sang was lost in a welter of brass. 'Respect' and 'My Girl' followed in quick succession and, apart from the varying tempo, there was little to distinguish between them. 'I Can't Turn You Loose' displayed what, to me, is Otis' number one talent. He possesses the most remarkable sense of rhythm. His body shook with every syllable and twisted with perfect precision to every loud but deft drum beat.

His other movements are like a slightly more energetic Ben E. King. He's very like the latter at times. Readers may know what I mean – all grins and smiles on what ought to be the most soulful of numbers! Otis will occasionally jerk his limbs at odd angles but is usually content with striding menacingly from one side of the stage to the other as if he were bent on thumping the saxophonist for playing a bum note.

He closed with a slow but uninspired 'Try A Little Tender-ness' and the audience clapped in ever-mounting crescendos as the rest of the bill came on-stage from the wings. I feel compelled to say that Otis is overrated. His reputation puts him amongst the top bracket of Rhythm and Blues artists but, strictly as a performer, he does not come within sight of Solomon Burke or James Brown, and any exciting Little Richard influence he might once have had has long since vanished.

Having said that I must add the show was worth seeing; very rarely do we have the pleasure of watching seven acts that we knew we would enjoy long before we had purchased our tickets!

Greil Marcus

WE CAN TALK ABOUT IT NOW: THE BAND AT WINTERLAND

Good Times, 23rd April 1969

*I wrote my first music column for the San Francisco
Express-Times, the best of the 1960s underground
newspapers. I started in December 1968, taking over
from the late Sandy Darlington; by the spring of 1969,
the paper had changed its name to* Good Times, *maybe
because, with the inauguration of Richard Nixon as
president, times were getting worse. 'This is it,' my
editor Marvin Garson said as he sent me off to cover
The Band's national debut at the Winterland Ballroom, where ten years later the Sex Pistols would play
their last show, then as before under the auspices of the
late Bill Graham. 'This is when we find out if there are
still open spaces out there.'*

*Marvin was a New Yorker; living in California
sometimes made him talk like Natty Bumppo, but
his words were accurate. By 'out there' he meant right
here, and he was talking about The Band because it
was obvious that they were committed to the very idea
of America: complicated, dangerous and alive.*

With the release of Music from Big Pink *the year
before, their music had already given us a sure sense
that the country was richer than we had guessed, and
by we I mean people then in their teens and twenties
and thirties, in their music part of what seemed an
America within the greater America in which they*

*found themselves trapped – trapped, as they saw it, as
I saw it, as we saw it, in a country conducting a
criminal war in our name, and if you stood against
it, did that make you a traitor, or a citizen?*

*In The Band's unique blend of instruments and
vocals, in the half-lost phrases and buried lyrics, there
was an ambiguity that opened up the world with real
force. The songs captured the yearning for home and
the fact of displacement that ruled our lives; we thought
The Band's music was the most natural parallel to our
hopes, ambitions, and doubts, and we were right to
think so. Flowing through their music were spirits of
acceptance and desire, rebellion and awe, raw excitement, good sex, open humour, a magic feel for history –
a determination to find plurality and drama in an
America we had met too often as a monolith.*

*The Band's music made us feel part of their adven-
ture; we knew that we would win if they succeeded and
lose if they failed. That was what Marvin Garson
meant. It was a good feeling.*

GM
– adapted from Mystery Train *(1975)*

THE BAND HAS BEEN together the best part of a decade, almost
nine years. Little Richard has been Little Richard for about
double that, but really, who else could he be? It's something
else to found a group that lasts. It's not a matter of I-Was-
There-When, though that's part of it; with so many bands
falling apart or kicking out members or just calling it quits,
The Band has stuck together.

A few years back, what was it like: playing favourite riffs,
the old and the new, picking up a new idea here and there,
maybe writing a few songs, playing great and nobody caring,
sometimes playing shitty no doubt and the nightclub drunks
heckling and walking out, spilling drinks on the stage if there
was one – that was The Band in the early '60s, when they

were called the Hawks. They all came from Canada, with the
exception of lead singer, drummer, and part-time mandolin
exciter Levon Helm, who hailed from Arkansas – but some
sort of Southern country tradition, a feeling for a frontier that
had moved on out West but was still really right there at
home, gave The Band its spirit and its tone.

They would gig all over the United States and Canada,
barnstorming like a baseball team during the off-season,
playing, says organist Garth Hudson, 'for pimps, whores,
rounders and flakeouts'. It can make you think of Mike Fink
and his riverboat, or saloons with board sidewalks outside.
Pick your own movie. Mine is by Charlie Chaplin; the music
of The Band reminds me of what you might have heard in the
mining towns of the great Alaskan Gold Rush. Did your
father ever read you the old Robert Service poem, 'The
Cremation of Sam McGee', about the 1890s gold-digger
from Tennessee who couldn't adjust to the freezing climate
of the Yukon?

> The Northern Lights have seen queer sights
> But the queerest they ever did see
> Was the night on the marge of Lake LeBarge
> When I cremated Sam McGee.

Poor Sam wasn't warm until he found himself on top of his
own funeral pyre. The Band has their view: 'I'd rather be
burned In Canada/Than freeze here In the South!' Maybe
The Band is just a group of hard-luck miners who decided to
try their band at something else. I told all this to Garth
Hudson and he smiled back, 'Well, I always have liked the
idea of reincarnation.'

In 1965 Bob Dylan was ready to tour the country and he
wanted a rock and roll band. He found the Hawks and they
were it. As Levon Helm, quoted in *Rolling Stone*, tells the
story, Dylan called them on the telephone at some nightclub
in New Jersey. 'We had never heard of Bob Dylan, but he had

heard of us. He said, "You wanna play Hollywood Bowl?" So we asked him who else was gonna be on the show. "Just us," he said.' They didn't know his music but they listened to his records and fooled around with Bob and understood what be was doing and it worked. The combination was magnificent: guitarist Robbie Robertson pushed Dylan to heights of musical fantasy that haven't been touched since. You can hear it on a single they recorded on tour in Liverpool in 1966, 'Just like Tom Thumb's Blues' (Columbia 4-43683, get it at Music City on Alcatraz in Berkeley).

'They're the greatest band in the world,' Dylan told Keith Richard of the Stones. 'What about us?' Richard wanted to know. 'Oh, you guys make the best philosophy, but . . .' 'What about US?' demanded Keith Moon of the Who. 'Well now, you make the best history, but . . .'

The tour was over, and after a while The Band came to Woodstock to live in the now-famous Big Pink. They'd play with Dylan at night, writing songs, inventing and refining their own sounds. *Music From Big Pink* came out of it – as Sandy Darlington wrote, 'it's like a good fishing hole, you can go back to it again and again and never be disappointed.' A great record. And now The Band was coming to Winterland.

Tickets went on sale a week early – there was some sense that this was a special chance for us, to have our spirits renewed, to hear and see what we hadn't ever come across before. *Good Times* received a very nice invitation from Bill Graham for 'a reception honoring The Band,' so I went. I don't know what I was expecting – reporters and cameras and floodlights, I suppose, but it wasn't like that at all. A few people were sitting around, and after a while members of The Band ambled in, chatted a while, and left. They were shy and friendly, and if someone had told them they were supposed to be big stars they'd most likely have been embarrassed.

The Band had not performed on their own in over four years. Thursday night was to be their debut, in a very important way. They're pros, but they were anxious and

worried. And Robbie Robertson, lead guitarist and composer
of 'The Weight', was terribly ill with the 'flu and a fever. The
Band was depressed and nervous, Robertson was fighting off
stomach pains and 103 degrees of temperature, and thousands of people were waiting for them at Winterland. The Ace
of Cups had done a delightful set and the Sons of Champlin
had completed their attack on the eardrums. Now the stage
was empty and records were playing – the crowd was getting
irritable. Winterland was crowded that night, but not
jammed; it wasn't hot and people were hip and friendly.
But it was eleven o'clock and nothing was happening.

Something like panic must have been in possession of Bill
Graham: Robbie Robertson was far too sick to play, but The
Band's management would not agree to Graham's plan to
cancel the Thursday night show in favour of a special Sunday
performance for those who'd shown up on opening night.
Finally, at eleven thirty, men began to set up The Band's
equipment, and we came alive. The Band came on stage in the
dark, tuning up, and it seemed like hours before they were
through. Then at midnight they were ready to play. We had
waited almost four hours, some of us. The lights went on,
everyone stood up, a girl behind me was screaming with joy,
yelling it: '*We LOVE you Band, welcome BAND, OOOOH,
BAND!*'

The crowd was with them but it wasn't working, not really.
Robertson looked weak and miserable, on the verge of
collapse, and the band, his friends, couldn't pretend he
was all right. They were worried about him. Off to one side
of the stage stood a big white-haired man in a dark suit, the
man who had hypnotised Robertson into 'forgetting' the
pains in his stomach. It was all very weird and uncomfortable, Robertson leaning against the piano and looking as if
he could not last another minute, playing minimal rhythm
guitar, his only attempt at a solo a shambles. Finally, on the
third or fourth song, they began to find themselves, and then
all at once it was over and they split. The Band done seven

numbers for 35 minutes, and after four hours it was clear that this was it for the night. The crowd yelled and shouted, at first for an encore and then out of frustration, some people screaming with hatred and rage. The girl near me who'd squealed out a welcome half an hour before was flashing cruelty: 'I hope you get sicker, Robbie Robertson!' At last the mood shifted, from astonishment to depression, from anger to bitterness. 'If they'd only,' a girl mumbled, 'If they'd only . . .'

The Band had been built up into heroes who couldn't fall, couldn't weaken, and now from the status of heroes they were not acceptable as guys who played music, they had to be shitheads and assholes. At least some people saw it that way, those who were yelling 'cocksuckers' as The Band stumbled off, Robertson in a daze. There was some kind of unholy disaster that night. It was wretched.

We were back again on Friday. The girls of the Ace of Cups had set things up perfectly (more about them next week), and as they were leaving the stage their bass player walked to the mic and virtually gurgled the words: 'Big Pink!' With all sense of time destroyed by a happy anticipation, it happened just like that (fanfare): The Band was on stage, the music was rising, and there was just no question, they had it all there before they'd even started to play. Robertson flashed a big grin at the crowd that wouldn't stop cheering, and then he bent deep over his guitar and The Band went into it all the way.

They are an amazing group of musicians. Not one of them stands out as a star, and yet they're each of them as distinctly different as the Beatles. They might be an accident of the frontier, a group of happy weathered outcasts who fell together in Tombstone, Arizona, and decided to give it all up and play music. Richard Manuel, lead singer, piano, organ, drums when Helm switches to mandolin – he might be the meal ticket, the card sharp who scrapes in the dough when no one wants to hear these guys play. He even looks a little like Hoagy Carmichael, who was (is?) a very cool-looking fellow. Robertson was wearing some sort of skull cap that night, and with his wire glasses and sideburns he looked like a Talmudic scholar whose scrolls had gotten lost on the prairie somewhere, and he had his younger brother, bass guitarist Rick Danko, along for the ride. God knows what they're doing here but there's no money to get back to Poland, so . . . Levon Helm – he might be a squaw man, a trapper who married an Indian only to find himself ostracised by the better citizens; that quality of toughness underneath the humour marks his powerful singing. He uses a very small kit of drums, so that every beat is solid and hard, no extra cymbal noise, it's all just too good to waste. Garth Hudson (organ, and piano on 'The Weight') would have to be The Old Man of Mountains, with his beard that nearly touches his chest; he wouldn't talk much, just peeking out over his organ every once in a while, no way to tell he's there at all save for the sounds he draws from his instrument.

They went through their repertoire, each song more exciting and colourful than the last, and then Hudson began to play the organ solo that leads into 'Chest Fever', perhaps their best composition, certainly their most effective performance in person. Hudson's playing was so dazzling that the audience actually gasped with amazement when he ended it and moved into the song itself. When the whole band took over the music seemed to expand, filling the hall to all of its corners, not blasting away the emptiness but simply making it impossible for anything else to occupy the same bit of space and time. Robertson heightened the drama of the song by hitting tough notes at the end of every line, and a tension grew up around the room, out of a realisation that something monumental was happening and we were there to hear and see it.

It just went on and on, into the second set Friday night and through both performances on Saturday. Richard Manuel's vocal on 'Tears of Rage' was probably the finest singing that has ever been heard at Winterland; so dramatic that you could see the song's story taking place on stage. Then Levon Helm left the drums to Manuel and strapped on his electric mandolin for 'Doncha Tell Henry' and he bent forwards and backwards while he and Danko played together, great lyrics with gruff laughter:

> Well, I went to the whorehouse the other night
> I was there all alone, I was outasight
> I looked high and low
> I looked up above
> And who did I see BUT THE ONE I LOVED!

They kept that first set on Friday night going for almost an hour, never missing a chance to take their music past where it had been before, and finally they ended it and waved goodbye. Our arms were weak from clapping and our throats sore from cheering, but we kept it up, storming and waving hats until they had to come back for an encore. Quickly, before his pals had even picked up their instruments, Levon Helm was laying down an irresistible beat, and the whole crowd was dancing, jumping, moving clapping, and then Manuel came in with these ever so familiar notes on the piano, no, they weren't REALLY going to play THAT, and Robbie Robertson literally dove for the microphone and they were all singing it:

> SLIPPIN' AND A-SLIDIN'!
> PEEPIN' AND A-HIDIN'!
> BEEN TOLD A LONG TIME AGO
> I BEEN TOLD
> BABY YOU BEEN BOLD
> WON'T BEEEEEEEE YOUR FOOL
> NO MORE!

People were getting off their feet, they were screaming with delight, yelling for the hell of it, Danko's bass moving the song up and down and back and forth. The Band playing Little Richard! It was one of the great moments in the history of rock and roll. Robertson took two extravagant solos, bobbing and weaving, coming up for air and a smile, dancing, hell, he might have BEEN Little Richard, and then Hudson came in on organ, Helm seemed to lose his mind without losing the beat, a frantic moment on the drums, kicking it off again, they just stretched it out until Little Richard was gone and you simply wanted to remember The Band. There is no chance anyone who was there will ever forget them.

Lenny Kaye

GIVE PEACE A CHANCE! GRAND FUNK RAILROAD TAKE SHEA STADIUM

Creem, 1st August 1971

The emergence of heavier-than-thou metal in the early 1970s was a tough stream for many rock writers to cross. Decidedly prole, not shaded with the avant-garde characteristics of groups on the Velvets/Stooges axis or the time signature convolutions of progresso-rock, it was easy to dismiss the bottom-up success of these bands – Black Sabbath from England, and Grand Funk Railroad from the American heartland – as base representations of the rock art.

I first saw Grand Funk opening for Canned Heat at some dimly remembered concert hall in New Jersey. Even though the audience hadn't heard of Mark Farner, Mel Schacher, and Don Brewer, their combination of hair-thrown theatrics and no-frills guitaristics had their target audience waving v-signs and cheering. I was initially dismissive, as were most other writers. The group's manager, Terry Knight, made the most of the critical immolation; as Grand Funk moved rapidly up their charts and into the hearts of their chosen fans, first selling out Madison Square Garden, and then Shea Stadium, he enjoyed watching the rock press chew and swallow their words. So did the rock press, for that matter, and as Grand Funk became mega, the back-and-forth barbs took on a life of their own.

The music seemed almost beside the point. The irony would come later, when Grand Funk jettisoned Terry Knight in a blizzard of lawsuits and recriminations and made a single produced by Todd Rundgren which must stand as one of rock's greatest anthems, 'We're An American Band'. In the end, they told their tale better than anyone.

LK

YOU GOTTA HAND it to Terry Knight. He never lost his touch. Two weeks before this event, full page ads ran in most of the New York entertainment sections, announcements of the impending occasion with big SOLD OUTs plastered gleefully on top. Within five minutes of each new development, everybody knew that the tickets had gone within 72 hours; that kids had camped before the box-office days before their scheduled openings; that extra lines had to be added all during the first morning; that the ticket sellers had 'never seen anything like it in all their years' of working at Shea.

And, lest it might have been missed in the wake of the usual round of strikes, murders, Paris negotiations, and controversy about the DeMartino family's epic battle to keep baby Lenore, that a press conference called by Terry in late May to announce Grand Funk's big date had a grand total of six attendees, with one leaving in the middle as if to prove an obvious point. 'It's the grossest case of nonrecognition in the history of the business,' he wailed to (among others) W. Stewart Pinkerton Jr. of the *Wall Street Journal*. 'How do we get press on a group that doesn't drop their pants or get busted?'

Terry should only worry. After all the gold that's rolled through his fingers, after all the sold-out engagements and top 20 albums, after not quite two years of watching Grand Funk scream inexorably to the top of American pop, he still paradoxically seems to be concerned with justification. Why else would so much emphasis have been placed on July 9th

being a historic occasion? Why else would he have exuded so
much concern over a negative and surly press, when a great
portion of it obviously backlashed in favour of himself and
the group? Why else would he have set up a press conference
where – if all one hundred fifty invitees had really shown – he
would have been proven golden, and if, as was the case,
nobody really came, he still would have come out on top?

Why? 'Cause, aside from any of the other diverse factors,
Terry Knight knows what he's doing, each sly-as-shit step of
the way; and if you want to give credit where credit is due,
you have to say that he's the only one yet who's had the skill
and foresight and insight to pull it off.

By the end of June, they were selling Grand Funk T-shirts in
the hip clothing stores up around Lexington Avenue. Blue
colors on white fabric. So you could go to Shea Stadium in
style, of course.

The phone woke me somewhere in the nines. It wanted to
speak to Jeff.

'No, Jeff doesn't live here anymore. I took over his place,
he's up in Vermont now. Can I help you or something?'

'My name is Albert Maysles and we wanted to get in
contact with him . . .'

'Well, I have his phone number up there . . . hold on a sec,
I'll get it for you.'

'Thanks a lot, I really appreciate it.'

Shuffle around a bit, looking for the scrap of paper that
might've been any number of places but probably wasn't.
Jeff's a filmmaker who does some work for the Brothers at
times, and I figured this was one of them.

'Here it is, blah blah blah, and take it easy, okay?'

'Right, thanks again.'

That was it. I had wanted to casually ask him where he'd be
that night, whether Grand Funk was going to do for 'Mean
Mistreater' what the Rolling Stones did for 'Gimme Shelter',
but never did. To be up in the bleachers is one thing, to get
just a minor glimpse of Mark astride his organ wiring every

possible combination of sound out of his well-worn axe while
Don and Mel create avalanches of mayhem around him. But
to be actually three feet from the stage, filming every last
rivulet of sweat as it drips off his arm bracelet, down his
elbow, slithering around each hair on his forearm to silently
rest between the third and fourth finger before being callously
brushed to the floor . . .

It wasn't much more than a typical day, at that. I stayed
home most of the time, listening to the radio, flipping a
station on and letting it lie there for a while, rummaging
the dial from AM to FM and back again. True to form, you
couldn't hear Grand Funk played once in all those hours. In
fact, if you hadn't been particularly looking for it, you might
never have caught the brief announcement around about six
when some lesser official from the great Queens Police
department came on WABC to say that they'd have about
two hundred men at the 'festival' (yep, that's what he called
it), and that no infractions of the law would be tolerated. I
divided two hundred into fifty five thousand and decided that
maybe a lot of infractions of the law would be tolerated.

And in that light, the ride out on the subway was extremely
promising. Whatever you do or don't do in New York, one of
the more sacred taboos of the city is that you never smoke in
the subway. You can jaywalk, amass any amount of pirating
tickets you like, even commit armed robbery now and again
with little fear of reprisal. If, however, you want to get busted
in a quick and efficient fashion, you have merely to light up
anytime after you put your token in the turnstile, and from
there it can be guaranteed that the long arm of the law will
wind you in within a mere thirty seconds or so.

But all the way out to Shea, through the factory wastelands
that border the East River and into the residential repetitions
that cover most of this great borough as it paves the way
toward the splendor of Long Island, the passengers on the
Flushing Special sat in little clusters, scarfing smokes like
they've done in school bathrooms from time immemorial,

cigarettes cuffed in their hands and smoke exhaled proudly into the air. A lot of the guys wore headbands, hair pulled down to cover as much of their ears and necks as possible; the girls eschewed high-fashion hot pants for the more practical garb of simple jeans and prominent bellybuttons. There were a lot of peace symbols in the air: sewn on jackets, hung around necks, carved into watchbands. The vanguard, you might say, of the American revolution.

The car emptied itself out at the Stadium, and everybody followed everybody else for a while. It wasn't hard to figure where you were going. Shea stands alone in the midst of what legend tells us was once a huge meadow in the heart of Flushing, surrounded by miles of superhighway and the ominous remains of the '64 World's Fair, and as you come up on it, it has that capacity to look mighty impressive. Big. Monumental, if you like, since that is exactly what it was designed to be. And there haven't been many coups in the history of rock'n'roll who have been able to fill it.

The Beatles once did, on a night in the summer of '65 (and again in '66) that I still hear in my mind as a high-pitched keening of hysteria, impossible to understand except for the moment and even then worth a second look. You couldn't hear them (at all: speaker technology was still in the primitive stages), you could barely see them, the few girls that broke through police lines to get at them seldom made it to much more than center field. But it was a strange and somehow indisputable spectacle, curiously cleansing and awe-inspiring, and I don't think anyone else in the world could have done it in quite the same way.

Surely not the Stones; even then, their darkness meant that the type they would attract would be hysterical in a different sense: a touch of the sexual, perhaps, with deeper and blacker passions. More loyal, as might be expected, but definitely smaller in number. Nor could a string of the British second level, such as Herman's Hermits and/or the Hollies. Too young, all too studiedly pop-star pretty and faceless. And, though there were great bands running around America during this time – topped by the Beach Boys in the west, and the Four Seasons in the east – most of them would have had trouble filling up a medium-sized theatre, not to mention a colossus like Shea.

The Beatles made their move at a perfect time, however, as their initial primary appeal not only cut across more lines of popularity than any of the other above groups, but they signed up at Shea when they had literally touched the peak of that popularity. The Moment was impeccably chosen. After more than two years at the top – and they'd never yet fumbled it, never yet made a wrong move which would have held them down for even the littlest of whiles – they'd begun to move toward a new audience, a more sophisticated one, a step which would one day signal the start of a thing called progressive rock.

On the other hand, it was before this growth descended from true eclecticism into sort of stereotypical try-ons of musical style, with a similar lack of success. In short, then, they were right in the middle of their most creative period, and they couldn't have maneuvered it any better if they'd tried. Shea filled slowly (a little bit over seven weeks, and that should tell you a bit about how far we've come), but it was packed to the gills by the time John, Paul, George and Ringo made their dash from the left field dugout.

And who would, or could, fill it today? Count 'em on the fingers of one hand. There are the Rolling Stones (almost the very same), for sure, since three Madison Square Garden concerts equal one Shea Stadium show anytime. Maybe a double bill of Black Sabbath/James Taylor (the 'Black/Jack Show' run by Warners-Reprise?). Maybe a full-scale presentation of *Jesus Christ Superstar* with the original cast? Maybe. But so far, and Terry Knight will be more than happy to tell you this in triplicate, the only American group to sell out Shea Stadium has been/is Grand Funk Railroad. In 72 hours. No more, no less.

The crowd moved peacably and even a mite happily toward the gates, and far from what anyone might have expected, there was little confusion. Hawkers were down to a minimum, the police – many of whom had their hair discreetly on the long side – were mostly young and friendly, and ticket scalpers were nonexistent. Somebody was selling glossies of Mark, Don and Mel, but he didn't seem to be doing a land-office business. There were no programs; not even a souvenir booklet. Maybe Terry figured these people knew who they had cone to see.

There was some inkling of trouble at the gates, where the police were confiscating contraband wine bottles and telling kids to put on their shirts, but it all seemed to be taken in good humor and nobody appeared to mind much. Up a couple of endless escalators, where a good system of hand-me-down ushers took everybody to their seats with a minimum of fuss and bother, and then you could first relax and look out over the field, with that sense of seeing it for the first tine, brighter and shinier than the TV image, in real full color life with a platform set squarely over second base like a squat frog, flanked by a truly crushing set of speakers. Enough to tell anybody that they'd gone just about as far as they'd ever have to go.

The sign on the scoreboard said 'Welcome from Mark, Don, and Mel', and to echo those sentiments, out bounded WNEW-FM (local Metromedia) disc jockey Scott Muni. 'Brothers and Sisters,' he said, a long way from the days when he used to ride the Electric Pogo Stick at 570 on the dial, and then proceeded to introduce his radio team. Happily, none of them talked or played records, and they got a pretty nice response from an enthusiastic crowd. WNEW, it might be noted, has been the only New York station to consistently program Grand Funk, and it was clear they were reaping the benefits of this here tonight. Muni then gave a little razzamatazz and waved his hand for Humble Pie, who took the applause up one better when they broke from the dugout.

With it all, though, it was not a particularly momentous opening. For one, the concert had started on time. It had been scheduled for eight, and that's precisely when it began, which meant that it was still fairly light and unmysterious out. In addition, the stadium was as yet only half-filled, and the large amount of empty seats gave one a little pause to wonder whether there actually would be enough bodies to fill them. Action outside the gates had slowed to a minimum.

Humble Pie are from the anguished school of British rock: a lot of striding about and wrenching at the microphones, an intense hang on every single note and mannerism. Maybe they felt that because of the large playing field, they had to exaggerate even their exaggerations; maybe they really knew that if they made a hit here, all those second and third billings would miraculously turn into firsts. Whatever, despite a good amount of effort, they never really put it over. Steve Marriott's claim that 'It's our job to get this intimate little gatherin' rockin'' seemed to vanish in the midst of an endless variety of dragged-out blues, and the group just managed to dissipate an already-low energy level due to the sweltering heat and humidity.

A short-lived rain shower added a touch of urgency to their set, and they used it to move into a version of Dr John's 'Walk On Gilded Splinters' that got the crowd clapping along; but in the end, nobody cared much if they took off their shirts or not (which they did). The cries for 'More!' that followed them off sounded less for pleasure than ritual, a sad note when you think that Humble Pie has all the making of being a mighty superior two-fisted band. For whatever reasons, though, they've just never been able to put all the pieces together in the right place, and at Shea, it just wasn't their time at all. As a grand finale, drummer Jerry Shirley flung his sticks out to the crowd. Too bad: with the nearest fan a whole baseball diamond way, there was no one around who had a remote chance of catching then.

Intermission rock revolved around Alice Cooper, Johnny

Winter, and a heavy dose of Sly. The scoreboard flashed
'Goodbye, Jim, We'll Miss You' to sustained applause, then
turned to 'Give Peace A Chance, Love Conquers All, Get
Funked'. An announcement from the stage advised those who
were throwing firecrackers to please stop: 'It may not affect
you in the same way it does me, but one of those might go off
and end up near somebody's ears . . . I couldn't work if I lost
mine.' It was greeted by a succession of loud explosions and
cheers.

Meanwhile, people had begun noticing the flashing lights
of a police car surrounding a black limousine behind a gate
over in left field. A line of ushers (kids, mostly) moved up in
double file toward the stage, forming a long pathway. The
gate swung open and the limousine moved through, stately in
its elegance, heads swiveling along its route, toward the stage,
finally disappearing behind it. The stadium, now suddenly
filled to capacity, went politely off the wall.

You gotta hand it to Terry Knight. No way to avoid it. He
takes something that would seem incredibly schlocky in the
hands of just about anyone else, something so corny and
melodramatic and obvious that you would never imagine
someone would have the actual balls to do it, and then he
simply does it, Just like that. And probably chuckles his ass
off in the process too.

Here's the set-up. They've turned out the lights, giving Sly
room to sing his simple song to the fade, and after, letting the
air hang silent and heavy for a while. The stage is sculptured
beautifully, white lights on the side framing a hulk of amplifiers, each graced by a series of unblinking red glows. A
long pause, the kind that is best referred to as 'pregnant'.
Then, at top volume, splitting the air arid gathering force like
a thunderclap, comes the opening majesty of 'Thus Spake
Zarathustra', the well-worn theme from *2001: A Space
Odyssey*. As it crescendoes, the lights of Queens rising
eternally over the moon that is the outfield fence of Shea
Stadium, three figures break into the gloom of the stage,

hands up in peace signs, getting met with a giant roar of approval from the assembled pack.

'Back From Europe and the Whole World! Grand Funk Railroad!' (Cup your hands over your mouth, open wide, and exhale hotly and noisily from the back of your throat: get the picture?)

There they are. God damn. They lose a bit of momentum tuning up, but with 8,000 watts of amplifiers kicking behind them, quickly gain it back with the opening slash of 'Are You Ready?' They're loud, much louder than the other times I've seen them, but also richer, not as ear-splitting and trebly. A volume you can live with, can thrive on, just on the threshold of distortion, and Terry Knight, up on a stand not far from the stage, playing with a set of mixing controls, is seeing that it stays that way. The first lead of the night is greeted by a major cheer, like a pledge of allegiance to a band that has proved themselves more a part of the people than the people themselves ever thought they had a right to expect.

They don't stop for a second. 'Are You Ready?' slams to a close, and Farner sheds his guitar. Grand Funk are a show band, first and foremost, and one of the finest parts of their on-stage ritual is the moment when Mark takes off his shirt, lightly chucking it behind an amplifier. The crowd's been waiting for it, primed by countless publicity stills and fond memories (some real, some imagined), and when he slips it from his shoulders, it's like a signal that the real gettin' down is about to begin. Covered by the uproar, he moves to the organ and the next song is launched into the air. 'Hello everybody,' he adds as introduction. 'We're going to have a *gooooood* time.' Obviously, to judge by the answering clamor, a self-fulfilling prophecy.

The thing which is surprising me through all of this, however, is not the flood-tide of response the group is receiving. I'd expected that, having seen it happen more than a couple of times since I first caught them in a suburban shopping center cinema in Teaneck, New Jersey, casually blowing the boogie of Canned Heat off the stage and into the parking lot. No, and it seems almost strange to be talking of Grand Funk in this light, what's setting me back now is how far group has come musically, how much broader the shape of their instrumental powers has become. They could still use some good material, since most of what they do is so supremely ordinary as to be instantly forgettable, and they do manage to touch on every cliché in the book at least once during a given night. But Don Brewer's drumming, far from the helpless flailing that might've been his lot at one time, is hard-nosed and rhythmic, and Mel Schacher's bass, gruff and simple and to the point, is near-perfect. Together, they lay a solid foundation for Farner to work from, and his guitar work avoids most lead exhibitionism in order to simply play strong back-up chords. It makes for a peculiarly powerful mixture, a totality of drive, and as they move from song to song, you can feel them was into the experience of playing at Shea, warming to it, building from it in a natural rise that never loses their rapt command over the audience.

Like clockwork, they can do no wrong. The opening chords of 'I'm Your Captain' are greeted with a loud ovation, as well they might be. It's possibly their most pop-oriented song to date, with good, non-bullshit lyrics, and a well-defined, simple melody: a side to the group which has been kept hidden to an extent, perhaps more by design than chance. They move through the final choruses, sliding the whole construct neatly into the next track, sharp and precise, a little philosophy for the masses:

> I don't care who you are
> I love the human race . . .

In the stands, the crowd is following their every move. A dozen or so kids have jumped to the top of the visitor's dugout and are dancing there, waiting for the inevitable moment when the police come to throw them off. Most everyone is on their feet, heads bobbing rhythmically, hands held in readiness for the moment when Farner asks them to clap 'em together. No doubt: there's a lot of enjoyment at going down at this show.

But if they're enjoying it, poking each other and nodding whenever one of the Big Three makes a particularly fine move, it still has to be admitted that there's a definite lack of hysteria in the air, a feeling that the whole night has still not passed beyond the bounds of control. Despite the rumor that a black belt karate guard stands ready to fortress the stage should any major rush develop, there seems to be little danger of such a prospect. Grand Funk fans are still at a concert, are still watching a show, and though they're rapturously in love with every outtasite minute, catching the fragments in each new song and using them to build a new high of fulfillment, they haven't once stepped over the edge. Here, as everywhere, almost doesn't count.

The drum solo begins like a sudden cut in the instrumental texture, and Brewer is off and charging. They love him, this heir-apparent to Ginger Baker, and he keeps it going for a long time, working the rhythm different ways so that it breaks nicely into the next set of waves. He's got a good start, and he doesn't lose the chain for a second, stopping for some towering applause, then blazing back where he left out. There's only one brief moment when he falters, dropping off for a little flash, and then he's returned to the beam, steady, waiting for Schacher to join him on the bass. The latter does, and they whiz through some nifty bits of simultaneous playing, following a complex progression that jerks to a halt after every series of phrases. It's so calculated that it's perfect, and suddenly the bleachers start shaking with the sound of stomping cadenced feet.

Farner holds it back, though. 'Can we have it quiet for a second?' The clamor cools down a bit. 'We'd like to play this next tune for one of our brothers, Jimmy Morrison!' There is a sustained, respectful applause, almost reverent in its warmth and honesty. Most everybody there, wherever they had gone after that unique part of time, owed a large debt to Morrison; he was one of the first, and one of the biggest, and in his own way, one of the best, and it was nice to get a chance to say some of those kind of things to him.

'The next tune' is Grand Funk's reworking of 'Inside Looking Out', and its reception, as the universally-acclaimed all-time fave-rave of Grand Funk live performances, wires everything into the socket. The crowd knows all the words, and sings them along without urging as Farner aims each one through the sound system. Ho moves from the microphone to the organ, steps to the bench, steps to the top, and stands there, scraping away at his guitar.

Back down to the stage, Schacher riding a runaway bass line, not letting it stumble for a moment. 'You know something?' *(roar . . .)* 'You people make us feel *daaamn* good!' *(louder roar).*

'Now I wanna know . . . do you feel *Alright*?' The answer rebounds back in a flash.

'Then Clap Your Hands!'

There's no stopping them now. The kids are in their glory, up on the chairs, leaning over the fences, joining in for all they're worth.

And then the lights go on. Not little spots, as had been running over the audience all night, or lights in the aisle, so you wouldn't trip over any loose bodies there. No, this is all the lights, the big stadium blinkers, a million little suns erupting into glory, all focused on fifty-five thousand who are rippling along like so many seas, a huge mirror reflecting the suddenly-small three people on stage, a true notion of where the party has been all along. An old trick, but it'll do it every time.

The song builds to a climax, turned up on full, pulling everything out as far as it will possibly go, then brought up close at the end. They make moves to leave the stage, but nobody's about to let that happen.

Farner comes back to the microphone. They've been on a good hour and he seems a little dazed and out-of-breath, 'Y'know,' he starts out saying. 'We're going to Tokyo, Japan, to play the Olympic Stadium there . . .' The crowd thinks this is just fine. 'I know I said this at Madison Square Garden . . . I've said this before, but when it's the truth you can't help but say it again.'

He stops for a second, and then: '*You're the Best Fuckin' Audience in the World!*'

This is a truly great band. After that kind of encore, even 'Gimme Shelter' and the *Space Odyssey* reprise that follow have to be somewhat beside the point.

The ramps are packed on the way down, dozens of conversations all centered about the same thing. *Weren't they fuckin' great? Did you see when Mark/Don/Mel . . . ?* A couple of firecrackers resound in the distance, but nobody seems to pay them any mind. The crowd is relaxed, energetic, and playful. Not drained, not even noticeably tired; rather, they seem pleased with themselves, bubbling over, noticeably quite happy. It's as if they've gone through an experience which allowed them to prove themselves to themselves, gave them reassurance that maybe what they were doing is right, is not as depressing and sick and tiresome as it so often turns out to be. Maybe their lives hadn't been changed, and maybe they hadn't been taken beyond the boundaries of time and space out to some other o-zone; but for once, they had been solidly treated to a good time, a time when no one was out to get them, to take advantage of them, to treat them like shit. It was their night, and no others. Something to savor, to take home and press into the *Survival* album cover for future use.

It's easy to extract a moral out of Grand Funk Railroad, simply because they've set themselves up as an extremely moralistic band. They give the people what they want, surely, and they're wise in this because I think they feel it's the only way to teach people what they need. Which is, among other things, that you should do anything you want, as long as you don't harm anyone else in the process, including yourself. Stay off hard drugs, 'We love ya just the way you are!' Dig yourself, without fail, any and every time. The solutions they offer are clear-cut. They don't deal in abstracts; whenever a situation comes up, they always plant themselves on the side of Right, each set of circumstances judged on its own. And they put it over, no hints of hypocrisy, mainly because they believe in what they're saying themselves; not because Terry Knight told them to, but because they're the living embodiment, the proof which seals the promise.

Rock'n'roll is built on a myth. That being a guitar flash or a wizard drummer or a laid-back bass player is better than being anything on this earth. That the American Dream didn't fade away when we ran out of West to conquer. That it doesn't take brains, or money, or position, or anything, really, to have that golden chance to go all the way. A realization that Elvis, or Buddy Holly, or Frankie Avalon, or anyone else you could care to name (John Fred and his Playboy Band?) started out just like you or me, and maybe, one of these days, just about as soon as the gettin' gets good, it's our number in the sweepstakes that's gonna come up next.

Grand Funk are from the midwest, the pit-bottom home of all this, from the urban clump up north that sits as one of its most prominent features. If you were a kid living there during its grey years, you weren't given much to believe in except for the everpresent fads and fancies of teenage America. Check out a particularly nice job of rolling and pleating in any '50s car magazine, and the address would be located somewhere outside of Gary, Indiana. Hear an especially trashy song on the radio, one just made for not more than eight transistors, and it's likely the group and its label would bail from the western edge of Ohio. If you cared at all about anything, and in those years, there were a lot who couldn't even get it up for that, this was where your hopes would lie. More often than not, that's where they'd stay: the big money was in the east, especially New York; the action out in California was equally distant. You could be lucky, but that's about all.

So Question Mark was lucky. Mitch Ryder was lucky. The Castaways were close but not real lucky. And Terry Knight, who had the best chance of any of 'em, who led his own group and made some fine music and was once rumored to be joining the Rolling Stones, he wasn't much lucky at all. His records would look strong, become regional hits, and then never move that extra inch which would have spelled the difference between failure and success. Left him with not much more than a lot of nice plastic and an album cover from which you can pick out a baby-faced Don Brewer. Taught him, in no uncertain terms, the rules of the game. How to move and when to jump. Made him a bit crazy, wary and driven, but I guess that's the price you pay as you pick up the necessity tools of trade.

Grand Funk know all this, and if they're not totally aware of their position in the myth, they certainly subconsciously sense it. Their strength doesn't lie on the stage, in their instruments, in their 8,000 watts of power. Their strength lies with their audience, who'll stay with them as long as the group remains true, as long as the group reflects a part of where they want to be, and then will split at the first sign of betrayal. It's a chancy proposition, to live totally within the expectations of your fans, letting them call your shots, trying to keep ahead and make your own directions while still keeping them in sight. But Grand Funk have chosen to live this way, to be one step ahead of the law at all times, and now that they've built it on a towering scale, have played the first of what obviously is destined to be a series of historic concerts, the question is: where do they go from here?

For they have to go somewhere. When you stop growing is when you become an institution, and institutions are meant to be thought of kindly and then put aside. Grand Funk isn't ready for that. Terry Knight isn't ready for that. So what they do is maybe write better songs, or plan a movie, or put together a concept album. Or, and here's a choice from the other side, maybe they don't do anything. Maybe they stay in the same spot and keep on repeating where they've been, falling backwards as the stream of time moves on. That's a flow of sorts, no? Shea Stadium was as far as the Beatles went, and that ain't a bad average.

Well, no, that's not really it, either. For Mark Farner has been giving red, white and blue garbage cans to his home city of Flint (not to mention a pair of polar bears donated by the group to the Central Park Zoo). Pretty soon, according to an interview with Terry Knight in *Crawdaddy!*, Mark will begin publishing his own newspaper called *Freedom Reader*. There are Grand Funk buttons and T-shirts already, and who hasn't got a Madison Square Garden poster of the group's last show secreted somewhere in his room? Will kids soon be able to buy a Mel Schacher model Fender guitar? Don Brewer drums (for those who like *more* than a *little* . . .)? Mark Farner-autographed armbands?

Grand Funk aren't a rock'n'roll band: They're a big fan club. The best fuckin' fan club in the world.

And why not? Grand Funk never disappoint, unless you happen to be looking for things that just aren't there. They're always square-shooters, on the level, up front and together. They believe wholeheartedly in their 'brothers and sisters', instinctively think of their audience in that light, and this in turn means that they will never treat their fans badly: never step on them or scorn them or take them by the heels and shake them until the last little bit of change falls out of their pockets. They realize that given another time and place, it might've been them down there rather than them up here; a sobering thought – for any musician. And if, in the end, it may come to mean that they'll never be more than the sum total of their audience, that Grand Funk will never be able to rise so far above themselves that they levitate a crowd beyond any of its other awarenesses . . . well, what the hell, rock'n'roll is only rock'n'roll, and it ain't too many who get to find God in a I–IV–V progression.

But even with all this, they haven't hit their peak yet, and I'll tell you why. They've saved the best for last, those sly l'il devils. You'll see: one of these days, they'll be finishing up a concert in some out-of-the-way place: Dekalb, Illinois, or something. The closing bars of 'Inside Looking Out' will shudder to a close, and they'll leave amid cries for more. After only a matter of seconds, though, they'll be back in their places, excited and energized, like kids who are about to receive an unexpected surprise.

'This is a very great moment for us,' Mark will say, his guitar slung down to one side. 'We'd like to introduce someone to you who's been with us from the very beginning . . . Some people call him the fourth Funk but we . . . call him our brother . . .'

Realization strikes the crowd an they begin to madly cheer.

The band drops back, striking up the opening chords to 'I (Who Have Nothing)'.

He moves from the shadows behind the wings of the stage, casual and unhurried, with the air of a man who has never missed once over the past two and some years and who doesn't expect to start now.

As the first spotlight touches him, they begin to scream, a shrill pierce never to stop throughout the rest of the night.

Terry Knight, man. You just gotta hand it to him.

Reprinted with kind permission of Creem *magazine*

Charles Shaar Murray

LIVE AT THE RAINBOW: THE RETURN OF ERIC CLAPTON

Cream, February 1973

After Cream and 'Layla', but before Ocean Boulevard *and* Enoch Powell, *Eric Clapton had vanished from the rock radar, laid low by junk and depression. With Hendrix gone, he was rock's most revered guitarist, and – after Pete Townshend had dived into the murk to retrieve him – it was an occasion of some moment when he returned to the stage. Possibly sentiment, and relief that Clapton was actually functioning again, had us listening through rose-tinted headphones: the resulting live album certainly didn't sound nearly as impressive as the gig seemed on the night. Nevertheless, on the night it mattered, big time. A couple of things which weren't in the piece: my opinion of Ronnie Wood went up by many a notch when I heard his recreation of the classic Duane Allman slide part when they played 'Layla'. And the* real *reason why the show was late was that Clapton had gained weight since the last time he wore his white suit, and he couldn't go onstage until said suit was let out.*

CSM

SO THERE'S THIS cat in the white suit smiling diffidently through his beard at the cheering hordes on the other side of the lights. He's feeling alright, because a special convocation of his buddies are all around and they've gotten it all nicely together for him. With a little help from his friends, right. And he raises the neck of his guitar just a little bit and cues in the band as he tears out the opening notes of the contemporary anthem that kept his name in the papers and his music on the radio.

The cheering redoubles because when his name had been announced, the people had paid tribute to a reputation, to something of a myth. As they heard the music, however, myth gave way to reality, and they applauded not what they wanted to hear and hoped they would hear, but what they were actually hearing.

What they were actually hearing was Eric Clapton's triumphant return to a public stage. Outside the Rainbow at around twenty past eight on that Saturday night were a few motley thousand folk, all crushed into the traffic islands and railings and corners that surround Finsbury Park's beloved Filmore surrogate, all squashed into a succession of singularly uncomfortable clumps, all cussing each other out as boots scuff, tempers fray, and the chilly winds of North London sting ever fiercer through the ethically impeccable tatters of the proud denims of yore. Inside, the first house is running 55 minutes behind time because Eric showed up late, and now an additional few thousand join the confusion as they leave the theatre.

Past the friendly man at the door frisking for tape machines, and inside looking for stars. There's Elton John, and Long John Baldry and George'n'Ringo, and – oh, wow – Mickey Finn and – hmmmm – Tony McPhee, not to mention Joe Cocker (who doesn't move a muscle during the whole two hours), Michael Des Barres who moves in his seat almost as if he was on stage. It's *Tommy* all over again – superstars' night out.

The Average White Band play an average white set that was mainly competent but occasionally hit some nice peaks. Then John Martin of Great Western steps out front and apologises for all the delays and then says, 'I have two words to say to you all: Eric Clapton.' Then the cheering starts. Despite all the heaviness outside, the cheering is unhysterical and thoroughly good-humoured: *Nice to see you back, Eric.*

Listen to the band: on your left, behind grand piano and Hammond organ is Stevie Winwood, clean-shaven, hair flowing down from a centre parting, looking absurdly young and boyish. Ronnie Wood, looking cockney hip with his chrome Zematis guitar, slide at the ready. Rick Grech on bass, whom we need not concern ourselves with further except to say that he played great. Jim Karlstein from Taj Mahal's band on drums. Pete Townshend, who set up the band, looking at his most Baba-Weer-All-Crazee-Now in an off-duty Indian cotton smock, and a lumpy orange Gretsch Anniversary, a far more informal guitar from his usual lean, tough Gibson SG, Reebop Kwaaku Bah on congas, and Jim Capaldi on drums.

So out comes the riff of 'Layla', and the reaction is the same as hearing Dylan at Bangla Desh. For whatever reason, for however short a time, someone we loved to listen to had stepped out to be heard again. Ronnie Wood's playing the Duane Allman slide bits, while Townshend underpins Clapton on the riff. Eric's singing nice: a rough-edged, dusty, well-used, but understated voice. Obviously, his vocal agility cannot match his dexterity on guitar, but something of the same phrasing is there. Then 'Badge'. God, it's just so nice hearing that stuff again, and hearing it coming from a bunch of cats with guitars and drums and pianos and shit standing right in front of you, instead of just from your trusty stereo.

Eric's looking happy and relaxed. You'd never know he was the man that a mutual acquaintance had assured me last year would never even be able to play again in his own front room. He is, as we hippies say in our quaint and colourful dialect, getting into it. Moving a little stiffly, he cues the band in for a few bars, playing a neat little flourish between beats. Then, in kicks the band and Eric leaning into the mike: 'Betcha didn't think I knew how to rock and roll . . .' Oh, come on, man! We didn't fool that easy. We knew you could all along. We just wanted you to come out and do it, that's all, and you did it real good.

Like when Stevie sang 'Presence Of The Lord', and you cranked up your wah-wah and blew that amazing solo, and after as we were all getting our breath back, some kid in the balcony called out, 'Nice one, Eric!' and we all cheered that as well. And your beautiful teamwork with Ronnie Wood on 'Key To The Highway', and that fine, fine version of 'Little Wing', and Stevie singing again on 'Nobody Knows You When You're Down And Out', and Traffic's 'Pearly Queen' and that final encore of 'Layla' even more shattering than before and . . .

God damn, you should have been there. It was sandwiched in between some pretty fine stuff, what with a sweaty evening of greasy superfunk with J. Geils the night before, and an unbelievably marvelous Steeleye Span show at the Albert 'All on the Monday, but the Clapton concert really was sump'n else. Even if Pete Townshend did most of the rapping and personality jive, we knew who that evening was all about. It was that guy in the white suit, who was blowing that sweet-biting ecstatic guitar, who was back in front of us after too long away.

Mike Des Barres said afterwards that it was the best concert he'd ever been to in his life. I know just what he means, and I'll second that anyday. Welcome back, Eric. We're glad we went and glad you came, and please don't wait so long next time. Thy hand sure hath lost none of its cunning, and Derek by any other name would sound as sweet.

See you again soon, Eric, and more power to your pick-ups.

6

AFTER THE FACT

Greg Shaw

MOD GENERATION: THE WHO'S *QUADROPHENIA* THROUGH THE YEARS

Phonograph Record, December 1973

This piece was written in 1973 for an American audience whose only exposure to the word 'mod' might well have been watching The Mod Squad *on television. This is the only justification I can offer for my ridiculous over-use of the word, not to mention the superficial, if not completely fatuous, attempt at a history and definition of the movement. Not only was I writing for readers whose main point of musical reference at the time was very likely the Allman Brothers, but also I had never been to England and had only a long-distance romantic fantasy of the whole thing myself. But at the time, nothing of any substance had been written on the subject besides Gary Herman's 1972 book, and it being told from a British point of view, I believed there was room for an American's perspective.*

The release of Quadrophenia *was of course the occasion for this article, and reading it now, I find it curious that in tracing the group's early history and assessing the place of 'mod' in some larger scheme of rock, I found such strong similarities in the contemporary glam scene, and felt that some kind of revival of the whole mod mentality might be in the offing. Little did I guess that a mere four years later The Jam would arrive on the scene, bringing with*

them a whole new generation of anorak-clad fashion
rebels!

GS

IF I COULD somehow live my teenage years over again, I think
I would choose to live them as a Mod. What it must have been
like to be a Mod in London in the summer of 1965! To walk
around the West End in a Carnaby Street parade, everywhere
kids blindly chasing the same absurd dream, lives surrounded
by and creating an atmosphere of the purest pointless pop the
world has ever seen.

Mod was, when you come down to it, the first outbreak of
the youth cult that grew to such immense proportions in the
sixties. It had already taken shape by 1964, a clearly-defined
lifestyle dominated by a rigorous code of trendy fashions,
picked instinctively on the basis of mere flash (op-art clothes),
snobbery (Italian motorbikes, French haircuts, American
R&B music), offensiveness to parents (Union Jack coats)
or just whatever seemed right. They couldn't explain what
they were doing or why, and they never even thought to try.
They preached no tiresome sermons like their later American
counterparts the flower children. They were Mods, that's all,
and their lives were the only statement they had to make.

The Mod's devotion to leisure time activities was not the
casual laziness, or 'dropping out', of America's hippies. Most
of them were in school or holding down jobs, it was just that
they derived no satisfaction from these activities. They
wanted glamour, excitement, action. So they created a sub-
culture all their own, and a rather large one at that –
according to reliable sources, there were at least a half million
self-defined Mods on the streets as early as 1964. And that
was just the first awakening of the movement. It kept on
growing through 1965, and by 1966 it had completely
engulfed British youth.

Of course it had become watered-down, commercialised
and acceptable by then. The original Mods were a fanatically

tight in-crowd, twisted with pent-up frustration, blocked up with non-stop pills, and totally obsessive. Come Bank Holidays they'd swarm down to Brighton and other seaside resorts, rampaging and brawling in the streets (like the American college kids who would annually destroy Ft. Lauderdale in the early '60s), and gathering in their numbers for pre-arranged rumbles with their teenage adversaries, the Rockers.

These battles made little sense on the surface. The Rockers were a minority of working-class kids from the North and less fashionable provinces, and their tastes ran to leather, booze, and Elvis Presley. The existed somewhere on the continuum between the Teddy boys and the Skinheads, but at the time their frustrations and complaints were pretty much the same as those of the Mods. Some say the conflicts were staged more for the sake of theatricality than anything else – easy headlines, the eyes of the nation, parents in outrage, etc. That seems as good an explanation as any.

Nik Cohn, who lived through it all, recalls these battles as 'ecstatic weekends – seventy-two hours without sleep, and all you did was run around, catcall, swallow pills, and put the boot in. For the first time in your life, the only time, you were under no limitations and nobody controlled you and you caught sight of nirvana. When it was all over, Rockers didn't change: they were solid, and they went on riding their bikes and getting lushed and brawling. But Mods were edgier, more neurotic, and everything that happened now was anticlimax. They were bored and they couldn't sustain. They lost their dedication. Very soon, they began to fall apart. At any rate, I have a memory of two fat years, 1964 and 1965, when you did nothing but run loose and waste time, buy new clothes and overeat and gab. It was futile, of course – pop has always been futile – but it seemed elegant, it was easy living, and English pop was better than it's ever been, than it's ever likely to be again.'

Another English writer, Gary Herman, went even further.

He wrote a whole book about Mod, and when it came time to put a title on it, his choice was clear-cut, he called it *The Who*.

In as much as music was a key ingredient in the Mod lifestyle, the Who were its focal point. They had been Mods from the very beginning, and were among the first of its spokesman to gain access to the media. 'I Can't Explain' was issued in January 1965 and jumped right into the Top Ten. Now at last the Mods had some faces of their own they could see on the covers of *Melody Maker*, *NME*, and *Rave*. And as you'd expect, they had the image to back up their position, and those images were seen everywhere.

The Who were archetypal Mods: small round faces, bobbed hair, and very high-contrast. Keith Moon was most often seen behind bullseyes or in his Elvis pullover, while John and Roger usually had on jackets of clashing patterns, and Pete sported a wardrobe that could well have been designed by Andy Warhol. I used to go crazy seeing those photos in *Hit Parader* and *Flip* – why didn't the shops in my town carry threads like that? The closest we had to that look was those surfer t-shirts with the wide horizontal stripes, worn with jeans or tight corduroys. But how I wanted a shirt with long tab collars and different prints on the sleeves and opposite sides! By the time the stores had them, of course, they were two years out of date.

One thing you could get, though, was the music, which meant the Who. Before the Who, Mods listened to American R&B, along with the Beatles, Stones, and other beat groups. Most of the groups around London were playing pretty straight R&B in 1964: James Brown and Sam Cooke and Arthur Alexander and Solomon Burke and Wilson Pickett. It had a certain exotic appeal, encouraging pop snobbery plus a strong beat for dancing. Dancing was all-important; it was the premier showcase for one's clothes, style, and overall sense of cool. The Mods had a pill-inspired dance called the Block, which went well with the chunky rhythm of R&B.

As early as 1962, Pete Townshend and Roger Daltrey and

John Entwhistle were playing together in a band called the Detours, which also included Colin Dawson and Doug Sanden, doing Cliff Richard, the Shadows, the stuff of the times. By 1964 they were called the High Numbers, with a record out called 'I'm The Face', full of references to fashionable discotheques, aimed at the Mod audience. They were already among the most popular groups with the Shepherd's Bush Mods, playing strictly R&B, when Kit Lambert and Chris Stamp found them and signed them to an exclusive management contract. Lambert recalls seeing them the first time and being impressed, not so much by their music as by the intensity of their audience, moving frantically in a small West End discotheque.

Lambert and Stamp initiated a crash image program for the group, starting with their name. The High Numbers had been pushed on them by a former manager, and now they reverted to a name they'd wanted before: The Who. It was perfect for them, catchy and opaque. With the name came new clothes, custom tailored by Carnaby Street to the tune of $500 a week, careful biweekly haircuts, and endless photo sessions and publicity releases. Then came 'I Can't Explain', an instant hit on the pirate stations, followed by a sixteen-week booking Tuesday nights at the Marquee Club.

At this point, not much more would have happened had the Who been almost any of the countless other bands around. Fortunately for us, they turned out to be a very exceptional group of musicians indeed. By early 1965 the Mod movement was well established and already becoming a bit stale to some. The Who sparked new life into it, and gave it a substance it had never known before by creating a style of music that was Mod, just as motorbikes and Carnaby Street were Mod.

It's an important distinction. Later in the year, groups appeared with songs about Mod, and none amounted to anything. All of them lifted their sound shamelessly from the Who, but made the mistake of writing songs about art school, fashions, *Ready Steady Go!*, and so on. Some of them were even good. The Eyes did a great rip-off of 'I Can't Explain' called 'I'm Rowed Out', backed by a Who parody titled 'My Degeneration'. The Creation made some classic records, 'Painter Man', 'Biff Bang Pow', 'Making Time', 'Can I Join Your Band', 'Nightmares'. They briefly included Ron Wood, now of the Faces, and an album containing their best material has just been reissued in England. None of them, however, can be considered anything more than genre records.

There were other Mod bands too, notably John's Children (of which Marc Bolan was briefly a member) who made a scorching pill stomper called 'Smashed! Blocked!' and the Small Faces, whose story is well known. But even the Small Faces, who were almost as archetypally Mod in appearance as the Who and shared a similar approach to music and song structure, fell short of the Who's mark.

When the Who first unleashed their sound it had two distinct qualities, each of which expressed in its way the Mod attitude in musical terms, both working together to created an impact that was shattering. Most striking was their sheer sound, a totality more monstrous than anything rock had yet seen. Keith Moon drove them on with his murderous assaults on the drums, his madman's eyes gleaming as he kicked his kit across the stage and sent sticks careening around the hall. Townshend fed off this, spinning his arm like a demented windmill, pulling the most amazing distortion and feedback from his guitar and producing an incredible chaos of noise. From this, the celebrated ritual destruction of equipment that ended each show for two years evolved quite logically, confirming the image Lambert and Stamp had been trying to build of the Who as conflicting, self-destructive egos. It was all very, very Mod.

This alone would have been plenty, but there was more. In addition to the James Brown numbers they still performed, the Who (or rather Townshend) were now writing songs of their own, and like the instrumental backings these songs were nearly all quintessential slices of the Mod sensibility. Like most great rock songs, they were all written in less than ten minutes, and without violating the basically inarticulate Mod stance they managed to say a great deal to and about their Mod audience.

'My Generation' is the one everyone knows, though probably the least of their early efforts in this style. I find it much too literal, rescued only by Daltrey's inspired stuttering, a little inside joke for the pillheads. During this period, for about a year, practically every song they wrote was a pop revolution. There was no formula beyond the hard chunky beat and feedback, except that most of them took a posture of arrogant teen braggadocio. What they were about, mainly, was an attitude, an outlook on life they shared with their audience.

Of their early singles, the most sublime are 'I Can't Explain', 'The Kids Are Alright', 'Out In The Street', 'Legal Matter', and 'Substitute', every one basically about one thing – finding self-image through the release of frustration-born tension. Tension and its release was the whole essence of the Who, both thematically and musically. Their singles were awesome bundles of charged dynamism, sparks flying off every chord, all threatening to explode into mayhem at any moment; somehow, though, a shaky control was usually maintained.

When that control slipped, we were exposed to a glimpse of pure chaos. Rock & roll had never been this terrifying before – and it was terrifying, in 1965, in a way nothing else, even the Stones, had ever hinted at. Like 'My Generation'; how could you react to a record whose ending was a minute or so of furious vandalism, with all instruments feeding back, amps and speakers blowing right and left, bringing up images of lightning bolts arcing across electrodes in some Frankenstein laboratory, and all the while this maniacal beat like eight baboons with heavy sticks in a tiny cubicle with walls of stretched drumskin, fighting for their lives to get out? And on the radio yet!

But that was their third single. The one before it was still more impressive. I shouldn't have to transcribe the lyrics to 'Anyway, Anyhow, Anywhere'; if you don't know them by heart there's not hope for you, although you might have a chance if you pick up *Meaty, Beaty, Big & Bouncy* without delay. At any rate, it's simply the definitive Mod anthem, some kind of ultimate brag song. Mod or not, every young person feels like making a statement like this sooner or later. Never mind the message, though – just listen to the record! They don't even wait for the end; two verses and a chorus, then . . . blam!!! A fuzzback space war unleashed before your very ears, seeming battalions of guitars vying to see which can self-destruct most spectacularly, Nicky Hopkins bashing away on his piano, and always that insane drumming. Really, just too much to take in. I still hear something new in this record every time I play it.

The Who were plain magnificent in those days. Huge as they were in England, they were legend here. All their early discs were heard on the air, all over the country at scattered times, though none did more than graze the national charts. So the Who became the idols of a large tribe of cognoscenti, who slavered over each new picture in a teen magazine, and lived for those infrequent appearances on *Shindig*. They made three in 1965. The first time they just did 'I Can't Explain', the second gave us an unexpected taste of 'Daddy Rolling Stone', a British B-side that never came out here. Third time on, though, they assaulted American eyes as well as ears with a performance I'll never forget.

It was a *Shindig* special, taped live at something called 'The Richmond Jazz Festival' and including Manfred Mann, the Yardbirds, the Animals, the Graham Bond Organisation, Gary Farr & the T-Bones (doing 'Wooly Bully'), the Moody Blues and the Who. Each group got only one song, and the Who didn't waste any time. They tore into a frenetic version of 'Anyway, Anyhow, Anywhere' that made the record seem pale. Townshend was battering his guitar mercilessly, hurling it around the stage, into the drums, through the amps and into the air, all the while producing storms of noise the like of which has never been equalled, not even by Jimi Hendrix, who at the time was playing 'Night Train' in some New Jersey bar. But the Who, there on TV in 1965, were more than just ahead of their time. Following the basically tame R&B reworkings of the other groups, they were like nothing any of us had been exposed to before, an inkling perhaps of the violence to which the younger generation would be driven in years to come by the same pressures of society and sheer teenage rebelliousness.

That was the early Who. Despite all efforts America was less than saturated with Whomania, and by the time they really broke through many things had changed. The legend was steadily growing, spurred on by the release here of their first album. As somebody said, it was like one great single, you just kept flipping it over and playing it again. Now, eight years later, it has lost none of its freshness. It is one of a very, very few albums I've had for that long and never ever, not once, grown tired of. Its only low points are two James Brown songs, 'I Don't Mind' and 'Please Please Please', but every Who original is a classic. 'It's Not True' and 'Legal Matter' were as good as any of the singles, while 'The Ox' was simply the first freakout instrumental in the history of rock. I was living in San Francisco at the time, feeling very smug about how avant-garde the groups there were, and when I heard 'The Ox' for the first time . . . well, it changed my thinking a lot.

It was almost mid-1967 before 'Happy Jack' became the first Who single to really hit in America. It made the Top 30, and many naturally assumed it was the group's first record. And in truth, it wasn't much like what had come before. Mod was dead, Swinging London was being taken over by Flower Power, and although the Who's orientation was still strictly Mod, it was no longer quite so violent or overtly genera-tional. In England, their previous hit had been 'I'm A Boy', a kinky little song about a young lad whose mum insists he dress up like a girl. The Who were broadening their scope; like the Kinks (with whom they briefly shared producer Shel Talmy) they were making the shift from raving rockers to more fully developed story-vignettes, some with greater subtlety (such as their next single, 'Pictures Of Lily', whose subject matter – masturbation – slipped right past most radio programmers – it got to No. 4 in England and No. 51 here).

The group's other interests were coming out as well. Pop Art was more than Union Jacks and auto-destruction, and it was all creeping into the Who's music. They released an EP cut live on *Ready Steady Go!* that revealed Keith Moon's absorbing interest in surf music; it contained versions of 'Bucket T' and 'Barbara Ann' as well as 'Batman'. John Entwhistle began his long series of odd B-sides: 'I've Been Away' (a man is sent to jail for a crime committed by his brother, who owns the local brewery), 'Whiskey Man' (the narrator is carried off to the mental ward because of hallucinations), 'Doctor Doctor' (hypochondria) 'Dr Jekyll & Mr Hyde' (schizophrenia), 'Heaven And Hell' (religion) and so forth. And in 1967, the group issued a single of 'The Last Time'/'Under My Thumb' in support of Mick Jagger and Keith Richard, whose drug case was then before the courts.

Much of their best material of this period was released in England only, but between *Magic Bus – The Who On Tour*, *Meaty Beaty Big & Bouncy* and an English compilation called *Direct Hits* plus various Backtrack LPs, most of it can still be obtained. The point is, though, once again we got only echoes of what the Who were doing. But at least 'Happy Jack' did well, which meant the subsequent album was also a success. 'Happy Jack' was the only single on it, the rest were uniformly excellent songs in a style that, in retrospect, occupied an all-too-short interim in the Who's development. Its best material consisted of simple pop songs, only peripherally Mod, such as 'Run Run Run', 'Don't Look Away', and the exquisite 'So Sad About Us'.

Of more lasting significance, however, was the album's
closing number, 'A Quick One While He's Away'. No mere
vignette, this was a full-blown mini-operetta, with the simple
theme of infidelity and redemption carried through several
movements and meant to be enacted on stage. This was an
extension of the theatrical leanings of the Mods as discussed
earlier, and it also signalled the Who's entrance into the
'progressive' era, that period of a couple years in which every
group felt compelled to invent things that had 'never been
done before' in pop music. The Beatles, Stones, and every
other major group with the exception of the Kinks fell into
some painfully pretentious experiments during this era, but
the Who alone proved able to explore the most valuable
products of progressivism (technical and conceptual) while
avoiding the pitfalls and turning the whole thing to their own
ends, which were still basically Mod.

Their next album was easily the best marriage of pop and
underground rock to take place in 1967. *The Who Sell Out*
was a pop-art concept from the start; with everyone doing *Sgt
Pepper*-copy concept albums, trust the Who to do one both
celebrating and chiding the commercial consciousness of
pirate radio (the British equivalent of our AM pop stations)
by linking each track with mock jingles, and including among
the tracks several numbers dedicated to commercial products
such as baked beans, deodorant, and zit cream. These were all
quite amusing and very much in keeping with Mod values
(and, incidentally, the mono and stereo pressings of the
album bore entirely different sets of jingles).

Among all this, and three songs in the Happy Jack style
('Silas Stingy', 'Tattoo' and 'Mary-Anne With The Shaky
Hands'), were seven numbers representing a new sound for
the Who, and a startling progression of the Mod mentality.
Originally, their songs had shared an extremely adolescent
frame of reference, implying much but expressing little more
than inchoate frustration and hot-tempered confusion, in a
musical setting tight and bristling with tension. Now they

returned to some of the same problems, but as older Mods, still desperately individualistic, but somewhat more mature.

'I Can See For Miles' was essentially a brag song in the same mould as 'Anyway Anyhow Anywhere' but using a whole new approach; the machine-gun guitar is still there, but contained in a structure that builds the tension more slowly and deliberately, over a wider range, so that when it is released the impression of omnipotence created by the lyrics is further underlined. This was one of what Townshend once described as 'plane songs', written during those many interminable hours flying above the Atlantic. *Sell Out* is full of them; according to Pete you can tell a plane song by the imagery of freedom and space. 'I Can't Reach You' is the classic example: 'I'm a billion ages past you, a million years behind you, a thousand miles up in the air, a trillion times I've seen you there . . .' And, on 'Our Love Was Is', 'our love was flying, our love was soaring . . .' 'Armenia City In the Sky' (written by Speedy Keen) and 'Relax', as well as an outtake called 'Grace Space Race', exhibit the same influences.

But these songs are of note for more than just these images. Lyrically, they show greater awareness of the complexity behind problems people have to face, though not (as other rock groups all seemed to do at this realisation) supplying what seemed to be easy answers. Mods still, they kept asking questions and insisting on their own right to a fair deal and a good time. Musically, the album also represented something new. To match the imagery, they created a sweeping, airy sound using orchestras and electronic devices, with Pete doubling on organ on many tracks, and altogether thinking in much broader terms when structuring the songs.

I say 'they' but of course I mean Pete, who wrote and arranged all the group's songs with the exception of the odd Entwhistle or Moon B-side. From the beginning he would make demo tapes, overdubbing all the parts including vocals, before presenting his ideas to the rest of the group. They didn't mind, recognising Townshend as the leading creative force; anyway, Entwhistle had his own plans for an album of children's songs and a symphony of sorts, being at heart a classical buff, while Daltrey took satisfaction in organising the band's stage act and Moon, well, Moon was just crazy.

Pete was always the intellectual in the group, the one looking for answers and posing all those difficult questions. And, like many of us in 1967, he began flirting with mysticism. 'Rael', on *Sell Out*, was a long yet incomplete work, structured in movements like 'A Quick One' but consisting mainly of repeating riffs and themes. It had no story line to speak of, aside from a confusing quasi-religious search ending in unresolved ambivalence.

The Who released no new albums for nearly two years. In this time there were some great singles, more Mod brag songs like 'Call Me Lightning' and 'Magic Bus', and a lot of touring. Everyone was expecting a live album, and many were fooled when Decca issued *Magic Bus – The Who On Tour*, which turned out to be a collection of studio tracks. At this time they were performing songs from all periods, mixing *Sell Out* material with songs from their High Numbers days like 'Fortune Teller' and Eddie Cochran's 'Summertime Blues' (a 1959 song with, like 'Blue Suede Shoes' from the same era, distinctly Mod sentiments) and closing with a medley of early hits including a smashup 'My Generation' in which, for the last time, guitars were destroyed and smoke bombs set off. As an interesting sidelight, both 'Summertime Blues' and Mose Allison's 'Young Man Blues' as well as another Eddie Cochran song, 'My Way', were recorded in the studio for *Sell Out* but never used.

All this time, Pete was devoting every spare minute to an idea that had been building in his mind for some time. Taking fragments from uncompleted projects – a minor-chord progression and guitar riff from 'Rael', and a song called 'Glow Girl' that he prepared three different ways for a single before discarding, plus another almost-single titled 'It's A Girl, Mrs Walker', he planned and meditated and fooled around with his eight-track home tape deck. A recent convert to Meher Baba, an Indian avatar claiming to be the incarnation of Jesus and all the world's highest spiritual forces (whose claim to fame was forty years without speaking – what better guru for an Mod who viewed himself as basically inarticulate!) Townshend quite naturally conceived *Tommy* as a spiritual parable.

Of course the story of *Tommy*, of how it became the world's first rock opera and changed the course of rock music and all that, needs no reiteration. Nor should the fact that many critics found it lacking in substance and indicative of the Who's downfall. What is interesting, in terms of this discussion, is the way in which *Tommy* can be seen as a still further extension of the Mod value system.

Those who confuse *Tommy* with the Moody Blues' brand of blarney are missing some important distinctions. Mainly, there's a big difference between pushing one's own opinions as gospel and trying to maintain integrity in a confusing situation. In other words, between giving answers and asking questions. *Tommy* raises more questions than it answers, and its intent is plainly to start others asking questions rather than to shove Meher Baba down their throats, as any lesser convert would have done. Baba is not mentioned on the album, nor is his philosophy there in any but the most circumstantial sense.

I think *Tommy* could be more correctly seen as the meeting of the questing Mod mentality with the world of metaphysics. 'Why am I not free?' asks the young Mod. First it's parents, girls, jobs . . . now, those forces vanquished, it turns out to be something a bit more intangible. It's interesting in this light, that the Who only turned to political questions after the spiritual quest – but hardly paradoxical considering that the Mod stance was so fanatically individualistic, even during the most collective phase of the movement. One person seeking his place in the scheme of things, whether at school or in the universe, is still a more Mod concept than the idea

or organised political activity or even politically-inspired
anarchy.

At any rate, *Tommy* concerned a young person's search for
meaning, in the broadest sense. That he was a most unique
individual, deaf, dumb, and blind, and that he found meaning
through something as unlikely and pop-art-absurd as pinball,
adds character and pop appeal to the story. There is also a
humorous irreverence running through *Tommy* that sets it
apart from every other rock concept album I can think of
(with the exception of *Arthur*) as a work of basic human
appeal whatever its ultimate message. It's also full of anomalies – Sonny Boy Williamson's 'Eyesight To The Blind', 'Sally
Simpson', and the great single 'Pinball Wizard'. And at the
end of it all, nothing has been resolved. Much has been raised,
much vivid imagery and some moments of very acute observation, wills have been asserted and desired thwarted. In
the very end, to quote a brief synopsis that came with the
original promo package, 'Tommy is completely isolated and
unable to communicate.' He can't explain, but he thinks it's
love. Mod to the very end.

The implications of *Tommy* were impossible to avoid. The
Who toured endlessly, performing it for growing crowds to
whom they were, at last, superstars. Imitation rock operas
appeared in profusion, and there was constant talk of making
Tommy into a film, a Broadway production, a ballet, a
ponderous institution. I found myself hoping that, having
done it, Townshend could put it behind him and get back to
the business of making singles – where, musically at least, the
Who had always excelled. Instead, Townshend announced
plans for another rock opera, mentioning a few song titles
including 'Water' and 'I Don't Even Know Myself'.

But it was not forthcoming. There was 'The Seeker', a good
rock & roll single with the same kind of chunky rhythms as
on their earliest records. It too was about the spiritual quest,
in more obviously Mod terms. 'I won't get to get what I'm
after, till the day I die!' laments the protagonist, frustrated

again. He's sharp, though, he knows better than to accept the simplistic explanations of the Beatles, Timothy Leary and the rest. He's lookin' out for himself all the way, and he won't be fooled.

Then came *Live At Leeds*. Everyone who'd ever seen the Who had wanted a live album immediately, and by 1970 it was ridiculously overdue. In interviews, Townshend claimed they'd been trying for years to achieve a usable tape, the Who being a very difficult group to record live. With the wide circulation of bootleg tapes, some far superior to *Leeds*, that seems unlikely, but whatever the case I found it to be a highly unsatisfactory album, completely lacking in the sense of dynamics that had been at the core of the Who's music from the beginning, substituting drawn-out guitar solos for those beautiful, smashing chords, and free of feedback save for a few token seconds at the end of an obese 'My Generation' stuffed with 'See Me, Feel Me'. Townshend, it seemed, was the electronic guitar wizard no longer; now he was merely another lead guitarist, and a rather ordinary one at that. For me, *Live At Leeds* was a tremendous letdown.

They bounced back, though, I'll give them that. 'Won't Get Fooled Again' signalled their entry into the realm of street politics, Mods on the march and all that. It also introduced Pete's latest sound, an organ-like beeping produced by an ARP synthesizer that ran through the song and most of *Who's Next*.

As rock politics go, 'Won't Get Fooled Again' was good. It took no stand except for the individual, asserted implicitly that all governments and forms of authority were not to be trusted, and suggested merely that people wise up. As much as Mod could be political, this was it.

And it was definitely Mod. Townshend knew it, too. He gave long interviews rhapsodising on the Mod movement and how it had influenced his thinking. He must have realised his unique position, as first and last spokesman for the Mods, former ace face of a movement already becoming history.

Mod couldn't have lasted on its own terms, of course; it was too alienated, and too existential to fight the current of youth consciousness, which throughout the late '60s was toward harmony and organised utopianism. And few Mods were as intellectually committed to (or conscious of) what Mod represented to care enough to try and keep its precepts alive through the increasingly complex ramifications of '60s youth culture.

Where were the Mods of yesteryear? Rod Stewart, Marc Bolan, David Bowie: all the rest had changed with the trends. The Who alone carried the mantle of Mod, and after all what can you do having immortalised a lyric as unequivocal as 'Hope I die before I get old!'? There's no way to back down from a statement like that, and growing old is the last thing you can allow yourself to do.

So you stay young – as young as you can, being 30-year-old rock superstar institutions, with operas, benefits for charity with royalty in attendance, millions of dollars, and a vested interest in an Eastern religious sect. And they've done all right too. No other rock group has managed to stay together so long without losing any of its personnel or its knack for rock & roll honesty, and it seems that no matter how far the Who digress they are always capable of jumping right back to the basics.

'Let's See Action' was such a return, a solid follow-up to 'Won't Get Fooled Again', and inexplicably it was the first Who single since 'Dogs' not to be issued in the US. Instead we had 'Join Together', a nice song with decent sentiments, which I hated. Maybe it was just that I remembered a time when it would have taken teams of doctors to remove all the drumsticks and guitar shards from anyone who tried to climb up onstage and 'join together with the band'. This was an open courting of the hippie harmonists, there was nothing Mod about it, and maybe that's what offended me. In any case, I was more pleased with 'Relay', which proposed basically the same thing but in a more indirect fashion, and sounded a bit more like 'Let's See Action'. And I loved the flip, a crazy Keith Moon song called 'Wasp Man' that recalled the days of 'Cobwebs and Strange'.

Whatever else, I'll always respect a band that puts odd cuts on flip sides to encourage people to buy singles. Almost every Who single has had one, right up to the present. 'I Don't Even Know Myself' turned up on the back of 'Won't Get Fooled Again', with nothing said of the rock opera it was supposedly written for. A sigh of relief; maybe we'll be spared. Then came 'Water', backing 'Love Reign O'er Me'. 'Water' had been touted as the best thing since 'I Can See For Miles' by those who'd had the tape for a couple of years, and of course it wasn't – too modern, no dynamics, and most disturbing of all, an official outtake from the forthcoming rock opera, *Quadrophenia*.

Uh oh, I thought, now we're in for it. I dreaded hearing it, expecting the worst, hoping for the best, knowing the Who still had it in them, but knowing better than to think that meant anything. Then I got the album. And it was the biggest surprise the Who have thrown me since . . . well, since I first heard one of their records.

Quadrophenia is at once nothing like *Tommy* and every- thing *Tommy* should have been. Its theme is also a young man's quest for meaning, and it is also a fully developed opera, with movements, themes, and roles assigned to each member. In fact, taken together it is meant to add up to the group's collective state of mind – schizophrenia split four ways: quadrophenia.

There's nothing abstruse or remotely arcane about it. Everyone will understand it, on some level. Those having some experience with Mod will revel in it. Plain and simple, it's a Mod nostalgia trip, set in 1965, the story of a young Everymod, the things he does, and the forces that make him do it. There are exquisitely apropos liner notes and a picture book of faultless imagery.

And the album is packed with in-jokes for those who know

enough about Mod and the Who's early career. The best of
these is buried in the middle of side three, in a song called 'Sea
And Sand'. One of the few real rockers in the set, it's a fine
song on its own terms. But there's more. As the last of the
lyrics on the libretto are sung, there is a moment of silence,
then a hard 'Got Love If You Want It' riff comes in while a
voice mixed low on the left channel starts singing 'I'm the face
if you want it, babe . . .'

Touches like that go a long way toward making up for the
album's deficiencies. Which, unfortunately, do exist. Reading
the lyrics gives rise to anticipations of an album full of
uncompromising mid-'60s rock & roll. The songs are full
of all the right references and attitudes regarding clothes,
pills, social relationships, and all they would need to have
been right at home on *The Who Sings My Generation*.
Musically, however, there's no mistaking that this is the
modern Who. They rock hard enough, when required, and
there are some nice riffs. But there is also a profusion of
symphonic and electronic sound effects, and a lack of really
blazing dynamism in even the most driving segments.

Which is not to say that Townshend should have tried to
recreate the group's early sound, just because that era is their
subject matter. Even if it might have resulted in a more
exciting-sounding album. I suspect he had something more
in mind. The Who have already dealt with the problems of the
adolescent Mod, from that side of the fence. Now, being
older, and having developed endlessly more subtle and complex means of expressing themselves, it could be they were
intrigued by the prospect of returning to that same theme,
from the other side, in third person rather than first as it were,
to see what further realms they could illuminate. That angry
feedback was all right for capturing the Mod's hostility, but
what of the great sense of aloneness and uncertainty that were
also part of the young rebel's life? For that you need those
orchestras and stately, sweeping movements, which the Who
have employed with great effectiveness.

Anyway, that's how I choose to look at it. Better this, I suppose, that an album like *Pin-Ups*. The old can stand on its own, pointless to try and mimic it. And it's a good album overall, even if I fear it'll be one of the last albums I pull out when I want to hear some Who, in the days to come.

One thing that would excite me would be a film based on *Quadrophenia*. A really intense black and white adaptation, like *Some People*, which drew a stark and fascinating portrait of English youth ca. 1962. Or in full Carnaby Street colour to match the brilliance of the times. It could be done any number of ways, and with the Mod movement as its theme, it couldn't fail to be great.

And the soundtrack, I'd like to suggest, ought to be done by a group like the Sweet, only not so well known. One of the new Mod bands that are beginning to appear around England. That's how I think of them, anyway. There has been some argument as to whether it's kosher to speak of Mod without meaning the whole social movement, but I think if there's one thing the Who have proven, it's that Mod can be reduced to an essential attitude that is applicable at all times and places . . . And from the look of it, that attitude seems to be gaining acceptance once again, as the last echoes of underground consciousness, pop's arch-foe, slowly fade out with the dead sixties. Suddenly the English pop papers are full of pictures of young groups with strings of flash-bam hit singles and the latest in bright, trendy clothes. And the look is very Mod as well, with neatly-trimmed longish hair, fresh scrubbed faces, clean new clothes, and image, image, image. Plus, the records these groups make are strongly rooted in 1965, hook and chorus songs with hard chords and dazzling guitar riffs, aggressive drumming, high harmonies, and lyrics about women who just won't behave.

So maybe Mod is coming back, and maybe the term Glam will stick, or maybe it'll be called something else. That's all very nice, but not terribly important where the Who are concerned. Because where these groups are just starting, the Who have been through it all.

Whether or not Mod returns in some form, the Who have already proven that there was more to it than most people thought. It was not merely another transient teen fad; rather, as Townshend maintained all along, it was a distillation of the basic value system every teenager has struggled to formulate since Elvis first shook his hips. In our culture, in 1974 as much as 1964, there's no need for any child of rock & roll to respond to his environment in any other way. We all experience frustration and alienation to some degree, and for those it hits most deeply, the adolescents, there can be no more correct or satisfying response, than to work it out through pop music, fashion, or whatever other channels exist in their own peer culture. No politics, no organised structures of any kind are to be trusted. Stick with your own and you won't be fooled.

That's the Mod outlook, and it has carried the Who through the years in good stead. Somehow, no matter what their age, no matter how subdued their music might become, I don't think anyone will be able to say the Who have gotten old as long as they keep it alive inside them. And in the end, when all possible follies of youth culture have come and gone, I wouldn't be the least bit surprised if they turned out to have been right all along.

Mary Harron

POP ART/ART POP: THE ANDY WARHOL CONNECTION

Melody Maker, 16th February 1980

I wrote this piece in Canada – I'd interviewed Warhol in New York and was holed up in the country writing it. The deadline for mailing it came and went and of course there were no faxes in those days. MM editor Richard Williams was holding the cover for it and I didn't know what to do. I thought I might have to fly back just to get the piece in. In the end I went to the Toronto airport and handed it to a guy who was lining up for the next flight to London. I gave him an envelope with the article inside and Richard Williams' phone number and begged him to call him when he arrived. The man did and Richard picked it up and it made the cover.

Looking back on the piece, which I hadn't read in twenty years, I don't think I gave enough credit to Warhol's work. He wasn't just a great designer, he was a great artist. I also underestimated the films. I cringe now at the article's rather pompous tone, but researching it and writing it was a real adventure – and where else could something like this have appeared but in the music press?

MH

Like to be a gallery
Put you all inside my show
– David Bowie, 'Andy Warhol'

'Because of Andy Warhol it's no longer possible to just do what you do and not have to act it out 24 hours a day. His style of doing things changed everybody's idea of what the values were that could make you a star. And as a result there's this self-consciousness going on everywhere, this use of the media. It's not just what you do now, it's what you say about it, the way you behave, who your friends are. Your life has to reflect it. And in a way a lot of trash has been produced because of that. Which was also part of his idea . . .'
                – Steve Piccolo of the Lounge Lizards

ANDY WARHOL IS one of the great unacknowledged influences on pop music. He influenced it in a very specific way, by fostering the Velvet Underground. But his influence spreads beyond that – you see it everywhere, but it's hard to define. It's a matter of style and attitude. Not only did Warhol leave his mark on Roxy Music, David Bowie, the Ramones, Talking Heads and every other New York art rock group, but he helped make them possible.

Warhol's influence on pop music started with pop art and what it did to America. He did not, in fact, originate pop art, but it's very typical of Warhol that most people now think he did. It was already news in 1959 when Jasper Johns exhibited two bronzed beer cans – a good three years before Warhol showed his silk screens of Campbell soup cans to the world. But it was Warhol who became the symbol of pop art, and who took it to its farthest edge.

Warhol's soup cans stood for everything that was trashy, disposable and mass-produced in American life. By bringing the supermarket into the art gallery, pop art discarded all prevailing values about what was good or bad, beautiful or ugly, art or non-art.

Pop art provided an exhilarating liberation. After all, not only was trash part of the modern landscape, but it had a life and beauty of its own. In American a lot of vitality, care and imagination has gone into producing trash. For artists, that whole bubblegum/comic strip/pop music/B-movie side of America had the excitement of forbidden territory. Children and teenagers could love it unselfconsciously, but artists had been taught to reject it as having no permanence or value. Pop art kicked down the barriers; now artists could admit to their secret love of trash. But because these artists were sophisticated adults, they celebrated bubblegum culture in an ironic, self-conscious way.

The age of pop art was also the age in which pop music lost its innocence. You can hear that innocence in the Ronettes and the Shangri-las and all those Twist songs, cheerfully fizzing away, never dreaming that anyone would take them seriously. But when the art world began to take an interest in pop, pop began to look at itself very differently. The two worlds locked; pop music acquired a history and influences.

Purely commercial pop continues to be produced, of course, as does purely 'art' music, but it was only after the two worlds interlocked that you had arty pop. Only after pop music had become self-conscious could you have a group like the Ramones, with their amazing ironic dumbness. The Ramones eternally stand back from themselves. They are both an expression of American teenagehood and a comment on it, and perhaps for that reason they have never been embraced by the mass of American teenagers. But then pop art was never truly popular either: reproductions of Warhol silk screens never found their way onto the living room walls of Middle America.

But if most Americans didn't approve of Warhol, and still don't approve of Warhol, everyone heard about him. The entry for him in *Webster's Biographical Dictionary* says: 'Perennially controversial, Warhol reached mythic proportions in the 1960s largely because his motives were almost totally obscure . . .'

Public fascination with Warhol revolved around two questions: *Why is he doing this? And How is he getting away with it?*

To the public he was a hustler, and in a way they were right. The way he manipulated the media was part of his statement – which makes you wonder whether Malcolm McLaren isn't one of his spiritual heirs. Both used the media – but, unlike McLaren, Warhol never had any subversive aims. Warhol has always had the greatest respect for money and fame and power.

The public must have been bewildered to see Andy Warhol, who seemed to be doing nothing, embraced by the Establishment – welcomed by the Museum of Modern Art, courted by Nelson Rockefeller. One reason was, quite simply, his talent. Warhol is a designer of great brilliance, and even when he seemed to be doing nothing but reproducing common American images – from dollar bills to Jackie Kennedy, from Elvis Presley to the electric chair – he did it with unmistakable flair.

Another reason was his talent for making the right social connections – at a time when art had become very fashionable. Tom Wolfe wrote in his profile of art collector Robert Scull: 'Abstract Expressionism was so esoteric it had all but defied exploitation by the press. But all the media embraced Pop Art with an outraged, scandalised, priapic delight. Art generally became the focus of social excitement in New York. Art openings began to take over from theatre openings as the place where the chic, the ambitious and the beautiful congregated.'

Finally, there was the fascination of Warhol's attitude, as seen in his occasional childlike, oracular public statements: 'In the future everyone will be famous for 15 minutes.' 'Business is the best art.' 'I love Hollywood. It's plastic, but I love plastic. I want to be plastic.' 'We're a vacuum here at the Factory. I think it's great.'

The Factory was his studio on West 47th Street. The name was both ironic and candid. The building had, in fact, once been a factory; now, by silk screening paintings and having most of his work done by assistants, Warhol was trying to produce factory art.

Warhol's Factory threatened the whole idea of art as individual, painstaking self-expression, and in this he went beyond his contemporaries. On the whole, pop art was fun. The work of someone like Claes Oldenburg – he of the enormous plaster hamburgers – could be seen as an affectionately satirical look at American life. Warhol himself was not satirical. He not only accepted the supermarket as valid subject matter, he accepted it for what it was. He may have outraged the bourgeoisie, but he *approved* of consumerism, of modern industrial life, in a way that the president of IBM in his most secret thoughts would not have dared to admit.

Warhol's blank acceptance, his refusal to make value judgements, had dangerous implications, but it was also liberating. Most people had become so frightened by the modern world that they couldn't even look at it straight. Warhol seemed to have none of the normal human reactions – no fear of alienation, loneliness, conformity.

Many of his pronouncements were witty: he was never totally sincere or insincere. The best source of these is *The Philosophy Of Andy Warhol (From A To B And Back Again)* – a book, which, characteristically, he did not write. His assistants wrote it up from taped conversations with Warhol: 'I like eating alone. I want to start a chain of restaurants for other people who are like me called ANDYMATS – "The Restaurant for the Lonely Person". You get your food and then you take your tray into a booth and watch television.'

At times, Warhol seemed to be looking at the world with the naïve curiosity of a creature from another planet. The only person I can think of now who shares this vision is David Byrne of Talking Heads. The title *More Songs About Buildings And Food*, the line 'Heaven is a bar where nothing ever happens' and the lyrics to 'Don't Worry About The Government' are all very Warhol. But Byrne seems more vulnerable. Throughout his songs, it's as if he's taking a correspondence course in modern life, learning step by step how to fit in.

Both Byrne and Warhol believe in the virtues of hard work,

business and success, and accept the status quo. But there's one big difference between them. Byrne worries about human emotions; Warhol doesn't or at least claims he used to but stopped when he discovered the television set and the tape-recorder:

'During the '60s, I think, most people forgot what emotions were supposed to be. And I don't think they've ever remembered. I think that once you see emotions from a certain angle you can never think of them as real again. That's what more or less has happened to me.' (*The Philosophy Of Andy Warhol*)

People did not forget how to feel during the '60s; this statement is about Warhol himself, and the solution he found to his problem in living. His problem seems to have been an extreme timidity, an almost pathological shyness that made it impossible for him to relate to people directly. He also loved and needed to be surrounded by people. His solution was to relate to them through tape and films. And because he was so famous, and could attract fame, his solution was a very public and influential one:

'The acquisition of my tape-recorder really finished whatever emotional life I might have had, but I was glad to see it go. Nothing was ever a problem again, because a problem just meant a good tape, and when a problem transforms itself into a good tape it's not a problem any more. An interesting problem was an interesting tape. Everybody knew that and performed for the tape. You couldn't tell which problems were real and which problems were performed for the tape. Better yet, the people telling you the problems couldn't decide any more if they were really having the problems or just performing.'

This only makes sense in the context of Warhol's social circle, where people wanted to sit around and put their problems on tape. This doesn't mean all his friends were rich and spoiled. Warhol hadn't yet become the full-time socialite he is today, and some of his entourage were social outcasts – hustlers and transvestites. But they all had a certain New York style of dealing with their neuroses by turning them into theatre – by developing an attitude and then acting it out full time in an amazing performance. Living theatre.

Warhol's entourage was also vulnerable and narcissistic. Warhol had spotted something about film and tape: they were an invitation to narcissism. You could act yourself out and record yourself and then play yourself back.

They don't necessarily function that way of course – most home movies are not narcissistic. But Warhol began to make a very sophisticated kind of home movie, in which his friends acted out themselves, and which were then shown to the public. And for some of his friends it was the most glorious thing that had ever happened to them, and for some it was ultimately destructive.

In 1963 Warhol and his assistants began making films at the Factory, which was a very large L-shaped loft with the walls covered in silver paper. The early films were silent, black and white, and had titles like *Eat, Kiss, Sleep, Blowjob, Haircut*: single camera shots, concentrating on a single activity, sometimes for many hours. The culmination of this was *Empire* in 1964, the eight-hour film of the Empire State Building which contained one action: a light being switched off.

What Tom Wolfe said about modern art in *The Painted Word* is also true of avant-garde film-making: the simpler something is, the more elaborate the criticism it inspires, until the explanation becomes more important than the work itself. Thousands of pages have been written trying to explain these films, and I don't want to add to them. Perhaps Warhol just became interested in the idea of film and approached it with his usual blank curiosity as if he had never seen anything like this before.

So there was no story, no acting, no artistic touch. Just – 'Here is a camera. See? This is what it does.' The films were stunningly boring (although they make beautiful still photographs) and were obviously meant to be. When questioned, Warhol said that he liked boredom. Boredom was great.

Gradually, the films became more elaborate, with sound-tracks and scripts. The performers were drawn from War-hol's entourage, the inner circle of the mad house of people who filled the Factory day and night.

As Warhol's *Philosophy* says: 'In the '60s everyone got interested in everybody else. Drugs helped a little there . . .' At the Factory members of the art establishment and rich debutantes like Baby Jane Holzer and Edie Sedgwick met the sexual underground of drag queens and Times Square hustlers. And the drug underground, too – amphetamines played a big part in the life of the Factory.

These 'underground' movies were made in a steady glare of publicity. Everything Warhol did at this time was news, and he could bestow the protection of his fame on the misfits who came off the streets to shelter at the Factory. In modern America, celebrity was becoming an end in itself; it no longer mattered what you were, as long as you were famous.

Movies, radio and TV changed the nature of fame. Until they were invented, fame had always been a matter of reputation; as long as it depended on word of mouth or on print, it was necessary to be or do something extraordin-ary to attract attention. You had to be very talented or very rich or beautiful or powerful or evil or saintly.

The advent of the electronic media meant that anyone's voice or image could be sent into a million homes (an advanced of sorts on the movies, which could only send them into movie theatres).

At the same time, celebrity watching became a full-time occupation for many people, because you could now 'get to know' anyone by seeing him or her on television, all by yourself in your own home. Actually, you wouldn't get to know them at all, or at least nothing beyond their public image, but still – there they were in your living room.

This teasing sense of intimacy made the public fascinated

by personalities; the emphasis shifted from what people did to what they were like. Rock music, which came of age with television, is totally obsessed by personality.

In the '60s, very few people were willing to admit that fame no longer depended on achievement. Warhol was quite happy to admit it, and to play with it. What he did was to take a group of unknown people and turn them into 'superstars'.

The word itself was invented by Warhol's friend Ingrid, a raucous blonde from New Jersey who began calling herself 'Ingrid Superstar'. The more she went to parties with Andy, the more her name was printed in the papers, and Ingrid Superstar became famous. Eventually, all the personalities in Warhol's films became known as superstars. Warhol's *Philosophy* defined them as 'all the people who are very talented, but whose talents are hard to define and almost impossible to market'.

Warhol was a great talent-spotter, and most of his superstars had wit and a kind of freaky glamour. (The transvestites' outrageous thrift-shop finery was an influence on glitter rock, at least the American variety, in the shape of the New York Dolls.) Some were great beauties, like Edie Sedgwick and International Velvet, some were great talkers, like Ondine and Taylor Mead – and some were both, like Viva and the drag queen Candy Darling.

In the early films they would just start with an idea – 'sit over there and eat a banana' – but even when they had scripts most of the action was improvised. The superstars would camp around or discuss their problems or reminisce, or just sit there, transmitting their presence onto the screen.

Cameras don't make judgements: they record everything, whether it's interesting or not. So, true to the nature of the medium, Warhol and his assistants let their cameras record everything; the early films were almost never edited. This made them boring, but life-like in a bizarre way. Warhol once called them 'documentaries'. It's true that even the most theatrical performers, the drag queens, were just repeating a performance they carried on in life; however, the camera was also inspiring them to perform.

Alan Midgette, who was probably the only professional actor to appear in Warhol's early films, says he remembers that once the fashion model Ivy Nicholson stood in front of the camera at the Factory and tried to slit her wrists.

'Those kind of people get demented when they become involved with movies, because they don't understand how powerful they can be,' he says. 'Something gets triggered off because they're not really acting. They haven't been given a part to play, so they start pulling these weird things out of their psyche and throwing them at the camera.'

Appropriately enough, the only real acting Warhol asked Midgette to do was to impersonate Warhol himself. In 1966 the artist was invited to go on a university lecture tour, and since Warhol was too shy, his assistant, Paul Morrissey, asked Midgette to go instead; there was a certain resemblance between the two, although Alan was younger and better-looking. So he sprayed his hair silver, like Andy's, rubbed the lightest shade of makeup on his face to imitate Andy's pallor, and borrowed Andy's black leather jacket.

Midgette impersonated Warhol at lectures, meetings with academics, and in interviews. 'I knew as Andy you could answer a question any way, and that the most ambiguous answer was the closest to being like Andy.' Eventually, the hoax was discovered, and the fees for the lectures had to be returned – but it also won Warhol thousands of dollars' worth of free publicity.

When questioned Warhol told a newspaper: 'Oh, well, we just did it, well, I, uh, because, uh, I really don't have that much to say. The person who went had so much more to say. He was what the people expected.'

Midgette thinks that it was seeing his replica accepted on the lecture tour that gave Warhol the confidence to appear in public. Warhol, who always delegated everything, had succeeded in delegating the responsibility for being himself.

Warhol was, at this point, probably the most famous and highest-paid artist in the world. And, ironically, his superstars became famous, too – real media celebrities. In a way, what Warhol had done was sick. He had let people expose themselves to the camera, and he had shown that not only did they want to expose themselves but that other people wanted to watch. He had made voyeurism chic.

Some of the superstars destroyed themselves, like Edie Sedgwick, who became a drug addict and died of an overdose at 27. But something good came out of those films, too. It was an attitude – tough, funny, sharp-witted – sustained by many of the superstars even when they were showing their scars. It was the attitude of people who had been through the mill and come out flaunting. Their detachment, the way they parodied themselves, was a form of courage – and if you were a drag queen in 1966, you needed all the courage you could get.

You can find the same attitude among certain personalities on the New York rock music scene today, like Lydia Lunch. You can also find the same sickness and affectation.

So many worlds converged at the Factory and Warhol knew so many people that it was probably inevitable that he should meet the Velvet Underground.

He was friendly with the avant-garde musicians la Monte Young and Marian Zazeela, in whose Theater of Eternal Music John Cale played when he first came to New York. Warhol also knew a conceptual artist named Walter De Maria, who played drums for John Cale and Lou Reed in an early incarnation of the Velvets called the Primitives.

According to Gerard Malanga, at one point Warhol was planning to start his own rock band along with Young, Zazeela, De Maria and Patty Oldenburg, the wife of Claes Oldenburg. The idea of Warhol fronting a rock band is irresistible but it never came to anything. However, it does show that rock was on his mind. By 1965 he had plans to open the first mixed-media show in New York, involving live music, dancers and film.

It was Gerard Malanga who actually led Warhol to the Velvet Underground. Malanga was Warhol's personal assistant during the mid-'60s, a poet and superstar, and Warhol's opposite in every way: good-looking, street-smart, an unabashed exhibitionist and extravagantly heterosexual. Warhol fired Malanga years ago, for some undisclosed transgression; this was after 1968, when the Factory had moved premises to Union Square and its whole style had changed.

It was easy to track Malanga down to his home on 14th Street at 3rd Avenue. It seemed appropriate to find this symbol of the old Factory still living here, on a block lined with cut-price stores, pawnshops and liquor stores. It is not one of the most dangerous streets in New York, just one of the sleaziest, like Times Square. Everyone, even the newsagents, looks like they are involved in something vaguely illegal and unsuccessful. It is also a drug street, where addicts of various kinds huddle in little groups, rocking back and forth, whimpering long, frenetic monologues.

Whenever anyone talks of the romance of streetlife I always think of 14th Street at 3rd Avenue and wonder if that's where they really want to be. But I also suspect that all the New York art undergrounds, from the Beats to the Factory to the rock scene, have been most alive when they connected with this world, maybe because it acts as a constant reminder of what you face when you put yourself 'outside of society'. Certainly, the Factory stopped taking risks after it closed its doors to Times Square.

When I met Malanga he still looked very much the way he does in photographs from ten years ago, down to the black leather trousers that he made into a fashion. Malanga explained that it was the first time in years that he had worn leather: he was leaving that night to appear at a poetry festival in Amsterdam and thought he should dress for the part.

It was the way he dressed when he went to see the Velvet Underground at the Café Bizarre at the end of 1965. He was also carrying a large whip at the time. Not because he was into S&M but as an accessory – it went with the leather. As the Velvets played Malanga began to do an extravagant whip dance, and afterwards Lou Reed came over and asked him if he'd come and dance every night.

Warhol's mixed media show, the Exploding Plastic Inevitable, opened upstairs at the Dom Theater in early 1966. Sometimes five films would be projected at once, running all over the walls and ceiling, and anyone from the audience could come up and run the projector. Sometimes the Velvets would all wear white so that they simply reflected the film images and became invisible onstage. The Velvets played ear-splittingly loud, Malanga did his whip dance onstage, and sometimes the entire cast of the Living Theater would come by after a performance and start leaping around the room.

This was the time when the whole Factory entourage hung out in the backroom restaurant at Max's Kansas City. Warhol's bill there was said to be $3,000 a month. Deborah Harry, who was a waitress there at the time, has said in interviews that not only were the Warhol crowd the rudest people she ever met, but they never left any tips.

The Velvets began to rehearse at the Factory, and did so nearly every day for almost two years. The phone was always ringing with invitations for Warhol and his entourage. This was an age of lavish parties, in lofts and art galleries, parties everywhere from discotheques to the Statue of Liberty. And so the Velvets wrote 'All Tomorrow's Parties': *'What costumes shall the poor girl wear / To all tomorrow's parties?'*

Malanga says, 'The Velvets were always invited to things, and usually they would show up. But they were very much in the background, and no one really paid any attention to them. Except for Nico, because she had a lot of social connections.'

Nico was then a successful fashion model who had appeared in *La Dolce Vita* and cut a single in London with Andrew Loog Oldham. Malanga says: 'It was Warhol's idea to bring Nico into the group; he wanted her in because he felt the Velvets on their own "lacked charisma".'

Of all the Velvets, Lou Reed spent the most time at the Factory and was closest to Warhol. In some way their attitudes were close. Warhol has often gone on record as saying that sex is too much trouble, but he is fascinated by the idea of sex, and many of his films were semi-pornographic in a distanced, ironic way. A friend of Reed's in the Factory days said to me: 'Lou is mostly a voyeur. In my experience he never had any sustained interest in either sex. You see, sex just doesn't offer Lou enough – he's just really bored by it.' But like Warhol, Reed was interested in the idea of sex, in the sexual role-playing of transvestism and S&M.

Reed drew on the Factory for his subject matter – the 'Chelsea Girls' are all Warhol people, 'Candy Says' is about Candy Darling, and 'Walk On The Wild Side' is a series of vivid superstar portraits – but he didn't share Warhol's passive, objective eye. 'Candy Says' is a very moving song, and Lou Reed had obviously been touched by these people; he identified with them.

Some of the Velvets' most important songs, like 'Heroin', 'Venus In Furs' and 'I'm Waiting For My Man', were already written by the time they met Warhol. He functioned less as an inspiration than as a source of financial and moral support.

Sterling Morrison, the Velvets' guitarist, thinks they might have broken up in six months if it wasn't for Warhol. Morrison says: 'He argued against restraint.' John Cale says: 'Andy's a good catalyst.' One reason why Warhol had such a powerful effect was that he created an atmosphere at the Factory where it seemed that all the old rules and forms had been broken and anything could be tried. His attitude was, 'Why not?' Or, when faced with a problem, 'So what?'

Walter De Maria says, 'There was a serious tone to the music and the movies and the people, as well as all the craziness and the speed. There was also the feeling of desperate living, of being on the edge.'

When I asked him if the people at the Factory ever thought about the future he said, 'No, I think the present was blazing and every day was incredible, and you knew every day wasn't always going to be that way.'

1966 is said to have been the great year at the Factory. By 1968 the Velvet Underground, after touring with the Plastic Inevitable, had come to an amicable parting of the ways with Warhol. That same year a lesbian feminist named Valerie Solanas appeared on the outer fringes of the Warhol entourage, and played a small part in one film, *I, A Man*.

Solanas, who seems to have had a certain sense of humour as well as a badly-deranged mind, had formed a group called SCUM – the Society for Cutting Up Men. When Warhol refused to produce a film script she had written, she became resentful. On June 5, 1968, she took the elevator up to the Factory, walked over to Andy Warhol, who was talking on the telephone, and shot him three times in the chest.

In his *Philosophy*, Warhol wrote: 'Before I was shot, I always thought I was more half-there than all there – I always suspected that I was watching TV instead of living life.' After being shot, he says, he knew that he was watching television: 'The channels switch, but it's all TV.'

Be that as it may, it affected him enough to cause a revolution in the Factory. The open door policy was stopped and the Factory moved premises to Union Square and became an increasingly professional organisation. Paul Morrissey, who had become Warhol's chief assistant (and who once managed Nico), took over the filming. The result was more commercial, and admittedly more entertaining, films like *Flesh*, *Trash* and *Heat*.

The new Factory, in Union Square, houses the office of *Interview* magazine. Glenn O'Brien, who edited it for three years and now writes its music column, says it was started to give Gerard Malanga something to do.

Interview began as a film magazine, but eventually concentrated almost entirely on interviews. They were all transcripts from tape recordings and like the early films, were interesting because they left in all sorts of things that a professional editor would have cut out. The interviews read just like conversations, sometimes boring and trivial, but with the fascination of eavesdropping.

Interview seems to have influenced the punk fanzines. *Punk* magazine, which started in New York in 1975, picked up the random, slightly surreal style of the early *Interview*. Mark P told me in the summer of 1976 that, although he thought *Punk* was too much of a comic book, it had given him the inspiration to start *Sniffin' Glue*. And the rest is history. Or not, as the case may be.

The editorial policy of *Interview* is avowedly to cover people who are doing interesting things, but it had concentrated increasingly on those who are rich or already famous. It's now edited by Bob Colacello, who contributes a rather arch monthly column about his social climbing. *Interview* has done a great deal for Warhol's own social connections, and he seems to appear at every important party. But then Andy Warhol – who was born Andrew Warhola 52 years ago, the child of Czech immigrants, whose father worked in the Pittsburgh steel mills, and who grew up in poverty – has always been infatuated with the rich.

The reception area of the new Factory is very quiet. There is a lot of polished wood floor, and polished tables, and the minute you walk in a young man politely asks you what your business is.

There are several of these young men wandering around the Factory, all remarkably alike. They are fair, well-dressed and very well groomed, rather sweet, but enervated. They have the kind of faces that appear in *Interview* magazine, and like all those faces they are faintly disappointing in the flesh – they only achieve perfection in photographs.

I sat down to wait. Fred Hughes, who is listed as the 'President' of *Interview*, walked in. He is small, neat, impeccably dressed, but brash. I suspect that brashness is his most likeable characteristic.

Hughes sat down at the telephone and smiled at me

suspiciously. Did I have an appointment? I was glad that I did, because there is a potential for nastiness at the Factory. If you did not have an appointment they could make it very clear to you that you were not beautiful, rich, amusing or in any way fabulous enough to have walked in there at all.

Warhol came in and we were introduced, not that I had any trouble recognising him. There was a slight shock at first when I realised how old he was – I had always thought of Warhol as permanently 30. At first sight he is unearthly. His skin is like nothing I've ever seen on a human being. His face, beneath the dyed silver hair, is so pale that it seems to have been modelled out of putty, ridged with little crevices that are, in fact, nothing more sinister than adolescent acne scars. He speaks very softly, and with a shy boyish charm that immediately begins to take effect.

Warhol explained that he had some business to take care of, and I sat down to wait again. I noted, with some satisfaction, that the paint was peeling from the ceiling. Warhol returned and we retired to one end of the room, past a huge vertical prism filled with rainbows, surrounded by black screens and potted plants, past a stuffed penguin on top of a marble table, surrounded by black armchairs. I brought out my tape-recorder.

'Is the radio on?' asked Warhol. He went over and switched it off, so that it wouldn't interfere with the recording. Warhol knows about tape-recorders.

I knew that a few days previously Warhol had been down at the Mudd Club filming a 'Rock and Roll Funeral Party' in progress there. The party ran for two nights in the upstairs room. The room was filled with shrines, each designed by a different artist. One was a replica of a trashed hotel room with a psychedelic poster on the wall and a lamp covered with a fringed shawl; on the floor lay a dummy in beads and feathers with a hedge of hypodermic needles sticking out of her arm – Janis Joplin.

'We have a show we're trying to do on cable television

called *Fashion*,' said Warhol. 'So we were filming it down there.'

What did you think was the best exhibit?

'I liked it . . . uh . . . well, I liked it because the party was for two days. I think the one I liked was the ham sandwiches in front of the candles.'

This shrine was to Mama Cass. Warhol said he thought the kids there wore great clothes. I asked if he thought the fashion had changed recently.

'Well, I think they're, uh, just . . . well, it looks like they're wearing the '60s, I don't know. Without being hippies.'

In England they're all wearing mod clothes now.

'They are? Oh, again? Oh, really? Oh, great. I like all the things the kids . . . the punk thing still looks great.'

This was all very nice, and very polite, and curiously paralysing. Partly it was the effect of Warhol's shyness; partly it was because I knew that he might walk away at any moment.

In your book, the one that's coming out now (*Exposures*), which groups have you . . . uh . . . have you got any groups in there? (Hesitation was catching.)

'I think so, yeah.' (Later, Glenn O'Brien would assure me that Andy really did have a bad memory.) 'I think we have the Talking Heads and, uh, we have Walter Steding, who works here. We have Lou Reed. Just, uh, anybody who usually comes up here.'

How did you come to . . . didn't you do an ad for Talking Heads?

'Oh well, I guess I met them a long time ago and I did an interview with them and I thought they were really terrific.'

We talked about the Palladium, which Warhol said was great, and then I asked him about the first time he saw the Velvet Underground. What were they playing?

'They were just playing loud.'

What did they look like then?

'Well, they always wore black. And Maureen played one

note and John wore black. They all wore black. They were great. But somehow they were in the New York kind of music, and California kind of won out with all the hippie kind of music.'

Didn't you take the Velvets out to California?

'Oh yes. We were there with Bill Graham at . . . what's the name of that place?'

The Fillmore?

'The Fillmore, yeah. Jim Morrison saw the show, and I think he picked up some of his style from that. He began to wear leather, like Gerard. Actually, Barbara Rubin wanted to bring us to London, so I guess if we'd really gone to London it might have been more successful. I'm sorry we didn't do that. She wanted to get the Albert Hall.'

Warhol couldn't remember how his involvement with the Velvets stopped.

'I don't know. I liked them so much, we might have had a contract, but it didn't matter . . . they just decided to find some other manager. Well, it was just too hard going around. It was fun to go around for a few months. And then we could have gotten another night club, and it would have meant staying up till seven every morning and it was just too hard to worry about that. So then the group broke up or something like that . . . and then it took years and Lou just kept on working. He's very good now, he's changed a lot.'

Do you ever go to his concerts?

'Oh yeah, I go to every one of them.'

Do you like his albums?

'Oh yeah, I think they're terrific.'

The Velvets were really the first art rock band, weren't they?

'Well, I think the Talking Heads are doing it better. They seem to be more sensible and they work at it. They were art kids, too. They went to Rhode Island School of Design.'

What do you mean – more sensible?

'Well, less crazy. It was a crazier time then, I guess.

Now they're doing it more like a profession. And they're good at it.'

You said something in *The Philosophy Of Andy Warhol* about how the '60s were very cluttered, and the '70s were very empty . . .

'. . . What are the '80s going to be like?'

Right.

'Oh, well, all I know is that New York is as fun now as it was then, but even more so. Well, the hippies were around then; that was sort of wonderful.'

I was stunned – in the '60s, Warhol and the Factory stood as a symbol for everything that was urban and cynical and decadent: everything that the hippies were not. Also, Alan Midgette and Sterling Morrison had both told me that everyone at the Factory used to laugh at hippies. But, on second thought, I'm sure Warhol does think the hippies were wonderful. He likes to see a lot of activity.

Do you think New York went dead for a while?

'Yeah, it did, it really did. Well, they kept pushing that New York was such a terrible place. There's just as much crime happening now as was happening then. There are the same people on the same streets.'

Do you ever go to London?

'Oh yeah, we were just there with Martha Graham and Liza Minnelli and Halston and Steve Rubell. Oh, it was wonderful.'

Does it strike you as having changed?

'Well it was really wonderful and, uh, great.'

I asked Warhol about his superstars. What was the difference between that kind of fame and other kinds?

'Uh . . . well, it was just such a good time for the kids. You got famous in one movie, and they didn't know that you had to go on to acting school if that was your career. It just happened too easy.'

I guess they didn't realise that it wasn't going to last.

'I always thought it was just sort of good training. And after you did it, you really had to go on to school to be an actor and really learn what technique was. Because it is technique.'

Did any of them try?

'Well, Joe D'Allessandro is in Rome. He makes a lot of movies. Not many of the others.'

But wasn't that part of it – that it was very easy fame?

'Well, it was just all right then, because everybody was supposed to do something new. And they all had the chance, but they just didn't know what to do with it.'

It's a bit like how people get famous in rock music.

'Yeah, like that group that was so great that just sort of fell apart and one of the boys died.'

The New York Dolls?

'No, no, no, the English one.'

Oh, the *Sex Pistols*.

'They were just so famous. But they were really talented. I guess the guy who killed himself was just the same kind of '60s . . . you get famous with something, and then you have to keep doing it because it's what you know. But the other one, the one that seemed to quit because he realised it had gone too crazy – what's he doing now?'

John Lydon? He's got a new group.

'It must be . . . a different theory, right? So you can change and do anything.'

I asked Warhol about Nico.

'Nico is really fat now. She's in town. Have you interviewed her?'

Do you think she ever cared about being famous?

'Well, Nico had like eight careers going for her, and every time they happened she changed. She was a French movie star, and as soon as she became almost successful at that she left and came with the Velvets. And then as soon as she was singing the right kind of songs and she was getting more work, she'd buy an organ and do chanting. Every time it's almost successful, she changes her whole style. I don't know why she does that.'

We talked about John Cale, according to Warhol the most talented of the Velvets. Just then a young man drifted past.

'Have you met Walter Steding? Want to meet him? He's great, Walter, do you want to do a little interview? He's the person you ought to interview, he's the one who plays the violin . . .' He beckoned Steding over and said: 'Why don't you tell her what you do, why don't you sit down and be interviewed.' He turned to me and said simply, 'Walter wants to make it, so . . .' So it made more sense for him to be interviewed.

Walter Steding, a rather shy and sweet young man, sat down by the tape recorder and told me about his first stage performance, in which he used electrical impulses from his brain to activate a synthesizer while he played the violin. Meanwhile, Warhol had disappeared. He had succeeded in delegating the interview.

Whatever Warhol did that was of real importance was probably between 1960 and 1968; once the shock of his refusal to make value judgements was over, he stopped being a radical force and became just an uncritical member of the Establishment. But we are left with his influence. It's particularly strong in the New York rock underground because he virtually created it by taking the Velvet Underground into his social world.

Andy Warhol's great virtues were his immense curiosity about people and the world around him, his open mind, his astuteness and his nerve. He could take almost any attitude and make it look cool.

This made him a great legitimiser. He legitimised the sophisticated use of bubblegum which would turn the Shangri-las into Blondie, and beach party music into the B-52s. He legitimised the ultra-naive but sophisticated celebration of America, and therefore made it possible for Jonathan Richman to write a happy song about a shopping plaza, and David Byrne to write a touching song about his apartment building, without being laughed at.

He made his entourage famous, and their outrageousness inspired the rock fashion for using transvestism and S&M leather for shock effect. With this came the whole idea of using decadence or a parody of decadence as a subject for rock music.

Warhol proved in his own life that no matter how fucked up you were you could survive through style – as long as you were never embarrassed. Warhol's particular style involved an emotional detachment that was based on a fear of emotion, and he helped make nonfeeling cool.

He understood the media brilliantly, and he showed how to use them before they used you, by *consciously* developing an image. His success also made it seem more important to have an image. He probably created David Bowie, and it seems right that Bowie, whose talent for celebrity rivals Warhol's own, should be the only rock star to write a song about him. And when Bowie was at his most famous the projected an invulnerability that like Warhol's was based on the sense that he wasn't quite human. He was a star personality who, in fact, had no personality, just a constantly changing image.

After Bowie, Warhol's influence seemed to fade in England. The Sex Pistols may have killed it. I think one reason why English groups are so concerned with taking moral stands and New York groups are positively hostile to them, is that Warhol's influence is much stronger in New York. Morality is contrary to the Warhol style. The advantage of this is that you are never self-righteous, and the disadvantage is that you are never sincere – or concerned.

At its best, the influence of Warhol's style means that the New York groups are witty and sharp and clear-eyed enough to express unpleasant truths; at its worst it means they will play with evil and not care about the consequences because, well, life is just a movie.

A few days after interviewing Warhol, I saw Glenn O'Brien. He'd just finished taping his cable television show, *TV Party*. Once a week Glenn and his friends, including

Deborah Harry, get together and have a party. On television. (Probably this could only happen in New York.) I told Glenn about the interview, and I asked him whether Warhol meant it when he said everything was great.

'Andy does like everything,' Glenn replied. 'The only thing he wouldn't like would be something that was boring or imposed on him. But it's also a very intelligent, Machiavellian politeness. If you say everything is great, some people will take you at your word and some people will think you're being ironic. The people who think it's great will think you're saying it's great and the people who think it's awful will think you're saying it's awful. So you're always saying the right thing.'

And that's where we have to leave it, because that's Warhol's message, that's what he's been saying all along: *Here is the modern world – and it's great.*

Robot A. Hull

SOUND AND VISIONS: PSYCHEDELIA

Creem, January 1981

Although some would argue that the heyday of Creem, *America's Greatest Rock'n'roll Magazine (or should that honour go to Holmstrom's* Punk *or* Hit Parader*?), ended in the late '70s, I feel* Creem *had as much impact during the '80s when it could be found in every 7-11 across America. By this time, the magazine was hitting its stride, and as a regular contributor and struggling freelance music scribe I felt that I was, too.*

Since I was writing regularly for The Washington Post, *then, as well as various alternative weeklies, I knew that the more serious publications would not be too gung-ho about essays on the Dave Clark Five or the tragic sensibilities of Gumby. So with* Creem *as my main outlet, I decided to formulate a series of quasi-histories of lesser-known music genres for the 7-11 crowd.*

I began this series with rockabilly, and then delved into garage-punk and bubblegum, genres which were then not featured in The Rolling Stone Illustrated History of Rock'n'Roll. *(When Lester Bangs called me up to brag that he had stolen from my original essays for his* Rolling Stone *version of history, I knew I had arrived.) My biggest challenge was the history of psychedelia, and I'm still not sure that I got it right; but for 1981 it seems okay.*

By the early '90s, with Rhino spearheading hip

nostalgia and the ageing boomers spending their loot on the burgeoning CD market, so-called rock history became its own marketable commodity. Every artist, every genre, every sliver of sound had to be codified, which perhaps reached its apotheosis with the advent of the Easy Listening radio format being marketed as 'lounge music'. Now, to be hip, you didn't have to create stuff, you just had to know about arcane stuff.

Five years after writing this history of psychedelia for Creem, *I co-wrote and edited a book of comix with my longtime friend and mentor the collector/cartoonist Mad Peck. In that book, we threw together every piece of flotsam and jetsom we had ever discussed during late-night phone calls about America's pop cultural debris. To me, this book,* Mad Peck Studios: A Twenty-Year Restrospective *(published by Doubleday, and, appropriately enough, instantly remaindered), says as much about the notion of pop music in the '70s and '80s than any other rock history I can think of. (And it's in cartoon form!) In his brief assessment of the book,* Greil Marcus said it best when he charted it at #1 in his 'Real Life Rock Top Ten' column in June 1987: 'The adventures of a band of comic-strip rock critics whose watchword is "It don't mean a thing if it ain't headed straight to cut-out heaven," this book picks up where Richard Meltzer's* Aesthetics of Rock *left off.'*

For me, pop music has always been about the cut-out bin, the LP no one saved or wanted, the one-hit wonder gone astray, the awkward voice, the trash we choose to ignore. That is the REAL history of rock. Whether it's easy listening schlock, '90s boy-band pop, or demented psychedelia, I firmly believe that we can never escape the cultural debris of our past because, deep deep down, we all sense that our future may very well depend on what's been lost in the bins.

RH

'OKAY. *You've swallowed the magic cube, downed a cup of organic tea with filigree leaves, and placed the diamond needle on the appropriate sounds. Now sit back and wait 20 minutes, until twinges of nausea herald the coming of the hereafter.*'
— Richard Goldstein, from 'The Psychedelic Psell,'
Village Voice, 1967

Chaos all around me
With its fevered clinging
But I can hear you singing
In the corners of my brain.
— 13th Floor Elevators, 'I Had To Tell You'

AT THE MERE mention of the term 'psychedelic rock', most folks turn livid — their eyes cross, purple dots splotch their rosy cheeks, and steam begins puffing in short snorts from their nostrils. Punk has become acceptable, and bubblegum can be considered a cute trend but acid rock . . . oh no, *never*! It is perhaps the only genre that can transform a solemn saint into a vituperative viper, hissing and lashing at an imaginary zonked-out world populated by Zen zombies.

The modern hatred of the psychedelic spell centres around a confusion over the exact nature of what many rock historians regard as a viable genre. In her *Rock Encyclopedia*, Lillian Roxon goes so far as to divide psychedelic music into sub-genres — 'acid' (LSD psych-outs) and 'head' rock (marijuana muzak). In an article entitled 'Psychedelic Rock: The World's Most Misunderstood Music', Greg Shaw suggests that real psych-rock was not only a direct outgrowth of '60s punk but also equally as demented. Most rock writers, though, have consistently viewed psychedelia with an unflagging cynicism *a la* Nik Cohn's definition of acid rock in *Rock From the Beginning* as 'a fairly meaningless phrase that got applied to any underground group, no matter what its style.'

Of course, these rock historians are correct in their assessments; they're just incorrect in their assumptions. Psychedelic rock was not simply a substantial genre nor was it a silly term used to collect divergent styles under a paisley umbrella: it was a mind-expanding consciousness, the first vestige of free-form experimentation, rock 'n' roll was restricted (whether for better or worse) by *form* – teen bands hacked out hits and atonality was taboo. As rock began to establish consciousness and to perceive its tradition, mentality became as important as physicality. Naturally it can be argued that rock 'n' roll would be better off today if this had never happened, but when one realises the contributions established by this movement toward the mind, the psychedelic experience no longer seems quaint but awesome.

Consider that this consciousness gave us the following: rock as a revolutionary force (social, political and sexual), the concept album, LP covers as art, rock criticism and its aesthetics, rock lyrics as poetry, and the notion that rock was every bit as intelligent (and as American) as blues or jazz. That's quite a formidable contribution from a supposedly footloose and haphazard genre, and certainly its major influences negate its minor irritations (body painting, incense, Ravi Shankar). In short, with the advent of psychedelia, rock began to be taken seriously, yet paradoxically, only as the acid style itself became increasingly comical.

Although it evolved during a period of musical transition during the summer and fall of 1966, there is no exact moment at which the Psychedelic Era began. In '66, while punk rock was demolishing the national charts, local bands in California (especially around San Francisco) had already been influenced by the psychedelic condition. Whereas it's true that many teenage punk bands, like San Jose's Chocolate Watchband (the first significant punk group to ponder the mysteries of the ancient pyramids), were walking the fine line between fuzz and strobe, psych-rock was not merely an outgrowth of the earlier genre; like punk, it can stand alone as an inspired testament of reaction and rebellion.

Briefly, the psychedelic vision was the sudden awareness that formlessness mattered. This reactionary enlightenment can perhaps be blamed on the Beau Brummels. Formed in '64 by vocalist Sal Valentino, the Brummels, despite their folk-rock inclinations, were able to create the illusion that they were a part of the British Invasion, scoring with 'Laugh Laugh' during England's reign in America. But they were actually from San Francisco, being the first Bay Area rock band to have a major hit (thanks to the assistance of two local DJs, Tom Donahue and Sly Stone). Attention began to be focused upon San Francisco as a musical mecca, yet many of the bohemians in bluegrass and jug bands resented the Top-40 plasticity that the Brummels represented. The folkies' alternative was to revolt against the Hit Machine, giving birth to the concept of 'underground music', a positive reaction against programmed formulae.

The very idea of underground music divided the rock culture. Punks and hippies were never enemies – both groups coexisted like fellow scientists testing mind-boggling experiments. The tensions always arose between what was perceived as 'artificial' compared to what appeared 'natural.' Artificial brainwashing tactics (i.e., Top 40 formats: 'Kill ugly radio,' preached Frank Zappa) were not condoned; only a free non-synthetic society was envisioned. Everybody (that is, except the squares) ignored the fact that the chief catalyst for this liberated consciousness was a chemical killer called lysergic acid diethylamide, a substance so powerful that it unleashed psychotic hordes all across America.

Some theorists, though, maintain that even without LSD the psychedelic sound would have emerged somehow . . . as an attack, in the form of a visionary quest, against the repression of a growing youth culture. In the loco Lone Star State, that's exactly what happened. With a pure desire for unbridled dementia as its catalyst, psychedelia first crystallized in Austin, Texas.

At the University of Texas around 1960, folkies began

growing their hair long and taking drugs (peyote, mesquite, mushrooms of all varieties) as a way of retaliating against redneck traditions. Tommy Hall, a psychology major at UT, was a freak leading a band called Lingsman; Roky Erickson, a 17-year-old high school dropout, was the singer for a punk band, the Spades ('You're Gonna Miss Me'/'We Sell Soul' on Zero). Like comets cork-screwing through outer space, the two collided, and this mystical act begat the messianic 13th Floor Elevators.

The Elevators recorded four albums for International Artists (a bizarre Houston company that, by offering artists an outlet for their innermost expressions of being, was the Psych Era's equivalent to Sun). Two of these works are absolute miracles. With its god's eye peering from a multi-coloured universe (there is no other LP cover that better defines psychedelia), *The Psychedelic Sounds Of* introduced 'that funny little noise,' the reverberating gimmick that became the Elevators' trademark. But what once sounded like electronic trickery, now sounds open and honest, like a pulse beat – like a voice in the wilderness almost 10 years later, responding to the heartfelt hiccups of Buddy Holly. With *Easter Everywhere* (its cover depicting a bright yellow sun blazing through a golden heaven), the Elevators painted their masterpiece: poetical and pulling toward a pastoral oblivion, like Dylan's *John Wesley Harding*, it quietly bespoke a renaissance.

Another IA outfit, the Red Crayola from Houston, was extremely anomalous, even for a psych-rock band. In the summer of '66, artist Mayo Thompson and Rick Barthelme (brother of writer Donald Barthelme) assembled a band to play 'Hey Joe' on the frat-party circuit. But whenever they'd perform their own compositions ('War Sucks', 'Hurricane Fighter Plane'), drunken fraternity brothers would hurl bottles and obscenities.

Red Crayola's desire for free-form experimentation was their vision (Barthelme even knew John Cage). Like the Pied Piper, the band attracted a cult, fifty-odd followers who accompanied the Crayola on assorted garbage. When 85 of these freaks crammed into a studio one summer's eve to provide background chaos for a Crayola recording session, the Familiar Ugly was born.

The result of this mess can be heard on the perplexing *Parable of Arable Land*. Rhythms clash as the multitude tries to play drums. Some buffoons slap parts of their anatomy; others stumble into the 15 mikes scattered around the deranged scene. Occasionally a song will rise above the madness only to be smothered by some lamebrain pounding a piano with a banana. Despite its obscure artiness, the Crayola's album signifies what the undercurrent of the psychedelic age: wholesome dementia.

Texas belonged to a demented tradition (Sam the Sham, Ornette Coleman, Doug Clark, Big Bopper, Question Mark, Groovy Joe Poovey), one that culminated in IA's psychie perceptions. In post-hallucinogenic times, a single Texas artist, the Legendary Stardust Cowboy, would encapsulate that tradition on a single recording ('Paralyzed' on Psycho-Suave) – but not before Texas had migrated to San Francisco, nor before America's then-emerging rock culture learned a valuable lesson that the prophetic crazy cowboy came too late to teach them.

Some of the music on the Elevators' LPs was recorded as demos as early as 1965, anticipating a meandering musical style often credited to rock groups from San Francisco, a city eponymous with psychedelia. Tommy Hall of the Elevators has claimed that his band was the first ever billed as playing 'psychedelic music' – when they performed in San Francisco's Avalon Ballroom (the dance palace of the Family Dog, a business commune formed by Chet Helms, another weird Texan). Regardless of who invented it, the spirit of psychedelia was definitely kept alive by the interaction between the intellectual communities of Austin, mangy and half-mad, and San Francisco, land of the cosmic giggle.

The so-called San Francisco sound was the greatest hallucination in rock history. From Ken Kesey's Trips Festival to the Monterey Pop media-event, the promises and publicity never ceased, yet the recorded proof was practically nil. The godfather of the movement in the folksy collegiate Bay Area was Timothy Leary, a Harvard pinhead who founded a religion based on the LSD experience. Because of its reliance on acid to enhance its significance, San Francisco's psych-rock remained inchoate, functioning as a musical stimulant for a stoned-out community. The bands existed to provide mellifluous vibrations for their audiences; further, they were usually indistinguishable from their wavering fans. Conse-quently, San Francisco bands required a freedom – an active interplay between performer and participant – that the re-cording studio simply could not offer.

Countless articles have been written about these groups, most of whom deserve only a footnote in rock history (considering their recorded *oeuvre* seems insignificant when compared to that of the snubbed Beau Brummels). The Charlatans, a folk band from the Haight-Ashbury neighbourhood, presented the Hippie Era with its symbol – they returned from a gig in Virginia City, Nevada, bedecked with the mythology of the Old West. The Grateful Dead (formerly the Warlocks), besides providing the background for Kesey's parties, were firm believ-ers in the free concert and the interminable jam. Big Brother and the Holding Company, owing to the Texas connection of Chet Helms, gave the world the Port Arthur blues of Janis Joplin. From Berkeley, a jug band known as Country Joe and the Fish (who pressed their own 7-inch LP on the Rag Baby label) mixed political humour with an acid soundtrack.

Organized by Marty Balin in '65, Jefferson Airplane was San Francisco rock fully realized. After Grace Slick joined the band (upon the dissolution of her own group, the Great Society), the Airplane garnered a national audience. The only hippie band to ever have hits, they could appeal to both the romanticism of the love generation ('Somebody To Love') and the hedonism of drugged deadbeats ('White Rabbit').

The importance of San Francisco's musical trip, however, was not its rock bands but its reawakening to the democratic principles of popular music. What united the Bay Area bands was their need to assimilate traditional American music, particularly the blues, into rock (which to them, had become too formulaic). Thus they shared no common sound (other than the sloppy, wandering jam) because their music was rooted in eclecticism. The California band that at least on record, defined this quality was the Kaleidoscope. On *Side Trips* and *A Beacon From Mars,* they mysteriously moved from Turkish drones to Cab Calloway without once referring to LSD, proving that the psychedelic vision was not strictly a consciousness induced by drugs. In southern California, this truth was given credence by crazies so caught up in the freak image that they forgot about acid altogether.

It began probably as a dream in the minds of two teenage companions, Don Van Vliet and Frank Zappa, isolated in the barren town of Lancaster. After their high school years, Zappa moved to Cucamonga and Van Vliet, quitting his job as a manager of a shoe store chain, soon joined him. The two made plans to form a band called the Soots and concocted Van Vliet's usual alias, Captain Beefheart. Eventually Zappa split for Los Angeles and invented the Mothers, but Beefheart, being more reclusive, returned to Lancaster. There, in '64, he assembled some 'desert musicians', the Magic Band, and began playing teen dances.

It must've been a shock boogalooing to the grinding blues-rock of a group dressed in black leather with matching high-heel boots. Beefheart's early band was raw and fundamental, true inheritors of Robert Johnson's dark vision. Their first single on A&M, 'Diddy Wah Diddy' (Bo Diddley transmo-grified), and *Mirror Man* (recorded one night in LA in '65) capture the abrasive intensity of this scabrous band.

Beefheart's other two pre-*Replica* recordings were tam-pered with by recording company moguls. Still, *Strictly Personal* playfully conveys the artist's unique vernacular

('Ah Feel Like Ahcid'), and *Safe As Milk* undeniably remains the most underrated album in rock history. Consistently disavowing the use of LSD and marijuana, Beefheart nevertheless was consumed by the psychedelic era; yet, he transcended the epoch's clichés through his poetic voice – but not without losing everything in the process. The age of acid simply could not contend with an authentic genius.

Beefheart's old pal Zappa, however, having been an adman, could objectify the times and, as rock's equivalent to Marshall McLuhan, could manipulate his audience via cryptic messages (usually satirical). Zappa's first opus, *Freak Out!*, was ugly, berserk, and quite intellectual – it defined LA's psychedelic frame of mind, embracing while lampooning the approaching banalities (multi-media events, happenings, grope sessions, concept albums) that, in '66, were not yet fashionable. The Mothers of Invention embodied the anarchic ritual of 'freaking out', a term that still best describes the ridiculous poses of LA's finest psychos: Kim Fowley's tongue-tied trips, the Seeds' flower power, Davie Allan and the Arrows' fuzzy soundtracks for a string of Hell's Angels movies.

Originally signed by MGM as just another folk-rock group (see 'Trouble Every Day'), the Mothers (thanks to Zappa's flair for hype and organization) denied God in rock 'n' roll, forcing listeners to re-evaluate their preconceptions. On 'The Return of the Son of Monster Magnet' (12 grotesque minutes of percussive cacophony and terrible noises from Godzilla's churning bowels), the band destroyed the barrier between rock and all other musical forms. Although his later work was too logical and too cynical, on *Freak Out!*, Zappa's music delineated a challenge alive with infinite possibilities. That Zappa could make the leap from his traditional R&B background to 'Help, I'm a Rock' is exactly what psychedelic awareness was all about.

Two other bands from LA during these garish times shared a fascination with the metaphysical: Love and the Doors.

Emerging late in '65, Love was an early underground success, their initial sound existing somewhere between folk-rock and punk. But as the band's leader, Arthur Lee, increasingly became an acid victim, Love's music drifted toward the pretentious realm of art-rock (i.e., 'Revelation', 19 minutes of boredom), finally (and tastefully) culminating in the ornate fragility of *Forever Changes*, an unqualified masterpiece.

Whereas Love were critical darlings, the Doors broke through the charts with seven minutes (!) of sexual teasing, 'Light My Fire'. The ghost of Freud was summoned forth in Jim Morrison's lyrics, and many fans interpreted his balderdash as poetry. ('Doors are between the known and the unknown' was the band's standard gobbledygook.) Considered within the kaleidoscopic network of psychedelia, the Doors seem daring; but regarded outside of that context, they seem as artificial as the Archies. Case in point: In the Feb. 10, '68, issue of a teen rag called *The Beat*, this contest appeared – 'The Doors need your help. Their new album contains one side *consisting of only one* song! Now, your problem is to name that song.' Of course, that lengthy ramble never materialized, but the Doors knew their gimmick and they whipped it to death. (For their post-'68 history, consult your textbooks.)

From the Chocolate Watchband to the Peanut Butter Conspiracy, mentally twisted music literally mushroomed throughout California during '66–'68, but even stranger were the warped sounds being released by a small folk/jazz label in New York City, ESP. ESP's first release (by artists not associated with free jazz) was from the Fugs, a group of poetical thugs from the Lower East Side, led by minstrels Ed Sanders and Tuli Kupferberg. Compared to the frivolous political humour of Country Joe's Fish, the Fugs' radical horseplay and scatological wordplay was filth from the sewers of the mind. Their three LPs for ESP included humorous classics such as 'Kill For Peace', 'Coca Cola Douche', 'I Couldn't Get High', and 'I Saw the Best Minds of My

Generation Rot'. (The group's later work for Reprise – *Belle of Avenue A; It Crawled into My Hand, Honest* – was equally as comical but less passionate.) Their phoney moments were few, yet in a 1967 interview Mother Zappa implied otherwise – 'The Fugs are not in good taste. They have bugs in their plan.' Time, though, has proven that Mr Freak Out (who still childishly titillates with song titles like 'Nanook Rubs It') is the nonpareil of poor taste.

Approved by Allen Ginsberg, the Fugs were applauded as artists (art being the most important ingredient of New York's psychedelic pastiche), while another rock group on ESP was largely ignored, the primitively profound Godz. No band during this era (not even the Elevators) can match their truthful vision: four grown men playing instruments they do not understand, struggling like children toward a musical high, losing their inhibitions and regaining their souls. A sentence from the liner notes of their first LP, *Contact High*, aptly defines their music: 'They are human, alive and hot in the blood, creating their own songs, forging their own sound with a beat like an elephant's heart.' The Godz chant, babble, pray, and surrender to apoplectic fervor on cantillations like 'White Cat Heat', 'Soon the Moon', and 'Permanent Green Light'. Their finest song, 'Radar Eyes', floats above the floss of psychedelia like a feather with wings. None of New York's No-Wave bands will ever approach the Godz' 'organic tribal F music' – today it seems unbelievable that their ESP debut was recorded on Sept. 28, 1966.

The other psych-rock groups from NY were distinctly tied to Greenwich Village's club scene. From the Cafe Au Go Go came Danny Kalb's Blues Project (Al Kooper's early band and Television's idol), playing a streamlined combination of blues and jazz that helped to articulate the meaning ot underground rock. Via Warhol's mixed-media perversion, the Exploding Plastic Inevitable, the Velvet Underground transcended the acid age by developing a torn-and-bleeding consciousness that would shape a decade's worth of rock and roll (conse-

quently, their story deserves a book). From the Night Owl
Café emerged the Blues Magoos, claiming to be the city's first
practitioners of psychedelics (their greatest moment, 'Dante's
Inferno', is merely an electrical distortion of the Godz' previous spiritual dissonance), as well as Lothar and the Hand
People, silly simps (whose groovy act relied upon the eerie
shriek of the theremin, used in horror films and on the Beach
Boys' 'Good Vibrations'). Unfortunately, the ascent of Lothar
the singing theremin signalled the inevitable: The trashy side
of mind-expanding was now attracting flies.

Unlike the urgent yet constrictive genres of punk and
rockabilly, acid-rock's fluctuating formula (alternating consciousness isn't a stable process) was incapable of encom-
passing both the ridiculous and the sublime – if, on the
surface, a psychedelic work seemed absurd then it assuredly
was. In short, there has never been a musical style so overflowing with bilge in the entire history of rock 'n' roll!

Consider: the infamous 'Bosstown sound', a hype insti-
gated by MGM to create the impression that Boston was the
next San Francisco. Beacon Street Union, Orpheus, Earth
Opera, and Ultimate Spinach were a few of the worthless
nightmares of the Bosstown hallucination. Even more crass
was a recording company called Mainstream. Primarily a
soundtrack label, it jumped on the acid bandwagon with Big
Brother and the Holding Co. From then on (the Amboy
Dukes excepted), Mainstream, a spineless ESP, released anything that wandered into the subterranean market (Tangerine
Zoo, Stone Circus, Growing Concern, Orient Express),
splashing albums with anaemic strains far removed from
the Elevators' colourful hypnotic eye: Gradually as various
scum crawled from the armpits of America, diluted psychedelia (or crapedelia) took over.

A prime example was Atlanta's Night Shadows (Mac Davis
and Atlanta Rhythm Section's Barry Bailey were once members), who pressed their own LP in '68, *The Square Root of
Two*, and dedicated it to the Marquis de Sade. Junk of the

lowest order, the album nonetheless anticipated the home-made cultism of the '70s and the selling tactic of including posters and 45s in the LP jacket. (Progressives from the conservative South, the Night Shadows recently reissued their album, billing themselves as 'a rock anomaly from Dixie.')

While acid-rock was fragmenting in the US, the British were revitalizing its essence. A chapter all its own, England's second wave produced what the cognoscenti feel are the supreme psychedelic masterworks: the Hollies' *Evolution*, Cream's *Disraeli Gears,* Traffic's *Mr Fantasy,* Pink Floyd's debut, Bee Gees' *1st,* the Yardbirds' *Little Games,* Procol Harum's first LP, the Move's early singles, *There Are But Four Small Faces,* Donovan's *Sunshine Superman,* and the Jimi Hendrix Experience's complete body of works. And then, of course, there are the forever tedious *Their Satanic Majesties Request* and *Sgt Pepper.*

The dissemination of American psychedelia was decidedly problematic. Perhaps it expired because the English were becoming experts at visionary fabulation. More likely, it was because the San Francisco scene was becoming over-exposed – Monterey Pop was a household word, Scott McKenzie preached floral salvation, and *The Mod Squad* popped on the tube. On Friday, October 6, 1967, a symbolic hippie was buried on Haight Street. Popular quote of the time: 'Well, the Grateful Dead just leave me cold,' snidely sputtered by the Rock & Roll Double Bubble Trading Card Company of Philadelphia.

Not surprisingly, what the psychedelic movement had originally rebelled against – the synthetic bubblegum men-tality – adopted the acid style. The electric Coral Sitar (pioneered by Decca recording artist Vincent Bell) seemed to be on every record. Typical of the artificial acid-rock sound were hits like the First Edition's 'Just Dropped In (To See What Condition My Condition Was In)', the Lemon Pipers' 'Green Tambourine', and Strawberry Alarm Clock's 'Incense and Peppermints'.

Outside the mainstream of Top 40, psych-rock was essentially evolving into a bad STP trip, becoming heavier and more ponderous, dozing into an awkward genre called (ugh) heavy metal. LSD chemist Owsley Stanley switched his patronage from the Grateful Dead to gutsier San Francisco band Blue Cheer, who murdered Eddie Cochran with decibels of sludge. From LA, the Iron Butterfly pounded themselves to the top with the 'Louie Louie' of metallic bedlam, 'In-A-Gadda-Da-Vida', and presented Atlantic Records with the bestselling LP in the company's history (pre-Led Zep, that is). International Artists even had its own HM band, Bubble Puppy (scoring with 'Hot Smoke & Sassafras'), and, from Long Island, Vanilla Fudge mastered the craft of 'psychedelizing' (recording tortuously slow-motion versions of others' hits, e.g. the Supremes' 'You Keep Me Hanging On').

Today, although its version has been forgotten, the delectations of psychedelia still subsist – in fact, the style perhaps was never lost but simply subverted by art-rock and progressive mood music. Its contemporary influence can be heard on Pink Floyd's *The Wall* and on recordings by such diverse artists as Chrome, Pere Ubu, Public Image Ltd., Suicide, Count Viglione, Half Japanese, Mars, and the reborn Red Crayola. Jamaican dub also offers a close approximation of the psychedelic experience (check out Burning Spear's *Garvey's Ghost*). In the '70s, though, the sound was best resurrected by one of its founders, ex-Elevator Roky Erickson. On 'Red Temple Prayer (Two Headed Dog)', Roky with his band, Bleib Alien, released a cosmic yelp from the fifth dimension and chased the devil back to his hoodoo kingdom.

The demise of psychedelia was inevitable, not just because it was absorbed by bubblegum or stomped by heavy metal, but primarily because of its image as 'hippie music'. Paul Revere, leader of the Raiders, once actually requested that DJs screen lyrics, warning America that many rock songs concealed LSD codes. (Subsequently, the Raiders released 'Kicks' as a protest against drugs.) In a '67 interview in a teen zine, actress Marcia Strassman (then a singing flower child), when asked about the hippies, had this to say: 'They turn my stomach. What parent would let such yuk walk into the house?' In short, acid-rock soon assumed the connotation of filthy musk for longhairs, and consequently met its doom – the reality of a clean-cut, peachy-keen Amerika.

'One guy wears beads and they all smell bad,' the imaginary Suzy Creamcheese once wrote about her favourite band, the Mothers of Invention. The nobility of psychedelic consciousness was never contained in light shows or in Jerry Garcia's magic fingers, but in what Suzy saw (and what America did not and still refuses to see): the recognition that rock 'n' roll, above all else, is an untidy revolution.

Reprinted with kind permission of Creem *magazine*

Simon Frith

JOHN LENNON: MY BRILLIANT CAREER

New York Rocker, March 1981

This obituary was originally written for Marxism Today, *the monthly journal of the British Communist Party which, under the editorship of Martin Jacques, had become an outlet for cultural politics, academic lefties, and many of the revisionist class arguments which fed into New Labour. I was never a member of its theoretical discussion groups (nor indeed of the Communist Party) but I preferred its earnest attempts to be open-minded to the self-righteous certainties of the various Trotskyist mags, and I was happy to be used as a critical counter to the usual CP pro-folk anti-disco line.*

The news of Lennon's death came through as the magazine was due to go to press, and I was cajoled by Martin Jacques (in a series of pleading phone calls) to produce a thousand words while he got a new cover together. I wrote it in less than an hour with little time for thought and must have dictated it to Martin down the phone, though I don't remember this. (It is generally forgotten how freelancers delivered instant copy in the days before faxes and email. I used telephone copy takers at the Sunday Times, *telex machines for the* Observer, *British Rail's Red Star parcel service for some magazines. Telephoning copy direct to the editor was probably the least reliable form of delivery.)*

I was writing for a political readership (hence the

quotes from Red Mole) and knew that my piece would
be read after Lennon had ceased to be news and when
people were likely to be tired of reading about him. I
was therefore as concerned to make sense of the media
response to his death as to explain his life, and I also
wanted to treat him as a living presence (in the music
of the Clash) and not just a historical icon.

At this time I had a column in New York Rocker
and, with a freelancer's interest in recycling ideas,
figured that this article would equally work there (if
changed a bit for a more knowing rock readership).
My approach to Lennon's death – political, academic,
instructive – would be so un-American.

                                                              SF

'DEATH OF A HERO,' it said in big black letters across the front
of *The Daily Mirror,* and if I hadn't known already I'd have
expected a story about a policeman or a soldier in Northern
Ireland.

The British media response to John Lennon's death was
overwhelming, and what began as a series of private griefs
was orchestrated by disc jockeys and sub-editors into a
national event, but it was difficult to decide what all this
mourning meant. The media themselves seemed less slick
than usual, more ragged in their attempts to respond to a
genuinely popular shock. What came through was not just
Beatle-nostalgia but a specific sadness at the loss of John
Lennon's Beatle qualities – qualities that never did fit easily
into British populist ideology. 'The idea,' as Lennon once told
Red Mole, 'is not to comfort people, not to make them feel
better, but to make them feel worse.'

John Lennon was a 1950s, not a 1960s, teenager and he
didn't have a great youth, but he did grow up in Liverpool
where there was an aggressive way of leisure that survived
television and the fifties rise of family consumption. By the
time I was a teenager, with the mods in the '60s, the young

were the only people left out at night and no one was very tough. The Liverpool sound was the sound of gangs and territory being claimed, and the Beatles always had to stand for something. They played their gigs in Liverpool and Hamburg clubs in which there was no space for subtlety or self-pity, no room for preening. The Beatles' noise was hoarse and harsh, an effect of the unrelieved nightly sets, and even the best of the '60s' live bands, the Stones and the Who, were indulged youth groups by comparison, with a flabbiness that the original Beatles couldn't afford. The Beatles sang American music in a Liverpool accent – nasal rather than throaty, detached, passion expressed with a conversational cynicism.

John Lennon was the only hero I've ever had. His genius is usually described with reference to the songs he wrote, but it was his voice that always cut through me. He sang with a controlled, forthright intimacy that demanded a hearing even on uninteresting material (like *Double Fantasy*). He was the only rock singer who ever sang 'we' convincingly.

The day John Lennon was shot in New York I got the Clash's *Sandinista!* I've played it incessantly since, as an exorcism of those old Beatles records that I don't want to hear again. *Sandinista!* is infuriating, indulgent, exciting and touching. It is packed with slogans and simplicities, guns and liberation, images of struggle and doubt, and it is a wonderful tribute to Lennon's influence – a record that would have been impossible to imagine without him. Jones and Strummer always were closer to Lennon and McCartney than their Jagger/Richards pose lets on.

John Lennon believed, more intensely than any other rock performer, that rock'n'roll was a form of expression in which anything could be said, and he believed, too, that rock'n'roll was the only form of expression in which many things – to do with growing up working class, mostly – could be said. His music (and the Clash's) involves an urgent need to be heard (a need which often obscures what is actually being said). In

1956 John Lennon found in rock'n'roll an anti-authoritarian voice that everywhere else was silenced, and most of his life afterwards was committed to keeping faith with this voice, preserving its edge, cutting through the ideological trapping of pop.

John Lennon refused to be trivialised and Yoko Ono was truly his partner in this, facing him with many of the issues that were later addressed by punk. She questioned the taken-for-granted masculinity of the rock'n'roll voice, rock conventions of spontaneity and realism, rock assumptions about the 'truth' of the singing voice and the relationship between the public and the private.

Since Lennon's death I haven't done anything much, but before it I was watching old films: *Top Gear* from 1964, a flat studio showcase of the year's British stars with two good incidents – the Beatles cheerful on stage, and the spine-chilling moment when the young Steve Winwood opened his mouth and that extraordinary white soul voice came pouring effortlessly out; and *Rude Boy*, a shoddy piece of flimflam designed to trivialise not only the Clash but the entire punk moment of 1976–9 – working-class 'experience' is mimicked though the medium of bourgeois realism and I walked out.

The Clash concert footage is good enough though, and does raise questions about the shifting rules of rock meaning. These days, for example, the annual berk of a British Christmas is Rod Stewart, who releases an album and goes on tour. Once upon a time his singing style (a refinement of the white soul vocal) was the epitome of emotional sincerity. Now he just sounds silly, and it is Joe Strummer's narrow range and tight-throated projection or John Lydon's wailing inarticulacy which are the sounds that mean it.

'Imagine no possessions,' John Lennon sang, but I never thought he could (John Lydon maybe). There was a sloppiness to John and Yoko's concept of peace and love and changing things by thinking them so, that concealed what mattered more – an astute sense of the mass market and how it worked. The central contradiction of John Lennon's artistic life lay in the uneasy enthusiasm with which he packaged and sold his dreams (which were, to begin with, real enough). The problem for the working class, he told *Red Mole* in 1971, is that 'they're dreaming someone else's dream, it's not even their own'. The problem for a working-class hero is that he too is defined in other people's dreams.

John Lennon was murdered by a fan, by someone who pushed the fantasies that pop stardom is designed to invoke into an appalling, stupid madness. But the grief that the rest of us Beatle fans then felt drew on similar fantasies, and the bitter fact is that John Lennon, whose heroism lay in his struggle against being a commodity, whose achievement was to express the human origins of pop utopianism, should be trapped, finally, by a desperate, inhuman, nightmarish version of the fan's need to be a star.

David Toop

SURFIN' DEATH VALLEY USA: THE BEACH BOYS AND HEAVY FRIENDS

Collusion, February–April 1982

I'd been a Beach Boys fan since my teens, first of all pepped up by the perfect pop of 'Fun Fun Fun', then mooching around lovesick to a backdrop of 'Warmth Of The Sun' and 'Don't Worry, Baby', finally turning into a Smile *obsessive, collecting bootlegs and speculating on what have been, given a little less acid, a little more application.*

When the Manson murders happened, I read all the articles and books and so became aware of this peculiar connection between Manson and Dennis Wilson. The shock was profound – Beach Boys music being all sorts of things, but never murderous – and somehow the story festered away in my subconscious until I had a context in which to develop it. Collusion was a magazine I co-edited, produced and published, so there were no editors demanding verification of sources or questioning whether anybody wanted to read such stuff in the New Romantics era.

Quite a bit of new information has emerged over the years: a profile of Bobby Beausoleil written by Truman Capote, the Bill Landis biography of Kenneth Anger, a few million words written on the tribulations of Brian, Dennis and Carl Wilson and the Beach Boys, plus a skip load of post-apocalyptic, Amok-type sleaze on Manson and the Family, their music, films and other hobbies.

A reader wrote to Collusion *in response to the piece, expressing an unhealthy interest in snuff movies. No doubt he went on to write for Creation Press. Plunderphonics composer John Oswald also contributed to the complexity of the narrative by suggesting to me that 'sexual processes' (and I don't think I misquote) were clearly audible at the end of 'Cease To Resist'. John later went on to become notorious for grafting the head of Michael Jackson on to the body of the Grateful Dead, thus proving that unusually close readings of the recorded experience can lead to greater things.*

Reading the piece again, 20 years after I wrote it, I just feel sad that an abundance of creativity, optimism and popular success failed to save the Wilson family from fates almost Biblical in their severity.

DT

'We'll get the roughest and the toughest initiation we can find'

The Beach Boys, 'Our Car Club' (1963)

WHEN THE BEACH BOYS released their 1969 album *20/20*, the biggest thrill for true fans was the inclusion of a *Smile*-era Brian Wilson/Van Dyke Parks song, 'Cabinessence', remarkable for signs it gave that Parks was the writer capable of focusing the mythical Americana that the group had embodied from their first single into something more substantial than teenage love, sports and identity crises. Tagged onto the end of Beach Boys product, it didn't make a lot of sense, but the feeling persists that in the context of the legendary *Smile* it would have clicked perfectly.

It was the last track, so unless you skip the stylus you encounter other aspects of Beach Boy/California preoccupations – the Ronettes/Phil Spector sound of 'I Can Hear Music', the Four Freshmen vocal blend of 'Our Prayer' (another *Smile* song) and a curious love song with a half-finished feel to it called 'Never Learn Not To Love'. This latter had been released the previous year as the B-side of 'Bluebirds Over the Mountain' with writer credits going to Dennis Wilson – drummer, surfer and symbol of West Coast sunshine simplicity.

Despite the disquieting intro to the song – silence into horror-movie creepy-crawlies – and the startling first line 'Cease to resist . . .' the song resolves into a two-tier regular patriarchal plea. On one level it cajoles 'give up your ego and let's fuck' and beneath that 'give up your world and join mine for the sake of true love' – the lyrics being sufficiently vague as to dilute these basic messages. The real origins of the song are interesting insofar as they betray not only the logical extension of this rather despicable philosophy but also show the eclipse side of California culture.

SUNSET BOULEVARD

The actual writer of the song – author and composer – was Charles Manson. Dennis first met Manson in 1968. The story goes that in a state of recent divorce he picked up two girls hitchhiking in Malibu. The second time he came across them he took them back to his Sunset Boulevard home (shades of Gloria Swanson) and went on to a recording session.

Returning at three A.M. he was confronted by a stranger – Manson – who responded to Wilson's fear by kissing his feet. On entering his home – courtesy of Manson – he found himself host to nearly a dozen guests (unknown to him and later known to the world as The Family). This little party outstayed its welcome to the extent of doubling its number over a period of months, wrecking Dennis's uninsured Mercedes-Benz, using his Rolls Royce for supermarket 'garbage runs', dumping him with the 'largest gonorrhoea bill in history' and finally driving him out of his own home –

formerly owned by Will Rogers – to live in one room at Gregg
Jakobson's house.

Jakobson, a talent scout married to Lou (of Abbott and
Costello) Costello's daughter, was impressed with Manson's
philosophy and introduced him to Doris Day's son Terry
Melcher, who was living at 10050 Cielo Drive at the time.
This address – previously occupied by Candice Bergen,
among others – became notorious as the location which first
drew Family activities into the full public gaze. This was the
scene of the murders that sent out the 'Helter Skelter' shock
waves. Many of the network of interconnections, ironies and
implications of the story are banal – simply to do with
geography, money and show business. Nevertheless, they
accumulate to form a distinctly obverse Moviola.

These Bel Air murders included Sharon Tate – star of
Rosemary's Baby (one of the first of the occult movies) –
and Jay Sebring a hairstylist who lived in the Benedict
Canyon mansion where Jean Harlow's husband Paul Bern
committed suicide in 1932 (as immortalised in Kenneth
Anger's book *Hollywood Babylon*). Sebring's salon was
located on L.A.'s Fairfax – an area name-checked in the
Beach Boys' unreleased 'H.E.L.P. is on its Way' – a hymn
to the health food restaurant on Fairfax and Third, H.E.L.P.,
and Brian Wilson's own health food store the Radiant Radish
(also the only pop song in history to mention enemas).

Melcher and Jakobson were satellites in the Beach Boys'
world – Van Dyke Parks met Brian Wilson on Terry Melcher's lawn, for example – and inevitably became involved in
Charles Manson's musical aspirations. Where the Manson/
Family album – released on the ESP label, an independent
that specialised in the emergent free jazz of the mid-'60s – was
recorded and who produced it remains confused. Some
material appears to have been cut at Brian Wilson's home
studio in Bel Air. Also, a Santa Monica studio was hired.
Dennis Wilson claims that these tapes – 'lust chanting, fucking, sucking, barfing' – were destroyed since he felt that 'the

vibrations connected with them don't belong on this earth'. There are other stories of film and tape recordings of the Manson Family music but whatever their circumstances the ESP album is a contradictory experience.

For much of the record Manson shows a vocal resemblance to James Taylor (odd in the light of Dennis Wilson co-starring with Taylor in the self-destruct car movie *Two-Lane Black-top* a few years later). In many ways it's an atypical psyche-delic record – the arrogance of the singer/songwriter genre interspersed by experimental stabs at formalistic breakdown. The lyrics 'distinguish' it, though.

Maybe the clearest exemplar of the Manson philosophy is 'Cease to Exist'. It demands a total capitulation to a higher or focal identity – really just an extension of ceasing to resist except in this case the 'higher entity' was advocating racial supremacy and mass murder.

It has been questioned as to why Dennis Wilson should have become involved in this nightmarish world in the first place. There are suggestions that he felt he had too much money. Harder to understand is his reason for taking over the 'Cease to Exist' song, especially in the light of his hindsight remark that 'Charlie never had a musical bone in his body'. Manson claims he gave the Beach Boys the song to soothe their differences and was furious when he discovered that the words had been changed (justifiably, from his point of view, since the quasi-magical psycho-dominance had been trivia-lised into boring old everyday sexual manipulation).

Dennis is quite clear that Manson sold the song for money and wanted no credit. Nevertheless, it's not much of a song and Dennis was beginning to show himself as possessing some considerable talent as a composer (check his solo album *Pacific Ocean Blue*).

WHO'S BEEN ROCKING MY DREAMBOAT?

Manson was in fact not the only Family member patronised by Dennis. In 1967 a full page ad was run in the *Village Voice* stating 'In Memoriam Kenneth Anger 1947–1967'.

This was not a death announcement, as might be expected, but a renouncement of film-making after Bobby Beausoleil, the original Lucifer actor in Anger's movie *Lucifer Rising*, had stolen 1600 feet of this picture from a locked trunk and taken it to Manson. At the time Beausoleil had fantasies of being a rock star and had been hanging out with Dennis Wilson in order to improve his chances.

Anger's story is that he gave Beausoleil money to buy musical equipment that was spent on grass – this caused the fracas that led to the theft of film footage. Manson is alleged to have demanded $10,000 for its return. Anger seems proud of the fact that this was the first example in history of film being held to ransom. He refused to pay.

Beausoleil became embroiled in the Family and eventually was convicted of the murder of Gary Hinman. His musical abilities came to fruition on Death Row in Tracy Prison where he recorded a sound track for *Lucifer Rising*. Others to have contributed soundtracks include Mick Jagger and Jimmy Page. The current music seems to be D.W. Griffith's organ soundtrack scored for *Birth of a Nation*.

Beausoleil claimed that Anger cast a spell on him and changed him into a toad. The other story is that he was so badly beaten up in jail that it disfigured him. Maybe the occasion was his struggle for the leadership of the Aryan Brotherhood – a cause not so far from the hearts of either D.W. Griffith or Charles Manson.

KUSTOM KAR KOMMANDOS

Naturally, there have been comparisons made between Manson's crude but effective psychosexual brain-washing (along with his inferred connections with the California Solar Lodge of the O.T.O.) and Kenneth Anger's self-professed devotion to Aleister Crowley ('I'm engaged in a long-term selling campaign. I have one product that I'm selling: the 20th Century's most misunderstood genius, called Aleister Crowley').

There are other parallels besides sex-magic and the rise of Lucifer. Hollywood-born Anger's most famous film is probably *Scorpio Rising* – a movie of complex symbolism whose imagery (biker gangs, torture, swastikas – you know the sort of thing) was like a reflection of the Manson world. It was, incidentally, one of the first films to use pop records ('Wipe Out', 'Torture', 'He's a Rebel' – no Beach Boys but close enough!) as soundtrack. Another (unfinished) film, *Kustom Kar Kommandos*, was described by Anger as 'an oneiric vision of a contemporary American (and specifically Californian) teenage phenomenon, the world of the hot-rod and customized car.' The cars were to appear 'an eye-magnet of nacreous colour and gleaming curvilinear surfaces' while the customisers would be presented as 'shadowy, mysterious – personages (priests or witch-doctors).'

It was as if Anger was filming the transition from the Beach Boys fun-fun-fun of 'Little Deuce Coupe' to the Rommel-inspired Manson attack battalions of customised dune buggies. Where Anger understood and cinematically portrayed the darker side of the Californian myth (he was to call Manson Uncle Sugar – the pilot of the Bad Ship Lollipop – in *Hollywood Babylon*) Manson himself was the living embodiment of it. Having helped create the myth, the Beach Boys fell victim to it.

For Dennis, the Manson persona must have seemed only too tempting. Revealingly, he described the attraction of Manson's music as being its spontaneity. Despite being the staunchest supporter of brother Brian's remarkable *Pet Sounds/Smile/Smiley Smile* writing, Dennis must have felt a strong nostalgia for the sparkling simplicity of earlier Beach

Boys records. The macho lifestyle, free sex, a philosophy supposedly based on love, male creativity supported by female servitude – irresistible to a macho romantic like Dennis.

This was all part of the ideal anyway. Manson raked beneath the skin of white middle-class California and revealed through himself the incipient violence, misogyny, antisemitism and hatred of blacks. Whether this occurred to Dennis later is impossible to say. His comment was 'I'm the luckiest guy in the world, because I got off only losing my money.' The sanitisation of 'Cease to Exist' into 'Cease to Resist' may have been a means of converting a terrifying glimpse of underlying realities back into socially acceptable human exploitation.

Nick Hornby

ABBA: WELCOME TO THE PALINDROME

Mojo, June 1997

*After writing this review of nine reissued Abba alb-
ums, I gave the CDs to a friend who runs a local music
store, and he placed them in his small and usually
impeccably groovy second-hand section. We agreed
that any monies received would be split between his
kid's school and my kid's school. That phrase 'usually
impeccably groovy' probably leads you to suspect that
you know how the story ended – with goatee'd Isling-
ton types, sick of staring at the same old Bill Evans and
Tom Verlaine albums, fighting with each other and
thrusting fistfuls of notes at the proprietor. Well, of
course that didn't happen. The nine albums sat there
for months, and I think we eventually shifted the lot
for less than twenty quid. Given that Abba were and
remain a supergroup, with successful West End shows
to their name, this must have been the least successful
reissue series ever.*

NH

WHEREVER YOU STAND on the Abba question (to which the
correct answer, incidentally, is 'Right up there with the
greats,' rather than 'Björn's mum, with a pudding bowl
and the kitchen scissors') you can't deny that this band
has legs.

When we watched – through tears of joy or our fingers,
depending on taste – the triumphant reprise of 'Waterloo' at

the end of the 1974 Eurovision Song Contest, only the most sapient of us could have predicted that 20 years later the entire Abba *oeuvre* would provide the backbone for post-modern TV chat shows (Aha!); or that camp pop groups would record tribute EPs; or that rap groups would sample their bass lines; or that the intro to 'Waterloo' itself would provide a thrilling moment in a hit movie. Abba became A and B and B and A over a decade ago, but our culture seems to have found a permanent place for them in its heart, which is more than can be said for, say, the Jam, who seemed more significant at the time.

Part of the explanation for this is that Abba have become an obvious and universal symbol of Naff in the same way that James Dean is a lazy exemplification of Cool: one would imagine that Alan Partridge, with his mock-Tudor home outside Norwich and his golf club membership, varies his aural diet with a little Shakatak once in a while, just for old time's sake, but basically Abba were his band in the way that the Beatles might be yours. (Any plans for an *Abba Anthology*, one wonders? Could Björn and Benny dust down the demos for 'Dum Dum Diddle' or 'Bang-A-Boomerang' and splice them together?)

It's the same for poor Muriel in *Muriel's Wedding*, but the moment in the film when she and her mate mime to 'Waterloo' at a holiday resort talent contest is complicated. Of course it's funny and tells us something about the central character (i.e. she probably hasn't got as many Nick Cave albums as she should have), but the scene has a real charge to it too, simply because the opening bars of the song sound so fucking brilliant. The film wants it both ways, and it gets it too, and there is the Abba paradox in a nutshell – they're great, but they're probably all dressed up as Napoleon.

A couple years ago, there was a pretty nifty BBC Peel-narrated documentary about the boys and girls, wherein the great and the good (Ray Davies, Ian McCulloch, Elvis Costello, the obligatory classical music scholar who had written a thesis about diminished 7ths in 'Gimme! Gimme! Gimme! A Man After Midnight' or some such nonsense) got together to tell us why Abba were the pop business. One listened with interest to what they had to say, of course, but one's attention was constantly distracted by the illustrative clips: did Abba really appear in a Mike Yarwood sketch? (Mike was doing Larry Grayson: 'You have a song called "Dancing Queen"? Shut that door', etc). And on *Seaside Special*? And Gerry Cottle's Circus? And did they really wear that, and dance like that? That they really, really didn't care at all, Abba, which probably means that they were the first and perhaps the only true punks: even Iggy cared a bit. He certainly never appeared on the *Mike Yarwood Show*, anyway.

I hope that you will forgive me, dear reader, when I tell you that I haven't listened to all nine of these remastered albums, um, all the way through, but actually you don't need to listen to them to work out what happened to Abba: the track listings tell the whole story. The first couple of albums, from '73 and '74, feature tracks called 'Ring Ring', 'Nina', 'Pretty Ballerina', 'Hasta Mañana', 'King Kong Song', 'Honey Honey', 'Dance (While The Music Still Goes On)', and 'Love Isn't Easy (But It Sure Is Hard Enough)': in other words, the song titles come in two languages, Eurobabble or a slightly strained intermediate-level English. (Love isn't easy but it's hard? What, precisely, is the function of that oppositional conjunction, guys?)

By *The Visitors*, their last studio album in 1982, all that has changed, and snappy Advanced English idioms are well to the fore: 'You Owe Me One', 'When All Is Said And Done', 'Slipping Through My Fingers', 'Two For The Price Of One', 'Head Over Heels' . . . I used to teach people like Abba. They were a pain in the arse. It only ever rained 'cats and dogs', and policemen were always 'bobbies'; there was something vaguely repellent about their desperation to become One Of Us.

That's what it did for Abba, if you ask me: they became desperate, because they had somehow got it into their heads that we didn't need Kitsch Scandinavian Eurovision hits. There was that brilliant mid-period, where they had taken off the Napoleon hats, and there was a bit less of the Ring Ding-A-Honey stuff, and they wrote 'Knowing Me, Knowing You' and 'The Name Of The Game' and 'Angel Eyes', pop classics all, without being afraid of going for the odd Dum Dum Diddle.

But then self-consciousness set in. It's one thing to be told that you're camp, it's quite another to actively court the description – by the end, Abba had got their own joke and effectively become their own Björn Again before tribute bands were even thought of. 'The Day Before You Came', their last hurrah, is a pop ironist's take on Abba, and pop ironists sure know how to pull the fun out of things.

Abba sold 240 million albums worldwide and ended up with serious money troubles, which seems somehow indicative of the peculiar nature of their genius (or Swedish tax laws). But genius it was: will there ever be another band which manages to mean so many things to so many people, to succeed through inclusion rather than exclusion? And, of course, those songs, the good ones, have stood the test of time, just about the only pop songs to do so that aren't built on guitars, bass and drums. If you only buy nine remastered albums full of jolly rinky-dink fairground synths and dodgy titles all at once this year, make it these. Failing that, a second-hand *Greatest Hits* will do.

RBP READER WRITERS

Al Aronowitz

Al Aronowitz, now known as THE BLACKLISTED JOURNAL-IST, has often been called 'the godfather of rock journalism'. His POP SCENE column in THE NEW YORK POST certainly turned him into one of the most powerful rock journalists in the world. Those columns – plus his writings in THE SATURDAY EVENING POST, THE VILLAGE VOICE and many other publications – set the tone for all subsequent coverage of rock and roll. He has collected some of his unpublished manuscripts in THE BLACK-LISTED MASTERPIECES OF AL ARONOWITZ. Some of them can now be found in his monthly e-zine THE BLACKLISTED JOURNALIST, at http://www.bigmagic.com/pages/blackj. As the man who introduced Allen Ginsberg to Bob Dylan, Bob Dylan to the Beatles and the Beatles to marijuana, Al has been known to boast that 'the '60s wouldn't have been the same without me'.

Mick Brown

Born in 1950, Mick Brown is a freelance writer and broadcaster who has written on music and other cultural affairs for a wide variety of publications, including the SUNDAY TIMES, the GUAR-DIAN, the OBSERVER, the SUNDAY CORRESPONDENT, ROLLING STONE and CRAWDADDY! He is now a regular contributor to the TELEGRAPH magazine and the DAILY TELE-GRAPH newspaper in London. Mick is the author of four books: *Richard Branson: The Inside Story*; *American Heartbeat: A musical journey across America from Woodstock to San Jose*; *Performance* – a study of the cult film; and *The Spiritual Tourist: A Personal Odyssey through the Outer Reaches of Belief*.

Richard Cook

Richard Cook was one of the major feature writers for NME in the early and middle '80s. He subsequently edited THE WIRE for seven years, and is currently editor of JAZZ REVIEW. He is the co-author of *The Penguin Guide To Jazz On CD*, now approaching its sixth edition, and in 2001 also published *Blue Note: The Biography*. He still enjoys a fair bit of rock music, though.

Caroline Coon
Artist, legendary founder of RELEASE and author of the seminal *1988: The Punk Rock Explosion*, Caroline was a regular contributor to MELODY MAKER and SOUNDS in the heyday of '70s rock. In 2001 her punk pictures formed part of the No Future?: Punk 2001 conference in Wolverhampton, England.

David Dalton
Key ROLLING STONE writer of the '60s and '70s and author of such bestsellers as *Piece of My Heart* (about Janis Joplin), *The Mutant King* (bio of James Dean), *Saint Vicious* (about Sid V.) and, with Marianne Faithfull, *Faithfull*, winner of a Ralph J. Gleason Best Music Book Award 1994. His novel *Been Here and Gone* came out in 2000. David is currently a regular contributor to MOJO and Gadflyonline.com.

Mick Farren
NME legend of the '70s, now a US-based author of great repute and contributor to MOJO and other magazines. Mick's many books include the cult *Tale of Willy's Rats*, countless science fiction novels, *The Black Leather Jacket* and the recent autobiographical *Give the Anarchist a Cigarette* (Cape, 2001). He lives in Los Angeles.

Simon Frith
Chairman of the Mercury Music Prize Committee, Simon was a key contributor to MELODY MAKER, LET IT ROCK, CREEM, the OBSERVER, THE VILLAGE VOICE et al in the '70s, and is the author of such revered books as *Sound Effects* and *Performing Rites*. He is now Professor of Film and Media at the University of Stirling.

Jerry Gilbert
Author of countless '70s pieces for MELODY MAKER, SOUNDS and ZIGZAG, Jerry also produced regular bylined columns for the DAILY MIRROR and MIDWEEK. He still writes widely on folk and other genres, and has recently been commissioned to undertake a book about the history and evolution of show technology.

Vivien Goldman

A pioneering SOUNDS and NME journalist during the 1970s 'Golden Age' of conscious reggae and militant punk, Vivien drew on a lengthy association with Bob Marley to write his first biography, *Soul Rebel, Natural Mystic*, and worked closely with visionaries like Ornette Coleman and Fela Anikulapo-Kuti. Described by *Rolling Stone* as 'a small miracle,' his most recent book, *The Black Chord* (with photographer David Corio) traces connections between African and Diaspora music. Based in New York, Vivien has written for INTERVIEW, the VILLAGE VOICE, ROLLING STONE, and HARPER'S BAZAAR.

Robert Gordon

Robert is the author of *It Came from Memphis*, *Elvis on the Road*, and *Can't Be Satisfied: The Life and Times of Muddy Waters*. His filmmaking includes the documentaries *Waters Waters Can't Be Satisfied* and *All Day and All Night: Memories of Beale Street Musicians*. Winner of a Deems Taylor ASCAP writing award, he has contributed to SPIN, DETAILS, Q, MOJO and many other publications; his essay on Jeff Buckley was included in *The Best Rock Writing of 2001*.

Mary Harron

Contributor in the '70s and '80s to MELODY MAKER, THE VILLAGE VOICE, the GUARDIAN and the NEW STATESMAN, Mary has subsequently become an acclaimed film director (*I Shot Andy Warhol; American Psycho*). She is currently working on two projects: a biopic of '50s pin-up star Betty Page and a film about the CBGBs punk scene she covered in the mid-'70s.

Nick Hornby

The world-famous author of four bestsellers – *Fever Pitch*, *High Fidelity*, *About a Boy* and *How to be Good* – Nick has written about music for the INDEPENDENT, MOJO and THE NEW YORKER. The film of *About a Boy*, with a soundtrack by Badly Drawn Boy, was released in 2002.

Robert (Robot) A. Hull

Robert (Robot) Hull began his illustrious career in the music biz when, as an 18-year-old whippersnapper, he submitted 50 record reviews in one fell swoop to Lester Bangs. Thenceforward he became a regular writer for CREEM during the '70s and '80s, also contributing to every rock rag known to man, from ROLLING STONE to TEENAGE WASTELAND GAZETTE. In the '80s, Robert became the pop music critic for THE WASHINGTON POST. He is now the in-house editor and historian for the ubiquitous direct-marketer Time-Life Music, where, as Executive Producer, he churns out over 250 music compilations annually.

Lenny Kaye
A living legend, both as a writer and as a musician/producer, Kaye wrote widely in the '60s for FUSION, ROLLING STONE, CRAW-DADDY! and other publications. He is co-author with David Dalton of *Rock 100*, and partnered the late Waylon Jennings on the latter's autobiography. Kaye compiled the seminal *Nuggets* anthology of garage punk and has long been the guitarist in Patti Smith's band.

Michael Lydon
A ROLLING STONE legend of the late '60s and '70s, Michael's seminal pieces on the Rolling Stones et al have been collected in *Rock Folk* and *Boogie Lightning*. *Ray Charles: Man and Music*, his biography of the Genius, received superb reviews. He is also a guitarist-singer-songwriter who performs in New York. Brite Records released his CD *Love at First Sight*.

Greil Marcus
Greil Marcus is author of *Mystery Train: Images of America in Rock'n'Roll Music* (1975; most recent English language edition from Faber & Faber, 2000), *Lipstick Traces*, *Dead Elvis*, *The Old, Weird America* (a retitled edition of the 1997 *Invisible Republic*), *The Dustbin of History*, *In the Fascist Bathroom* and *Double Trouble*. Greil has published columns, essays and reviews since 1968 in ROLLING STONE, ARTFORUM, INTERVIEW, SALON.COM, COMMON KNOWLEDGE and many other publications. In 2000 and 2002 he taught an American Studies seminar at Princeton University. He lives in Berkeley, California.

John Mendelssohn
'If not the father of American rock criticism, at least its nephew!' Thus spake the cover of Mendelssohn's *I, CARAMBA: Confessions of an Antkiller* (1995), an hilarious account of his life as a writer for

ROLLING STONE, CREEM and other publications, not to mention of his career as lead singer with '70s cult band Christopher
Milk. John lives in Santa Rosa, California. In 2002, he composed
and produced the debut album of Mistress Chloe, supreme domi-
nant goddess of all London, as well as ghostwriting her memoir
Dominatrix: The Making of Mistress Chloe, and finally finished his
own second solo project, *Sex With Twinge*. He is currently at work
on his own sexual autobiography and on a nonfiction book about
the failures of his relationships with his first wife and only daughter.
He is old and weary, but implacable.

Barry Miles
Barry Miles, born 1943, spent four years at Gloucestershire College
of Art before moving to London in 1963. In 1966 he was the co-
founder of Indica Books and Gallery where John Lennon first met
Yoko Ono. That same year Miles was co-founder of INTERNA-
TIONAL TIMES (IT), the first European underground newspaper,
where his first four interviews were with Paul McCartney, George
Harrison, Mick Jagger and Pete Townshend. He specialises in
writing about the Beat Generation and is the author of, among
other books, *Allen Ginsberg: A Biography* (Simon & Schuster,
NYC, 1989), *William Burroughs: El Hombre Invisible* (Hyperion,
NYC, 1992), *Jack Kerouac: King of the Beats* (Holt, NYC, 1998),
and *Beat Hotel* (Grove, NYC, June 2000). His bestselling *Paul
McCartney: Many Years From Now* (Holt, NYC, 1997) was
written in close collaboration with McCartney.

Bill Millar
The author of books on the Drifters and the Coasters, Bill Millar
was also Consultant Editor on Panther's *Encyclopedia of Rock*
(1976) and Orbis' *History Of Rock* (1981). His 'Echoes' column
was a feature of RECORD MIRROR, LET IT ROCK and MEL-
ODY MAKER. His exhaustive liner notes for the Bear Family label,
and other companies, will provide key content for RBP. Bill, who
was awarded the MBE in 1996, lives in Dartford, Kent.

Charles Shaar Murray
One of the NME's '70s superstars and the author of magnificent
books like the recently reissued *Crosstown Traffic*, about Jimi
Hendrix, and *Boogie Man*, about John Lee Hooker. Charles writes
for MOJO, the DAILY TELEGRAPH, the GUARDIAN, the IN-
DEPENDENT and other publications.

Glenn O'Brien

A key observer on the New York pop scene, Glenn was the music writer on Andy Warhol's INTERVIEW and has written for SPIN, ARTFORUM and countless other publications. His books include the anthology *Soapbox*, the poetry book *Human Nature* (dub version). He is 'The Style Guy' at GQ magazine and editor-at-large of ARENA HOMME +. He wrote and produced *Downtown 81*, the film starring Jean-Michel Basquiat. His literary and arts magazine THE BALD EGO debuted in summer 2002.

Simon Reynolds

The widely acclaimed author of *Blissed Out*, *The Sex Revolts* (with his wife Joy Press) and *Generation Ecstacy* (aka *Energy Flash*), London-born but now New York-based Simon started out as a MELODY MAKER staff writer in the late '80s and has since gone on to freelance for SPIN, THE VILLAGE VOICE, THE NEW YORK TIMES, THE WIRE, and UNCUT. He is currently working on a book about post-punk music, 1979–84, to be published by Faber (in the UK) and Viking Penguin (in North America) in early 2004. His Blissout site can be found at http://members.aol.com/blissout/front.htm.

Jon Savage

Author of the award-winning social history of the late '70s, *England's Dreaming: Sex Pistols and Punk Rock*, *The Kinks: the Official Biography* and co-editor of the acclaimed *The Faber Book of Pop*. In 1997, Jon wrote the BAFTA-award-winning BBC2 *Arena* documentary on Brian Epstein. A key punk-era writer for SOUNDS, and later for the FACE, the OBSERVER, the GUARDIAN, THE VILLAGE VOICE, and MOJO, he writes and lives on the island of Anglesey, Wales, where he is working on a history of 20th-century youth culture.

Will Self

The brilliant novelist, short-story writer and broadcaster has also written a number of scabrous, insightful music pieces in the course of the last decade, mostly for the OBSERVER. Will's latest novel, *How the Dead Live*, was recently issued in the UK as a paperback by Bloomsbury.

Greg Shaw

Founder of the legendary MOJO NAVIGATOR R&R NEWS, one of the earliest rock zines, based in San Francisco in 1966–67, and

then of the ageless (WHO PUT THE) BOMP in L.A. during the
'70s. Greg is one of the godfathers of rock writing and chronicling.
His other writings include books, liner notes (recently the Rhino
Nuggets boxes) and the sprawling, ongoing Bomp website
(www.bomp.com). His Bomp Records label has issued (and reissued)
countless classics of psych, garage and power pop, and launched
many musical careers, including that of Iggy Pop. His most recent
endeavour is 'Bompbooks.com', which aims at being the definitive
online rock bibliography. Further details and more biographical
stuff may be found at the site.

David Toop
An experimental composer/musician who has worked with musicians ranging from Brian Eno to Prince Far I, David has written many
exceptional pieces for the FACE, ARENA, MOJO, THE TIMES and
his own early '80s magazine, COLLUSION. He is the author of *The
Rap Attack* (now in its third edition), *Ocean of Sound* and *Exotica*.
He also curated Sonic Boom, a major exhibition of sound art for the
Hayward Gallery in 2000. He once appeared on *Top Of The Pops*,
though has yet to see this performance on *TOTP2*.

Steve Turner
Experienced interviewer who began writing for BEAT INSTRU-
MENTAL as features editor and has subsequently written for
NME, ROLLING STONE, Q and countless newspapers. Steve's
books include *Conversations with Eric Clapton* (1976), *Hungry for
Heaven* (1988), *Cliff Richard: The Biography* (1993), *Van Morri-
son: It's Too Late to Stop Now* (1993), *A Hard Day's Write* (1994),
Jack Kerouac: Angelheaded Hipster (1996) and *Trouble Man: The
Life and Death of Marvin Gaye* (1998).

Penny Valentine
Penny was one of the first British pop writers of note, writing in the
'60s for DISC AND MUSIC ECHO, and then later for SOUNDS,
CITY LIMITS and many other publications. She was also the first
female pop writer in the British press. Most recently she co-wrote
(with Vicki Wickham) *Dancing With Demons: The Authorized
Biography of Dusty Springfield*.

Cliff White
As well as NME, during the '70s Cliff wrote regularly for BLACK
MUSIC, BLACK ECHOES and SMASH HITS, and during the '80s

was product manager for key reissue company Charly Records, then briefly Demon Records. He also spearheaded a prolonged campaign of James Brown reissues for PolyGram/Universal and was awarded a Grammy in January 1993 for his contribution to the JB *Star Time* box-set. In recent years Cliff has managed a team of repertoire researchers for the MCPS-PRS Alliance in London.

Paul Williams

The founding father of rock and roll writing, Paul's CRAW-DADDY! was the first real publication dedicated to pop music. He has subsequently written many acclaimed books on music, from *Outlaw Blues* and the two-volume *Bob Dylan: Performing Artist* to *Rock and Roll: The 100 Best Singles* and *Love to Burn* (about Neil Young) and *How Deep is the Ocean?* (about Brian Wilson and the Beach Boys). His most recent books are *The 20th Century's Greatest Hits* (books, films and paintings as well as records), *Back to the Miracle Factory* and *The Crawdaddy! Book* (an anthology from the 1960s issues). He still publishes CRAW-DADDY! now (www.cdaddy.com)

Richard Williams

Former editor of MELODY MAKER and currently chief sports writer for the GUARDIAN, Williams is among the most respected music writers of the past 30 years. His books include *Out of His Head*, about Phil Spector, and *The Man in the Green Shirt*, about Miles Davis. *Long Distance Call* (Aurum Press) collects some of his best work. Richard's latest book is a biography of Enzo Ferrari.

The work of these and many other writers can be read on Rock's Backpages, the Online Library Rock & Roll. Join today at www.rocksbackpages.com

INDEX

A NOTE ON THE EDITOR

Barney Hoskyns is the author of several books including *Say it One Time for the Brokenhearted*, *Across the Great Divide: The Band and America* and *Waiting for the Sun: Strange Days, Weird Scenes and the Sound of Los Angeles*. He has written for *NME*, *The Times*, *Vogue*, *Arena*, *Rolling Stone*, *GQ*, the *New Statesman* and the *Independent on Sunday*, and was US Editor of *Mojo* for four years. He lives in London and co-founded *Rock's Backpages* in 2001.

A NOTE ON THE TYPE

The text of this book is set in Linotype Sabon, named after the type founder, Jacques Sabon. It was designed by Jan Tschichold and jointly developed by Linotype, Monotype and Stempel, in response to a need for a typeface to be available in identical form for mechanical hot metal composition and hand composition using foundry type.

Tschichold based his design for Sabon roman on a fount engraved by Garamond, and Sabon italic on a fount by Granjon. It was first used in 1966 and has proved an enduring modern classic.